Federalism, Power, and Political Economy

A New Theory of Federalism's Impact on American Life

Christopher Hamilton
Western Kentucky University

Donald T. Wells
West Georgia College

JK
325
.H35
1990
West

Prentice Hall, *Englewood Cliffs, New Jersey 07632*

Library of Congress Cataloging-in-Publication Data

Hamilton, Christopher, [date]

   Federalism, power, and political economy: A new theory of
federalism's impact on American life/Christopher Hamilton and
Donald T. Wells.
     p.   cm.
   Bibliography: p. 321
   Includes index.
   ISBN 0-13-313685-X
   1. Federal government--United States. I. Wells, Donald T. [date].
   II. Title
JK325.H35 1990
321.02'0973--dc19   88-27464
                                            CIP

Editorial/production supervision and
   interior design: Shelly Kupperman
Cover design: Ben Santora
Manufacturing buyer: Pete Havens

©1990 by Prentice-Hall, Inc.
A Division of Simon & Schuster
Englewood Cliffs, New Jersey 07632

Printed in the United States of America

10 9 8 7 6 5 4 3 2 1

ISBN   0-13-313685-X

Prentice-Hall International (UK) Limited, *London*
Prentice-Hall of Australia Pty. Limited, *Sydney*
Prentice-Hall Canada Inc., *Toronto*
Prentice-Hall Hispanoamericana, S.A., *Mexico*
Prentice-Hall of India Private Limited, *New Delhi*
Prentice-Hall of Japan, Inc., *Tokyo*
Simon & Schuster Asia Pte. Ltd., *Singapore*
Editora Prentice-Hall do Brasil, Ltda., *Rio de Janeiro*

For Chris Hamilton, this book is written in the deep shadows of certain extraordinary human beings:

the late Gwendolyn Fletcher of Concordia, Kansas—teacher of literature, master sculptor of minds, and weaver of dreams for four generations of Kansas young people

Jarek Piekalkiewicz—master of logic and human character

Robin Remington—exemplar of wisdom, perception, and grace

Elaine Sharp and Mike Harder—wizards of subtle insight

Mom and Dad—for their courage and patience

Katharine Jeanne—who teaches souls to imagine, to create, and to peer into mysteries

For Don Wells, reminded by Voltaire's observation that "if this is the best of all possible worlds, imagine what the second best must be like," the book is dedicated to his grandchildren, Jessie Leigh Wells and Jacob Alexander Wells, and to other grandchildren still to be born, in the hope that this world will hold the best for them.

Contents

4   Subnational Federalism: The Interstate Pattern 94

5   Subnational Federalism: The Substate Pattern 122

PART II Power, Policy, Economics, and Society:
The Bigger Picture of Federalism's Impact
on America

12 *The Winds of Change: Cycles, Trends,
and Directions in Federalism 303*

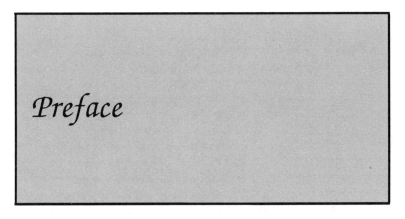

Preface

"As long as the reason of man continues fallible and he is at liberty to exercise it, different opinions will be formed" (James Madison, The *Federalist*, No. 10). In many respects, this well-known explanation of the development of factions is one of the best comments on the study of federalism. The study of federalism is a lively field, and one in which many different opinions exist regarding both fact and interpretation. We find this situation healthy, exciting, and just plain old-fashioned fun.

In part, that is why we wrote this book. Perhaps it is not too much to say that much of the academic treatment of federalism has found itself lodged in the dusty corners and shadows of the legalistic, fiscal, and historic methods. Only recently have efforts been made to introduce and build on the power of newer social science concepts and theories to create a more potent, fuller picture of federalism. Such approaches have helped to highlight the bigger, extraordinary significance of federalism for life in America (see, for example, Elazar 1984 and Henig 1985).

What we attempt in this book is to extend, deepen, and further enliven the study of federalism by putting to work some of the newer theories and concepts of the social sciences. The guiding question in our minds throughout the book was this one: What difference does federalism make in the lives of average Americans? And what we found, by putting social science theories to work, is that federalism has an incredible range of effects, and that it makes a powerful difference in the political, social, and economic life of Americans.

Federalism, Power, and Political Economy is an attempt to write a truly innovative text on American intergovernmental relations. It uses policy concepts, political economy and social science theory, commentary on power, and the analysis of policy impacts to reinterpret federalism as a vital, powerful, and underestimated factor in our politics and economics. Specifically, the book explores how policy, implementation, economic market functioning, and political and community life are dramatically influenced by the "great political, invisible hand" of federalism. The broad, main theme is that federalism, if it is properly understood, is the major arbiter of power, policy, and economics in America.

This is truly a different picture of federalism, one that is hardly stodgy. As a *direct* result of using the newer concepts, federalism appears "bigger" than previously thought. The political economy approach used here understands federalism as a complex political economy, arranged in seven related traditions or patterns. This new concept of federalism, we think, may stir up a little controversy about the nature and meaning of federalism, and open up some new insights. Chapters 1 and 2 develop the basic political economy picture of federalism. In these chapters, we present the idea of federalism as a political economy and explain how the political economy view helps us unlock an understanding of the profound significance of federalism. In particular, we describe seven political economy patterns of federalism and sketch the historical roots, effects, and evolution of the three great federalist traditions.

These first two chapters are crucial to the argument in the rest of the book. We start from the point that what you think you see when you look at federalism (or any phenomenon) is partly dependent on the conceptual tenses through which you look. Thus, the previous approaches to the study of federalism are reviewed, and shown to be building blocks in an unfolding picture of federalism that includes the political economy approach. We compare the idea of federalism as a complex political economy with the older ideas of federalism that come from the institutional, pluralist, organizational, and legalistic perspectives.

Using the political economy picture of federalism, Chapters 3–7 describe and relate the remaining patterns of federalism to the three national federal traditions outlined in Chapter 2. Thus Chapter 3 discusses the nation–state pattern, Chapter 4 the interstate pattern, Chapter 5 the substate pattern, Chapter 6 the interlocal pattern, and Chapter 7 the national–local pattern. We wish to alert the reader that the way we describe federalism in each of these chapters is quite different from material found in most previous texts on federalism. We seek to emphasize how the economic, representation, policy, and power systems of each pattern work, and how they are organized as part of federalism's larger reality. We emphasize the historical and the current effects of each of the seven patterns of federalism on economics, power, representation, and public policy in America. Each of the chapters also contains what we call a "nuts and bolts" section, which should help the student understand the practical workings of the system. Again, we place these practical aspects of each pattern into the larger political economy picture, in order to understand the *meaning* of federalism.

Chapters 8–11 continue to build the political economy view of federalism by introducing important information and thinking about power and policy in federalism. We stress that federalism is the major arbiter of power in American politics. In Chapter 9, we attempt to show how federalism "fights back" and influences public and private power. And we emphasize that it makes no sense to summarize social power systems without demonstrating how power has policy effects on people, and how federalism alters all this. All of this builds up to Chapter 11, which in many ways is the capstone chapter in the book. In it, we describe the bigger picture of federalism's social significance in American society. As sociologists would express it, we try to show how federalism has important social functions in politics and economics.We stress the idea that federalism "does big things" that have fundamental significance for life in American society.

Finally, in Chapter 12, we use the political economy approach to reflect on some of the major recent trends in American federalism. We end the book by suggesting the directions the study of federalism might take in the future. Through it all, the political economy approach reveals *how* federalism makes for profound and pervasive differences in American life. If at the end of the book, people are more aware of the differences federalism makes, we will judge the book as having done its job.

In a very real way, this is a coauthored book. After seemingly endless drafts, neither of us can identify whose language is present in several of the chapters. We have collaborated so much on the theory, content, wording, and style that the product is in fact a joint work rather than a sum of two individuals efforts. Certainly, the concept of the book, its organization and structure, its development of ideas, and the overall political economy approach itself, and the interpretation of facts, practices, and events to which it leads are all the result of our joint interaction. The book is far better for this, and we are better students of federalism for it.

Although the book is written with a systematic approach, we labored mightily to bring the approach down to earth with a clear, lively, direct writing style aimed at upper-level undergraduate and graduate students, as well as "thinkers" and "theorists" of federalism. The book is accessible to students and scholars alike.

We would be criminally remiss if we did not recognize those persons who made special contributions to the development of the book. Claire d'-Essery and Karen Horton of Prentice Hall were helpful in seeing potential in the book. Rhonda North of the Political Science Department at West Georgia College went well beyond the call of duty to prepare the manuscript. To her we are deeply indebted. We appreciate the assistance and support of Richard Dangle, dean of the School of Arts and Sciences, and Joan Artz, government documents librarian, both of West Georgia College. Kathy Hamilton worked with us as a research assistant during a critical period in the "survey of the literature stage" and performed a superlative job. Our wives, Kathy and Jewel, were not only loving and patient but supportive and helpful in a number of ways. They no doubt heard more about the ideas and theories expressed in the book than they wanted to hear, but they listened not only with tolerance but in critically creative ways as well. To the anonymous reviewers of Prentice Hall whose comments were so useful for content and style improvements, we express sincere thanks. We ask that as many readers as possible contact us with their suggestions for future work in this important area of study. While we are indebted to many, all matters of fact and interpretation in the book are our sole responsibility.

Chris Hamilton and Don Wells

The Forgotten Force:

1

Federalism in American life

THE IMPORTANCE OF FEDERALISM

Federalism is simply too often forgotten. So before we try to describe federalism, perhaps we should see what important differences it makes. Consider the following three questions. They help illustrate the pervasive influence of federalism in American life.

What explains the recent, remarkably widespread efforts to solve social problems such as drunken driving, child abuse, and educational quality in America? One answer is that these issues, and innovative solutions to them, have spread from state to state. Typically, these problems first gained attention in the states through the agitation of small, initially powerless interest groups. Later, attempts at policy reform were copied from one state to another. This illustrates the impact of *interstate relations* in federalism. Later in the book we will explain further how public policies spread from state to state because of the influence of the structures of federalism.

Another question. Why do divorced working mothers with children receive liberal financial help from some states (Wisconsin and Minnesota, for example) but virtually none from others? It is small comfort for unfortunate mothers to learn that *federalism* has allowed states to set their *own* levels of benefits, independent of the level of benefits in other states and the national minimum levels required by the national program of Aid to Families with Dependent Children.

A third question. Who was responsible for providing weather information to the incoming Delta Airlines plane that crashed in Dallas in 1986, killing dozens? Again it is small comfort to the survivors and the relatives of the victims to learn that *federalism* has created a patchwork of government agencies responsible for managing such critical services. Thus a national weather service had provided weather information to the pilot, but the *local* airport authority (a municipal agency) had decided to leave the airport open in spite of a severe thunderstorm. Such fragmentation of responsibility among agencies is sometimes (graciously) called *cooperative federalism*.

THE BASIC PICTURE OF FEDERALISM IN THIS BOOK

Federalism is a thread in almost all aspects of public policy and economics in the American political system. For example, all public policies involve actions by myriad governmental agencies at each level—national, state, and local. And whenever people in and out of government debate welfare, education, and other issues, they always debate the role that federalism, local or national, should play in the solutions. Thus federalism, economics, and public policy are intertwined.

The basic theme of this book is that federalism dramatically affects economics, public policy, political power, and representation in America— to the point of making a difference for drunken drivers, abused children, working mothers, airline crash victims, and all the rest of us. The perspective and information we present should lead you to the conclusion that federalism is one of the most important forces in our collective life. We will develop a fresh view of federalism based on the ideas of policy studies, power perspectives, political economy theories, and other social science concepts. Using these newer concepts, we will reinterpret federalism as a complex **political economy** that presents itself in seven related traditions or patterns.

We will argue from this political economy viewpoint that federalism is a considerably bigger deal than the concepts usually used in studies of federalism would lead us to believe. We will portray federalism as much more than pluralist politics and grants played out over different levels of government—the meaning of the currently popular term *intergovernmental relations. Thus, our main task in this book is to describe federalism as a complex political economy and to show how it affects economics, power, representation, and policy in America.*

Our beginning argument is this: How we understand federalism—what we think it "really is"—is a subtle but crucial point. Federalism is not often fully understood as having profound effects on policy, representation, power, and economics. Too often it has been viewed restrictively in terms of intergovernmental fiscal affairs, politics, or court cases. And sometimes federalism is simply misunderstood. For example, both liberals and conservatives have seen federalism as a cumbersome dinosaur, blocking policies they wish to see implemented. Thus, liberals object to obstacles in federalism that slow enforcement of civil rights or environmental policy, while conservatives may wish there were not so many federal courts to block their antiabortion or school prayer proposals. And in the 1980s the Reagan administration revived the old states' rights view that the national government has created an overly powerful, faceless bureaucracy that runs roughshod over state and local interests. The national government, so they say, is a problem. These various views of federalism, whether academic or rhetorical, fall short of presenting a full picture of federalism in American life. And thus the need to interpret federalism as a complex political economy.

From our political economy perspective we will try to show the bigger picture of federalism by presenting three major themes: (1) federalism is a treasure chest of cultural ideas about politics and economics, (2) it is the main arbiter of power and policy, and (3) it is the regulator of power, market, and elite forces in America. This kind of federalism should hardly be a dry subject or a back-burner course offering.

In the first two chapters we put together the basic concepts, ideas, and themes underlying a political economy understanding of federalism. We will fill in this portrait of federalism in increasing detail throughout the remainder of the book, so that by the end of Chapter 11 the big picture of federalism can be understood. We then summarize our ideas in Chapter 12.

In this first chapter we will try to develop a basic feel for political economy thinking. To do so we will:

- define federalism as a political economy;
- outline previous approaches to understanding federalism;
- explain how a political economy understanding adds more "parts" to the picture of federalism;
- describe how this broader perspective on federalism helps us understand the real significance of federalism for society and economics;
- introduce the seven political economy patterns of federalism; and
- illustrate the preeminence of federalism as a social force by discussing the essential issues and policy cycles of federalism.

Thus this chapter describes the major features of the federal system *understood as a complex political economy.*

Chapter 2 introduces the basic method used in Part I of the book to describe the **seven political economy patterns** in federalism. It sets the tone of thinking about and describing federalism. In particular it:

- presents the "big picture" of national federalism—the three important national traditions of federalism (compound, dual, and centralist), which underlie everything else about federalism and intergovernmental affairs;
- analyzes the roots and design of these three patterns;
- shows the effects of these patterns over time—on politics, society, economics, power, representation, and public policy;
- explains why the roots, design, and effects of federalism are political and economic; and
- describes the *present* features of the national traditions, introducing their nuts and bolts.

The method used in Chapter 2— describing roots, historical effects, and current features and political economy impacts—is repeated in Chapters 3–7. Chapters 2–7 also discuss the relationships between the patterns themselves.

Today federalism is usually seen as the constitutional design and interplay of various government levels in the middle of a tug of war among various groups and cultures. But this view does not do justice to federalism's real complexity and policy power. In the 1960s and 1970s the term *intergovernmental relations* replaced *federalism*, calling even more attention to the pluralist forces in federal operations. We think the idea that *federalism is a complex political economy* should replace this simpler understanding of federalism, by calling attention to federalism as a system of forces and patterns that dramatically affect economics, representation, power, and policies in America.

To a considerable extent, federalism was designed as a complex political economy. We do not mean by this that all aspects of federalism were intended, or that the Framers of the new American system fully realized that they were setting in motion a complex political economy. Instead, we suggest in Chapter 2 that the Framers (especially Madison, Hamilton, and Jefferson) were partially aware of the direction in which they were pushing federalism and the development of politics and economics. Thus, we concentrate in this book on how federalism has come to function in society, politics, and economics. The goal of this approach is to better appreciate federalism's role and power in American life.

A Quick Review of Political Economy Approaches

But what precisely do we mean by a political economy approach? Generally, such approaches concentrate on describing how political and economic systems overlap and affect each other, and how they affect policy making, the allocation of resources, and the quality of life in societies (Frey

1978). One of the difficulties in using political economy concepts to study federalism is that political economy traditions are fragmented into several schools of thought. Bruno Frey has identified four such traditions: (1) social, policy, and political systems analysis (Dror, Jones, Boulding, Easton); (2) Marxist and neo–Marxist theory of the state (O'Connor, Robinson, Sweezy); (3) public choice theory (Ostrom); and (4) institutional political economy theories (Lindblom).

Which of these approaches should we use in analyzing federalism? Frey has argued that the systems, Marxist, and public choice approaches have certain general weaknesses. Systems theories, for example, often exaggerate system stability without explaining specifically what real-world policy processes, changes, or impacts are (Wood 1970, 503). Marxist theories often exaggerate deterministic economic and social-class forces. And public choice theory, which stresses rational individual choices, does not adequately recognize the various functions performed by political and economic institutions in modern societies. Because of such problems, these perspectives would not allow us to cast much new theoretical light on the nature of federalism.

Our approach to understanding federalism rests on the fourth option: **institutional political economy theories**. These theories seem more useful because they focus on *the relations among federalism, politics, economics, and society*. The institutional political economy approach we adopt is based on three essential points:

1. All major features of life in society are affected strongly by two semi–independent spheres: *politics* (political institutions, values, and policy processes) and *economics* (economic institutions, values, and processes). Specifically, our approach tries to describe how these two spheres influence each other and society through federalism.
2. The structures, values, and institutions in politics and economics overlap. The most important part of the overlap is federalism. Specifically, this approach will describe *how* federalism affects society through both political and economic means.
3. Federalism as a *complex political economy* is much bigger than intergovernmental pluralism, institutions, official legal and fiscal affairs, and so on.

The strength of this approach is that it helps us to see the bigger picture of federalism—the relations among federalism's institutions, traditions, and environmental influences, and what difference these features of federalism make for society and public policy.

The Political Economy Definition of Federalism

From the political economy view, federalism is a complex *system* of seven patterns in politics and economics that operate and interact at both the national and subnational levels, with very important effects in economics, representation, power, and public policy. It is important to think about how all the parts of federalism work together as a system in politics *and* economics. These relationships are pictures in Figure 1-1. A full description of this view of federalism is given in the last part of this chapter.

Most important is to see that federalism has seven political economy patterns or traditions. (See Table 1-6 on page 19.) Three of the seven political economy traditions of federalism—compound, dual, and centralist federalism—operate at the national level. At the subnational level there are four patterns—interstate, state–local, interlocal, and national–local federalism. These seven patterns derive from the original *design* and *evolution* of federalism.

These seven patterns consist of political institutions and their important policy, economic, and social functions. These components of federalism interact with one another and are affected by interests and groups *across government levels*. The idea of intergovernmental relations conveys this aspect of *official or pluralist federalism* very well. The institutional aspects of federalism have always been easy to see; such things as the national versus state and local levels of governments, specific institutions (Congress, governors, mayors, and so on), elites and interest groups, and grants and fiscal relations are some of the more common topics in traditional textbook descriptions of federalism. But the other parts of federalism have *not* been given much attention in the literature. These include federalism's environments, political economy patterns, regulation of power, social significance, and policy phases (see Table 1-1). We will give a lot of attention to these

Figure 1-1 *The American federal system as a complex political economy*

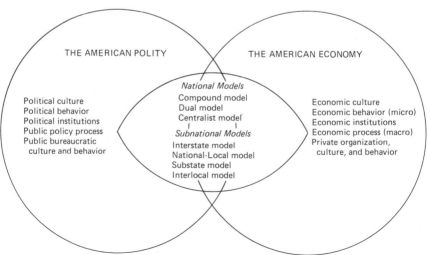

THE AMERICAN POLITY

THE AMERICAN ECONOMY

Political culture
Political behavior
Political institutions
Public policy process
Public bureaucratic
  culture and behavior

National Models
Compound model
Dual model
Centralist model

Subnational Models
Interstate model
National-Local model
Substate model
Interlocal model

Economic culture
Economic behavior (micro)
Economic institutions
Economic process (macro)
Private organization,
  culture, and behavior

TABLE 1-1 *Major Features of American Federalism*

Environments	The Seven Federal Patterns	Institutions	The Policy Process	Outcomes and Policy Cycles
National Level				
• national political culture	• compound model	• Congress	• policy content and direction	• socioeconomic impacts
• national cultures of federalism	• dual model	• the president	• policy phases [1]	• structural impacts
• democracy and capitalism	• centralist model	• bureaucracy	• IGR innovation spread	• system evolution
• elite and interest group systems		• federal courts	• policy change across levels	
• contemporary political ideologies		• parties		
Subnational Levels				
• regional political cultures	• interstate model	• governors	• policy content and direction	• socioeconomic impacts
• state and local political cultures	• substate model	• legislatures	• policy phases	• structural impacts
• elite and interest group systems	• interlocal model	• bureaucracy	• IGR innovation spread	• system evolution
	• national-local model	• courts	• policy change across levels	
		• municipalities		
		• parties		

[1] These include formulation, legitimation (or enactment), output, implementation, outcome, readjustment and evaluation, and cycles. See Jones 1970.

neglected topics in this book. But first we wish to build up to the view of federalism as a system of seven political economy patterns, and relate this view to the study and evolving understanding of federalism. So for now we will go back and reconstruct how federalism has been understood (and underestimated) by political scientists. We will have then laid the basis for a better understanding of federalism as a complex political economy.

WHAT'S IT ALL ABOUT? WHY THE STUDY OF FEDERALISM NEEDS THEORY

Perhaps the most important idea to keep in mind while building a bigger picture of federalism is that federalism *cannot* be separated from ideas and theories about it. This means that anybody's understanding of federalism rests on his or her assumptions about what it is and how it affects us. It also means that any interpretation of federalism is based on previous work on federalism. This rich store of ideas and concepts can be brought together to form a more general and powerful interpretation, such as our political economy interpretation. To understand how theory, concepts, and ideas have advanced the understanding of federalism, it is necessary to understand how the theory of federalism has developed.

The Muskie Committee, a prominent and extremely competent congressional panel, conducted a comprehensive overview of the literature on federalism. Among its important conclusions are the following:

> The field of intergovernmental relations might be characterized as the hidden dimension of government...performing as almost a fourth branch of government in meeting the needs of our people, it nonetheless has no direct electorate, operates from no set perspective, is under no special control, and moves in no particular direction. (U.S. Senate Subcommittee on Intergovernmental Relations 1965, p 2.)

At least two of these conclusions are remarkable. The first is the description of the federal system as a "hidden dimension"— even though the Muskie Committee knew of the mountain of academic literature on federalism. The second conclusion that stands out is the assertion that the federal system "moves in no particular direction." Both conclusions point to the critical need for systematic interpretive theories of federalism.

The federal system appears to be hidden precisely because we have made study after study of it without developing an interpretive theory of it. We know an almost bewildering array of facts about the system. Indeed, one of our problems may be that we are suffering from information overload. But we do not possess much in the way of *theory* capable of explaining these facts. Theories simplify large bodies of data by categorizing and explaining facts by their major characteristics.

Thus, the federal system has appeared to the Muskie Committee and others to "move in no particular direction"—to operate randomly—because of the scarcity of interpretive theory. Whatever else theories do, they allow us to "describe the beast." Theories allow us to identify patterns in social phenomena. And if the theories are powerful enough, they eventually allow us to develop and test propositions about future behaviors and events (although this is extremely rare in the social sciences). As far as the study of federalism is concerned, these developments are still a long way off. But there are patterns in federalism, and the study of federalism would do well to develop more theories, based specifically on newer social science approaches, that attempt to interpret these patterns.[1]

Does It Matter What We Call the Beast?

Yes, it certainly does. For example, the question of whether a distinction should be made between federalism and intergovernmental relations has been widely debated in recent decades. The basic issue was whether such a distinction is needed to more fully describe and understand federalism. Most scholars have come to accept the view that a distinction between the two concepts is valid. One scholar expresses the difference this way:

> *Federalism*, as we understand the term today, means a system of authority constitutionally apportioned between central and regional governments. In the American system, the central or national government is often called the federal government; the regional governments are the states. The federal–state relationship is interdependent; neither can abolish the other and each must deal with the other. *Intergovernmental relations* is the more comprehensive term, including the full range of federal–state–local relations. (O'Toole 1985, 2)

In this view, *federalism* is a more narrow, legally based term. Most scholars today regard *intergovernmental relations* as the more satisfactory term.

But the distinction between the two ideas points to a more revealing fact. What political scientists mean when they use the concept of intergovernmental relations, or IGR, is something much more than the relatively simple legal and institutional relationships that by and large have been the subject of older studies of federalism. But describing just how "much more" federalism "really is" has been beyond our capability, because scholars have still not brought to the study of federalism the newer and more powerful theories such as policy analysis and political economy theory. Such approaches will enable us to capture more of the bigger picture that scholars have seen by using the newer idea of intergovernmental relations.

But despite the current preference for the term *intergovernmental relations*, we primarily use the term *federalism* in this book, for two reasons. First, *federalism* is rooted in political philosophy and American history. Second, we prefer the term because Madison, Hamilton, and Jefferson understood *federalism* to mean something much closer to a political economy concept, which is actually much broader and more profound than the concept of intergovernmental relations. (We will develop this argument in Chapter 2.)

Somehow this broader meaning of *federalism* got lost in the twentieth-century stereotypes of federalism. For years, the word federalism conjured up to students visions of dry tomes of law or artificial lists of the "dual" powers of the states and the national government. Despite the evolution of the idea of intergovernmental relations, these stereotypes are still quite strong. Elsewhere in political science, the new notions of policy phases, the political economy, and political and bureaucratic decision making and environments have come into wide use, especially since the 1960s. But the study of federalism remained untouched by most of this until the 1970s, and even now, as we shall see, relatively few of these new concepts and theories have been applied to it. Instead, the study of federalism has been dominated by three approaches–institutionalism, pluralism, and organization theory. A brief account of the evolution of these approaches is important because each reinforces our point that how we understand federalism depends on how we look at it.

PREVIOUS APPROACHES TO UNDERSTANDING FEDERALISM

Institutionalism, pluralism, and organization theory each have a fairly distinct set of assumptions about what federalism "really is." In Table 1-2 we contrast

TABLE 1-2   *Four Approaches to Federalism*

	Federalism	*Key Concepts*
Institutionalism	• official activities across levels of government	• government structures
	• balancing of national and subnational functions	• dualism • cooperative federalism
	• legal structures and levels of government	• divisions of powers • stages of representation, federalism
	• structures for controlling power, limiting representa-, tion and providing for efficient government functions	• centralization or decentralization

TABLE 1-2   *(Continued)*

	Federalism	Key Concepts
Pluralism	• "federalism" is really intergovernmental relations • interest-group activity across governmental levels • representation structures for diverse interests	• governmental levels and roles • interest-group politics • citizen preferences and satisfactions • implementation through decentralization
Organization Theory	• institutionalism with better management • officially sanctioned goals • coordination and control of intergovernmental activities • efficient program performance	• efficiency • implementation • intergovernmental bargaining and consensus • environmental control • policy evolution
Political Economy	• subsystem of politics and economics • complex pattern of political economies • seven patterns	• power theory • compound theory • policy phase • macrosocial functions • federalist cultures • federalist cycles • microsocial functions

these three approaches and the political economy approach. The oldest approach, **institutionalism**, blends federalism with constitutional law and fiscal relations. Institutionalists generally define federalism as official activities across the various levels of governments, which balance and mix national and subnational government powers. Ultimate power is said to lie with the national government. Institutionalism derives primarily from James Madison and The Federalist Papers. Since the 1950's, the second approach, **pluralism**, has guided not only the study of federalism but much of the rest of American political science as well. Pluralists see federalism largely as a tug of war among many roughly equal groups acting across government levels. It is rooted in the ideas of John Dewey and Joseph Schumpeter, as considerably modified by Robert Dahl, David Truman, and David Easton. The institutional and pluralist ideas of politics are the roots of the term *intergovernmental relations*. The third and most recent approach, **organization theory**, is concerned primarily with describing how to improve coordination and management efficiency in the federal system. It combines the ideas of institutionalism and pluralism with a "how-to-keep control" perspective. This approach can be traced to the work of Frederick W. Taylor, Chester Bernard, and Herbert A. Simon.

Institutionalism

In describing federalism, institutionalism has focused on constitutional history, government design, fiscal affairs, and legal relations between governments. Its key idea has been that federalism should be designed and adjusted legally to get the best means of curbing excessive political power.[2] Thus, federalism as understood by this approach is largely a system of legally designed institutions for the control of power. Like the other approaches, institutionalism has guided both what has been studied about federalism (description) and how the federal system can be adjusted to solve governmental or public problems (reforms or prescriptions). The way institutionalists view federalism is shown in Table 1-3.

Clearly the institutional viewpoint allows us to see only certain key elements in the *structure* or *design* of federalism. That is, institutionalism sees federalism in terms of government structure, reorganization, statutory and fiscal relations, policy centralization, and government fragmentation. For example, those concerned with describing governmental structure continue to debate how to describe the levels, policy functions, and development of federal relations (see Chapter 10). The discussion has produced some colorful metaphors indeed. Morton Grodzins, for instance, popularized *marble-cake federalism* as a description of widely mixed powers shared cooperatively by the various levels of government (1960, 265). Deil Wright used the metaphor of a *picket fence* to emphasize the alliance between program specialists at all levels of government (1982, 63). However, a zenith was reached with Aaron Wildavsky's characterization of the federal system as *fruitcake federalism*:

> Of glutinous texture, it hardly seems to diminish by the cut, falling back into its former shapelessness as the earth into its primeval void. And, for suitable social occasions, when it becomes a collective enterprise, added to as it is diminished, it grows, like the appetite, with the feeding. Simmered, suet style, just short of boiling over, it accommodatingly absorbs all inputs, its bubbled surface conveying glimpses of goodies, soon disappearing beneath the not quite comprehensible outer form that appears to change only as it remains the same. (1981, 80)

As you can see, metaphors have their limits as useful ideas about federalism. So many metaphors purporting to describe federalism were put forward

TABLE 1-3 *How Federalism Is Understood by the Institutional Approach*

Descriptions of Federalism

1. constitutional history, law, and regulation (Diamond, MacMahon)
2. shared sovereignty (Diamond, Riker)
3. governmental reorganization (Zimmerman)
4. structural, statutory, and fiscal relations of governmental levels (Wright)
5. government fragmentation, multiple authority, and separation of decision making from enforcement (Pressman and Wildavsky)
6. a series of stages (Grodzins, Wright)
7. centralization or decentralization of political power (Beer, Pressman and Wildavsky, MacMahon, Farkas)
8. representation through the federal structure (Diamond, Beer)
9. grants, revenue systems, and distribution of resources by level of government and functional area (Derthick, Wright)

Reforms or Prescriptions for Federalism

1. legal reforms as general solutions (MacMahon, Zimmerman)
2. structural or reorganization reforms as general solutions (Pressman and Wildavsky, Farkas, Zimmerman)
3. centralization of decision making for effectiveness (Pressman, Wildavsky, MacMahon, Zimmerman)
4. decentralization for effectiveness through increased responsiveness (Zimmerman, McDavid)
5. antitrust regulations (Lowi)
6. fiscal reforms (Derthick, Wright, Pressman and Wildavsky, Farkas)

that scholars began to analyze the metaphors themselves (Stewart 1979). All the metaphors tended to assume that "official-looking federalism" was made up almost exclusively of government levels and their relations.

Reforms of federalism, or *prescriptions*, have been limited in most institutional writing to legal or structural reforms. Institutionalists have concerned themselves with such questions as whether to centralize or decentralize the federal system to get "what's best" from it, whether to increase or decrease government regulation, whether to adjust fiscal relations between the nation and states, and so on. Thus, to institutionalists, how to reform federal design and structure is the key to solving problems in the complex federal system. For example, Zimmerman (1983) has proposed metropolitical consolidation as a means of improving "weak" local governments, and Wright (1982) has spent lots of time discussing the details of reform proposals, fiscal relations, and administrative effects of the grant system.[3]

These topics are not unimportant in the study of federalism, but they are only part of the picture. The institutional approach has generally called insufficient attention to how federalism *includes* and affects many other political and economic phenomena, such as political cultures (typical political activities and belief systems), the political behaviors of people, and private economic markets. It also neglects how public policies, under the influence of federalism, affect society. (*Public policies* are generally defined as what governments do or do not do with the resources at their disposal.) Thus, whether people, groups, or government districts are richer, cleaner, or better off because of federalism and public policy is still a weak area in institutional theory.

Pluralism

Like the institutionalists, pluralists have been concerned with how to properly concentrate and control excessive political power. They have emphasized the federal structure as a system of *representation* that allowed many diverse groups access to the political arena. Early pluralists, especially those influenced by the philosopher and educator John Dewey, argued that political power could and ought to be in the hands of the participating "average citizen." Later, in the 1950s, pluralists modified this proposition, arguing that political power was and ought to be in the hands of either interest groups or competing elites. The pull of roughly equally powerful groups was assumed by pluralists to safeguard democracy by preventing any one elite group from controlling politics; no single group could dominate all the others and thus control the public decision process. Contemporary critics of pluralism, represented by Lowi, agree that the competition of groups controls excessive power, but it does so by paralyzing government. In this view, government, pressured heavily by all, can respond to none. This is what Lowi (1969) calls *hyperpluralism,* or the end of interest-group liberalism. The pluralist view of federalism is shown in Table 1-4.

The pluralists, who seek to transfer more political power to the common person, have tended to see federalism primarily as a representation system (Beer, Diamond). William Riker has convincingly demonstrated the inaccuracy of this perception. He argues that most analyses of federalism have consisted of moral evaluation rather than accurate descriptions (Riker 1975).

As such, they are based on certain assumptions, which have never been proved. Among those assumptions is the assertion that federalism promotes a democratic political system. Riker has argued convincingly that such has not always been the case (1975, 155). Responding to Lowi's—and, later, Riker's — criticism, the pluralists began describing federalism more as a government structure that affects interest-group liberalism. This view, common by the late 1960s, emphasized federalism as a complex thicket of

TABLE 1-4 *How Federalism Is Understood by the Pluralist Approach*

Descriptions of Federalism

1. group and territorial representation (Diamond, Beer)
2. agent of democratization (Beer)
3. the artifacts of democracy (decentralized parties, electoral systems, party competitiveness) are related to the efficiency of government structure (Reagan, Zimmerman)
4. historical phases (Grodzins, Wright)
5. public choice theory: the federal system responds to the needs and preferences of the individual through such means as voting, lobbying, and decentralization, which are assumed to be necessary to democratic processes
6. interest-group liberalism models, including the marble cake and picket fence metaphors, containing the premise that no one power group is dominant

---

Reforms or Prescriptions for Federalism

1. politics ought to be responsive (Farkas)
2. public choice theory that politics ought to be built on citizen satisfaction (Bish and Ostrom)
3. decentralization can lead to inequality of services and social inequities (Elazar 1972: 4–10); it thus has ambiguous effects (Farkas)
4. fiscal federalism ought to be decentralized revenue sharing (Reagan)
5. decentralization is difficult to implement (Pressman and Wildavsky)

---

governments at various levels that repressed different interests and "slowed down" politics and policies. This perspective also led to the rise of the organization theory view of federalism.

Organization Theory

Although the institutional and pluralist approaches have dominated the study of federalism, organization theory has grown more influential since the mid 1970s. Of all the branches of organization theory, only the classical (Taylor, Gulick and Urwick, Mooney and Reiley) and the neoclassical (primarily Barnard and Simon) have had an enduring impact on the understanding of federalism. Both of these branches try to spell out those principles of management that will achieve organizational goals with the least worker resistance. This how-to-maximize-control bias has colored organization theorists' discussions of federalism, and especially their studies of policy implementation in the federal system (see Sharp and Polumbo 1980). These theorists tend to define federalism as an obstacle to the attainment of political leadership or national goals. The way organization theory views federalism is shown in Table 1-5.

Organization theory primarily describes intraorganizational process—what happens "inside bureaucracies". It advocates and tries to explain the use of management techniques for more effective leadership in the federal system. Its recommendations for federalism emphasize methods of

---

TABLE 1-5 *How Federalism Is Understood by Organization Theory*

Description of Federalism

1. executive coordination, decision making, incrementalism, uncertainty, and constraints imposed by human psychological needs across government levels (Elmore, Berman, Pressman and Wildavsky, Mc-David)
2. internal conflict over goals; the impact of roles and specialization across government levels (Elmore, Berman)
3. buffering of the environment, control of the domain, and organizational exchange across government levels (McDavid, Derthick)
4. the effects of the general environment, including the political economy and social forces across government levels (Van Meter and Van Horn)
5. government fragmentation and degree of coordination (Pressman and Wildavsky, Zimmerman, McDavid, MacMahon, ACIR)
6. management control, efficiency and planning needs, and problems across levels, from a "top-down" perspective (Wildavsky)

Reforms or Prescriptions for Federalism

1. greater coordination between levels of government in the area of federal aid (MacMahon)
2. reorganization as a solution to the problems of coordination and span of control (Zimmerman, ACIR, 1961b, 1976)
3. policy execution by means of new organizational machinery having more direct means of coordination (Pressman and Wildavsky)
4. better means of coordination of fiscal accounting (U.S. Senate)
5. A-95 review process (IGR Cooperation Act of 1968)
6. comprehensive planning, specifically in health (Partnership in Health Act (1966)
7. consolidation of grant programs in Comprehensive Employment and Training Act (1973) and in housing and community development Housing and Community Development Act (1974)
8. planning, Programming, Budgeting System and the general growth of policy analysis, especially cost–benefit analysis

---

increasing executive power for program coordination, consolidation, control, and reorganization. Its primary assumption is that if public managers or other decision makers can better control and design government structure and process, successful intergovernmental bargaining is possible in the federal system (see Sharp and Polumbo 1980). This assumption has also been embraced by most implementation theory treatments of federalism (Pressman and Wildavsky 1973). Better control and design will supposedly make federalism function more efficiently—but that the control advocated is largely for national program managers' goals is never quite made clear. And the organization theory picture of what federalism "really is" is largely that of pluralism and institutionalism—pluralist politics across government levels (but under better-organized national policy management and control). The thing federalism needs, according to organization theorists, is better management and centralized but bargained control.

One of the major weaknesses of organization theory is its inadequate concern for outcomes, or what difference federalism makes for society. By limiting its analysis to *bureaucratic* or *enforcement* issues, organization theory reflects a bias found in institutionalism and pluralism.

The Need for a More Comprehensive Approach

The problem is that none of these three traditionally dominant approaches helps us thoroughly understand federalism as a social and policy force. To be sure, the progression of "what federalism is" from simple legalism (early institutionalism) to the richer idea of politics across levels (pluralism) to ideas about "getting things done" (organization theory) was very important. But these ideas have simply not carried federalism as far as other topics in political science have gone. The policy theory and political economy "revolutions" in political science —with their concern about policy problems, the impact of government on social conditions, power, and the need of citizens for greater control of government have left the study of federalism largely untouched. By the late 1980s, political scientists were still not emphasizing what policy difference federalism makes for most of us, or what relationship it bears to power and economics, despite decades of considerable analysis of the federal system.

It is only somewhat easier today to get the argument accepted that federalism is *not* just simply institutional or official roles, group politics, grant flows and fiscal affairs, or lists of evolving formal powers. But federalism is slowly getting recognized as something larger. In fact, as this book will show, it is more pervasive, more a part of our everyday thinking, and more influential in economics, society, and politics than is evident from the older approaches. We can start to make our case by introducing the picture of federalism presented by the political economy approach.

THE POLITICAL ECONOMY APPROACH TO FEDERALISM

From the political economy perspective, federalism in the United States is a complex system of seven patterns of specific political and economic relations, institutions, cultural characteristics, legal principles, and political relations between people and organizations across different governmental levels. The major features of this system were presented in Table 1-1.[4] Before we look at the seven political economy patterns, let's briefly survey the "parts" of federalism.

The "Parts" of Federalism

The "parts" of federalism certainly include (1) national institutions, such as Congress, and their important political functions. But at a higher level of thinking, federalism also includes (2) the political, fiscal, and other relations between political interest groups and those institutions and (3) the important social and policy functions and effects of these relations. Previous textbooks on the federal system have concentrated on the first and second of these elements. But the social and political– economic significance of federalism cannot be understood unless the third "part" is also clearly in mind.

Another important part of the federal system is the environment. This consists of national and regional political cultures, national cultures of federalism itself, elite and interest-group systems, parties and contemporary ideologies, and the tensions between "free-market" capitalism and democratic values in America. Subsequent chapters will detail these environmental elements and their influence.

This book also discusses the topics normally found in textbooks about federalism (such as shared powers, the balance of power, dualism, and fiscal affairs). But perhaps a little less familiar to the student of federalism and the specialist alike will be our description in Chapter 10 federalism as going through **policy evolution and processes** (formulation, implementation, and so on). Even less common will be our description of federalism as having **policy cycles** (centralization versus decentralization, national versus state innovation, and so forth). This discussion, which draws on policy studies and the literature on power, is perhaps one of the more novel parts of our description of federalism.

The parts of federalism are grouped into the seven general political economy patterns mentioned previously. Let's turn to them now.

The Seven Political Economy Patterns of Federalism

In addition to their unique characteristics, the seven patterns of federalism have similar aspects. Each has a political and social environment that directly influences *federal political relations*. We have identified the environmental elements in Table 1-1. In addition, each pattern involves specific *government* institutions, the arrangements of *power elites and interest groups* in society, and the processes and cycles of the *public policies* that federalism produces and affects.

The **national patterns of federalism** are those patterns of politics, economic intervention, and public beliefs that are linked to the practices of the national government; they have influence from coast to coast. The **subnational patterns of federalism** are influenced by the national patterns but mostly have their roots and major influence in regional and local societies

---

TABLE 1-6 *The Seven Patterns of Federalism*

The Three National Patterns

1. *Compound federalism* is the tradition of fiscal politics and economic and social regulation under the constitutional system, which recognized dualism but revised it in favor of strengthening the functions of the national government. Compound federalism also embodies the widespread influence of James Madison's ideas on government design, public cultures, and socioeconomic regulation in the American political economy.
2. *Dualism* represents the very old traditions of national, state, and local levels, the cultures of different regions, economic regulation, and the political sovereignty of the national government.
3. *Centralism* involves the traditions of blended elite and national government powers, which serve to justify the "insider" role of economic elites and the business class in culture, politics, and economics. This pattern was strongly influenced by the politics of Alexander Hamilton.

The Four Subnational Patterns

4. *Interstate federalism* involves the politics, economics, and social life of regions, and the politics of national and state-based political groups and government agencies.
5. *Substate federalism* involves the expression of dualism within states viewed as *civil societies.* Substate federalism includes state–local relations in the areas of the politics, economic and social regulation, and societal and political institutions.
6. *Interlocal federalism* involves the politics, economics, and social life of cities and the relations between the urban and rural areas of states over various issues.
7. *National–local federalism,* probably the newest "kid on the federal block," involves the ways in which the national government, national politics, and national public policies influence local life, and vice versa. Often described merely as "grants and regulations," this pattern really involves much more.

---

and politics. They interact and often compete with national influences at all levels. Table 1-6 offers a brief comparison of these seven patterns.

These seven patterns of politics, social life, and economics are the ways in which federalism operates in American life. In the succeeding chapters we will describe federalism in America by summarizing how these seven political economies affect each other and how they work as a whole to affect politics, economics, and society.

THE MAIN THEMES OF THE BOOK

We will now try to outline the ways in which federalism is a preeminent social force and give a big-picture introduction to the major themes of the rest of the book.

One thing that makes the federal system important in American life is its effects on economic and social life. The effects of each of the seven patterns are described in Chapters 2–7. Another very important characteristic of the federal system is its evolution from a complex constitutional and ideological bargain that has produced public cultures *of* federalism itself. The evolution and important effects of the three national federal traditions and cultures are described in Chapter 2.

The three national traditions and public cultures of federalism (compound federalism, dualism, and centralism) are very significant socially in a number of ways. They have great stability, staying power, and policy effects today. Most of the issues that polarize America today, such as school prayer, abortion, and the Equal Rights Amendment, show the influence of "these three patterns" of federalism. They show how federalist beliefs are durable, cyclical, and often full of unresolved tensions about the power of the Supreme Court, or about local or state rights to regulate life versus national power. We will argue in Chapters 2, 11, and 12 that conflicting public cultures of federalism play themselves out again and again in our politics as different elites and interest groups rise to power only to be frustrated by the structural and cultural obstacles in the federal system. Federalism, in short, "fights back." The polarizing issues just cited also show clearly how federalism's institutions, contradictions, and kaleidoscopic national and local cultures affect American policy, life-styles, and interest-group power. A greater appreciation of federalism's social role can help explain these effects.[5]

Finally, the issues just mentioned illustrate how federalism evolves slowly, in response either to executive initiatives or to requirements placed on it by social or economic crisis. The civil rights era, the New Deal, World War II economic planning, and today's industrial policy debate are examples of major social turning points that have altered federalism. Yet federalism *always* evolves within the limits of its public cultures, which themselves are surprisingly stable. This argument will be developed in Chapters 2 and 12.

Federalism's Issues and Policy Cycles

Public expectations about federalism itself produce policy patterns and policy cycles. These policy cycles occur when proposals to "reform" federalism return to themes that reflect alternative public cultures and patterns of federalism. For instance, a federalist policy cycle seems to have resurfaced in the 1980s, in the form of proposals for a return to dualism and increased state powers. Under President Reagan's inspiration and in response to long-standing complaints from conservatives, states, and cities, the Jeffersonian political culture and dual federalism came back into vogue in the 1980s in debates and trends in federalism and public policy. Whether this latest cycle of ideas is being implemented in a transformation of the federal system is a question to be addressed in the final chapter (we think it largely is not).

Policy cycles that involve federalist issues may be initiated by presidents (such as Johnson or Reagan) or brought to the public agenda by state or interest-group backlashes (today's New Right). Often "new" issues reopen what actually are frequent, cyclical debates about federalism. Often the debates are simply about **federalist issues**, such as increased state powers. At other times the debates are about an effect of federalism (should a nationally enforced school-prayer ban continue?). Either way, the debate is about federalism—as an issue itself or as an arbiter of power and public policy.

Types of Policy Cycles.   One policy cycle involving federalism is the old debate over the proper locus of innovative power in public policy. Should policy power be decentralized or centralized? Should it reside in the states, local government, or the national government? This issue cycle haunts the realm every decade or so (compare Johnson in the 1960s with Reagan in the 1980s). Thus, the 1960s public consensus on pursuing new national goals was reversed with the Carter–Reagan grant reforms, the 1980s civil rights retrenchment, and deregulation in the economy.

Less obvious is a second type of cycle, one that appears when political coalitions at different levels collide. This collision usually involves executive, local, and socially powerless alliances, as in the New Deal, the New Frontier, and the War on Poverty. These alliances become "cycled out" of power years later when interest groups disgruntled over issues of federalism form different executive – elite and regional or state alliances. This happened in the Carter–Reagan years, when social-program reduction, tax cuts, and antiabortion policies, for example, gained public support in reaction to a complex of liberal trends in the 1970s. These ideas were favored by western and southern conservatives, libertarians, social elites, and New Right populists, all of whom gained prominence with the 1980 election of Ronald Reagan (see Chapters 9 and 12).

Seeing such issues without recognizing how they have been influenced by federalism is risky. Federalism *by itself* is often a public issue. But most of the time, federalist issues and policy controversies are blended inseparably. To see that the issues of federalism are usually involved in controversies over other issues is to see how this second type of cycle —that of federalist alliances —works.

Public issues often "arise" through and/or use federalist reforms and rhetoric ("cooperative," "creative," "new federalism," and so on). Proponents of different policies often want to change the direction of public policy and even the role of the courts in the federal system. The changes almost always imply a redirection of the federal bargain itself. It seems almost inevitable that if these advocates of change can get policy "to go their way" for a while, resistance to their policies will arise somewhere in the federal system, and the opposition usually uses the federal system in one way or another to build this resistance. The anti–Equal Rights Amendment movement is a recent case in point: the 1982 deadline for ratification passed with the ERA short of the required number of ratifying states.

Federalist Issues Are Cultural and Unresolvable.   These policy cycles and public debates about federalism and public policies are *never really resolved*. In fact, their consequences are redebated, perhaps years later, as the policy effects from a previous period are felt by today's parties, elites, legislatures, and other impact groups. For example, public housing programs involving direct federal subsidy or construction were virtually eliminated in the early 1980s by the Reagan administration, which held that such programs were outdated failures and that the "housing function" had to be returned to the private sector. But by the spring of 1988, Congress and the media were debating the need for a strong government role in providing public housing, and policy action seemed imminent (MacNeil, Lehrer News Hour, March 28, 1988).

Recurring debates such as these occur within the limits of public cultures of federalism; indeed, this is one reason the debates and policy readjustments are never fully resolved, since Americans like to reintroduce the ideas of centralist federalism versus some other kind of federalism after a few years of policy experimentation. Americans seem to have only so much patience with federalist patterns, coming to feel after several years or decades these patterns yield either too much national interference or too little progress on "real" national goals. Thus federalist issue cycles are common, resulting in swings between federalist rhetoric and policy.

The effects of federalist issue cycles not only on policy but even on party evolution, social structure, and economic developments is one of the least explored areas of the American social landscape. It is crucial to see that these cycles involve recurrent debates about both federalism itself and federalism's policy role, and to realize that politics and the economy in America cannot be discussed fully just in terms of "today's issue agenda," "the administration's policy," or "changes in American economic conditions."

Something New Is Always Old: The Oldest Issues of Federalism

The usual controversies about federalism usually raise the issues that dominated the first uneasy agreement about federalism made in the 1787 Constitutional Convention. The federal "deal" of 1787 was an attempt to cope with a number of divisive social issues, which remain important today. What are these federalist issues? First, federalism is partly about an elite-designed but bargained consensus about how to *distribute power*. Second, federalism is partly about *regulating and representing* an increasingly broad set of social interests. Third, federalism is partly about *stabilizing political* power shifts and trends. Fourth, federalism is also partly about *regulating and undergirding* an entrepreneurial capitalist class in *politics and the economy*. These issues are what makes federalism a complex political economy. And debates about the federal "deal" (from the time of *The Federalist Papers* until today) are an ongoing part of the disagreement in America about how to regulate and resolve disputes about this political economy.

What is not obvious is that these recurring debates *always* concern specific federalist issues. The debates arise over the "more proper design" of the system. (For example, how should power be distributed between subnational and national structures?) The *legitimacy* of the basic structure of federalism is rarely at issue, but the role and power of federalism in policy making at different levels are. The debate is always couched in, if not obscured by, talk of temporary policy goals (slavery, discrimination, economic intervention by the state, welfare, and minority rights are examples arising over the last 150 years or so). But aside from these specific issues "at issue" at the time, the essential federalist issues *concern the ultimate purposes or operations of federalism*. A summary of these essential issues follows.

The Essential Issuses of Federalism

1. *Efficiency*. Here the issue is whether some aspect of policy implemented by a level of government is "working right" achieving ostensibly social goals. This leads in turn to the issue of whether the "faceless" Washington bureaucrats periodically have too much or too little power.
2. *Effectiveness*. Here the issue is whether what was done years ago by states, Congress, or some other "villain" has accomplished what was intended by law, court decision, or executive action.

3. *Responsiveness.* Should power and policy be in the hands of someone or something "distant" or "close," "central" or "local"?

4. *Representation.* This is a core function of federalism. This complex idea is about who speaks for whom at what territorial level. Representation, naively or not, is seen in America as "getting real power". Thus certain issues of representation carry great emotional and symbolic value about having or not having power — such as getting the right to vote, getting the election district drawn fairly, getting your "*somebody*"on official councils, etc. Whether various official bodies or decision processes are "inclusive" or "exclusive" is a great issue. It is often a source of race, sex, or labor controversy, and sometimes violence.

5. *Democracy.* In journalism and common parlance, *democracy* most often means majority public opinion, or the "public interest,"—even though most political theory and some research express much doubt about the necessity, purpose, strength, and general trustworthiness of public opinion as a sole guide to decisions. "Doing what the people want" has become a battle cry in debates over federalist tinkering, and especially over government power. The tendency of European democratic socialists to see democracy as proportional representation, or as economic, work, or social-group consultation through the government or legislatures, is *not* an idea affecting the American mind. Some aspects of federalism in America (such as the separation of powers and the electoral college) limit democratic expression in various ways.

6. *Social regulation* means a lot. It means efforts by government to redistribute advantage so that all persons, rather than a few, enjoy wide resources, and to control individual or business behaviors in public life in ways decided by Congress and the public regulatory agencies. These agencies are often tied to economic elites. Mostly, it is the regulation of business or social behavior that is really controversial (at least to business executives). Regulating people (or resisting government regulation) involves tackling states, Washington, and courts of all kinds, and many levels of bureaucracies. Less often, civil liberties are at issue on a national plane, but they too involve a complex diversity of conditions among states, especially the conditions of crime and education. In fact, most social regulation lies with states and localities. Which level should perform this function is always a controversial issue.

7. *Economic regulation* means a lot too, since courts make decisions about the economic functions of states *and* the federal government, at least regarding policy powers. Almost as complex as social regulation, this issue involves single-industry or industry-wide efforts by governments to control hazardous business practices, usually by indirect means (fines, blacklists, and so forth). Federalist debates about business regulation and the limits of various levels of government power are perhaps more contentious and visible simply because economic elites and business usually oppose state power (or even public criticism). Or perhaps, economic regulation is more "shaped" by various levels of government and is thus more truly intergovernmental. Again, which level should do the regulating is a hot issue.

8. *Power and elite control* are usually overlooked. No function of federalism is more important or more often forgotten by elitist or Marxist interpretations of power. All kinds of national and regional majorities and economic elites are frequently stymied in their attempts to control the various levels of public office, to sway federal or state bureaucracies, or to grab influence in the various courts. Many theorists fail to see how federalist structures can impede overt, ideological, or even covert forms of social power. Compound federalism was

designed partly to tilt power toward an aristocratic, wealthy class at the national level and especially at the state level (see the descriptions of the three national traditions of federalism in the next chapter). Still, the federalist design had features built into it to frustrate *both* tyrannical majorities and national elite consensuses on most issues most of the time, *primarily within* the structures of government. Federalism, and virtually everything else about the constitutional design, was *not* intended to limit the power of economic organization. However, the First Amendment was, among other things, meant to control religious threats to the state and democracy. Only recently have a few theorists started to explain how federalist structures, myths, and cultures affect economics, society, and elite and majority power in America.[6] This topic, how power is exercised by elites and others to get around federalist obstacles, and to what extent these groups succeed are summarized throughout the book, and especially in Chapters 8 and 9.

9–10. *Equality and justice.* Crime and its definition and prosecution are generally decentralized, and so is inefficient, unconstitutional, or unjust law enforcement. Unfortunately, the federalist patterns make it somewhat harder for the "down and out" and the socially unpopular groups to get redress, just as they make elite dominance a difficult thing to pull off at the national level. Inequality and injustice become issues only slowly, grabbing attention and money when proposed solutions are not too socially costly. Federalism is a paradox, allowing conditions of inequality to be tackled if localities are inclined, yet allowing injustice to worsen if the opposite is the case. Always a "top-burner" concern in the federalist debate, the implementation of equality and justice is lodged largely at the bottom of the "structural thicket" of governments, where it is at the mercy of local economic conditions.

The recurrent debates about these ten federalist issues are usually raised in the context of proposals for institutional reform, as if all the problems of the complex federal system could be cured with "a better federalist design" (Nixon) or by "returning power to the states" (Reagan). Such slogans are part of the political symbolism of reform. They drive most of the debates in institutional terms, building on the theme of "redesign it a little and it will be better." In fact, federalism is much more than the simple engineering of laws and the reshuffling of organization powers. Even more important is that the debates about federalism are debates not only about the *means* of implementation (as we casually think), but are about the distribution of power in society, as well as the criteria of "good" public policy. This is what the ten issues just listed are really about! So, federalism in America is linked very tightly to all of policy, all of economics, and all efforts to achieve the "good society." A reading of Chapters 10 through 12 should make this abundantly clear.

Policy and Power in Federalism

In Chapters 8 through 10 we will introduce two other social science innovations not usually applied to federalism—policy theory and power theory. The most important interpretation we introduce is that federalism exhibits the phases of policy development (see the footnote to Table 1-1) in at least two ways. First, the patterns of federalism strongly affect the way policies arise, are enacted, and implemented. Perhaps the most interesting of these effects is that public policy formulation, enactment, and enforcement are inherently intergovernmental. This idea is developed in Chapter 10. Second, federalism's role in the policy process has many economic, social, and political effects (Chapter 11). Sometimes these effects in turn have cyclical policy effects. This means that policies on welfare, health, and housing, for example, swing between experiments that variously emphasize market versus public approaches, or national versus state or local innovation. These cycles sometimes prevent local solutions to public problems from being completely, or at least consistently, applied. In other words, federalist policy solutions are developed within the limits of public cultures of federalism, and are somewhat subject to cycles of federalist issues. Thus, the social effects of federalism, particularly on policy cycles, are important in another vital way—by regularly limiting policy choices and their implementation.

Of course, policy scientists will recognize the importance of exploring federalism by means of policy concepts other than those of phases and cycles. It is important to know, for instance, whether the nature of public policy determines the degree of conflict over federalism. Certainly the question of who gets policy benefits and how policies evolve is a front-burner federalist concern. Given the complex nature of the federal system, it is also important to discuss whether the level of policy origin (state, national, or local) makes a difference in the scope and effects of new experiments. How policies are spread around in the patterns of federalism, and what social difference this makes, are summarized in Chapter 10.

Perhaps most important for society is the question of how federalism sets up representation systems and how it regulates private power and interest groups in the political arena. These functions are related—because representation systems establish forms of public influence (through elections, the separation of powers, institutional makeup, and so on). At the same time, the design of federalist institutions, we shall show, has a central role in channeling and limiting power and majorities in politics. This, in turn, has profound policy and economic effects. These important functions of federalism, often underestimated, are discussed in Chapters 8 and 9, which draw on research about power, economic policy, and federalism.

Finally, federalism should be seen as having more social significance than it is currently credited with. Our findings and views on this important topic draw from various pools of research and theory and are presented in Chapter 11.

SUMMARY

The importance of federalism has been underestimated. But it is possible to identify the significance and power of federalism in American life by using conceptual and theoretical advances common in other fields of social science. To do so may well mean a potential revolution in the study of federalism. We believe that if we conceptualize federalism as a complex political economy (as Madison, Hamilton, and Jefferson did), we can identify its true socioeconomic significance.

Ironically, what we find when we redefine federalism as a political economy is very close to James Madison's understanding of compound federalism. Why it has taken 200 years to return to a view that emphasizes some of the vision of Madison is anyone's guess. It is high time to reexplore federalism through more powerful social science concepts and theories. This book attempts to do this, to look at federalism as a political economy and its larger role in American life.

KEY CONCEPTS AND THEMES FOR REVIEW

federalist issues
institutionalism
institutional political economy theories
intergovernmental politics
organization theory
patterns of national federalism
patterns of subnational federalism
pluralism
policy cycles
policy evolution and processes
political economy
seven political economy patterns

NOTES

[1] There is another important reason why a political economy conceptualization of federalism is needed: Studies of federalism need to adopt a more standard base of modern social science theory. The political economy concept of federalism has the advantage of resting on a universe of social science theory about complex organizations and social structures. Since midcentury certain prominent scholars (Weber 1964; Dahl and Lindblom 1953; Parsons 1954; March and Simon 1958; Lindblom 1977) have developed the common structural view that human social behavior is organized by social and political cultures, bureaucratic traditions, economic markets, and political systems. The views of federalism developed in this book rest squarely on those ideas, concepts, and theories.

Not only do studies of federalism need to pay more attention to the rest of social science theory, but the social sciences need to pay more attention to federalism, whose social significance they still underestimate. For example, social scientists sometimes fail to realize that federalism *is a network of patterns that stands largely by itself, straddling politics and economics*. It is a subsystem that penetrates the larger political and economic systems. Its seven patterns involve very specific political and economic relations, institutional and cultural characteristics, and rules and regulations governing people and public organizations at different governmental levels and locales. In short, social scientists need to take a much deeper look at federalism.

[2] For example, the legalistic school of federalism, represented by the conservative wing of legal scholars at the University of Chicago Law School, would take this view. This school is strongly affected by old-line institutionalism, laissez-faire ideology, and strict legal constructionism, and lies well outside mainstream theory and research in history and political science. We hesitantly label it a form of establishment scholasticism.

[3] The 1987 edition of Wright's text still devotes four of twelve chapters to government fiscal relations alone.

[4] Clearly the model of federalism we present in Table 1-1 is based in systems theory. Our descriptions of the environmental parts of federalism are influenced by theories of political culture, organizational networks, and normative political theory.

[5] We want to be clear that we are treating American federalism from the standpoint of social science *functionalists*. This means that we are looking at what *emerged* as American federalism by approximately the 1820s and how it functioned thereafter in society, economics, and politics. The key figures (Madison, Hamilton, Jefferson) cannot be understood merely as "all-seeing, collusionary wizards" (indeed Hamilton and Jefferson were at each other's throats much of the time) during the early evolution of federalism. Instead we are using the modern concepts and theories of the social sciences to reinterpret how their somewhat divergent but collective effects on federalism's cultures and political economies *emerged* as permanent features of our political system, and *what difference those features make*.

[6] It is more than significant that leading neo-Marxist and mainstream sociological works on power and the state neglect James Madison, *The Federalist Papers*, and their collective effects on the political economy in designing the structure of the new government and creating public myths and a public culture of federalism. That a complex theory of political economy worthy of today's best comparative and functional theorists was inherent in the thought and influence of the founders is finally being recognized. See, for example, Epstein 1984.

The Design and Evolution of National Federalism:

2

The three traditions of a national political economy

In this chapter, we will describe the three national traditions of federalism in America— compound federalism, dualism, and centralism. We will do something a little unusual with these three traditions: we will trace them back to the ideas of the Founders, then through the formative events of the past, and up to their present state of evolution. We will focus on the difference each tradition has made—on politics, economics, and policy—over time. We will attempt to show how the traditions compete with one another, causing America to swing from one tradition to another at different points in its history. We will also begin to show the power of federalism in determining public policy, economic development, political conditions, and regional differences. In this way we can demonstrate that federalism really is a complex political economy having major effects in American life.

As we saw in Chapter 1, compound federalism is traceable to James Madison. It is the most complex national political culture of federalism,[1] and also the most powerful and widely shared one. Even so, it is often misunderstood, or omitted entirely, in discussions of federalism. Dual federalism is older than compound federalism as an idea. It originally blended the early ideas of confederation with the thinking of Thomas Jefferson. To the extent that dualism has a "godfather," that individual would be Jefferson. Centralist federalism was articulated by and later associated with Alexander Hamilton. It is the federal culture that has the most variations.

THE COMPOUND FEDERALISM OF MADISON

No doubt the great winner in the federalism design contest surrounding the Constitutional Convention of 1787 was James Madison with his conception of **compound federalism.** This federal tradition has what looks today like both dualist and cooperative features. But it stands alone, if only because it was built into the Constitution itself and took on life in the opinions and actions of the new government. It is the most pervasive and generally accepted public tradition of federalism.

The thing most interesting about compound federalism is that it truly was a *compound.* A compound is a blend of elements that is different in the end from the characteristics of the elements by themselves. This is true of compound federalism: it is a blending of (1) tensions, powers, and functions, sometimes shared by national institutions and sometimes not, and (2) the nation versus the states. This blending has political and economic effects that really are a "social sum greater than its parts." Table 2-1 lists the essential elements of compound federalism as a political economy. As is clear from the table, Madison and the Constitutional writers and delegates whom he influenced were not just tinkering around with national political institutions.

It is not just what Madison said or thought at any particular time that is crucial to the genesis of compound federalism. This tradition derives not only from Madison's direct contributions at the Constitutional Convention of 1787, but also from what emerged from his arguments at the convention and took shape later in both cultural and political institutions. In this respect, as others have shown (Diamond 1974; Epstein 1984), Madison influenced the federal system to become something different from what federalism had meant before. Before *The Federalist Papers,* federalism was much closer in meaning to "confederation"; after, it meant "compound."

Today, Madison is usually credited with re-creating the separation of powers among the executive, legislative, and judicial branches. But he is also largely responsible for re-creating the powers of the central government and determining the division of the levels of government, with certain powers shared by the states and the national government and certain powers held separately. The central government, in Madison's view, would assume a superior role in economic, defense, and constitutional issues. Actually, Madison's ideas are quite close to today's idea of cooperative, or picket-fence, federalism with its emphasis on intergovernmental action often with a national "lead role."

More important, Madison's compound federalism, the main features of which were largely worked into the Constitution, had more to it than just politics; it also had to do with economics. It was a *political economy* not just a representation scheme. It involved not only a *plan* for sharing and separat-

TABLE 2-1 *Elements of Compound Federalism as a Political Economy*

Centralized civil liberties *and*	The proposition that only the national government has sufficient power, capability, and responsibility to achieve the prime goals of government: "the protection of human faculties, the security of private rights, and the steady dispensation of Justice" (*The Federalist* (hereafter *Fed.*) 37,227; *Fed.* 10).(For example, the Constitution gives the national government the power to suppress rebellions, but does not eliminate state militias; the Constitution declares itself the Supreme Law of the land; the Supreme Court is given original jurisdiction over state disputes.)
Social order functions	States, in contrast, are too small to avoid domination by strong factions or interests. Looked at from a national standpoint, this means that states cannot guarantee all citizens basic liberties or justice. (Diamond, 1974 in O'-Toole, 1985 on Madison's Convention speeches). (The addition of the Bill of Rights secured basic civil liberties, at least at the national level, thanks to the anti-Federalists.)
Separation of powers and the control of social power	Human nature leads people to form essentially self-interested factions, which can misguide public opinion, especially if the factions themselves are composed of misguided passionate elites or uneducated and volatile social groups. Majorities are thus essential to democracy yet constitute its greatest threat, since they are often unstable, uninformed, and easily misled to repress minorities (*Fed.* 10; the last paragraph of *Fed.* 51). To guard against these dangers, certain features of government design were established: limited representation, such as the indirect election of the president by state elites and the election of the Senate by state legislatures; the separation of powers; different terms for House and Senate members; and the requirement that three-fourths of the states ratify amendments.
Separation of powers and its effects on the forms of limited representation	The protection of minority rights and democratic stability requires a balance among those who are wise (the Courts), those who are powerful (the Senate) and those who "represent" more of the common interest (the House) (see *Fed.* 51,323; *Fed.* 53; and *Fed.* 57). This is accomplished through separation of powers in the central government (see *Fed.* 78,465–70; and *Fed.* 47–51).

TABLE 2-1 *(Continued)*

Revised dualism	The protection of rights and the maintenance of democratic stability required a careful revision of *shared* and *dual* powers of the states and the nation (*Fed. 51, 323; Fed. 17; Fed. 20; Fed. 27, 176–7; Fed. 29, 187*). (This included roughly determining which government level should have the powers of economic development, regulation, commerce, trade, finance, and defense; outlining these and other functions; and incorporating them in the Constitution.)
Centralized economic and international functions	"Lesser" functions of governments that are vital to the survival of the whole society are best handled almost exclusively by the central government, since the states may not be inclined to cooperate. (These include treaties, defense, regulation of domestic commerce, trade between states, foreign commerce and foreign affairs, including war, and national economic development and regulation of interstate business. See Diamond, 1961, in O'Toole 1986, 32–33; *Fed. 30; 198.*)

ing mere powers between government levels, but also priorities for economic, social, and political order and a notion of the macroeconomic functions of governments. *Madison's compound federalism was, in fact, designed to produce a complex, multi-level political economy.* The widespread public acceptance of his ideas he did not foresee, but it certainly has helped maintain his version of federalism.

The Goals of Compound Federalism

Madison intended his version of federalism to accomplish four main goals for the new order: (1) to provide limited representation of the public, (2) to provide varied representation of different elite groups in different institutions (separation of powers), (3) to guard against both elite and social tyranny, *while* (4) safeguarding a stable, emerging capitalist, social, and economic order. The separation of powers and Madison's recognition and revision of dual federalism were the keys to these goals. Madison formulated most of the important principles in the new constitutional system with the intention of achieving stability in the new order. These principles emphasized how to manage social order, representation, *and* economic development simultaneously, through *political* methods. (See Epstein 1984, 162–65. This important book summarizes these goals of federalism, which are explicit in *The Federalist Papers.*)

The Meaning of Compound

In this sense, *compound* meant that dualism was merely revised in the Constitution. *Compound* also meant that dualism and the new separation of powers were to act *in concert* with other features of federalism. These other features included a central government responsible for national economic development, national representation, and social order, and states responsible for crime, social life, and state representation. The joint purpose of these various elements was to isolate national development and the political sphere from any danger that might confront the limited democracy in the new federal system, while centrally guiding national economic development. Thus the design and the goals were all compound.

The Ideas behind the Compound Design

Madison's ideas about compound federalism were complex, and they take some explaining. Madison had a complex skepticism about human nature, factions (interest groups), and the *states*. This skepticism lay behind his ideas about the design of the federal system and the national government. One of the central goals was for the new system to allow limited public input and representation, *while* throwing up institutional barriers to elite and majoritarian power within the political sphere of life.

For Madison, the national mix and the balance of powers were inextricably combined with and as much a part of federalism as were the somewhat less critical rights and powers of the states. This is because, for him, federalism was explicitly compound—a true mixture of states and nation that was "a whole greater than the sum of its parts."

The separation of powers was to be the key to accomplishing the four main goals discussed previously, but it was to act in concert with other features of federalism to isolate the political sphere of life from dangers to limited democracy. Madison was especially concerned about such dangers as a tyranny of the majority, disputes based on property and wealth, and sectarian interests within the states. To Madison (and Hamilton, as well), these dangers might arise from the passions of human nature, from *within* the institutions, *and* from *external* social elites and misguided public opinion. In their view, expounded in *The Federalist Papers,* so many historical dangers threatened representative government that conservative protections were needed.

But stability of representation was not the only purpose of the new order. Madison and Hamilton also developed general views about how to manage social order and economic development through *political* methods. For example, they persuaded the delegates to the Constitutional Convention that a strong central government was the only trustworthy source for protecting private property, insuring justice, and managing economic development. Other functions of governments, such as defense, treaties, internal order, foreign commerce, and diplomacy, were also best handled by a national government, because states might not be inclined to cooperate with each other. To Madison the states, where "faction and oppression would prevail" ultimately, were *not* to be trusted with the most important social-order and economic functions.

However, this is not to say that state powers were abolished. Compound federalism also meant that the states would remain essentially self-governing in terms of administration, social life, intrastate commerce, law, crime control, and civil liberties. (The national constitution, though, would eventually prevail on this last item. See Epstein 1984.)

Thus, Madison's view of federalism—that sovereignty over some matters was shared by the two levels, while sovereignty over other matters was exercised solely by one level—also meant that *dualism was maintained*, even if revised. Thus, some of the roots of today's cooperative federalism and dualism can be found in Madison's handling of some problems with compound solutions and other problems with dualist solutions. The states and the courts may well have gained as much influence as they have today because some areas of politics and policy were left undefined, or were shared; *not* all issues were settled in the original federal bargain.

Madison and Hamilton from Today's Perspective

It is not fully recognized today that Madison (and Hamilton) dabbled not only in the design of America's politics but in the arrangement and direction of its economy. They spent somewhat more effort in working out goals for the political sphere. In Madison's case, this was certainly because the political theory of the design was much more elaborate than the economic ideas. Both emphasized political control because they were what we would call **democratic elitists:** they believed that an enlightened, democratic-minded economic elite should have more say in politics and economics than the average person. Also, many if not most of the Founders wanted a stable democratic order primarily as a basis for ordered economic expansion. Finally, the government role in economics was developed before the age of industrialization. There was no crystal ball to tell Madison of the coming of big business and large-scale capitalism. Because of their contributions to the politics and economy of the new republic, Madison and Hamilton—and not Smith, Ricardo, Malthus, or other celebrated economists—were probably history's most successful designers of a political economy.

The Fate of Compound Federalism over Time

Compound federalism has always been the main force in determining the *sharing, balancing,* and *distribution* of power and functions among the levels of government. It tilted the dualism of the Articles of Confederation toward national power in economics and social-order maintenance. Finally, it had broad, somewhat veiled effects on policy making, creating new institutions that came to have important institutional perspectives, which were rooted most often in the *representation* of different interests. To some extent, the compound institutional design means that the Senate is still a relatively elite "club," the House is more a representative of grass-roots perspectives, and the courts are a sort of legal "guardian class." And all the states remain in competition with the national government over policy control. These tensions are echoed within the states, forty-nine of which adopted the separation-of-powers design.

What has been the fate of compound federalism over time? (Figure 2-1 traces its evolution, and that of the other patterns of federalism, from 1750 to 1988.) The answer is best understood (as Madison foresaw) against the background of battle for political power by various elite, mass, and regional interests. In this battle, compound federalism was either the object of direct attack by groups wishing radical change of the system or it was the battleground itself.

The political struggles arising from attempts by groups and important figures to overcome compound federalism (either directly or as the result of pursuing other goals) have marked some of the rites of passage in our development as a society. Alexander Hamilton (with considerable irony) was one of the first to attempt to alter the terms of American federalism (since it was the prime obstacle to his goals), by further "nationalizing" the powers of the federal government so that it could control the direction of the economy. Hamilton succeeded in this, at least until the late 1840s, by which time his national bank had sunk beneath the combined assaults of Jackson and regional banking interests. In altering the terms of federalism, Hamilton set up an *alternate model of federalism* that survives today—and that forms the basis of elite involvement in politics. Thus, from 1790 to the 1830s, compound federalism was challenged seriously by Hamilton's new centralist model which ran a close second for dominance.

In the 1860s and 1870s, the compound model may have operated in a narrow, national, and institutional sense that is, the national balance of power, was maintained, but its full force was quite diminished after the Civil War. This was because the Yankee victors used the centralist model in those two decades to impose northern constitutional, political, and economic requirements on the South. Lincoln was right when he concluded that the fate of the federal bargain was put in question by the Civil War.

In the 1890s compound federalism began to reassert itself in politics as urbanites, farmers, white elite separatists, populists, and progressives worked within the compound framework pressed Congress and ultimately the presidency for satisfaction of their extremely divergent needs. As a result new features of subnational federalism, especially local–local and

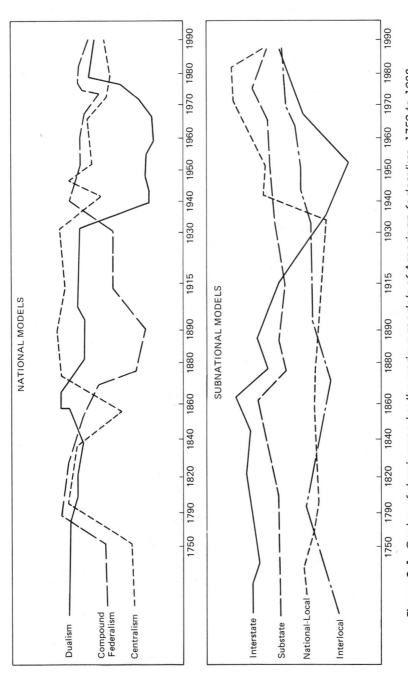

Figure 2-1 *Cycles of dominance by the various models of American federalism, 1750 to 1988*

[1] No evaluation of the relative importance of subnational versus national models is intended in this chart (see Chapters 10 through 12, and especially twelve on this issue). The chart is based not on quantitative analysis but rather on historical interpretation of the relative influence of the models.

NATIONAL MODELS

Dualism
Compound Federalism
Centralism

SUBNATIONAL MODELS

Interstate
Substate
National-Local
Interlocal

national–local patterns, appeared by the 1920s. But, at least until 1910, centralism was dominant, as Dolbeare (1986) has argued, because Yankee capitalist elites had reasserted national control of the economy and polity in the 1890s.

In our view, this meant that compound federalism was displaced once again, from the 1880s until at least 1915, by Yankee big business forces, with one exception—the interests of southern economic and political elites. By the 1890s, southern elites had gotten what they wanted out of the federal system—reassertion of white elite dominance in politics in the South, growing southern control of Congress, reassertion of segregation and racism, and a new, extensive order of white upper-middle-class control of local politics and social life. The general result was that by the late 1890s compound federalism had failed to fragment national elite power in order to aid the causes of "lesser forces" such as populists, labor unions, farmers, women, and blacks. The technical and fiscal aspects of compound federalism reflected its decline at this time. Hamilton-style elites were back in the federal saddle (despite the progressive inclination of Teddy Roosevelt), and would remain there until the Wilson era.

Some writers picture the late nineteenth century as an era when "democracy was at risk," sinking beneath the rising power of Yankee business elites (Dolbeare 1986; Kolko 1963). But we see this time more as a complex struggle between federalism and new political, economic, and cultural forces, such as growing urbanization, progressive and big-city machine politics, and economic and ethnic complexity. These forces were the engines of change in local and state politics, and by the 1930s they had clearly led to the emergence of new patterns of federalism.

By 1915, compound federalism had been reestablished and invigorated at the national *and* subnational levels with the advent of the powerful democratic progressivism of Woodrow Wilson (See Wilson, 1908). As it did the presidency, Wilson's long shadow touched federalism. As a result, compound federalism began to reemerge on a par with centralism. Specifically, after Wilson power in policy, politics, and economics began to shift to bureaucratic, regional nonelites in the federal system.

Wilson's policies had this effect because they stimulated agricultural stabilization and subsidization, urban grants for improved basic services and planning, women's suffrage, city management reform, and marginal activism in monopoly regulation. This meant that compound federalism was again beginning to fragment elite power, allowing cities and local, nonelite, disadvantaged groups to "get some action" through Congress and the presidency, if not the courts. (For a good review of federalism in this era, see Degler 1986, 11–13; and Colella 1986, 42–52.)

Later in the twentieth century, this reinvigorated compound federalism began to function hand in hand with the centralist New Deal of Franklin Delano Roosevelt. FDR's new brand of federalism involved a com bination of new programs. Some involved the innovation of direct grants to local governments, primarily for public employment, housing, and unemployment relief. These grants formed the first stable basis of national–local federalism. Other developments, such as social security, the public-works programs, which built roads, schools, and bridges, and the right to strike under the Wagner Act, involved very significant increases in the role of the national government in the economy. These developments generally worked to the advantage of labor, including child laborers, blacks, and other minorities, and boosted Keynesian types of economies for stabilizing the economy. But these were not merely new policies or new presidential roles in politics. They also meant new subnational patterns of federalism, which began to guide political, economic and social life in new ways (see Chapters 3 through 7).

The Concrete Forms of Compound Federalism

Today, compound federalism has certain prominent features:

1. *It creates constitutionally rooted* **policy dualism.** The Constitution specifies that certain features of public policy are to be handled by different levels of government. These effects are *dualistic* in nature. For example, court rulings have given Congress the lead role in national fiscal policy and government regulation while retaining opportunities for substantial state involvement. The dual legal systems of the United States are also rooted in the compound pattern, which created new federal courts while allowing the states to retain their own legal systems.

2. *It has led to an increased institutional* **balance of power.** Both the national and subnational balance-of-power systems (49 states copied the national Constitution) are rooted in Madison's compound design.

3. *It has created a number of other means of* **political-power balancing.** In addition to the separation-of-powers systems in virtually all governments, compound federalism fosters certain kinds of power competition in the American polity. Along with the important guarantee of a "free, unfettered press," these include the following:

1. *The watchdog role of the mass media.* At all levels of government today, the press is important as an exposer of government and corporate power abuses, corruption, policy mismanagement, neglect of the disadvantaged, and so on.
2. *The interest group struggle.* Interest groups in America are organized and active on an *intergovernmental* basis. They *must* be so. They are intergovernmentally active because compound federalism created a shared system of policy control and political sovereignty among the various states and the newly strengthened central government. So, since governmental policy making and policy enforcement are usually intergovernmental, interest groups must act at many levels to get what they want. Usually the interest group struggle in-

volves intergovernmental lobbying, court litigation, attempts to alter or obstruct policy administrators and regulations, and other strategies. These efforts focus on *both* policy-making and policy-implementing agencies from top to bottom in the federal system. Forcing the interest group struggle through different layers of institutions dilutes and alters interest group power. Precisely how this is done will be described in Chapter 9.

3. *Institutions and election systems that balance regional and state interests with national ones.* Most of the writing on federalism emphasizes this. It conceptualizes federalism largely as a struggle between legitimate, representative institutions on the one hand and levels of government surrounded by their political environments on the other. In this view, policy is made, implemented, and power-balanced *between* institutions and *between* the states and the nation. Certainly this is part of the picture—how a governor perceives and acts on a problem in relation to different bureaucracies, the national administration, and so on. But elite and power theories and studies show that institutions do not exist in a power vacuum; rather, they may sometimes be indistinguishable from the elites themselves and come to be dominated by one or several interests. Despite elite power, there is something to be said about *representative* institutions and public bureaucracies having a life of their own, with independent identities and powers and competing turfs. The founders, and particularly Madison, designed institutional fragmentation to work just in this manner. How this works, because of compound federalism, is described in Chapter 10.

4. *The fragmentation of national and regional power elites.* Researchers such as Dye 1980 and Domhoff 1978 have uncovered the tactics elites use to obtain consensus among themselves and to unify their control over the economy, the policy-making process, and government institutions. Domhoff, Dye (1980), and other elite-power researchers have demonstrated that sometimes this unanimity and control does allow elites to attain their goals. But their research does not reveal that elites split up only on the basis of their differing interests; they also split because the compound federal structure divides their attention among different government levels, bureaucracies, and institutions—"keeping 'em on the run," so to speak. So, for example, several allied elite groups might be busy lobbying Congress and getting the president to be their "water boy," but they will be giving up on the federal courts, or even ignoring whole institutional sectors, such as state courts. It's tough to play the ball in half a dozen courts at the same time, even for the Rockefellers or the Morgans (see Figure 2-2).

The *political-power-balancing* consequences of compound federalism's structure have not been highly visible in power research or in treatments of federalism. But they are not to be underestimated. Chapters 9 and 10 explain these consequences in detail.

4. *Compound federalism has an important, nationally shared belief system about federalism.* Madison virtually created a *national* political culture that has been widely accepted in this society. The two key elements of this culture are that public and elite opinion alike generally support (1) the courts' power and independence and (2) the necessity of national dominance in policy perceived to have national scope.

Thus the acceptance of national solutions long predates FDR, Wilson, and Lyndon Baines Johnson, and really is traceable to Madison's success in

Figure 2-2 *Representation and political power in federalism*

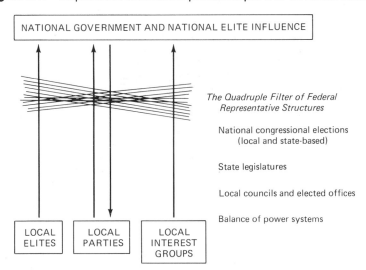

altering the issue agenda in favor of more national power. Wilson, FDR, LBJ, and like-minded presidents have merely capitalized on and enlarged this cultural consensus—indeed as had Lincoln, whose rhetoric for protecting the Union did not fall on deaf ears. Madison and Hamilton had created this consensus long before. It is the dominant political culture of federalism.

5. *It has practical, administrative, and technical forms.*

Compound federalism has given rise to certain procedures that maintain themselves or have compound kinds of effects. For example, block grants and revenue sharing—grant mechanisms popular since the Johnson years—are innovations in the spirit of compound federalism. This is because they feature clearly shared authority, shared implementation, and monies shared by the states and the nation, with perhaps a lead policy role for the national government.

Often called **cooperative federalism,** these aspects of practical federalism are really motivated by compound federalism's political culture. This is because they feature what can be described as joint nation–state policy control with substantial policy independence for local levels, including subnational discretion in implementation, standards, and distribution of monies to recipients. Other expressions or features of compound federalism that illustrate this are the joint decision and consultation processes among Federal Regional Councils, and the coordination functions served by regional economic development commissions, regional planning commissions, and other forms of intergovernmental executive consultation. Thus, much of today's compound federalism is rooted not only in constitutional bodies but in a political tradition that is firmly established in American practice. (See Chapter 3.)

THE DUAL FEDERALISM OF JEFFERSON

Often treated today as if it were out of date, **dual federalism** has had a strong influence on federalist culture and practice. As we shall see, dual federalism is not dead but lives on in belief, governing traditions, and public policy.

Dual federalism is a set of beliefs about both politics and economics. For politics, dual federalism is the belief that having separate and equally powerful levels of government is the best kind of macropolitical arrangement. In fact, most dual federalists believe that the more separation, the better the government. As a set of beliefs about economics, dualism prescribes a particular decentralized political order for the better management, growth, and enhancement of both national and regional economies. Dualism comes from the older federal design of a confederation of strong, loosely associated, sovereign states, a design that also had business priorities and goals in mind from the beginning. But dualism was not, as some picture it (Charles Beard, for instance), simply government succumbing to business elite interests.

The Roots of Dual Federalism

Dual federalism has two main sources. The first was the tradition of confederation—the first arrangement between states and nation—established under the Articles of Confederation. The second source was the towering influence of Thomas Jefferson, the great synthesizer and patron of dual federalist culture.

Under the Articles of Confederation, power was *state-centered*. The states were sovereign and the central government was dependent on them. This situation increased the strength of local cultures in national life. It certainly magnified the power and privilege of state elites (almost exclusively white male property holders in those days) in politics and economics. Most important for the forming of a dualist political culture, this arrangement contributed to an enduring American state of mind about what is proper in politics and economics. President Reagan's "New Federalism" certainly attests to the durability of dual federalism as an American federalist culture.

Helping keep dualism alive over the years has been the great influence of Thomas Jefferson, the godfather of dualism. It was Jefferson's thinking that crystallized into the federalist culture of dualism (see Peterson 1962 on Jefferson's immense influence).

Three important elements of Jefferson's influence on dualist culture are (1) his belief that populist democracy was possible, (2) his emphasis (stronger than that of Madison, Hamilton, or his erstwhile allies the anti-Federalists) on both liberty and equality in the American order, and (3) his loose association with more radical anti-Federalists. Jefferson also called for smaller, self-governing civil communities. This last point differentiated

Jefferson from the anti-Federalists (and perhaps Reagan, who may best be labeled a surviving example of them), who often stressed individual and community self-rule and decentralized government, but downplayed civil liberties and civil rights in the process. Jefferson equally stressed *both* sets of values as necessary for a democracy. Dualist philosophies have a very strong appeal for southern, midwestern, and rural people of libertarian, populist, and conservative persuasions (Maddox and Little 1984).

The Evolution of a Political Economy

As a political economy, dualism has meant for American life a number of important things over the years. First, it meant that economic and social life and political liberties in the first century and a half of the Republic were largely controlled at local and state levels. Consequently, their development was uneven, and they were generally reactionary in nature. Examples include slavery, late-nineteenth-century Jim Crow laws, lack of rights for labor, and limited national protections in practice under the Fourteenth and Fifteenth Amendments. Until the 1930s, these spelled a considerable lack of equality for minorities and women, and a limited role for the national government in state economies despite efforts at regulatory laws (Degler 1984).

Second, dualism had significant economic consequences, at least until the Civil War. The majority of Americans probably supported Madison's revision of dualism. And most of the elites supported most of Hamilton's centralist efforts, which revised federalism at the national level through the mid-nineteenth century. What this meant was that two federalist traditions were at work on the economy in the nineteenth century. First, Hamilton's centralism (and Jefferson's land purchase) accelerated national growth and business expansion, which in turn helped northern capitalism to emerge from the 1820s through the 1840s. Meanwhile, dualism reasserted itself as a national political and economic force by the 1850s with the rise of slavery and regional banking, and it resulted in a mixed plantation and capitalist southern economy and expanding western farms. The southern economic system was substantially damaged by the war for some fifty years or more. But the dominant surviving Yankee economy after the Civil War was even more "industrialized." It experienced rapid industrialization in the late nineteenth century simply because national economic elites were given an "inside track" on government means of accelerating this growth, such as land grants, western homesteading, and rail subsidies. Thus, Hamilton-inspired centralism promoted economic expansion again in the post–Civil War years (Degler 1984).

Thus, throughout the nineteenth century federalist forces, such as Hamilton's centralist traditions and Jefferson's purchase of the Louisiana Territory, combined to lessen state government dominance over major economic development functions. Central banking, westward expansion, subsidization of railroad and canal construction, elimination of the Indians, lease, sale, and grants of government land and resources, and the eradication of slavery are all evidence of the growing economic role of the national government under Hamilton-style federalism.

By the end of the 1800s, all of this had redefined and weakened dualism by clarifying and strengthening economic and social-order powers in the hands of the national government. This centralization of power also fostered national elite political influence (what Dolbeare 1984 calls **Yankee capitalism**). Some of these aspects of nineteenth-century dualism are good descriptions of centralism versus dualism today, in the basic arrangement of the political economy functions of governments. Today, however, the New Deal and the Great Society have certainly meant large redefinitions and expansions of these roles in controlling the economy, regulating business, expanding civil rights and political participation, and so forth. So in fact, dualism evolved from a strong states-rights position in the early 1900s, lost force between 1865 and 1912, and finally gave way to the centralist federalism by the 1930s. This short history of dual federalism demonstrates again how federalism has much to do with political economy in America.

Dual Federalism and Social Evolution

In practice, dual federalism meant that even through the mid-twentieth century the national government infrequently interfered in the local business or social life of individual states. The major exceptions were the initial constitutional recognitions of political inequality and slavery, the Civil War and Reconstruction, and the "maintenance of order," which meant occasionally suppressing Indians, restive farmers, and labor unions with federal troops. Otherwise, such national interference in local social life was limited until the 1930s, when dualism experienced a precipitous decline with the Great Depression and the presidency of Franklin Roosevelt.

The Decline of Dualism in the Political Economy, 1930–1980

Dualism was extremely powerful in American politics and economics until 1930 (see Figure 2-1) but began a precipitous decline in the late 1930s. This decline was due to several developments. First, there was the failure of the economy in the 1930s. This required macroeconomic intervention by the Roosevelt administration and Congress, and later even the Supreme Court. Second, FDR's new centralist categorical grants and New Deal programs set the stage for later government expansions of grants-in-aid, expanded state–level regulation of the economy, and, eventually new interventions in the politics of the states (civil rights and reapportionment, for example). A third factor is the widely recognized "change of heart" of the Supreme Court after

1938 on the constitutionality of such issues as government arbitration of labor disputes, the guarantee of the right to strike, and racial discrimination. All this amounted to, or at least accelerated, FDR's great 1937 victory in obtaining Supreme Court sanction for a new activism by the national government in the economy and in subnational politics. A fourth factor surely has to be that economic and business elites came to recognize the various ways an expanded role in government serves elite interests and general public acceptance of that expanded role (Domhoff 1978, 1982, 1983)

What's the significance of this midcentury decline of dualism? All of these trends did not mean simply a growing acceptance by the public and officials for more government grants and an expanded national economic role. Nor did they mean merely an acceptance of simplified Keynesianism, or political acquiescence in the tactics and programs of the New Deal. Primarily these trends spelled a shifting of the ground upon which American beliefs about federalism stood (in fact, a new federalist cycle) and its role in the political and economic orders. This shift in federalism was in favor of an expanded national government; it constituted nothing less than a permanent shift in our view of federalism's role in political and economic life. Even today, most Americans favor a strong national role in providing social security, and want strong national action in environmental protection, civil rights, and a host of other activist programs (see Ferguson and Rogers 1984; and Chapter 12.)

From the New Deal to Reagan, compound federalism rose to its former status as perhaps the most powerful culture, and the new alternative of centralist federalism displaced dualism, which fell to a weak third position. In short, the mid-1930s marked not just the beginning of the New Deal, nor merely the first party realignment since the Civil War, but also the beginning of a new cycle of federalism—and the decline of dualism, at least until the 1980s.

The Concrete Forms of Dualism Today

The various forms of dualism are treated throughout the book. They can be summarized as follows:

1. dualist culture
2. public policy dualism (things that for all practical purposes are monopolized or dominated by one level of government versus another)
3. dual legal systems
4. dual institutional and representation systems
5. social life in local context
6. dual power and interest group systems (including the "New Federalism" experiments of President Reagan)

Dualist beliefs have had profound effects on federalism, which are identified in Chapters 3 through 7. Policy dualism has to do with public policies monopolized by either the national government or the state governments. Dualism affects primarily the tendency to have semiseparate national versus state areas of influence and function. But it also has a tradition of influencing the division of responsibilities and functions between state and local levels. Thus, dual legal, institutional, and representation systems are primarily state–national divisions, whereas culture, policy, and social-life dualisms are reflected both between the states and the nation and between the various states and their local regions and jurisdictions. Dual legal, regulatory, and social-life systems and policy effects are discussed throughout the book.

The Resurrection of Dualism: Reagan's "New Federalism"

Today, dualism has made a minor comeback. From 1972, when President Nixon sought through his "New Federalism" to cooperatively decentralize the administration of fiscal sources and grants, through the Reagan administration, the political cry from Washington was to decentralize government powers with an accompanying policy dualism. Perhaps for domestic policy at least, Reagan could best be described as the first twentieth-century anti-Federalist to occupy the White House. The strong appeal of old-line dualism (Reagan's phrase: Get the national government off your backs) explains much of the appeal and efforts of the Reagan approach. Reaganites, like the early anti-Federalists, are highly suspicious of national government power. At least in rhetoric, administration spokespersons favor a general decentralizing of power and policy control to the states and localities (except for religion and personal morality issues, such as drug use and abortion). They also stand rather clearly for market solutions to economic disruptions. At its core Reagan's New Federalism called for a dualistic swap of responsibilities with the states and a return of power to the states.

It is no coincidence that these ideas strikingly parallel those of the early anti-Federalists. Federalist issues have been cycled back out of American dualist federalist culture into the New Federalism. Reagan's New Federalism was introduced in 1981 but was strongly opposed in Congress by lobbies for the states and cities. Thus, administration efforts had to aim at overcoming the liberal legacy of the New Deal. Equally important, they had to overcome powerful obstacles posed by the Madisonian compound culture. The Reagan era may be seen at least in part as a struggle between the contrary and intractable institutions (the courts, Congress, and the rest) of Madisonian federalism and the rather radical dual federalism views of Jefferson. The account of this struggle fits into the much bigger picture of power in federalism (see Chapters 8 and 9).

Why the resurrection of dualism? First, although dualists' views have from the beginning constituted a minority culture of federalism, such views have never really died. Periodically, they are quite popular. They seem to be unconsciously recycled back into prominence from time to time, though not often at the presidential level. Second, with the demographic, economic, and electoral pendulum swinging toward the South and the West in recent decades, it may have been inevitable that western and southern (and therefore new-wealth and dualist) perspectives would filter back into national politics. This demographic time bomb thrust back into prominence many dualist ideas and the political figures who espoused them. Thus the New Federalism should not be seen as representing anything new. It certainly should not be improperly squeezed into simplified "conservatives-versus-liberals" conflicts, as some innovative analysts have noted (Maddox and Little 1984). Rather, the New Federalism should be seen for what it is—a resurrection of dual federalism.

Insofar as the Reagan years have seen a shift in certain areas of public policy, the areas of greater success rather closely resemble the primary goals of classic dual federalism. The Reagan influences have been primarily in five areas. *First,* there has been a shift in the patterns of public issues emphasized by leadership and the media, although general public opinion has not shifted significantly. National problems such as poverty are emphasized less, while cutting budgets and social spending is discussed more. *Second,* there has been a reduction in the national capacity for taxing. The tax-gathering capacity of Washington is lower now than in the 1970s because of lower individual tax levels, lower business tax rates, and the 1986 "tax reform." This latter law merely shifted around the generally lower tax burden. It kept the "tax capacity" of the federal Treasury at low levels but returned the tax *share* of burden roughly to what it was in the late 1970s.

Third, public spending in Washington has experienced some reduction in its *rate* of increase since 1980, and changes in what receives emphasis. The trend has been towards smaller percentages of revenues for social welfare, and greater percentages for defense, with cuts in federal grants to cities and states and a shifting of regulatory enforcement and tax burdens to those entities. A *fourth* trend has been a slight deemphasis on national business regulation and federal economic clout over business. A *fifth* trend has been a considerable weakening of labor rights and bargaining (Palmer and Sawhill 1985).

Most of these programs and changes have not gone nearly as far as were desired by the Reagan administration, because of opposition from Congress, interest groups, courts, and state and city officials. Reagan seems to have been a rather instinctively pure dual federalist, and his views seem to have done battle with all the historic, embedded "devils" of Madison's compound federalism and Hamilton's centralism. With constraints such as these, perhaps it is not surprising that policy change has not gone as far or as quickly as the Reagan administration's true believers wanted. (See Chapters 9 and 12 for the full story on the limits of change under Reagan.)

What Dualism Explains Today

The social significance and various impacts of federalism on society, economics, and politics will be fully summarized in Chapter 12. But here we will briefly mention some of the more important effects, to round out our picture of the evolution and meaning of national federalism.

Several researchers have recognized the political–economic impacts of dualism (see Henig 1985, Chapters 4–11; and Smith et. al 1985, 181–201). Despite this, some prominent theorists prematurely announced the demise of dualism in the early 1970s (see Elazar 1972). Among the most important of these impacts is that dualism is the most significant cause of fragmentation in public policy. A lot of public policy, social regulation, and economic policy is by and large dominated by one or another level of government, despite a trend of joint action in most policies. It is clear that the national government still largely dominates defense, civil rights, and macroeconomic policy, for example. On the other hand, states still dominate education, welfare, social values, and crime (see Henig 1985). Research on implementation (Williams 1982) has shown that dualism is the most important cause of complex fragmentation troubles in the implementation of public policy, particularly at the local level.

Dualism is the root cause of why policy is formulated and implemented at separate government levels. This is because when policy emerges from Congress or the states, it is the result of compromises between national and local perspectives (colored deeply by national and local elites and groups). What members of Congress perceive back on the farm or what governors carry to Washington often conflict with national programs or budget philosophies.

But dualism reaches back even further in time to explain why initial policy decisions (new laws and regulations) seem "compromised" or "poorly drawn up," when judged by the criteria of scientists or economists. Administrators, representatives, and senators cannot for long simply ignore home-state politics and interests, despite presidential pressures or the outcries of number-crunching scientific advisers. So, because of pressures from lower, dual levels, the national budget cuts get softened, balance-the-budget cries get neglected, and presidents' policies get reworked deep in congressional committees where there are conflicts between national and local (and not merely public and private) interests.

Chapters 8 through 11 will explain more about the various other influences of dualism and those of the other six patterns of federalism. These chapters will show how dualism influences issue agendas, how it helps limit elite power in politics, and how it explains some of the regulation of economic and social life.

THE CENTRALIST TRADITION OF HAMILTON

America during the formative period was not seriously affected by the specific economic ideas of Adam Smith, for the simple reason that few people had heard of him before the growth of the economics profession in American universities in the late nineteenth century. Alexander Hamilton, an intense and brilliant student of economics, was one of the first Americans to read Smith, and he rejected Smith's laissez faire views of government intervention in the economy. In the 1790s, as secretary of the Treasury, Hamilton enticed business elites and government officials alike into accepting a much more interventionist role of government in the economy. His purpose was to secure a degree of government power for business growth and national stability greater than the orientation of Smith and the conventional economic wisdom would ever have permitted in England.

In his extensive influence, Hamilton may be regarded as the "American Adam Smith" but with very different effects on America than Smith had on England (Hacker 1957). The Federalist party, which Hamilton virtually created, persuaded Congress and the nation to accept central bank controls, stable government finances and taxes (largely regressive), government subsidies for business elites, and central control of imports and currencies. Hamilton was even the primary supporter of judicial review.

By 1800, Hamilton had "won the war" for many of his favorite ideas about government intervention in the economy in support of business growth. Perhaps most importantly, he established the secure expectation (almost a tradition) among entrepreneurs that business ought to have a guiding hand in governmental, economic, and political affairs (Veblen 1904, Warshow 1931). Today, this expectation is the basis of business elites' political power and social status, and to some extent is the basis of the appeal of the Republican party and conservative politics in America, for example, big-business biased the Grace Commission of 1984 on federal reforms.

As a political culture of federalism, **centralism** is the belief that relatively strong national control of economics and politics by national elites is necessary to produce the most efficient and effective socioeconomic system. It includes the belief that political, economic, and policy functions of a national government should be guided by a national economic elite. The elite's policy control should be especially strong in the following areas: maintenance of social and political order, management of public involvement in politics, maintenance of capitalism and national economic development, and the securing of economic stabilization and subsidization of private enterprise. To centralism, and to most business elites, the representative function of government is meant to be limited but not eliminated. Centralism favors the national elite and business goals even at the sacrifice of state and local elites and certainly nonelite groups. In short, the centralist view of politics and public policy is that (1) economic and business elites "know best" and should manage overall economic, social, and political development, and (2) elite power is, and ought to be, built into the Constitution and into the institutional decision-making process of governments.

The Concrete Forms of Today's Centralism

The practical elements of centralism have involved use of the powers of the federal courts, control of fiscal relations, determination of economic development and economic regulatory policies, and top-level staffing of government appointments and positions to pursue centralism's basic goals. The specifics of how centralist goals affect these things are covered in Chapter 8.

As we have seen, the technical aspects of modern federalism are often labeled by political scientists with such folksy phrases as "picket-fence" "cooperative," "competitive," or even "marble-cake" and "fruitcake" federalism. But the technical elements of federal grants and regulations have less to do with culinary delights than with specific strategies guided by the broad grip of centralist methods and goals. The Advisory Commission on Intergovernmental Relations (ACIR) and many state and local officials began to complain of excessive centralism by the late 1970s. They claimed that the purpose, or at least one of the purposes, of the methods of grants and intergovernmental regulation that have become widespread since the New Deal is to manage the complexity posed to national goals by the "restless folks" below (see ACIR 1984a, 184, Figure 5-2).

These terms, which have become a part of federalist jargon, are unsatisfactory on several counts. For one thing, it seems clear they can be described more completely by the centralist model as features of elite "bargaining," strategies aimed at increasing national policy control, since they all merely refer in the final analysis to the *degree* of centralism in the federal system. More important, these picturesque terms tend to obscure by directing too much attention to the supposed balance of powers among *official* levels of government. Certainly these tensions exist. But the "official nature" of federalism is overemphasized by these terms while the more basic complexity of federal politics is neglected. Actually, public policy and power in federalism are a blend of public and private power and interest groups. But these terms point largely to the relationships of official governments in federalism, masking the *political stakes* and *consequences* of federalism for groups in the social order. Describing the centralist tradition is a better way of summarizing the centralizing tendencies of grants and politics in federalism, particularly since centralism has operated throughout the history of federalism.

What are these centralizing tendencies behind many federal grants and other programs? Centralist practice in federalism means that national macroeconomic and intergovernmental regulation policies are often guided and managed by elites. A classic example is the Federal Reserve. The Fed's powerful commissions virtually control interest rates and money supply in the U.S., yet it is made up largely of personnel from Wall Street, Ivy League economics departments, and big eastern insurance, banking, and financial combines. Its activities are secret for the most part, and its people are not subject to election, recall, or even as much media coverage as Supreme Court justices. The chair of the Fed is generally called "the second top job in American government." In fact it is perhaps the most powerful position.

The most important trend-setter for this pattern was Alexander Hamilton. Hamilton altered the features of compound federalism by administrative practice and early national economic policy, putting tax and banking policy in the hands of economic elites by 1800. In the process he established and strengthened the pattern of Yankee capitalist power in various important ways that live on today, as in the Fed. These lasting elements include elite expectations of power and influence, rationales for elite power, traditions of promoting policies favorable to big business interests in party programs, and ways of guiding the regulation of the economy and monetary system through public bureaucracies (Dolbeare, 1984).

But in spite of Hamilton's preferences, elite power operates in the context of Madisonian design, which serves to limit that power and cast certain practical obstacles to successful collusion among elites. The obstacles to centralist policy inherent in compound federalism are important factors in our later argument that federalism is the great arbiter of power in the American system (see Chapter 9).

Evolution: Hamilton, the Federalist Party, and the Yankee Capitalists

What affected the evolution of the centralist model in its earliest years? Most important were, no doubt, Hamilton's ideas and practices. Hamilton's major accomplishments included the national bank and regressive taxes, the centerpiece of Yankee elite management of national economic development. He also proposed an unapproved but breathtaking plan for economic planning (it gave the Yankees and Wall Street certain early ideas that they seem to echo today). And last, but not at all least, he started the Federalist party, which became the model of elite politics and perspectives in America.

Centralism became one of two dominant federalist ideas (the other being compound federalism) affecting politics and economics from 1787 to the early 1800s (see Figure 2-1). As a federalist culture, it was very strong from the 1820s until the 1840s during the beginnings of national economic expansion and the era of the national bank. But from the 1840s to 1865 it seemed to fade somewhat in favor of dualism. The major factors explaining this shift to dualism are Jackson's populist democratic and economic policies, the rise of southern economics and power, the collapse of the national bank into private banking, and westward expansion. All these developments increased the political and economic power of southern and western interests. However, this shift did not mean that the Yankee capitalist class had fled politics. It simply found that its economic and political preferences did not always win out on a national basis against southern, western, and other economic elites.

From the Civil War to the New Deal, centralism vied with dualism for the main ground in politics and economics. Dualism certainly made itself felt in profound ways with the secession of the southern states and the Civil War. But the Yankee victory and ensuing Reconstruction can be said to have emphasized severe centralist methods in both politics and economics over the South, at least until the mid-1870s, when the South turned back toward southern white elite rule.

Although centralism lost to the interstate model in the South in the latter part of the century (see Chapter 4), it gripped the rest of the country's politics and social order with a vengeance from the 1880s until Wilson. Elite control over politics and economics at the national level was legitimized through the ideas of centralism. Centralism became the prime cultural justification for laissez faire economics, northern reconstruction of the South, and the Supreme Court's "protectionism" of big business and its limits on economic regulation by government.

The ideas and practices of centralism rose to prominence at the turn of the century because of several factors. The defeat of populism as a national party in the 1890s and the weakening of the Progressives occurred as a result of the growing power of monopoly capital and industrialization. Others have demonstrated (Kolko 1963; Weinstein 1968; Dolbeare, 1984) that in the 1880s and 1890s government regulation of business through Congress's new laws on railroads and monopolies had blunt teeth. This is because the Supreme Court struck down many of the new regulatory powers, under the tortuous reasoning that regulation was an unfair restraint of trade or a restriction of the "civil liberties" of business corporations. Further, the decline and crushing of labor unions and the extreme laissez faire ideology of the Supreme Court after 1880 contributed to the ability of national economic elites to use features of the federalist system to dominate politics and economics for centralist goals. Labor unions were unable to collectively bargain and were rendered in effect virtually illegal and ineffectual in court decisions before 1937, when the Supreme Court upheld the National Labor Relations Act.

The evolution of centralism is a very long story, which can be summarized only briefly here. But several things should be remembered. First, centralism has fewer constitutional roots than the other federalist cultures. Most of the "elitist" features of the Constitution, identified by Charles Beard (1941) in his famous book about the economic self-interests of the Founders, were actually worked into the Constitution as part of the creation of compound federalism. But centralism, as a culture and political economy of federalism, emerged from these features. It took on different forms, first under Hamilton, then under the Federalists, and later under the Yankee capitalists of the late nineteenth century and beyond. For the most part, centralism is now manifested in intergovernmental grants, fiscal policy, and institutional domination by national and economic elites.

Enlightened Centralism

Centralism has undergone a major transformation in the twentieth century. It has experienced a certain "mellowing," beginning with the influence of Woodrow Wilson and culminating in Franklin Roosevelt. The Great Depression of the 1930s provided the economic conditions conducive to the modification of a major federalist pattern. We call this modified form of centralism **enlightened centralism.** Enlightened centralism has resulted in major differences in American life:

1. a vastly increased policy role for all intergovernmental levels, due in part to the lead roles of the national government in providing services, and in part to macroeconomic policy;
2. a vastly increased complexity of *operational federalism* (grants, fiscal relations, dependencies, bureaucratic administration and power, etc.);
3. an explosion of new grants and related interest group activity after World War II, accelerating especially in the 1960s—*regulatory centralism;*
4. many new efforts at *intergovernmental* grants, policy, and bureaucratic *management reforms,* which were all at least partially targeted for improving intergovernmental performance, responsiveness and efficiency; and,
5. a major effort to accomplish *state-level institutional reforms,* executive–bureaucratic reforms, and reforms of state legislatures (increasing the power, staffing, planning, budgeting, and bureaucratic supervision of both state legislatures and governors' offices).

Franklin Roosevelt had the most influence in changing centralism to the more "enlightened" system just outlined. Roosevelt's approach was to refashion the political economy of federalism. To accomplish this in fact (although he probably didn't fully understand his tactics in doing so), Roosevelt blended the new enlightened centralism often inextricably with a reinvigorated compound federalism. This complex approach had lasting effects on the American political economy.[2]

First, Roosevelt's programs and politics helped maintain a softened and enlightened version of Yankee capitalist political power at the national level for perhaps two generations (at least until the Nixon years). This loosely structured coalition of elites (see Dye 1980; Domhoff 1983; and Dolbeare 1984) maintained national dominance most of the time over ideology and culture, policy appeal to the population at large, and the basis of the new Democratic party majority. The loose New Deal coalition of minorities, labor, and have-nots, including the South, allied with Yankee elites to support the Democratic party. This coalition still has not completely faded.

Second, the new grants and relief programs, aside from alleviating the worst aspects of the Depression, boosted the evolution of today's subnational patterns of federalism. Interlocal and national–local patterns of federalism in particular received a boost, in part because the many new-style grants were explicitly designed by national elites to involve state and local implementation (see Chapter 7). The new "enlightened and collaborative" centralism was simply one more policy tool of the New Deal strategy of change.

Third and most important, the new centralism became *legitimized* in the public's eyes. Many new things about federalism, viewed suspiciously in earlier eras, became common. These included new labor rights and federal power to protect them even at local levels; social welfare; and welfare bureaucracies at *all* intergovernmental levels. This in itself laid the early foundations of the "interest group liberalism" so prominent in postwar America.

Last, the newly invigorated blend of centralism and compound federalism also had quite profound consequences for economics and the public policy process and policy outcomes. One was that it considerably altered the policy agenda in American politics. Primarily, it established a new pattern of links between the White House and state and local groups and institutions. These "alliances" are often put together by the White House to advocate policy change. These intergovernmental political links have merely been revised by different presidential administrations to benefit different goals and groups. The issues that come up are the ones seen as linking the White House with "lower segments" of society, however these might vary. Recent examples are Nixon's forgotten majority and New Federalism programs, Johnson's War on Poverty and civil rights programs, and Reagan's supposedly disenchanted taxpayer and his proposed social-budget and tax cuts and military increases. The point is that the programs of presidents are often pursued through intergovernmental alliances and political strategies. As a result, the attention of the mass media in America is often shifted to the issues arising primarily from these strategies. This is one reason there is not much national media coverage of what happens in the daily implementation of programs, the distribution of wealth in society, and the operation of the legal system, legislatures, or bureaucracies.[3]

The transformation of centralism also helped produce the widely discussed shift in the federal courts from a conservative laissez faire economic and constructionist dualism before 1937 to liberal judicial activism. This shift in judicial philosophy, so often narrowly understood as a "new liberalism," is really part of the larger new social consensus about the New Centralist Federalism and its role in political economy.

The new shift also had certain concrete policy effects that are worth reinterpretation. It helped lay the basis for more centrally directed (if minimum) macroeconomic intervention by the federal government and an expansion of the regulatory powers of federal agencies over business operations and hazards to the public. It accelerated, across intergovernmental lines, national elite-guided assistance to urban, agricultural, and neglected economic sectors. As a result, much new policy, political, and economic power was being generated in subnational federalism, at both the state and urban levels (see Chapter 7).

In economic terms, not only did "practical Keynesianism" and increased regulation become acceptable at the national level, but the new centralism ironically inspired an important new era in state-level policy innovation in these same policy areas (new labor laws, welfare, mine safety, and so on). Thus, it became "all right" for states to practice more active economic regulation, since the "feds" were now doing it. What should be recognized is that all this was not a result merely of the filtering down of the new "Keynesianism," as certain economists would have us believe, but involved a shift in the definition of what was proper for federalism in the macropolitical economy.

Finally, enlightened centralism explains in part why development capital and resources were being shifted, at government behest, to the South and West through such means as regional development grants, the TVA, and later the interstate highway and farm subsidy programs. Thus, the shift in federalism may in fact have accelerated the demographic and political shift to these regions, a political factor urban sociologists and demographers have perhaps overlooked. The shift occurred because the "new centralists" (Roosevelt's grants and program "barons") were sensitive to the new potential for national economic growth, the inequitable conditions prevalent in the South and West, the national and regional needs for political and economic stabilization, and last but not least, the demands of representatives in Congress from those regions. All these developments were not merely old Yankee centralism in new clothing; rather, they represented a new shift across the board in Americas' conception of how to arrange their political and economic order under federalism.

SUMMARY

That the key figures in the development of federalism—Madison, Hamilton, and Jefferson—differed in their conceptions of economic and political order helps to explain the fractured and ambiguous beliefs that most Americans hold about politics, economics, federalism, and government power. However, there is no doubt that the Founding Fathers were trying to reach a consensus about both politics and economics for the new order—and that federalism was the heart of that debate. The admittedly self-appointed leaders of the Constitutional Convention of 1787 were strenuously attempting to reach some minimum common ground for the future conduct of politics and economics within and between their territories and with other nations.

Of course, numerous theories of what the Framers were "really up to" have been offered. Some theorists (Beard 1984) emphasize that the Framers were economic elites attempting to reconstruct government to enrich themselves or advance the most effective system of government to directly aid industrial development (or—a more cynical view, their own economic interests). Other theorists (Diamond 1974) emphasize the key role of towering figures such as Madison, Hamilton, and Jefferson in crafting compromises and arguments that persuaded both the public and the delegates to opt for a stronger national government. Still other theorists (Hofstadter, Miller, and Aaron 1959) emphasize that these men were "wizards" of political theory, crafting the good society for future generations, with an eye to both classical Greek and eighteenth-century liberal democratic theories. What can we make of these conflicting theories?

Probably all these interpretations have some merit. But they can best be understood, and somewhat reconciled with one another, by focusing on "who won." That is, which arguments, which people, and which proposed features of the new system "won out" in the end? "What mattered" for the majority of those at the Convention and later during ratification? What mattered was a design of federalism that provided for securing the economy and for achieving self-government balanced between state power and the power of the new central government.

The idea that federalism, and what people thought they were getting with the new order, was *both* political and economic is lost on most of us today. Federalism was about *political economy*. The design answered the following question then (and answers it now): What are we committed to in politics and economics? Thus to look at federalism's design means not merely to study our roots in history but to find out why we believe and act the way we do about politics and economics.

Public cultures of federalism are at the root of the seven patterns of federalism described in Chapter 1. It is these seven patterns and how they function within federalism's complex social structure that we continue to discuss in the next several chapters.

KEY CONCEPTS AND THEMES FOR REVIEW

balance of power
centralism
compound federalism

cooperative federalism
democratic elitist
dual federalism
enlightened centralism
policy dualism
political-power balancing
Yankee capitalism

NOTES

[1]A *political culture* is a shared set of beliefs and governing traditions (Almond and Powell, 1980).

[2]McGregor Burns (1956; 1970) recognized many of the policy implications of this.

[3]See Van Meter and Van Horn 1976 on implementation; Henig 1985, 146–59, 200–206, and Chapter 7, on growth and economic-development roles of cities and states; and Smith et al. 1985 on the economic effects of the tax policies of state and local governments and for an important review of the literature on the economic role of states and locals.

Nation-State Relations:

3

Unscrambling the elements

In this chapter, we present the material that is the major emphasis of most textbooks on federalism. Our purpose is to examine the primary features of the relations between the nation and the states. However, our treatment will depart significantly from the way books have approached nation–state relations in the past. It will differ both in what it will include and in what it will leave out.

The primary objective of this chapter is to describe the major features of nation–state relations and relate them to the three national federalist traditions discussed in the previous chapter. We will concentrate on such things as the representative system, governmental institutions, and fiscal and regulatory systems. In this way, we can relate the "grass roots" and practical details of the federal system in a larger analytical framework in order to bring *meaning* to nation–state relations.

It is important also to explain what our treatment of nation–state relations will not include. Most important, we make no claim to explain all the operations of federalism from day to day. For example, we will not examine all the many types of grants-in-aid, nor the mechanics of regulatory federalism. There are excellent summaries of these topics elsewhere. Indeed, we have already mentioned the problem of information overload created by the numerous, detailed studies of parts of the American federal system (see the reference list at the end of the book).

One problem for any approach to federalism is that the many features of federalism are too complex to all fit neatly into categories. A given practice—revenue sharing, for example—is inspired by and is often a mixture of political cultures and traditions. But it is possible in most cases to identify the dominant set of causes and patterns of the major features of federalism. What we must urge the student now is to look for overall patterns which bring meaning to dry facts rather than search for pure examples which neatly fit all the characteristics of the seven political economy patterns of federalism.

PRACTICAL FEDERALISM: THE POLICY FUNCTIONS OF GOVERNMENTS IN THE FEDERAL SYSTEM

Usually a description of federalism starts with a breathtaking statement of the scope of it all—cultures, regions, policy functions, 60,000 municipal governments, fifty states, and so forth. A good way to start understanding all this is to get a picture of how policy responsibility is "broken up" in the federal system. It should be emphasized at the beginning that no policy today is the *exclusive* domain of a single level—not even defense, which is often seen as the purest national function. Certainly, as we shall see in Chapter 10, public policy in the United States involves a broad sharing of responsibilities between levels. On the other hand, it is possible to carry the idea of shared responsibility too far. For example, in the late 1960s it became something of a fad in academic circles to describe federalism as involving all policies at all levels. This was part of the scholarly idea that it was time to announce the death of dualism in the days of Lyndon Johnson, which were marked by a national euphoria for national action to solve problems. As a result of this fad, many analysts, (for example, Elazar 1966:53) downplayed the idea that policy responsibility is located a little differently at different levels. Thus an important question was neglected—how general responsibility for policy control operates in the federal system.

What is important to see is that general policy control is *more or less* the primary responsibility of one of the various levels of government. By focusing on which level *more or less* has dominant responsibility for a policy area, we understand a lot more than we would if we argued that federalism has no levels, or that policy is fully shared in such a way that no level performs any distinctive function. Responsibility for policy shifts over time, and to picture policy control as being sealed off between levels is like skating on thin ice. Therefore, a common-sense description should emphasize who *primarily* does what at which level and with what effects. As Table 3-1 shows, some policy functions are monopolized by a certain level—national, state, or local—some functions are shared by the nation and the states, some are shared by states and locals, and some are shared by all levels.

A number of very interesting things can be pointed out about policy functions in the federal system as a whole. It is most interesting that the strongest powers monopolized by the national government (macroeconomics, defense, natural resources, foreign relations, and constitutional issues) very closely resemble the design of Madison's compound federalism.

TABLE 3-1 *The Distribution of Policy Functions in American Federalism*

Monopolized by the national government

macroeconomics, defense, immigration, social security, labor–management disputes, civil rights, workplace safety, regulation of monopolies and banking, wilderness areas and land conservation, atomic power and waste, airlines, railroads, broadcast licensing, outer-space exploration, international trade, foreign aid, foreign relations, postal services, counterintelligence

---

Shared rather evenly by the national government and the states

medical care for the elderly and disadvantaged, welfare benefits, environmental protection, social order, scenic recreation facilities, farm subsidies, industrial incentives, taxing, civil liberties (although supremacy lies in the national Constitution and in judicial review), highways

---

Monopolized by the states

welfare administration, control of insurance, regulation of professions, nursing, higher education, regulation of utilities, definition of crime, justice administration, marriage, property rights, powers of municipalities

---

Shared rather evenly by state governments and local municipalities

primary and secondary education, public finance, roads and highways, public transportation, airports, welfare administration

---

Monopolized by local municipalities and jurisdictions

most important aspects of primary and secondary education (personnel, curriculum, programs, facilities, etc.), city growth and zoning, land use, public sanitation, fire and water services, parks, recreation, libraries, maintenance and provision of streets and roads, crime control, cultural life, political party organization and participation, property taxes

---

Shared rather evenly by all governmental jurisdictions

taxes, housing, urban growth and services, highways

TABLE 3-1 *(Continued)*

Important areas of systematic nondecisions

competency requirements for presidents, other executives and media figures, reduction of powers of Congress or powers of the federal courts, changes in the constitutional basis of representation, control or regulation of the mass media or of religious practices, anything beyond moderate regulation of business activities, socialization of production or services, or national economic planning, such as legislative or other public controls of private finance (banking), drastic reduction in civil liberties except during war or crisis, mandatory wage and price controls or direct intrusion into international marketing

---

For a comparison over time of the degree of centralization within more traditional policy functions, see Riker (1964:82–83).

Second, business, social, and intergovernmental regulation are mostly shared today, although because of the Supreme Court's interpretation of the interstate commerce clause and the independence of state regulatory bodies over the years, some of these functions (such as regulation of insurance, professions, and property rights) have become intrastate functions. Other functions are almost exclusively in the national domain (arbitration of labor disputes, constitutional rights, atomic power and waste, airlines, and so on).

What is most prominent about policy functions in the federal system is the power and functions of states and locals. In his text on subnational government roles in public policy Jeffrey Henig (1985) has correctly emphasized the influence of subnational federalism on policies and social life in America. Henig clearly shows that states and locals dominate such things as basic-service delivery (water, garbage, and so on), education, provision and regulation of health and social services, provision of physical infrastructure (streets, public buildings, sewers, and the rest), business and professional regulation, economic development, and law enforcement. We would emphasize that some of these functions are divided between states and locals, with such things as business regulation, regulation of health care delivery, licensing of professions, higher education, and social life controlled largely by the states. Yet many of these areas are shared by municipals, especially law enforcement, cultural life, and education.

What is *not* done in the federal system is very significant. As political scientists have long emphasized, it is perhaps more important to know what is systematically not done or avoided or even *suppressed* in politics, than it is to know what is decided. The kinds of things that are consistently not done, avoided, or suppressed are public policies called **nondecisions** (Bacharach and Baratz 1970). At first this distinction may seem a trifle silly, but upon reflection it is seen to be truly profound. In your private life, for example, if you avoid a person of the opposite sex who is pursuing you with a sexual or marriage purpose in mind, you are making an important "non-decision"—you are *systematically* deciding *not* to do something important with that person. And you may avoid this person in very subtle ways which are not easily seen or interpreted by others. The same is true in politics: decision makers often systematically avoid or even suppress things in brazen, subtle, or even devious ways that have potentially profound effects but go virtually unnoticed quite often.

In American federalism, for example, it is almost never "decided" to change the constitutional basis of representation, which rests mostly on territorial units (states or election districts). The mechanics of elections may be changed, but the territorial basis of elections is not switched to proportional representation, or representation of social groups in legislatures, as is commonly the case in Europe and a few of the socialist countries (Yugoslavia, most prominently). Nor is it ever decided to increase the competence of the president by placing additional requirements on the office, such as requiring that a new president take a seminar in international affairs from competent specialists and scholars, or receive periodic briefings from past presidents—although these might be very useful things to do. Controlling the mass media or private religious practice, reducing the powers of the courts, or socializing major sectors of the economy come up for discussion in the federal system only rarely, through state innovations. Many of these things simply lie outside the tolerable range of issues in federal cultures. Expecting "reforms" in these areas, therefore, is rather dreamy, unless you happen to live in a city where there are some pretty innovative public officials, or in a state where beliefs, practices, and leadership can break away sometimes from the traditional areas of nondecision.

REPRESENTATION

A basic political effect of federalism is that it fragments power without democraticizing it (see Chapter 10). It would be difficult to argue—and we know of no reputable scholar who does—that the Framers intended to establish a democracy. In the Constitution we see instead a design that expressly limits political participation. For example, the Constitution left in place the state laws which limited voting to white male property owners. It also set up the Senate as a body elected by white male state legislatures (and not by popular vote) and established the electoral college and other obstacles to public influence and majority rule (Manley and Dolbeare 1987).

In the systems of representation in our federal system, this political effect of federalism is still important today, despite constitutional reforms. It reflects clearly two important questions concerning the political nature and consequences of the federal design. First, does the federal system itself determine who has power and who is powerless? This question is the central concern of Chapters 8 and 9, and along with the question of policy impacts considered in Chapters 10 and 11 goes to the heart of our interpretation of federalism. Second, what does this effect of federalism imply for representation? Who originally was to be permitted to participate in the federal design and who was not? How does representation work today? For whose interest was the system designed, and how well does the system serve those interests or other interests today? These questions we will treat now, because we need to appreciate how the design of the federal system affects nation-state relations today.

The description of the constitutional **representation system** could not sound more like James Madison and compound federalism. On the one hand, the main privilege of establishing representation systems—at least with regard to the "times, places and manner of holding elections"—was vested in state governments. On the other hand, Congress was given the power to regulate such systems "at any time by law" (see Article I, Section 4). In this regard, Hamilton concurred with Madison. He argued forcefully that to vest exclusive power over elections in the national government would be a "danger" and that allowing total control by the states would be a "hazard" (*The Federalist*, Nos. 59, 60). On the practical level, this provision meant that the states established most of the electoral system. Yet Congress has exercised its regulatory power on behalf of matters of crucial national concern, such as equality. The first such instance occurred in 1842 with the requirement that representatives to Congress be elected by districts rather than by a statewide "general ticket."

The point is that this federal design created a representation system consisting of multiple, self-sustaining centers of power, privilege, and profit. Since E. E. Schattschneider's seminal 1942 work, it has been common to view the representative centers of power as "natural monopolies" that "plunder" the political system (Schattschneider's words). The representation system is the purest reflection of "who gets what, when, and how" in politics. Schattschneider (1942:134) saw political parties as the natural organizations through which governance and "plunder" could be carried out: "As an extractive enterprise for the extortion of patronage and plunder from the government, the party acts with great precision. The party as the formulator of public issues is something else again." Schattschneider found it hard to believe that the representation system was inextricably linked to federalism. He argued that it "seems to be a synthetic product manufactured by the local political machines for purposes of their own" (Schattschneider 1942:142). Nevertheless, it is vital to emphasize that the institutions of the representation system (the parties, the electoral system, and the rest) are rooted in localities in the United States *because of* federalism's fragmentation.

The political economy implications of a fragmented representation system are endless. Perhaps they all reduce to an indifference to wider public interests in favor of the abuse of power for sectional or private gain. Certainly they mean that the representation system established in the American federal design provides greater access for some and less for others. In comparison with more recent European representation systems, the original American federalism is almost an oligarchy. Even today, although some "democratic" reforms have penetrated the national representation system (direct election of the Senate, minorities' rights to vote, Supreme Court–ordered electoral apportionment), others have not. Thus we have no national system of petition, recall, or referendum, the Constitution remains difficult to amend, the president is still not directly elected, and most U.S. senators are millionaires who rose from state politics and fortunes.

These oligarchic tendencies have many political economy effects, of which two are critical to an understanding of the representation system. In the first place, as we have seen, these oligarchic tendencies make access to high posts and the largesse of government easier for some groups and individuals and more difficult for others. Second, they still allow some of the claims of local socioeconomic groups to be channeled upward, as does the electoral college, which favors southern and western interests in presidential and congressional elections. At the same time, they limit the leverage of those state or regional groups against federal action, because this leverage is perceived by government or in big business and elite circles as "encroachment" on *their* vital interest (see *The Federalist*, No. 57, and compare Truman 1979:107). The legacies of biased representation can allow *local* oligarchs to have their cake and eat it too. They can get nearly all of the local cake–in the form of the public largesse in their area of monopoly. And they are provided links to the largesse of the larger system beyond their monopolies' boundaries while retaining enough clout to sometimes prevent national or group encroachments. Some of the latest research on local urban elites now suggests this is all too common. White (1982), for example, found that local business elites largely controlled mass transit policy in Los Angeles and San Francisco after World War II. Other studies show that urban business and government elites typically control policies on urban economic growth, land use, and social service agencies (Domhoff 1983: chap. 6; Molotch 1976; Ostrander, in Domhoff and Dye, 1987).

THE ELECTORAL SYSTEM

There have been a number of revisions in the original electoral system, which leads us to somewhat different conclusions about its current meaning for federalism. The original national electoral system was designed in 1787 to prevent the democratization of the federal system by fragmenting the electoral base on which public officials would be elected. The major problem of design, then, was to prevent *majoritarianism,* or dominance of the electoral process by "popular majorities." The design problem had a horizontal dimension—preventing majorities from developing cohesion—and a vertical dimension—preventing emerging majorities from exerting upward influence. Federalism was the key to both problems, as Madison pointed out in *The Federalist*, No. 10. Madison argued forcefully that it was necessary to prevent a uniting of public sentiment into a common cause. In a sentence reflecting both despair and hope, he wrote that "the *causes* of faction cannot be removed and...relief is only to be sought in the means of controlling its *effects*" (p. 80). Thus majorities are an unavoidable and frequently undemocratic condition with which government must deal. How are the effects of majorities controlled? In a remarkable passage, Madison explained:

> Either the existence of the same passion or interest in a majority at the same time must be prevented, or the majority, having such coexistent passion or interest, must be rendered, by their number and local situation, unable to concert and carry into effect schemes of oppression. If the impulse and the opportunity be suffered to coincide, we well know that neither moral nor religious motives can be relied on as an adequate control. (p. 81)

Where morality and religion fail, the federal design can prevail!

Madison believed, in other words, that the federal design could do two things. First, it could prevent any one interest from uniting in a majority. This could be accomplished, Madison argued, by creating a larger political system. The larger the political system, the greater the "variety of parties and interests" and the less likely it would be for any one interest to unite. Majorities could then be prevented from uniting if the larger system were compartmentalized into geographically insulated political communities. Thus a "wicked project will be less apt to pervade the whole body of the Union than a particular member of it" (*The Federalist*, No. 10:84). This combination of a larger polity and electoral divisions, Madison thought, would take care of the horizontal dimension of the problem of majoritarianism.

Second, the federal design could ensure that a majority, having formed, would be unable to exercise upward influence. Madison's contribution toward this end was to provide for indirect forms of election for all national offices except membership in the House of Representatives (see Madison's defense of this view in *The Federalist*, No. 63:384).

Some of the Framers opposed any involvement of the people in elections. John Mercer, for example, argued that he found nothing in the proposed Constitution more objectionable than "the mode of election by the people. The people cannot know and judge of the characters of candidates. The worst possible choice will be made" (quoted in Farrand, 1966:200–201). In any event, the electoral scheme that came into being required that all national officers other than House members come to their positions by a process that involved state legislatures. Until 1913, for example, state legislatures elected members of the Senate. They also determined the method of choosing members of the electoral college, who directly elected the president. They even indirectly influenced Supreme Court nominations, in that the president, chosen by the electoral college, nominated Supreme Court justices for confirmation by the Senate, whose members were *also* chosen by state legislatures! Thus if a certain "wicked project" pervaded a particular state, it would not necessarily find support in other states and thus would have difficulty influencing national politics and policies.

As a result, James Madison was confident that the complex electoral system in the federalist design would protect against both the baneful influence of faction as well as the tyranny of misguided majorities. What Madison did not foresee was the fact that factions could dominate at the decentralized level as well as at the central level and could form enough horizontal cohesion to sustain a thrust upon a higher level of government. The result was that the fragmented electoral system in the federal design allowed local elites (normally economic "factions") to carve out natural monopolies. Then, through collaborative networks (similar to today's interlocking corporate directorates), these elites could form the horizontal cohesion necessary for centralized effort and control.

Certainly, this tendency was strongest in the earliest years of the Republic, when state laws allowed only about 15 percent of the population (white male property owners) the vote, and when so many aspects of the constitutional design gave weight to this minority, especially in the election of the Senate and the president. By the mid-twentieth century numerous developments had weakened this tendency, including the rise of interest group pluralism, legal recognition of women's, minorities' and eighteen-year-olds' right to vote, legalization of the right to strike, and the direct election of the Senate.

Thus by the late 1960s, at least, the fragmented electoral system was no longer such "easy game" for elite interests. But ironically, some of the most important measures of public control over politics began to decline at this very time that the franchise and political pluralism became most extended. Research identified several aspects of this decline—the decline of parties, declining political participation, increasing apathy, the much discussed decline in readership of newspapers, declining SAT scores, and other indicators of lower public education and involvement in politics. Elite power, by default, seemed to be on the rise again in American politics by the mid-1970s, along with such things as campaigns based on big money from political action committees (PACs) and on television advertising, and the decline of public interest groups' power (see Chapter 9).

Because of these converging trends, it may be that the electoral system is quickly becoming once again the most "elite-captured" aspect of American government. Evidence of this, among other things, is that the cost of Senate and even House campaigns is dramatically escalating, that local elites are recruited by parties or run as independents, that presidential campaigns are increasingly becoming financially "hostage" to big PAC donors and to media manipulation of voter opinion, and that local and administrative elites are still disproportionately recruited from business elites' social networks (ACIR 1982A).

From a political economy perspective, the increasing influence of national elites in the institutions of representation means several very important things. First, it means that macroeconomic monetary policy is made "from the top" by a few elite business interests that are responsible to no one through the electoral process. This occurs whichever political economy is in vogue at the time. For example, consider the following developments. The centralization of macroeconomic powers in Congress is linked to the compound model of political economy. Thus the management of the economy through fiscal policy, industrial policy, and trade policy led by Congressional acts is now largely a national function, whereas the states are to provide a healthy environment for local business activity. How this takes place differently in the seven models of federalism is described in Chapters 10 and 11.

Under the influence of the dualist political tradition, there have been recent calls for decentralization in federalism and a rhetorical revival of "laissez faire" economics. And under the influence of the centralist political economy there has been a weakening of enforcement of regulatory federalism (which often appeals to both private firms and subnational governments but also serves wealthy and corporate elite interests). For example, despite fierce consumer lobbying and media opposition, the giant Georgia Power Company recently won a $480 million rate increase to help defray multi-billion-dollar cost overruns it had allowed in constructing one of the last nuclear power plants licensed in the U.S. No election was scheduled to allow voters the option to "recall" this decision. Therefore, it is important to keep in mind two questions: Who directs these policies, and in whose interest are they formulated?

A second significant political economy effect of increasing elite "capture" of the electoral system is that policy generated and supported from below is often blocked or neglected at the central level. No policy area more illustrates this point than the environment. Public opinion polls during the Reagan administration showed that Americans overwhelmingly supported tougher environmental protection laws *even when* such laws meant fewer jobs or higher taxes. Nevertheless, that administration reflected an indifference bordering on hostility to environmental concerns (Lash, Gillman, and Sheridan 1985). Certainly, the national record thus far on environmental protection is characterized by many ecologists and environmentalists as a disgrace. How is this difference between public expectations and national action explained? The answer is that while national elites, especially big corporate elites, cannot prevent environmental concerns from becoming part of the political agenda, they may be able to block or neglect those concerns.

Third, increasing elite capture of the electoral system has far-reaching significance for what political scientists call the **issues agenda.** Controlling what the public is concerned about is one of the most important techniques of political dominance. On the one hand, this technique requires control of those things that *do* become a matter of public concern. Determining the issues agenda in this respect involves articulating the "legitimate" problems of society and proposing solutions. According to Harold Lasswell, it also requires a slight variation in his definition of politics as who gets what, when, and how: controlling the things that get placed on the issues agenda requires determining who says what, through which channel, to whom, and with what effect (Lasswell 1960:117).

Controlling the issues agenda also requires preventing unwanted issues from becoming matters of public concern; this is the process that Bacharach and Baratz graphically referred to as a nondecision. On the surface, federalism's many centers of political activity and its institutional diversity would seem to make a nondecision difficult, if not impossible. In classic Madisonian terms, compartmentalized political communities and national structures of government should prevent "dangerous" national factions from arising, but these separate units should also be fertile ground for the raising of issues. And in many ways they are. It was in the states that many of the "social experiments" were first attempted. States had the first social security system, the first unemployment compensation system, and much more. When these policies became popular, the national government assumed responsibility for them—a process we might term *policy cooptation.* On the other hand, the federal system sometimes lends itself readily to nondecisions, as with the failure of the Equal Rights Amendment in the 1980s.

Federalism affects issues in the broad political economy, because federalism was from the start built upon a broad, sometimes fragile consensus about representation, economics, and politics in America. And over time it has largely sustained, bolstered, or broadened that consensus. In a word, the federalist design and political culture usually guides and often shapes national policy debates (for more on all these themes, see Chapters 10 and 11).

There is, however, another "face" to federalism. As we have seen, one of the many complex and sometimes seemingly contradictory purposes of federalism was to control the elite. Even though the federal design deliberately biased access to power toward a wealthy aristocracy at the national level (this bias was even more pronounced at the state level), it also had features built in to frustrate both tyrannical majorities and national elites. These features were primarily subnational federalism and (especially in the form of the balance of powers) institutional complexity. Thus federalist structures were viewed by the Founders as obstacles to overt and excessive control of social power. However, what the American experience with electoral systems clearly demonstrates is that elites have sometimes found effective methods for circumventing such obstacles (see Chapter 9).

Thus federalism is a paradox: it limits democratization, it biases access to national power, but it also creates state and local politics and institutional complexity such that national or elite goals may not always be realized. These seemingly contradictory aspects of federalism have led to what we might call a creative tension with one another. What are the results of this tension? Among other things, elite power is tempered with a sense of dependency on mass support, lower-level forces can "float" new ideas and policies in the federal system, and federalist obstacles tend to moderate elite dominance. This paradoxical nature of federalism is explained in more detail in Chapters 9–12.

POLITICAL PARTIES

Many observers have commented on the effect of federalism on political parties in the American system. This effect is best summed up in three words: *local, fragmented,* and *undisciplined.*

Federalism creates a climate in which it is almost impossible to have party unity. Each state has developed a unique party system that is little subject to national party direction. The state pattern has in turn filtered down so that the "locus of power" in the party is at the county level. The power of the party apparatus and party officials at the county level has been greatly reinforced by the political tradition that statewide patronage be distributed as evenly as possible among the county chairs. This localism stands in stark contrast with the general mobility of the American people: most Americans are probably less attached to the localities in which they live than any other people in the world. Yet political parties have always been rooted more in the decentralized, multiple centers of power, privilege, and profit created by the federal representative system than in the "sentiments" of the American people.

This symbiosis between political parties and the representation system increases the power of local party activists. To return to E. E. Schattschneider's theme, local party organizations gained control of the natural monopolies created by the representation system. Each party organization, then, has a certain geographic monopoly. Thus the second primary characteristic of national party organization—fragmentation. Each local party apparatus is a "power unto itself." As David Truman has remarked, political parties are leverage against federal action by interests which are only tactically local (1979:107). Thus we see what to many observers is one of the most puzzling effects of our party system. How can local interests, with only local tactical resources, resist national efforts? The answer is by utilizing their symbiosis with political parties and the federal representation system (see Figure 2-1 on p. 36).

This emphasis on fragmentation is not to imply that political parties are never concerned about the "bigger picture" or are never involved in larger federalist functions. Indeed, many analysts point to the "integrating functions" performed by political parties as the "cement" of the federal system (see, for example, Grodzins 1960 and Riker 1964). Some, such as Robert Lineberry (1982), argue that parties are pure *linkage institutions,* which pluralistically connect the demands of people with government institutions. But things are not so simple. It just is not clear that political parties have either the effect or the strength to make the fragmented federal system "hang together." How well parties might do this would, of course, depend on the strength and interests of these political institutions at any particular period. Thus some of the analysts just cited now decry the weakening of political parties by the direct primary and other progressive reforms, precisely because of what they perceive to be a weakening of the parties' capacity to glue together an otherwise disintegrated federal system (see Leiserson 1958).

Such a view is, of course, partly accurate. But the political economy approach highlights several important points beyond this initial conclusion. In the first place, political parties and their leadership certainly have not overexerted themselves in an effort to "glue" the disjointed federal system together. The natural monopolies created by federalism are simply too unwieldy to be glued too closely to another power center. Thus, it may be that over the long stretch of American history, local party activists have expended more energy insulating themselves from influence from above than integrating the disjointed parts of the federal system.

Schattschneider was correct: The party as formulator of public issues (that is, the issues of larger, not purely local, concern) is weakened by many forces in the federal system. Local party activists and interests have tried to strengthen their leverage against persons and elements above—a political economy function of no mean significance for policy, power, and representation. A good example today is the grass-roots influence of Christian fundamentalists on the national Republican party.

The parties in federalism are thus "undisciplined." At best, they are loose confederations of natural monopolies. To put the matter simply, even if the national party had the will to do so, no effective means has been found by which it could establish a rival organization for removing party officials in a given local area. Aside from the absence of a strong central authority within political parties, there is very little connection between state and national parties.

Given the local, fragmented, and undisciplined nature of political parties, what are their political economy effects in our federal system? More than for any other institution, the answers to this question depend on the level of government involved. Because of federalism, the most important functions of political parties are their "micro–political economy functions" at the state and local levels. At these levels, political parties serve as agents of socialization, reflecting the dominant federalist culture in an area or locale. This function, in turn, affects local and state policy choices. See Chapter 11 for an elaboration of this view. We have illustrated also how political parties channel the claims of local elites both within the natural monopoly of their area and upward to larger jurisdictions. Perhaps most important, political parties function as extractive forces, extracting demands, goods, and services from others within the self-sustaining centers of representation and private power created by the federal representation system.

INTEREST GROUPS

This century has seen not only an expansion of the number and kinds of interest groups but also a dramatic increase in a special type of interest group—the intergovernmental lobby. This lobby now consists of approximately seventy local, county, and state associations, of which the National League of Cities and the National Governors Association are probably the most visible and best known. These formal government lobbies attempt to supplement the formal representation system of federalism with interest group "power." (Add to this the fact that particularly through Congress, the formal representation system gives heavy weight to subnational and local interests.) Federalist issues often dominate the agendas of these various intergovernmental interest groups. Finally, there are hundreds of nongovernmental interest groups operating across government levels as pressure groups.

    From another angle, the multiple, self-sustaining centers of representation and private power created by the federal system are both a boon and a curse to average, citizen-based interest groups and elite interest groups. On the one hand, federalism has multiple **access points** for groups pressing their interests on governments. That is, if pressure groups lose at one level they can simply transfer their activity to another. This way, they never totally lose. Part of the strategy of groups raising new issues has been to shop around for the level and branch of government most sympathetic to their interest. This has been the strategy of the antiabortion, prolife lobby. Fairly new to the scene, and confronting no less an obstacle than the Supreme Court's *Roe* v. *Wade* decision (1973), which made abortion a matter of a woman's right to privacy, the prolife forces have fought in Washington *and* the states to rewrite laws and policies and to overthrow the *Roe* decision. And while the states have increasingly tried to redefine abortion procedures, the courts have held to Roe. By thus blurring the distinction between winners and losers and by giving hope to those who perceive themselves as having gained nothing in a particular political battle at one level, federalism contributes to the diffusion of social conflict. This diffusion of conflict is one important social function of federalism (for others, see Chapter 11.)

On the other hand, the representation system created by federalism is a curse for interest groups because it makes it more difficult for them to win—at least in the sense of getting clear, sustained action for what they seek. The multiple, self-sustaining centers of representation and power function not only as access points but as obstacle or veto points as well. Thus to win a *policy decision* somewhere in the system is not necessarily to win a *program outcome*. Official prayer in school has been banned since 1962, but it is still widespread in southern and western schools, for example.

The clearest example of this difference between decision and outcome is the so-called authorization—appropriation gap. In nearly all policy areas, American legislatures annually authorize more money than is actually appropriated. Thus interest groups may win big in the authorization process but win much less in the appropriation process. For example, in 1975 Congress appropriated only 42 percent of the authorized amount for education. Education groups thought they had won a significant percentage increase in the amount authorized education, only to be "blindsided" in the appropriations process. In addition, policies are modified and redefined as they filter down through the federal system to field-level implementation. What comes out of the intergovernmental meat grinder may be drastically different from what was put in. These two factors—the possibility of being "blindsided" in the federal system and the system's capacity to alter policy as it percolates down—help blur the distinction between the winners and losers in interest group competition.

In fact, this blurring may be one of the most significant political economy effects of the federal system for interest groups. Maurice Stans, former director of the Office of Management and Budget, once defined budgeting as the "uniform distribution of discontent." Perhaps "Stans's Law" should be restated more broadly. Federalism creates a rather uniform distribution of discontent among competing interest groups. It provides an environment in which no group loses totally. Each group wins something— even if just a symbolic statement or an additional supporter. And each group loses something. In particular it loses control over a policy decision as it filters through the federal system. Thus the system contributes to the diffusion of social conflict. In a world in which there are no clear winners and losers, the intensity of the conflict—and thus, in Schattschneider's extremely descriptive term, its contagion—is lessened. In a system in which not everything can be provided for everyone who asks, this is an important effect.

Socially, however, it may mean that few problems are ever resolved fully. As a result, federalism is the context for what we will call *recurring policy cycles* (see Chapter 11).

CONGRESS: THE MIRROR OF SUBNATIONAL FORCES

Some studies of federalism have emphasized the responsiveness of Congress to state and local interests. Nice summarizes this point nicely: "Members of Congress are generally willing and able to speak for and protect the interests of their states or districts, and a number of features of Congress enhance that ability" (1987b:35). In large part, this is true because of the representation system. Senators often do in fact represent states, and representatives often do in fact represent districts.

To put it differently, every senator has a "governor" in his or her constituency, and analysts agree that the "district role orientation" is the most frequent self-perception among members of Congress (Fenno 1978). The representation system and the self-perception factor are reinforced by a number of internal features of Congress. No member of Congress could neglect service to constituents, for example.

This powerful influence of subnational forces in Congress is what we mean when we say that Congress is the mirror of subnational forces. Congress mirrors the myriad interests of the subnational level in national policies. To put it differently, Congress has substantial difficulty developing a coherent, unified, long-range policy on federalist issues or on any policy, because Americans generally have been unable to choose among the three political economy cultures of federalism. Trends in American opinion and policy have oscillated among the federal cultures over time. In a perceptive article, David Walker concluded that congressional actions in the 1970s reflected a "distinctive mix of drastic change and no real change...," and that this "explains why this system simultaneously appears to be merely an extension of the Cooperative Federalism of the Eisenhower era to some and a totally transformed system to others" (1980:54).

Walker's insight dramatically emphasizes the basic thesis of this book. What you see when you look at federalism depends a great deal on the conceptual lenses through which you look. Although congressional actions on federalist issues may look disjointed and ad hoc, a careful examination of those actions could make sense of them by tracing them to one of the three political economy cultures and to the interplay between national and subnational political actors. What looks like repressive federalism to some looks like civil rights enforcement to others. One man's repressive federalism is another woman's civil rights!

Walker also makes the important point that Congress is the "prime architect of the contemporary pattern of intergovernmental relations"

(1980:54). What this means is that state and local interests have been strong influences in the development of federalism in this country. The prime mover in the swings among the three political cultures over time has been the prevailing opinion of state and local political actors. In this regard, it is perhaps not quite accurate to refer to an "unworkable intergovernmental system," or a "dysfunctional federalism" (Walker 1981:57). The system is working well (too well?) in reflecting the diverse positions flowing out of the three dominant political cultures.

In this book it is not possible to sort out all that Congress does or all that nation–state relations involve and relate those actions to the three political economy cultures. But we can sort out the main patterns. A few examples will illustrate. (See also Table 3-2.)

The compound model has apparently been guiding congressional action in the areas of civil rights, congressional "advice and consent" on foreign and military policy, and macroeconomic policy. The centralist model has been guiding executive and congressional action in the areas of regulatory federalism, the shifting in budget priorities from human resources to defense, crime, and law enforcement. (There has been conflict between Congress and the president since the late 1970s on how far to carry those

TABLE 3-2 *Policy Areas Guided by Federalist Traditions*

Compound	Centralist	Dualist
• most civil rights and liberties	• monetary policy	• block grants
• "advice and consent" on military, foreign, fiscal, and macro-economic policy	• international trade	• education
	• New Right social agenda	• regulation by states
	• categorical grants	• taxes
	• centralized, nationally preempted regulation	• crime, justice
• general revenue sharing	• defense, intelligence, covert operations	• substate IGR and fiscal relations
• cooperative inter-governmental social and economic regulation	• abortion (*Roe* v. *Wade*)	• regulation of social life
• regulation of interstate commerce		• regulation of the professions
• environmental regulation		• management of natural resources

trends.) The dualist model has been guiding state and congressional action in the areas of education, regulation, and taxes. Dualism still produces pretty big differences between the national and the various state programs in these policy areas. An interesting question, but one that must be left to another work, is how much stability a political economy culture will have in a specific policy area over time. The dualist political culture has dominated congressional action on education, for example, for well over a century now.

We estimate that there is more stability within these guided issue areas than a casual observation of congressional behavior would suggest. For example, William Riker's older study (1964:82–83) of the degree of centralization in the United States by "substantive functions" over time suggests that the basics of nation–state policy sharing is strikingly similar between today and 25 years ago (dualism). This suggests stability in basic federal traditions. Whatever the degree of policy stability, the point is that the major actions of Congress are very frequently rooted firmly in the three major federalist political traditions.

THE PRESIDENT: FEDERALISM'S PERSONIFICATION
AND PSEUDOMANAGER

The American presidency occupies center stage in federalism's theater. The president is at once the most visible actor in the federal system and the focal point of federalist pressures. It is in the president that federalism can move out of the domain of structures, patterned relationships, and the like and be personified in an individual.

In part, it is the peculiar American process for electing presidents that places them in such a powerful, if precarious, position. The general political effects of the electoral college are well known (power to the "big" states, influence to urban areas, and so on). What is of interest here is that the electoral college has two very important effects for federalism. First, it ensures continued dominance by subnational interests (however divided between big and small states) of the election of the president. The essential problem for presidential candidates is to put together a combination of states that will result in a majority in the electoral college. This problem affects campaign strategies, from the decision to concentrate on some states to the neglect of others, all the way to decisions on what to do in the final election days. Perhaps most important, this need for an electoral college majority affects the posture candidates take on issues. Barry Goldwater, for example, could lambaste the Tennessee Valley Authority when campaigning in TVA states, yet praise the Bonneville Power Commission when campaigning in his own Southwest. Second, the electoral college, at least in practical terms, makes the president the only national official with a "national constituency." Even though they vote in state units, voters see themselves as casting their ballots for the president (actually they vote for members of the electoral college).

The combination of these two effects suggests in turn one of the most important political economy effects of federalism on the presidency—its powerful role in structuring issue debates and agendas (for more on this, see Chapter 11). With the states as the basic units of the electoral college, the president, even more than Congress, is the focal point for all the crosscurrents of the federal system. Almost all federal forces converge on the presidency—national and subnational elites, party units, interest groups, governmental officials, and a host of others. And they weigh a ton.

The proper coalition of these forces is a major factor in a winning strategy for gaining the presidency. It also helps the president influence Congress, control the bureaucracy, and so on. So while these federalist crosscurrents may be a heavy burden on presidents, they are also one of their most important political resources. As the Hollies put it, federalism "ain't heavy, [it's] my brother." Certainly, federalist forces are major determinants of the issue agendas of presidents.

But it is important to take this view one step further: the election of the president is the nearest thing to a plebiscite in the American system. It may not be strictly accurate to say that the constituency of the presidency is the American people, but the appearance is there. So the president is expected to reflect a "national perspective" on the concerns of the day. And, as we have seen, the "concerns of the day" involve the cyclical debates about federalism that pervade the American political system. Thus virtually all twentieth-century presidents, and particularly the most recent ones, have had federalist reform agendas as a central priority. There were, for example, two "New Federalisms" (Nixon and Reagan) in the 1970s and 1980s. And the key feature of President Johnson's Great Society was *creative* federalism. More significantly, it is nearly impossible to understand contemporary federalism without knowing about the profound modifications of the federal system during Franklin Roosevelt's New Deal. Thus federalism both shapes presidential priorities and is affected by them.

The president's own preferences are also powerful forces in determining the federalist agenda. Presidents are usually committed to one of the three federalist cultures. Although there are probably no purely dualist, centralist, or compound presidents, the dominant postures of recent Presidents toward federalism can be identified. Take Ronald Reagan. In many respects he was one of the purist dualists since Thomas Jefferson. In his acceptance speech at the Republican National Convention in 1980, for example, Mr. Reagan declared forcefully, "Everything that can be run more effectively by state and local governments we shall turn over to state and local governments along with the funding sources to pay for them." Jefferson could not have put it better. But at the same time, Mr. Reagan's support for the New Right moral positions sounded very centralist. Still, the point is to look for overall trends. Lyndon Johnson was a centralist in most respects. The explosion of categorical grant programs in his presidency in part reflected Johnson's desire to set national policy to benefit minorities and cities through stiff requirements for grants-in-aid and through regulatory federalism. Richard Nixon, on the other hand, showed a preference for compound federalism. His major federalist accomplishment—general revenue sharing—was an effort at "devolution." In Nixon's thinking, this involved revitalizing the states so that they could play a more active role in the federal system. Jimmy Carter continued the compound tradition with his "New Partnership." But Mr. Carter reflected a mix of political culture traditions in that he substantially accelerated direct federal–local relations by keeping a heavy urban focus to his federalist policies. And, as we have noted, Ronald Reagan was a dualist almost to the point of being an anti-Federalist in his beliefs and goals, if not always in his administration's actions.

In the title of this section we referred to the president as the "pseudo-manager" of the federal system. Nearly all reviews of presidential effectiveness in managing federal issues and processes have concluded that the record varies substantially among presidents (Wright 1982; O'Toole 1985; Nice 1987b; Dilger 1986). The most important reasons for this variation include the amount of time the president devotes to federalist issues, the president's general political leadership qualities, opposition to the president in Congress (a feature of compound federalism), and the nature and intensity of federalist issues at the moment. Our interest lies more in the political economy effects of presidential actions than in the effectiveness of the president as a manager. We will return to the presidency and its representation, policy, and economic effects in Chapters 9 and 12.

THE BUREAUCRACY: FEDERALISM'S PROFESSIONALS

It is in the bureaucracy that the most complex patterns of intergovernmental relationships occur. In analyzing the bureaucracy and the federal system, it is all too easy to simplify. Thus, it is common to find the proposition that bureaucrats (or *policy professionals*, in more recent usage) provide the cohesiveness necessary for intergovernmental action. They do so, so the theory goes, because of shared expertise, shared values, and because of common commitments and professional expectations (see Peterson et al. 1987:160). This view is partially correct as far as it goes, and this cohesion has some important political economy effects. For one, relations between bureaucrats at different levels override jurisdictional considerations. Furthermore, it has been amply demonstrated that such relations result in frequent bypassing of political decision makers at the respective levels. These things are important, but they are not the full story.

Bureaucratic behavior in the federal system can best be understood as a political economy "game." In one of the most famous social science studies, Graham Allison (1970) borrowed from philosopher Ludwig Wittgenstein a general **game approach** to analyzing the Cuban missile crisis during the Kennedy administration. The parallels between the findings in that study and studies of bureaucratic behavior in the federal system are striking. Bureaucratic behavior in the federal system is a complex series of simultaneous, overlapping games among players at various points in the system. These games, as Allison found in the Cuban missile crisis, are neither random nor "at leisure." Rather, they are structured by what Allison calls **action channels**. Action channels are regular patterns of action on issues. Allison summarized in excellent fashion the functions performed by these channels: they (1) preselect the major players, (2) determine the players' points of entrance into the game, (3) distribute advantages and disadvantages for each game, and (4) determine who "gets a piece of the action" (control and benefits) in the first place. Allison found that the fourth function was the most important one for the outcome of the Cuban missile crisis.

It is difficult to avoid the conclusion that the most important function of action channels in federalism is the same—to determine who gets a part of the action. Many studies of *functional federalism* have been done which shed light on these issues. One of the best is a book entitled *When Federalism Works* (Peterson, Rabe, and Wong 1987). The authors of this important work examine the outcomes of nine federalist programs in the general policy areas of education, health care, and housing. One of their more important findings was that "these programs operated more effectively than earlier observers realized or acknowledged possible" (p. vii). But from a political economy viewpoint, the most interesting finding was that there is a major difference between what the authors call *development programs* and *redistributive programs*. Intergovernmental development programs promote economic growth or the advancement of certain industries or professions which benefit directly from public funded projects such as highways, riverways, and hospitals. Redistributive programs, such as medicare, serve one group at the expense of others. The authors refer to the "simple" task of administering development programs and the "complex" task of managing redistributive programs. In some policy areas the action channels are mature and thus regular; in other areas they are evolving, volatile, and more politically open. Peterson, Rabe, and Wong refer to the "maturation of redistributive programs," by which they mean that intergovernmental administrators learn how to do the difficult (train workers, reduce poverty, and so on) quite well over time, just as automakers "work out the bugs" in a new line of cars. One of the most important conclusions of the book is that "federal professionals find local counterparts who seem as committed to the redistributive objectives as national policymakers" (p. 140). The authors interpret the significance of this development as the securing of local compliance. We interpret its significance from a political economy viewpoint as the establishment of regular action channels which determine policy control and benefits.

This leads us to the most important political economy effect of bureaucratic behavior in the federal system. Simply stated, the stakes in the federal game are limited and may be claimed before all willing participants are allowed access to the game. This effect, perhaps best illustrated in economic development and redistributive programs (described by Peterson et al. 1987), is particularly important when one looks at the list of programs defined as developmental—hospital construction, vocational education, impact aid, and community development, education, health care, and housing. These "development" programs usually have redistributive outcomes (that is, someone or some group typically loses). And these outcomes are often determined without the opportunity for some to play the game.

THE SUPREME COURT: CONSISTENCY IS THE HOBGOBLIN OF LITTLE MINDS

If the quotation from Emerson that forms the heading of this section is correct, the United States Supreme Court has been the repository of some of the greatest minds in American history. Following the Court's convoluted course through federalist issues is much like following the "bouncing ball" in the child's game. The Court has bounced from one dominant culture to another both between periods and between issues during a given period. Cynthia Cates Colella (1986:30–71) has provided an excellent summary of the Court's federalist-related decisions over time. Although she did not relate Court decisions to our federalist political economy cultures, her survey makes it clear that there have been periods when one of the three cultures was dominant: the Marshall Court for compound federalism (although Marshall's specific problem was the institutionalization of national power), the dualism of the Taney Court, and the centralism of the "converted Court" of the New Deal period. The Court, like the other branches of government, has oscillated among the dominant cultures over time.

Colella's analysis also makes it possible for us to see the oscillation of the Court between political economy cultures during a given period, depending on the issues. This oscillation is particularly clear in what she labeled the New Judiciary, specifically the Burger Court. Colella concluded that:

> the Burger court often has tended to appear inconsistent, if not incomprehensible....Clearly, all concerned—...even the Court itself—are confused. Nor is it immediately apparent whether this confusion is the

symptom of a wrenching Constitutional transition, a genuine attempt to balance the protection of individual rights with...traditional institutional relationships such as federalism, the legal manifestation of an overloaded society, or merely the product of faulty judicial logic. (1986:71)

We suggest that an important additional factor in this confusion is the inability of the Court to apply a single federalist culture consistently across all policy areas.

This last point deserves greater explanation. The Advisory Commission on Intergovernmental Relations (ACIR) has identified the primary areas of Court action on federalist issues. Among the most active policy areas are the environment, equalization of municipal services, and taxation and finance. Upon examination we find that the Court is applying different federalist cultures to each area. Thus the rulings in the three policy areas appear inconsistent when viewed as a whole (according to a standard such as judicial activism). But when viewed separately as embodying a dominant federalist culture, they are quite consistent indeed.

Consider the leading cases in each policy area. First, decisions on the environment reflect the dualist political economy. The Court has ruled that states may not impose standards less strict than the national standards (*Pennsylvania* v. *EPA*); may impose standards more stringent than those of the national government (*Huron Portland Cement Co.* v. *Detroit*); and may not impinge upon a "national purpose" in environmental regulation (*Northern States Power Co.* v. *Minnesota*). There is no clearer application than this of the dualist notion of separate spheres of government doing separate things without impinging on one another's integrity.

Second, the equal provision of municipal services is rooted in enlightened centralism. The Court has ruled that unequal provision of municipal services (sewage, streetlights, and so on) violates the equal protection clause of the Fourteenth Amendment (*Hawkins* v. *Shaw*) and that municipalities must make a good-faith effort (equal efforts but not necessarily equal results) to equalize services to their citizens (*Beal* v. *Lindsey*). On the other hand, the Court refused to hold that an unequal tax base for public education—another very important program of local governments—denies students in the "poorer" districts the equal protection of the laws (*Rodriguez* v. *San Antonio Special School District*). This ruling came after a state supreme court (California's) had decided that unequal financing violated the equal protection clause of the state constitution (*Serrano* v. *Priest*).

In the third area, taxation and finance, the Court's decisions appear firmly rooted in the compound federal culture. The Court has attempted to meld national and state action into a true compound. It recognized the legitimacy of the equal protection clause of the Fourteenth Amendment in *Louisville and Nashville Railroad* v. *Public Service Commission of Tennessee,* holding that Tennessee could not apply different assessment standards to similar property. Protecting the interest of the states (even in the face of a seemingly clear constitutional prohibition of state import duties), the Court held that a tax applied nondiscriminatorily to both domestic and imported goods does not violate the Constitution (*Michelin Tire Co.* v. *Wages*). And, protecting states from intrusion by other states, the Court declared that a tax on commuters only violated a citizen's right to travel (*Austin* v. *New Hampshire*).

Within these three policy areas, then, there appears to be some consistency in the application of the three federalist cultures. The problem is, of course, sorting out the Court's decisions across all policy areas.

The political economy effects of the Court's oscillation among federalist cultures over time and between issues are significant indeed. The best statement of this significance was provided by Felix Frankfurter, a member of the Court. Before he was appointed to the Court, Frankfurter wrote that:

> the raw material of modern government is business...all our major domestic issues...are phases of a single central problem, namely, the interplay of economic enterprise and government. These are the issues which for more than a generation have dominated the calendar of the Court. (1961:41)

Frankfurter's observations certainly could be applied to federalism. The central thesis of this book is that the dominant feature of federalism is the structures it provides for the interplay of economic enterprise and government. Indeed, we would go farther than Frankfurter: issues concerning the interplay of economics and governments have dominated the Court not simply for a generation but since the founding of the federal system.

The oscillation of the Court among the three federalist cultures has enabled the Court to choose at random the basis for any given decision. If it suits the Court's fancy to root environmental decisions in the dualist culture, the Court does so. A fruitful line of inquiry would be to identify the reasons the Court bases decisions in a given policy area in a specific federalist culture. For example, why has the Court rooted environmental decisions in the dualist culture? Who or what influenced the Court in this decision? In whose interest was the decision? What implications for representation, power, and policy does such a decision have?

The oscillation among cultures certainly has implications for evaluating the Court. The Court is frequently pointed to (for example, by the ACIR) as the "umpire of the federal system." If this is so, then the Court has had a difficult time "defining the strike zone." Its random hopping from federalist culture to federalist culture, like its bouncing among policy areas, leaves the confused observer with the impression that the Court is guilty of "faulty judicial logic."

But the compelling advantage of the Court's federalist posture is that such oscillation enables it to adapt its decisions to the prevailing values of the time—and with a speed that is sometimes dizzying (as with the Court's "change of heart" during the Great Depression). The oscillation enables the Court to accommodate its rulings to the "political branches of government." With a few notable exceptions, the United States has not been characterized by severe political confrontation among the three "equal" branches of government. The oscillation among federalist cultures has enabled the Court to tailor its decisions to powerful political interests—validating Frankfurter's conclusion that the dominant issue on the Court's agenda has been defining the interplay of economic enterprise and government. And it has enabled the Court to walk the fine line between national and subnational power and interests without undue confrontation with either level. In all these respects, then, the Supreme Court has demonstrated that it is the "supremely political" institution in the federal system.

FISCAL FEDERALISM

No area of federal relations has provoked more study and writing than fiscal relations.[1] This writing has concentrated on both general trends in intergovernmental transfers and the specific grants, spending requirements, and so on, found in the programs. The ACIR continually monitors fiscal federalism and publishes an excellent summary of major trends in the annual edition of its volume *Significant Features of Fiscal Federalism*. However, as we mentioned earlier, it is not our intention to summarize this vast literature. What we seek is to create a wider analytical perspective on the major issues and political economy functions of fiscal federalism. Thus the brief descriptions of intergovernmental transfers that follow will emphasize how each relates to the three political economy traditions and what political economy meanings or effects each has.

Categorical Grants

The oldest and most numerous form of intergovernmental transfer is the **categorical grant**. A categorical grant is a money payment, usually requiring some level of matching by the recipient, for a specific program or project and in accordance with specific standards.

Government data are not such as to allow us to estimate the share of the different forms of grants. We do know, however, that all national aid to states and locals in the 1980s dropped under the earliest Reagan budgets from a high of $94.6 million in 1981 to $86 million and $88 million in 1982 and 1983, but rose dramatically after congressional restorations in 1984 to $99 million (ACIR, 1986:60).

Categorical grants take four forms. *Formula-based categoricals* are allocated according to a group of weighted factors specified in legislation or administrative regulations. *Project-based categoricals* are allocated to specific projects on the basis of individual applications. *Formula–project grants* combine features of the first two types. Finally, categoricals may be *open-ended reimbursement grants*. Here the funding jurisdiction reimburses specific proportions of recipient costs. The amount of reimbursement is usually determined by a formula, so in many respects it is difficult to tell this fourth type from a formula grant.

Two policy areas—public assistance and highways—have received the lion's share of categorical grant funds—approaching 70 percent. Employment security (approximately 6 percent) and contributions of surplus agricultural commodities (about 3.5 percent) are a distant third and fourth. Among a number of other programs aided by categoricals are the national school lunch and milk programs, school construction and operation, hospital construction, low-rent housing, slum clearance, and urban renewal. Thus a wide range of policy areas have received assistance through categoricals.

Categoricals are rooted in the centralist political economy. Their basic purposes have been to enable the feds to accomplish program objectives thought to be in the national interest, to raise the level of services in the states, and to specify what the states would and would not do by way of administrative or process standards. The basic conclusion in the literature, at least until the late 1980s, was that the conditions attached to categoricals substantially broadened national direction of state activities.

Indeed, in the 1980s this interpretation was elevated by many to the level of dogma. Governors, mayors, and other subnational officials decried "intrusive Washington," which seemed to them to be threatening the prerogatives of states and their political subdivisions. Academics frequently joined the chorus. Consider the following statement from a noted analyst of fiscal federalism:

> A federal government that began in an atmosphere of some suspicion, whose every activity was scrutinized by zealous defenders of states' rights,…has become…so much the arbiter of individual citizens' lives that it seems to many that the Tenth Amendment has been reduced to the status of a vestigial remnant. Many forces participated in this evolution, but none more important than fiscal ones. (Break, 1981:60)

Are there no limits to what "grant money" will buy?

The answer is that of course there are limits. Although it is clear that categoricals are rooted in the centralist political economy, many data indicate that the conditions of aid attached to them are not as effective intrusive agents as many have assumed. While characterizing the formal conditions attached to categorical grants as "extensive, expensive and intrusive," Carl

Stenberg (1981) has identified four problems with national control over their administration. First, many of the funds are highly *fungible.* That is, recipients can use them for purposes other than those specified in the grant authorization. Obviously, if the grant funds are highly fungible, then the states retain substantial discretion over their use.

Second, Stenberg found no clear "audit trails" in most grant programs. George Break (1981) found that categoricals splinter responsibility and obscure the lines of authority to such an extent that meaningful accountability is precluded. We agree. How then, do we know that the conditions of aid have been so intrusive?

Third, Stenberg found that grant agencies cannot do effective review because of the large number of recipients, the range of the programs, and the inadequate staff of Washington review offices. This finding is consistent with the conclusion of an excellent study of the conditions attached to categoricals. The authors of that study observed "limited federal enforcement efforts and large variations in accepted levels of performance by local governments" (Massey and Straussman 1985:292). The determinants of the level of enforcement were the degree of emphasis given enforcement by Congress, the president and the agency itself, the degree of controversy about enforcement among the public or interest groups, and the history of the activity. The authors also found, however, that the granting agency often depended on the grant recipient to implement the federal legal requirements for aid. Thus, any review by officials in the granting agency would be "no harsher than necessary" to enforce these requirements.

Finally, on the basis of these findings Stenberg concluded that information supplied by grant receivers was often subject "to cursory review, filed away, and forgotten" (p. 37). This conclusion is important, since much of the 1980s academic picture of the conditions of aid has depicted recipients as "powerless victims" whose choice is reduced to "take it or leave it." Such a view is surprising, even naive, since it contradicts much of what we know about intergovernmental politics and policy implementation. It is much more accurate to say that a mutual dependence regarding grants and their "conditions" exists between granting and recipient agencies. This dependency is one of the most important political economy effects of categorical grants. Substantial intergovernmental bargaining has been stimulated by categoricals, and this bargaining in turn often overrides the centralist goal in grants (see Chapter 10; see also Pressman and Wildavsky 1973).

Block Grants

Block grants are funds provided chiefly to general-purpose governments in accordance with a statutory formula for use in a broad functional area. The specifics of the use are largely at the recipient's discretion. There are five basic design characteristics of block grants. First, aid is authorized for a wide range of activities in a broadly defined functional area. Second, recipients have substantial discretion in identifying problems, designing programs to deal with them, and allocating resources. Third, nationally imposed requirements (the administrative "conditions" in categoricals) are kept at a minimum. Fourth, aid is distributed on the basis of a statutory formula. Finally, eligibility provisions are statutorily defined and favor general-purpose governmental units as recipients and elected officials and administrative officers as decision makers. The major block grants are the Partnership for Health program, the Omnibus Crime Control and Safe Streets program, the Comprehensive Employment and Training Act (CETA), housing and community development programs, and Title XX (social services) programs.

Block grants are rooted in the dualist political economy. They were born in a concern for maximizing the discretion of state decision makers and are nourished by the continuing appeal of dualism as a federalist culture. The Reagan administration's emphasis on limiting federal involvement in state and local policy is an excellent example of the strength of the dualist appeal.

Block grants have important political economy effects. Among the most important is that they can ensure that our modes of meeting human needs remain largely state-centered. One of the most important features of contemporary fiscal federalism is that grants have aided activities that not too long ago were assumed to be entirely state responsibilities. Aid had extended to the major areas of "national concern" from the 1930s to the 1950s, and in the 1960s and 1970s it spread to areas traditionally thought to be of state concern only. David Walker has provided an interesting list of "state concerns" now assisted by federal aid: rural fire protection, libraries, jellyfish control, police pensions, preservation of historic landmarks, urban gardening, training for use of the metric system, arson control, home insulation, meals-on-wheels, snow removal, aquaculture, displaced homemakers, education of gifted children, development of bikeways, aid to museums, pothole repair, runaway youth school security, and art education (1981:53). **Block grants** provide national financial assistance while state governments retain control over disbursements and implementation of specific program areas.

General Revenue Sharing

General revenue sharing was an important fiscal feature from the 1970s until the mid-1980s. Started largely by President Nixon in 1972, GRS was to allow states and localities to receive monies from the national government in the form of transfers or grants which minimized national restrictions. By the late 1970s, all forms of revenue sharing made up between 10 and 12 percent of all local revenues. But by 1985 revenue sharing had been virtually eliminated by Reagan administration budget cutting, despite strong local resistance.

General revenue sharing consisted of funds distributed by formula with few or no limits on the purposes for which they could be spent. Additionally, there were few restrictions on the procedures by which they might be spent. The formula, established in the State and Local Fiscal Assistance Act of 1972, consisted of three factors—population, tax effort by state and local governments, and income level of the population. The formula immediately raised the question of whether GRS rewarded poorer states that taxed their populations heavily. Thus, the formula became a factor in the debate between Sunbelt and Frostbelt politicians on the distributional impact of intergovernmental transfers generally. One third of the money was allowed to be retained by the state for state use; two thirds had to be distributed to local governments on the basis of the same formula used to determine the state's allocation. Funds from general revenue sharing also were used for practically all recognized state and local functions except that they could not be used as matching money for other national grants.

General revenue sharing had its roots in compound federalism. What the program envisioned was the welding together of the nation and state in a fiscal relationship that tapped the capabilities of both. The assumption was that the national government is better at raising money, and there is some justification for this assumption. A study in Georgia, for example, found that for every growth factor of 100 in the economy, national taxes in the state increased by a factor of 140, state taxes by 95, and local taxes by 70 (Quindry, 1971). It was further assumed that state and local governments, as the direct providers of the broadest range of services, were better at spending money. General revenue sharing, then, is assumed to be the mechanism by which the superior capacities of both levels are united in a "true compound."

Even though general revenue sharing was used in virtually all state and local functions, its political economy effects have been difficult to pinpoint. One effect was that at the local level, much of GRS was used for "one-shot" physical improvements rather than for antipoverty, housing, or other social programs. Another effect was that each periodic Congressional reauthorization produced intense lobbying by representatives of state and local governments. Despite this lobbying, GRS on several occasions (most notably in 1979) came within a few votes of defeat, and at the end of Reagan's second term it appeared dead.

Unscrambling the Elements

What we have tried to show is that fiscal federalism represents the "playing out" of the three dominant federal political economies in the area of intergovernmental fiscal relations. The proliferation of categorical grant programs (there are about 500 of them) is largely an expression of the centralist belief that the national government wields the power of the purse so as to direct state and local activities toward nationally determined purposes. Block grants reflect the dualist notion that relations between the units must protect the integrity of the states and the national purpose. General revenue sharing is predicated on the compound assumption that the nation and states can be brought together in a fiscal relationship that taps the superior capacities of each level. How one views each type of program, then, depends to a large extent on what one believes about federalism.

In an exceptionally insightful study, Shannon and Calkins (1983:23–29) observed that the early 1980s witnessed a new direction in fiscal federalism, which they described as a significant acceleration of national fiscal activity and a deceleration of state fiscal action. The increase in national expenditures had numerous causes, especially the increased interest on the national debt, the defense buildup, and various demographic trends, particularly the aging of the population, which required expenditures such as increases in social security and health care. So by the mid-1980s, in spite of the cutbacks in intergovernmental programs, national spending was still experiencing "great acceleration" (one huge "trigger" was the massive antirecession automatic spending in the mid-1980s for unemployment compensation).

On the other hand, state deceleration in spending resulted from the reduction in federal aid flows, the 1981–82 recession (which further limited national budgets for IGR aid through 1984), and the taxpayer revolt—all of which limited state tax increases for a few years. By the mid-1980s, however, state and local taxes were again on the rise as states tried to respond to needs and demands.

Shannon and Calkins argued that national acceleration and state deceleration in spending in the early 1980s resulted in a change in traditional concerns and goals in fiscal federalism. Traditionally, there has been a lot of concern for an "intrusive Washington" (the ACIR's term), a national government that so intrudes on state discretion that it ultimately reduces the states to administrative units of the national government. We have pointed out that the evidence for this effect is slim and that the conditions-of-aid effect has varied widely among programs, time periods, and jurisdictions. In any case, Shannon and Calkins argue that the concern now should be for an "extrusive Washington"—that is, for a national government that is so revenue-hungry in the constraints of current tax laws that it may preempt the tax base by pulling grant money and tax exemptions away from the states in order to finance rapidly expanding national expenses.

Is such a development likely? If so, how concerned should policy makers be with an extrusive Washington? The political economy approach to federalism suggests that the answer to the first question is "Not very likely." The latest trends in this issue are covered in Chapter 12. But just as the federalist culture and design have prevented the national government from "intruding" too greatly on the states, they are likely to prevent it from excessively preempting financial resources from the states. Again, the "ex-

trusive" concern rests on the same assumption as the "intrusive" concern—
that the states are passive units within the federal system. A realistic ap-
praisal reveals that such is simply not the case. In spite of the political
message of the taxpayer revolt, for example, the states were busy expanding their tax bases in the period 1981–83. By 1985, increases in income and
general sales taxes had peaked, but thirteen states were still raising motor
fuel, alcohol, and other excise taxes to shore up revenues (ACIR, 1986:4).
And certainly the states did not relax their claims on national government
grants and other transfers, receiving $24 from the feds for every $100 raised
on their own in 1985.

REGULATORY FEDERALISM

Although **regulatory federalism** has received much more interest in recent
years (see Reagan 1987 for an excellent review), national regulation itself is
really nothing new. The national government has been regulating private
firms since the beginning of the nation. Further, it has been regulating states
and their political subdivisions at least since the passage of the Fourteenth
Amendment. It is this type of regulation—national regulation of the states
and localities, and state regulation of localities (Chapter 5)—that we term
regulatory federalism.

Regulatory federalism experienced a radical transformation in the
1970s. In the first place, there was a quantum leap in the number of federal
regulations aimed at or implemented by state and local governments.
Second, the scope of such regulation has increased significantly. As a noted
commentator on the subject has observed, "the federal regulatory presence
has spilled over from the traditional economic sphere to include the nation's
states, cities, counties, school districts, colleges and other public institutions.
What was quite unthinkable (and seemingly politically impossible) a few
decades ago has both been thought of and come to pass." (Beam, 1981:9)
What are these "unthinkable things" that have come to pass, how do they
relate to the three national political economies, and what are their major
political economy effects?

Regulatory federalism takes four forms. The first consists of **direct
orders.** These are regulations that must be complied with under the threat
of civil or criminal penalties. The best-known example of this type of
regulation is the Equal Employment Opportunity Act of 1972. This statute
prohibits job discrimination by state and local governments on the basis
of race, color, religion, sex, or national origin. A similar prohibition had
been placed on private employers in 1964. The direct order that has
provoked the most controversy, however, is one that is contained in the
Fair Labor Standards Act. In 1974 Congress amended the FLSA so that it
applied to almost all employees of state and local governments (the

amendment also covered federal employees). A series of cases challenging the constitutionality of this amendment ensued. In *National League of Cities* v. *Usery* (426 US 833, 1976) the Supreme Court held that "Congress may not exercise power in a fashion that impairs the States' integrity or the ability to function effectively in a Federal system" (at 252). The 1974 amendment did impermissibly interfere with the integral governmental functions of states, the Court concluded.

After several cases in which the Court searched for definitions of the "traditional" and "integral" functions of states, it concluded in *Garcia v. San Antonio Mass Transit System* (469 US 528, 1985) that its efforts to do so were "unsound in principle and unworkable in practice" (at 1031). Thus the Court reversed the *Usery* decision and held that Congress was regulating the states in a permissible way in amending the Fair Labor Standards Act in 1974. What the court seemed to say in the *Garcia* ruling is that when Congress amends its own laws to regulate states, it is impossible for it to act unconstitutionally, even when that action might diminish the role and status of states. If this is so, then the scope and frequency of direct orders are to be determined mostly by the legislative branches of government, rather than by the courts.

The second form of national regulation of the states consists of **crosscutting requirements.** These are regulations imposed on grants across the board. Because they apply to all federally assisted programs, they are sometimes referred to as *horizontal mandates,* and they have a pervasive impact. The late 1960s and the 1970s witnessed a flood of new crosscutting requirements.

In an inventory of crosscutting requirements, the Office of Management and Budget identified thirty-six socioeconomic policy requirements and twenty-three administrative and fiscal policy requirements (OMB 1980). Within the socioeconomic policy requirements, nine dealt with nondiscrimination, sixteen related to environmental protection, three provided for protecting the advancement of the economy, three dealt with health, welfare, or safety, two required minority participation, and three set labor standards. The statutes involved are a roll call of some of the most important, and in some instances controversial, legislation in recent decades: the Civil Rights Act of 1964, the Age Discrimination Act of 1975, the Rehabilitation Act of 1973, the Comprehensive Alcohol Abuse and Alcoholism Prevention, Treatment and Rehabilitation Act of 1970, the Drug Abuse Office and Treatment Act of 1972, the National Environmental Policy Act of 1969, the Clean Water Act of 1972, the Safe Drinking Water Act of 1974, the Clean Air Act of 1970 (as amended in 1977), and the Wild and Scenic Rivers Act of 1968. This partial list reflects both the range of crosscutting regulations and their significance in our political economy.

A third, and less frequently used, form of regulation is the **crossover sanction.** This is a fiscal penalty that is imposed in one program area and applies in a second area. Thus a failure to comply with the requirements of one program can result in a reduction or termination of funds for a second, separately authorized program. In this way, the penalty "crosses over" from the first program to the second.

Two examples illustrate the crossover sanction. The first is the Highway Beautification Act of 1965. Prior to the passage of this act, Congress had tried to motivate the states to beautify their highways (specifically through removal or "setback" of billboards) by offering a bonus to states that complied. Only about half of the states took any action whatsoever. Then Congress passed the act. This act imposed a 10 percent penalty on any state receiving highway construction funds that did not comply with the standards established in the act. All the states quickly came in line. The second example is the Emergency Highway Energy Conservation Act of 1974. The purpose of the act was to lower highway speed limits to fifty-five miles per hour. To do this the act prohibited the secretary of transportation from approving any highway construction money for states that did not impose a fifty-five-mile-an-hour speed limit. All fifty states quickly adopted the limit. But by 1987, under a new amendment passed by Congress, most states were raising their speed limits in rural areas.

The most complex form of national regulation of the states is the fourth type—**partial preemption.** Partial preemption rests on the power of Congress to preempt a policy area (remove it from state activity). Since *Gibbons v. Ogden* (1824) and its doctrine of preemption by implication, this power of the Congress has been assumed to be rather broad. The power works like this: Congress identifies a policy area in which there is a strong national and state interest. Then, through legislation, it creates a situation in which the states either must act on a policy (usually in conformance with congressionally established standards) or have their involvement in the policy preempted at the national level. In essence, Congress says to the states, "If you act, we will not, but if you do not act, we will and then you cannot." The preemption, however, is only partial. The national government establishes base-level standards, but the states may in most instances, establish higher standards, and the states will implement the program in question. As we shall see, implementation is sometimes the political "dirty work" that has to be done in highly controversial areas, such as the environmentally safe disposal of hazardous chemical wastes.

The three best examples of partial preemption are the Water Quality Act of 1965, the Clean Air Act of 1970, and the Resource Conservation and Recovery Act of 1976. This last act has to do with the identification and disposal of hazardous chemical wastes. All three acts require the states to devise plans to implement federal standards for clean air, water, and the environmentally safe disposal of toxic chemicals. In the Clean Air Act, for example, federal authority is sweeping. The administrator of the Environmental Protection Agency can require states to change their transportation policies (for example, to give additional support to mass transit systems) or to regulate private individuals (for example, to establish an emission control and inspection program). Thus from the bottom looking up, it may be difficult to tell the difference between partial preemption and a direct order.

REGULATORY AND FISCAL FEDERALISM AS MIRRORS OF THE THREE NATIONAL PATTERNS

What do these details about intergovernmental grants and regulation mean in a political economy sense? In particular, how do the three national federalist traditions affect these things?

The effect of dualism on fiscal and regulatory federalism is fourfold. Dualism results in *dual legal systems* (national and state), *dual institutional and representation systems, dual public policy traditions,* and *dual power and interest group systems.* The specifics of laws, budgets and agency activities in regulation and fiscal relations are strongly influenced by these four dualist forces. Dual legal systems means that we have national and state legal traditions and institutions which are at least semiindependent of each other—different courts and different bodies of regulatory and civil law. Dual institutional and representation systems means significant differences between the national and various state political parties, differences between the dual "tracks" of legislatures, courts, executives, and bureaucracies. They produce corresponding differences in regulation and fiscal relations. Finally, there are somewhat distinct power elite and interest group systems at the national, state, and interstate levels. The result, dual regulation and fiscal traditions, means that what "plays well" in Washington may not be widely accepted in Peoria.

Compound federalism affects nation–state fiscal and regulatory relations most in two areas. First, the overall direction of macroeconomics (fiscal, monetary, and labor policy, regulation of interstate business, and international trade) has traditionally fallen to the national government. However, in recent years policies in these areas are increasingly the result of a contest between state and national political forces (this is seen especially in congressional economic policy making). Second, the compound tradition has very powerful political and economic effects through the influence of federal courts on lower courts and local life. This influence has been especially strong since the 1960s in defining the balance between intrastate and national (interstate) regulation of business and, through court intervention, in creating and strengthening reforms in civil rights and representation (affirmative action, one-person-one-vote, redistricting, and so forth).

Centralism affects nation–state fiscal and regulatory relations most in two ways. First, since the mid-1960s it has increasingly taken hold in the country as a philosophy of public policy, power, and nation–state relations. Most recently it is reflected in the rise of the political power of big business, the emergence of the New Right, and the struggle between national elites (a topic covered in Chapter 9). Enlightened centralism first accelerated the reforms of the late 1960s in civil rights and business regulation. But recently centralism has come to adopt a probusiness agenda of deregulation, with the possible outcomes of lessening civil rights enforcement, weakening labor priorities, and scaling back occupational, health, and product-safety regulations.

Second, centralism has significantly increased because of the growing phenomenon of bureaucratic discretion in making and enforcing public policies, determining the budget, shaping the nature of legislation, and redirecting the goals and activities of state or local bureaucracies. There has been some preemption of state regulation of various policy areas (labor safety, environment, product safety, and civil rights, for example), but the degree of national preemption is much exaggerated. And there is little recognition of the ability of state and local interests to preempt national activity through policy innovations when the feds don't act, or through their profound influence on policy implementation (see Chapter 10). In this case, centralism is at war with dualism and the subnational patterns of federalism. It is a war that the centralist tradition does not always win, especially in implementing public policies.

SUMMARY

The relationships between the nation and the states present a rich and varied mosaic. We have observed that many of the major features of federalism do not fit neatly into categories. But it is possible in most cases to identify the dominant causes and patterns of these features.

When all the elements of national–state relations are unscrambled, what are the key features? First, general policy control is more or less the primary responsibility of the various levels of governments. Thus different structures have responsibility for determining what governments will do and what they will not do (nondecisions). Second, the federal system fragments governmental power without democratizing it. In Chapter 9 we will develop this thesis, arguing that federalism is the chief arbiter of power in the American political system. Additionally, the federal design has created a representation system consisting of multiple, self-sustaining centers of power, privilege, and profit.

All of these features "make it tough" on political institutions in this country. For example, federalism has created an environment in which party unity is almost impossible. Political parties, largely because of federalism, are loose confederations. Federalism has been both a curse and a boon for interest groups. To obtain a decision at one place in the system does not necessarily mean that the group has won a policy outcome. For many interest groups, following a policy through the maze of federalism is a difficult if not impossible task. But federalism allows interest groups many access points, so they can shop around a bit until they find a sympathetic institution. Thus federalism makes it possible for most groups to win something while ensuring that few groups get everything they want.

Within the basic institutions of national federalism, Congress most clearly mirrors subnational forces. However, the president is the focal point for all the crosscurrents of the federal system. On the one hand, these crosscurrents are a liability for the president (a federalist meat grinder of sorts), but they are also powerful assets in structuring and channeling issues, debates, and agendas. Chapter 12 analyzes the effectiveness of the president as the pseudomanager of federalism. Game theory is one of the most effective ways to understand the complex patterns of intergovernmental relationships within the bureaucracy. It is even more difficult to explain the inconsistent, almost erratic posture and functioning of the Supreme Court in the federal system.

It may be simply because "money talks," but no area of federal relations has provoked more study and writing than fiscal relations among the various levels of government. Our approach was to examine the various intergovernmental transfers within the broader framework of the political economy approach to federalism. This was also our approach to the important topic of regulatory federalism. By relating fiscal and regulatory federalism to the three national political economies, it is possible to obtain a broader picture of what these things mean.

As we stressed in Chapter 2, the several subnational patterns of federalism rival, and in some policy areas outweigh the national pattern in importance. In Chapters 4–7, we analyze these subnational patterns.

KEY CONCEPTS AND THEMES FOR REVIEW

access points
action channels
block grants
catagorical grant
crosscutting requirement
crossover sanction
direct order
game approach
general revenue sharing
issue agenda

non-decisions
partial preemption
regulatory federalism
representation system

NOTES

[1]See Chapter 1, note. d. Wright (1982) is an important source for this kind of treatment of federalism.

Subnational Federalism:

4

The interstate pattern

In the previous chapter, we indicated that national federalism is much more than what Walker (1981) has called a "nonsystem." From the standpoint of the three dominant federal traditions, we see distinct patterns of relations that might otherwise seem capricious. Federalism is a system—and one that makes patterned sense.

In Chapters 4 –7, we view the four subnational patterns of federalism in similar terms. Again, we start by describing "official federalism" and then build in a political economy view (which will be enriched in Chapters 8 –11). In each case, we attempt to describe the pattern. Then we try to identify its roots in the early political history of this country and broadly trace its evolution to the present day. Next we describe the "nuts and bolts" of the pattern, stressing how it functions as a political economy. Finally, we examine its meaning in politics, policy, and economics. In this chapter, we concentrate on interstate relations.

RELATIONS BETWEEN SEPARATES AND EQUALS

Whatever the winning design in the relations between the central government and the states, the federal bargain struck at the Constitutional Convention provided that states should in some respects be "separate and equal." In the beginning, at least, states were assumed to be entirely sovereign. W. Brooke Graves (1964:60) has argued that the Declaration of Independence created thirteen sovereignties that merely acted together to declare independence and protect themselves. Indeed, the language of the Declaration is the language of sovereignty:

> We, therefore,…solemnly publish and declare, That these United Colonies are, and of Right ought to be Free and Independent States;…and that as Free and Independent States, they have full Power to levy War, conclude Peace, contract Alliances, establish Commerce, and to do all other Acts and Things which Independent States may of right do.

Little would be added to our approach to federalism by entering the debate over *where* sovereignty rests in the American political system. At least in their relations with one another, however, states are practically islands unto themselves. Interstate federal relations are relations between virtually separate sovereignties and between constitutional equals.

In a very important sense, this virtual sovereignty in interstate relations rests in the antifederalist political tradition. The records of the convention of 1787 show clearly that the antifederalists there were silenced, if not converted to federalist thinking. But as we have seen, the antifederalist culture did not die. Antifederalism stressed the strengthening of states over the strengthening of a national government. As a way of thinking about federalism and the management of politics, social life, and economics, the antifederalist political culture is seen most sharply today in the relationships between the states. As we have observed, what this mode of thinking means is that public policy was **state-centered,** for much of our early history. And since states characteristically maintained a posture of isolation sometimes bordering on hostility toward one another, most day-to-day public policy during the early period was centered in *specific* states.

However, as a result of the long reach of the compound federal culture, there are two important exceptions to this last situation. First, the Constitution did provide certain limits on state actions. The "supremacy clause" (Article VI) serves to make every provision of the Constitution apply to states in a constraining way, particularly when connected with Supreme Court rulings, such as *Gibbons* v. *Ogden* (9 Wheaton 1, 1824) that national law might preempt state law in a policy area. In our view, which emphasizes what the federal bargain means in terms of the political economy, more specific features of the Constitution better illustrate the impact of its limits on the states.

For example, Article I, Section 10, prohibits any state from "impairing the obligation of contract." Charles Beard has skillfully documented the private economic motives that led the Framers to include this provision in the Constitution. From a political economy viewpoint, the provision served to protect economic arrangements for national economic elites (see discussion of compound federalism in Chapter 2). Specifically, the prohibition protected these elites from too great an influence by the masses through state legislatures. It also functioned as one of those checks "against the excesses of democracy" so feared by Framers such as Edmund Randolph. Thus, the contract clause both secured economic interests for a national elite and protected "political order" in such a way as to discourage mass challenges to elite power. The latter point was demonstrated by the infamous Shays's and Whiskey rebellions (nothing discourages the masses like the army showing up). The clause is an indicator of the idea that federalism is a system of polities within a complex political economy. It also clearly indicates that federalism, from the beginning, affected who wins and who loses in the competition to acquire political power, conduct business, and amass wealth.

The second practical limit on state domination of public policy in the early era was interstate cooperation, sometimes for the purpose of limiting individual freedom of action in politics, but mostly to achieve regional economic and social objectives. This cooperation gave life to interstate federalism early on. The major problem in understanding these early examples of interstate cooperation is that early history is looked at from an urban-industrial perspective. Thus, several interpretations of federalism have pictured interstate cooperation (or *regionalism*, as most sources have it) as a relatively recent phenomenon. This assertion overlooks early interstate cooperation, some of which had very important *potential* if not actual political, social, and economic consequences.

ROOTS AND EARLY EVOLUTION

One of the earliest examples of interstate political cooperation (one that would have had profound implications for American history if it had worked out differently) was the 1814 convention of New England states known as the Hartford Convention. Eager to protect its merchants, who along with merchants from Rhode Island had benefited substantially from the War of 1812, the Massachusetts legislature called for a convening of all the New England states. Massachusetts, Rhode Island, and Connecticut sent official delegates, and Vermont and New Hampshire sent observers. More moderate delegates gained control of the convention and scaled down what would have been rather extreme proposals to protect the political power of New England states and to further the economic interests of New England merchants. These merchants already had a virtual stranglehold on critical commodities and the supply of hard money. Extremists talked of seceding if Congress failed to meet the demands of the convention (the demands took the form of amendments to the national Constitution). Subsequent events quieted secessionist talk, but did little to assuage the regional economic struggles in the country.

Many of the same Yankee merchants involved in the Hartford Convention had rallied earlier under Alexander Hamilton to support the establishment of the national bank in 1791. Representative James Jackson of Georgia quickly identified the essence of the bank plan: "This plan for a national bank is calculated to benefit a small part of the United States, the mercantilist interests only; the farmers, the yeomanry, will derive no advantage from it" (quoted by Hofstadter, Miller, and Aaron 1959:268). This emerging Yankee capitalist class succeeded in getting the bank's charter renewed for an additional twenty years in 1815.

From the 1830s to the Civil War, western and southern states were able to weaken the national bank and ultimately replace it with an essentially private banking system. This invigorated private bank system served to increase the wealth of other regional elites and allowed other regional economies to expand and compete with New England. Again, *subnational interstate federalism* had worked behind the scenes to produce profound social and economic change.

Interstate federalism has had several other economic and social outcomes. One is in the area of race relations. William Riker (1975) has argued that one of the most important historical uses of federalism has been racial suppression. In policy analysis language, racial suppression was one of the most important outcomes of interstate relations. C. Van Woodward (1966) has demonstrated clearly that a genuine reconstruction of southern society by the North was under way immediately after the Civil War. This transformation continued into the 1870s and 1880s. During the 1880s, however, a mass alliance between poor whites and newly enfranchised blacks known as the **southern Populist movement** began to threaten the entrenched political and economic power of Bourbon Democrats in the South. In an interstate effort of grand proportions, these landed elites moved in state after state to obtain passage of so-called Jim Crow laws. The effect of these laws was to disenfranchise and isolate *both* poor whites and blacks and virtually cancel the Fourteenth and Fifteenth Amendments for some eighty years. Passage of the Jim Crow laws solidified the dominant political power of Bourbon Democrats in the South, established the one-party system in that region, stifled Reconstruction, established a social order unknown before the Civil War, and created an economic underclass in the South that is visible even today. Thus stories in Georgia newspapers in 1986 frequently characterized that state and Atlanta as a "mini–New York in a sea of Mississippi poverty"— an unkind but still partly true picture.

When we look from the vantage point of our theory of federalism at how Reconstruction was strangled in the crib, what we see is a replacement of the centralist model of federalism with the interstate model. The

1890s in the South may be taken as a case of the ascendancy of subnational federalism in one region of the country.

Having said this, we must immediately make two points. First, we are not saying that what resulted from the ascendancy of interstate federalism in the South in the 1890s was *inevitable*. Strong regional preferences, or antifederalist ideas, are hardly dead in America. Ronald Reagan's popular "antifederalist" rhetoric called for a situation that, so far as the structure and function of federalism is concerned, would mean the return of the interstate model to dominance. The appeal of Reagan's federalist rhetoric certainly affirms the durability of anti-federalist ideas. Certainly this means, among other things, that the concentration of research on the national models of federalism skews our perspective of the American political system and distorts the political history of the country.

The second point is that from the 1890s forward, the interstate model has taken many forms—different from the relatively raw regional economic self-interest expressed in the Hartford Convention, and more like the highly "public interest group" forms reflected in interstate reciprocity laws. In short, we can say of interstate relations that they are sometimes prominent in politics and economics; that they have been very influential from the beginning of the American political system; and that they have taken some new forms but have many social effects of the same *magnitude* as those of the patterns of national federalism. The social significance of the patterns of federalism is summarized and compared in Chapter 11.

LATER EVOLUTION: THE MODERN ERA

Developments beginning in the 1890s illustrate the link between the interstate model and its function in the political economy in the most direct ways possible. From the 1890s to 1937, the concept of states' rights was construed by the federal courts in such a way as to virtually institutionalize laissez-faire economics in the legal precedents of this country. Key cases that illustrate this period include *United States* v. *Knight* (156 U.S. 1, 1895), *Hammer* v. *Dagenhart* (247 U.S. 251, 1918), *Schechter Poultry Corp.* v. *United States* (295 U.S. 495, 1935), and *Carter* v. *Carter Coal Co.* (298 U.S. 238, 1936). Cynthia Colella sums up her incisive review of the courts' role in the period in this way: "It was an era that saw small entrepreneurs locked out of the competitive process and the public locked into the stranglehold of rampant industrial expansion. The states were helpless to control the transnational arrogance of the 'robber barons' and, by the turn of the century, the court had badly curtailed even their internal controls" (1986:42).

The height of this distortion of the Constitution came in 1895, when the Supreme Court struck down a government suit against a big sugar monopoly by making the preposterous distinction that "manufacturing and selling sugar across state lines at unfair prices was not interstate commerce" and not a direct restraint of interstate trade (*United States* v. *E. C. Knight Company*, 156 U.S. 1:1895). The Court "had turned dual federalism upside-down...it had created a Constitutional 'no-man's land' in which no one could act to protect the public, small business and increasingly the economy itself." Progressivism from 1900 to the 1920s was characterized by a number of Court rulings that restricted monopolies, and by new laws that set up regulation of meat inspection, mine safety, and drugs. But by the 1920s the Court had returned to its role as guardian of unregulated capitalism, and "the powers to tax and spend, regulate the economy, and to police may have been relegated to a state of dormancy" (all quotes from Colella, 1986:49).

As we have pointed out, Adam Smith had little influence in the construction of our constitutional system and the foundations of our political economy. Alexander Hamilton had much more influence in determining these things. But by the 1890s, social Darwinism and laissez-faire economics had combined to form a new and enormously popular dogma among the national elite. Social Darwinism was a crude amalgam of Darwin's theory of biological evolution and Herbert Spencer's social views. According to its advocates, whatever happens socially must be what's best, or it wouldn't have happened that way. There was also the vulgar notion that the fittest survive, so they must have created the best kind of society. These ideas helped justify the rise of the truly powerful Yankee capitalist class in the late nineteenth century as America underwent an astonishingly rapid industrialization.

The new national economic elites became interested in "constitutionalizing" laissez-faire economics (partly, to be sure, because of their puffed-up self-concept of their "right to rule," fed by class power and social Darwinism). They found in the courts the idea of dualism, which became another principle on which to base laissez-faire rulings. This principle was extended by the Courts to affect interstate regulation. In numerous cases, by emphasizing "states' rights"—to avoid regulating child labor practices and abuses in industry, for example—the courts could play the advocate for the economic elites and give them a dualist reason for having their centralist cake and eating it too. The Supreme Court merged interstate supremacy with centralist interests, fashioning a double standard that protected "legitimate" big business and capital against state and national action. Wallace Mendelson expressed the constitutional-law nature of this powerful development very clearly:

> This double standard is an aspect of what has been called "dual federalism." It meant that states' rights somehow limited even the *expressly delegated* national powers *for some, but not for all purposes.* Thus

dual federalism protected "reputable" business in its more modern transgressions [e.g., trusts and child labor] but not in such old-fashioned immoralities as prostitution, gambling, impure foods, liquor, narcotics, or "fraudulent" margarine....

It would be erroneous to suppose that the sudden new concern for states' rights in the 1890s brought the states new freedom to manage their own affairs. Quite the contrary! States' rights in this context was merely a device to hamstring national government [note: the compound model]. Contemporaneously with dual federalism, as we shall see, the courts developed the doctrine of "substantive due process" to save "reputable" business interest from the "sovereign states." Thus did laissez-faire economic doctrine find expression in the Constitution....(1965:94)

This is one of the clearest examples of the interstate model functioning as a political economy. In the 1930s, the interstate pattern was to be dramatically changed by the Depression and the New Deal (see Chapter 2). The features of interstate relations today (which survive largely from the time of FDR) are what we will now summarize.

NUTS AND BOLTS: THE PRACTICAL VIEW FROM THE STATES

The constitutional equality and the economic-resource inequality among the fifty states have created a complex environment for interaction among the states. In effect, an infinite range and variety of interstate relations is possible. The relations between officials and political interests of state A and state B are usually not the same as those between state A and state C. In some respects, the kaleidoscope of interstate relations is more difficult to sort out than the more patterned relations between the states and the nation. But the sorting out of interstate relations provides a rich source of insights into the federal system. Chapter 10 develops the ideas of interstate political networks and regionalism and how they work in politics and power systems. Here we concentrate on relations between state governments themselves.

Within the political economy of federalism, interstate relations are a dialectic of conflict and cooperation. A review of the 200-year history of American federalism suggests that of the two patterns of interaction, conflict relations have been more frequent and more significant than cooperative relations. And a good case can be made that conflict relations between states are in flux. For example, it is one thing to struggle with other states for advantage in licensing corporations or banks. It is quite another thing to be locked in conflict with other states over environmental or health issues that have intergenerational effects. Faced with issues that are intergenerational and global, states are digging in their heels in an increasingly combative posture toward other states and the national government. We will get to these issues shortly. But first, there are certain areas of cooperation mandated or prescribed by the Constitution. These interstate obligations are an important legal basis to a larger understanding of the relations among the states.

Constitutionally Prescribed Obligations

In Article IV, the Constitution prescribes three legal "obligations" that each state owes to every other state. These are the full faith and credit obligation, the privileges and immunities obligation, and the obligation to extradite. They are the foundation below which interstate cooperative relations cannot go. But what do they mean in practice?

The **full faith and credit obligation** requires each state to give validity to "the public Acts, Records, and judicial proceedings of every other State" (Article IV, Section 1). Public acts consist of civil laws passed by state legislatures. Thus an individual in Georgia who has entered into a divorce decree that includes child support payments will find upon moving to New York that New York will enforce the terms of those payments according to the Georgia laws.

However, this obligation does not extend to criminal laws. No state is obligated to enforce the criminal laws of another state (*Wisconsin* v. *Pelican Insurance Co.,* 127 U.S. 265, 1888). The required exchange of records applies to the official documents of the state, which (by terms of an act of Congress) are authenticated by having the seal of the state affixed to them. Such documents include deeds, birth certificates, death certificates, mortgages, and marriage licenses. States must also abide by the judicial proceedings and decisions of other state courts in all civil matters over which they have jurisdiction. The one significant exception to this rule is divorce. Since *Williams* v. *North Carolina* (325 U.S. 226, 1945), the status of a divorce is somewhat unclear where one or both parties resided in a state the *minimum* length of time required to fulfill that state's residence requirement. In the *Williams* case, North Carolina was upheld in its refusal to accept the Nevada divorce of an individual who lived in Nevada for only the minimum time required for residency in that state (at that time, six weeks).

As inclusive as this first obligation seems to be, the **privileges and immunities obligation** is stated in even more inclusive language. Article IV, Section 2 reads, "The Citizens of each State shall be entitled to all Privileges and Immunities of Citizens in the several States." The intent of the section is clear. The Framers wanted to ensure that citizens could travel (and do business in) other states without encountering discriminatory treatment. A state cannot favor its citizens over the citizens of other states in such matters as the acquisition and use of property, the transaction of business, the pursuit of interests in the courts of the host state, and the taxation of income and property (*Corfield* v. *Coryell,* 4 Wash. C.C. 371, 1825). One emerging variation of this is that the states of the upper Middle West are considering entry into a Great Lakes states compact that may require member states to collect sales taxes on property bought in member states and return part of those monies to the state of *residence.* In general, however, the Constitution simply uses the word *all* and makes no list of the privileges and immunities protected by this clause.

This word "all" has produced several difficulties of interpretation. Two areas have been especially troublesome. First, one of the more important categories of privileges, of course, is the various political privileges —voting, running for and holding public office, and access to state facilities. Every student knows that out-of-state tuition is higher than in-state tuition. But not many know that a state could limit the number of out-of-state students it will admit to one of its institutions — a law school, for instance. By law, for example, the University of Colorado in Boulder cannot admit more than 22,000 students. And most Americans learned in high school civics classes that all fifty states have residency requirements for voting and require citizenship as a qualification for running for office.

More important for young college students is the privilege of practicing a craft—electrician, undertaker, or "southern planter" (as we call it here in the South), and so on—or a profession—lawyer, doctor, and so forth. Such a privilege is granted in the form of a state license, and is commonly withheld by states from citizens of other states. This situation obviously poses difficulties to a people as mobile as Americans are. Probably the most common difficulty is illustrated by a young married woman with a teaching certificate in state A whose husband is transferred to state B, where she finds herself unable to teach. Or—a more absurd example—a doctor from state X who is vacationing in state Y may be unable to render medical aid in an emergency in state Y because to do so would be to practice medicine without a license. The medical example spawned "Good Samaritan laws" in most states. These are reciprocity laws that allow medical personnel (doctors, nurses, and paramedics) to render medical assistance in emergencies. Some policy areas have seen the extensive application of the reciprocity concept. Teaching is a good example. States that are parties to the National Association for the Accreditation of Teacher Education statute agree to recognize teacher certificates from member states. Other areas, though—law and accountancy, for example—have experienced little application of the reciprocity technique.

The third interstate obligation is that of **extradition** (or *rendition*). The language of the Constitution appears to make the obligation mandatory: "A person charged in any state with treason, felony, or other crime, who shall flee from justice, and be found in another State, shall on demand of the executive authority of the State from which he fled, be delivered up, to be removed to the State having jurisdiction of the crime" (Article IV, Section 2). However, it is in the extradition section that we see most clearly the meaning of the question "What is the Constitution among the states?" particularly when interpreted by the United States Supreme Court? One situation presented a stark federalist contrast—the national "supreme law" required state action (the fugitive *shall* be given up), but the State of Ohio simply said no (it would not give up the fugitive) (*Kentucky* v. *Dennison*, 24 Howard 66, 1861). Alas, what was the Court to do? John Marshall knew, as is commonly known, that the Court has no direct enforcement powers. In this instance the nature of the federal system forced the justices to be creative. Their decision allowed the Court to slip out of a potentially very embarrassing situation. The Court held that extradition is a "moral" obligation and not a judicially enforceable one. This ruling, to say the least, could have turned the Court into an "irrelevancy," to use colorful term of Bushrod Washington, a member of the Marshall Court. Ironically, the Court was not loath to disparage, if not embarrass, governors. In his opinion, Chief Justice Taney argued that the assignment of "federal duties" to a governor "might overload...and disable him from performing the obligations to his state." Governors, however, simply did not find the press of this "federal duty" too demanding. Having been relieved of the *legal* duty to extradite, states have established routine processes for the return of fugitives, and those processes function as a matter of course in all but the rarest instances. It remains interesting that the legal *obligation* to extradite is apparently missing.

Conflict Relations: E Pluribus Unum versus All Other Unums

In a very real sense, the Constitution of 1787 and thus the American federal system was born out of conflict between states. Many factors had produced dissatisfaction with the government under the Articles of Confederation, but it was interstate conflict in the area of commerce that triggered the Constitutional Convention of 1787. Specifically, states passed laws governing commerce that were in conflict with each other. The problems created thereby were especially contentious between Virginia and Maryland. The navigable channel of the Potomac River was on the "Maryland side" of the river. Taking advantage of this, Maryland passed a number of laws giving advantage in shipping to Maryland producers. Several efforts were made to settle the resulting dispute—including the Alexandria Conference and a meeting in George Washington's home. Delegates to those meetings recognized the general problem of conflict between the states and called for a general conference to be held in Annapolis for the express purpose of resolving commercial difficulties among the states. The Annapolis Conference became the immediate precursor of the Constitutional Convention. Though unable to agree on a plan to resolve commercial difficulties, the delegates instructed Alexander Hamilton to draft a call to all states to attend a convention in Philadelphia "to render the constitution of the Federal Government adequate to the exigencies of the Union." It is commonly noted in American history books that Virginia sent the most serious and competent delegation. There is nothing like the pocketbook to inspire seriousness of effort.

Over time, the range of interstate economic conflict has been broad indeed. There has been minor conflict between the states on such commercial issues as the quarantine of agriculture products. Anyone who has read a seed or plant catalog has seen the phrase "may not be shipped to ____ state." It is difficult in the modern world to justify the prohibition of shipping apple trees from Missouri to Washington on purely quarantine grounds. On a more serious level, there is conflict between the states on intergenerational issues—problems that pose costs for future generations, such as environmental pollution—on development issues, such as water rights, and on such regional issues as the Sunbelt–Frostbelt rivalry. And as we have pointed out, the intensity of these conflicts does not seem to have abated; in some areas, such as economic development, it clearly has increased.

We want to set the story of interstate conflict in a context of federalism viewed as a political economy. We are therefore most interested in two questions. First, what are the major areas of interstate conflict, and what do they involve? Second, what are the political economy effects of interstate conflict? To illustrate these concerns, we turn now to three policy areas that involve major aspects of interstate conflict—hazardous waste, water rights, and economic development.

Hazardous Waste: A Strange Brew of Legislative Cooperation in a Cauldron of Conflict.   Hazardous waste is a policy area of intensive interstate conflict. The extent of this conflict has been well documented.[1] Because hazardous waste is a policy area of intergenerational importance, the conflict is likely to increase rather than lessen over the next several years. Hazardous waste may be divided for classification purposes into solid waste, toxic chemical waste, and nuclear waste (itself divided into low-level and high-level nuclear waste). Solid waste has long been viewed as the most "settled" of the three areas.

Responsibility for solid waste disposal is clearly with the states. However, the states have mandated that the primary service providers will be substate jurisdictions (cities and counties with a few instances of special-district providers). Finally, there is national monitoring of state and local facilities. As we shall see shortly, this long-settled policy area has become somewhat unsettled in recent years.

As we saw in Chapter 3, legislation on toxic chemical waste is an excellent example of the regulatory device known as partial preemption. States generally have primary responsibility; if they do not assume responsibility, the national government will. The Low Level Nuclear Waste Act is more on the order of direct national regulation of the states. In addition to requiring state responsibility for storing low-level waste, the act sets national standards below which the states may not fall. In all three areas of waste, there is no shortage of legislation—both national and state.

As in most other policy areas, the federalist culture that underlies legislation in each of the three areas is fairly clear. Solid-waste legislation is rooted in the dualist culture. There is the assumption of rather separate spheres of action with a preference for a direct service provider as "close to the people as possible." The role of the national government is one of underwriting local efforts and monitoring the program to ensure that national interests are met. Policy on toxic chemical waste and legislation on low-level nuclear waste are rooted in the centralist political culture. The first is an example of partial preemption and the second most closely approximates a direct order; both reflect the belief that national power is an appropriate lever to use with states, triggering state action even in previously inactive states (Wells 1982). Much of the conflict in hazardous waste management and much of the inaction in the areas of toxic chemical waste and low-level nuclear waste are traceable to the influence of federalist traditions and cultures as political economies. The primary political economy effects in these policy areas, then, are conflict in all three areas and inaction in two of them.

Conflict in hazardous waste policy is explainable in large part in structural terms. Hazardous waste legislation, as with environment policy generally, has enabled Congress to act "nobly" by taking the high ground of principle while leaving the messy work of implementation to the states and localities. This structural factor is seen most clearly in the Resource Conservation and Recovery Act, the most significant legislation in the toxic chemical waste area. In the RCRA, Congress was careful to provide that the official responsible for hazardous chemical waste policy was the director of the national Environmental Protection Agency. Substantial power for promulgating standards, certifying state programs as being in "full compliance," and so on, were vested in the director. Congress then expressed its intent that states assume primary responsibility for implementation and management of chemical waste programs. But that intent was so constrained that serious questions can be raised concerning the discretion actually left to the states and the options available to them. In short, Congress reaped the political capital while leaving the states with the political risks of actually siting facilities (Wells 1982).

Structural problems take more specific forms, which have to do with relations among the "semisovereign states." For low-level nuclear waste, the conflict centers in the question of which state will host the site. Efforts to create a regional capacity to manage wastes have failed largely because no state wants to become the host state. In toxic chemical waste, conflict revolves around the shipment of waste to existing sites in other states (which raises the question of whose site is best for a particular "dump zone"). In short, interstate conflict is so extensive that no adequate documentation of its extent has yet occurred.

Perhaps the most revealing and amusing illustration of structure-based conflict is the case of the "wandering garbage barge." It was probably not very amusing to those directly involved. The garbage barge was called *Mobro 4000* and its tugboat *Break of Dawn*. In the spring of 1987, some 3186 tons of "clean" garbage from Islip, New York, was loaded on the barge with a destination of Morehead City, N.C. Islip's landfill had reached capacity and a private firm had contracted to haul the trash to the North Carolina site. When the barge arrived in Morehead City, the captain of the tug was told in good southern style "to get the hell out of North Carolina's waters" (*Time*, May 4, 1987, p. 26). In explaining the state's reasoning behind its order, Stephen Reid of North Carolina's Solid and Hazardous Waste Management Bureau commented, "We have enough garbage of our own. We didn't need New York's" (*Time*, May 4, 1987, p. 26). This set the barge and its cargo on a series of rejections that involved five other states (Alabama, Mississippi, Louisiana, Texas, and Florida) and three foreign countries (Mexico, Belize, and the Bahamas). The captain of the *Break of Dawn* summed up the situation nicely: "There's a sneaky feeling that I have. Something greater, something bigger is controlling all this…and not letting us unload the bloody thing and get done with it" (*Atlanta Constitution*, May 4, 1987, p. 9). That something bigger was the long reach of federalism. Specifically, that something bigger was interstate conflict over a particularly noxious public problem. The emotions of the conflict were rooted in the dualist federal culture. Consider that, whether half in jest or not, Governor Edwin Edwards of Louisiana threatened to call out the national guard with orders to shoot if the barge tried to dock in his state.

On the international front, Mexico put its Navy on alert in the event the barge approached the Mexican coast too closely. In these two parallel actions, we see the meaning of the phrase "the states are semisovereign entities." When a policy issue is rooted in the dualist federal culture, the states may "exercise their sovereignty"—even to the point of calling out troops. And in this kind of conflict posture, the states can hardly resist taking potshots at the feds. The attorney general of Louisiana, William Guste, complained to the press that "the Environmental Protection Agency was not watching at all. If that barge tips or runs into a storm, the garbage could end up on our shores" (*Time*, May 4, 1987, p. 26). The relatively "settled area" of solid waste policy fostered some pretty unsettled relations between the states, and between the states and the nation, over New York garbage.

The hazardous waste policy area not only is fraught with possibilities for interstate conflict but also reflects clearly the intersection of the political and the economic in the distribution of the costs and benefits of public policy. The distribution effects of hazardous waste policy are clear (even if they are difficult to trace precisely in how they can affect individuals). Hazardous waste programs concentrate the risks and disperse the benefits. The risks associated with the implementation of hazardous waste control—say, the siting of a chemical waste facility—are concentrated in the geographic area of the facility. Thus the individuals who bear the costs of the facility are those who live near it. It is this concentration of risks that produces the intense opposition of "locals" to all siting attempts—a kind of conflict sometimes called NIMBY ("not in my back yard"). While the public favors the environmentally safe disposal of toxic waste, it does not want the facilities "next door" or even elsewhere in their state.

But such facilities also disperse the benefits. A wide range of people benefit from hazardous waste policy implementation. The general public benefits from the environmentally safe storage of toxic residues. Operators of specific sites profit from commercial operation of the facility. Firms producing the dangerous residuals benefit from a publicly acceptable means of disposal. And political decision makers benefit from the public perception that they are able to solve difficult and complex problems (although the decision maker certainly is seldom popular among the folks who live near the facility).

Beyond the question of who benefits and who pays, there is the complex intergenerational problem associated with an uncertain technology. The technology for most solid waste (placed no longer in "dumps" but in what are euphemistically referred to as *sanitary landfills*) provides a reasonably high degree of probability that it is environmentally safe. However, the technology associated with toxic chemical waste disposal— *cell technology*—is not as convincing (Wells 1982). Also, the technology of low-level nuclear waste disposal—*trough technology*—has been subjected to severe criticism for its "bathtubbing" effect: water seeps into the concrete troughs in which low-level waste is stored, filling them much like water fills a bathtub, and spilling over, carrying radiation with it. Even more substantial criticism can be levied at the *burial technology* associated with high-level nuclear waste disposal. The long-lasting radioactivity of the waste leaves this technology suspect. For example, it has long been rumored that tons of dangerous radioactive stuff are "buried" off the shores of Washington State—the by-products of military nuclear waste dumping.

Such uncertain technologies pose some of the most difficult ethical decisions that policy makers in the federal system have faced. In the first place, the uncertain technology of hazardous waste management moves policy makers away from traditional kinds of decision making—compromise among competing factions (pluralist theory) or elite decisions "behind closed doors" on the basis of experts' advice. The NIMBY syndrome has virtually become the Eleventh Commandment, prohibiting the compromise so essential to traditional pluralist politics. The uncertain technology also denies the "informed expert" sufficient scientific grounds on which to give clear, informed advice. Consequently, political decision makers have a very tough time choosing between the political signals they receive from the public and the scientific evidence they receive from experts.

Thus what are made virtually ineffective by the volatile issues in hazardous waste management are *process norms*. These are the generally accepted "rules of the game," the ways in which policy decisions are made. The process norms characteristic of each of the three federalist cultures are relatively clear and surprisingly stable. But they are inadequate in the face of the decision complexity involved with hazardous wastes. Therefore, the federal implementation strategies used—whether centralist direct orders to control low-level nuclear waste, or compound partial preemption of the control of chemical wastes—are also ineffective in reducing conflicts in politics or in getting viable programs of waste control.

In short, the federal system has yet to develop a set of process norms that can guide the implementation of the large body of legislation on hazardous waste. This vacuum is not likely to continue indefinitely, if only because of what is at stake—the manner by and the degree to which the system must eventually achieve a very important policy objective—the environmentally safe disposal of hazardous waste.

Western Water: The Desert Winds of Reality.   Conflict over water has been a major factor in the economic development and political life of the West since the frontier days. Much of the conflict has revolved around the uses of available water. Historically, the successful participants have been ranchers and farmers. Thus water was available, often in superabundant quantities, for agricultural purposes. But with the growth of the Sunbelt, cities are starting to challenge that traditional allocation. The distributive politics of water has taken a new twist.

Historically, the politics of water development in the West was a distributive politics that transferred wealth between regions. Numerous studies have been made of this development. Among the best and most insightful of these studies was one by Beattie and associates (1971). This study assumed four types of regions—the region of water origin, the region of water destination, the region(s) through which water would be transported, and the regions unaffected by the transfer (that is, the remainder of the United States). The study took into account both direct and indirect effects. Its primary conclusion was that water development projects resulted in enormous regional shifts of income. Most interesting, those income transfers were positive in all areas except the region that the authors called "the rest of the United States." That is, although water transfers did produce losers in the region of origin, the losers' losses were exceeded by the gains of others in that region. The losses for "the rest of the United States" were large in the aggregate but small on a per capita basis.

This study should modify the conventional wisdom on income transfers resulting from water development. According to such thinking, water development is a zero-sum game: for every winner there is a loser of equal proportion, so that the sum of wins and losses is zero. Such a situation may be true of western water in the aggregate. But it is not true among the direct, small-scale competitors for water. Western water development, historically, has meant the extraction of substantial income from the "rest of the nation" for distribution to the West, both in the region of water origin and in the region of destination. Thus, in a separate report one of Beattie's colleagues asserts correctly that "in a political sense, it really is income rather than water that is being transferred" (Castle 1983).

Two factors have combined to place in serious question the nation's willingness to continue such income transfers to the West. First, the water development potential of the West has been realized for all practical purposes. The only future development that could involve distributive politics on the order of the past is the interbasin transfer of water. Most analysts agree though, that such a scheme is highly unlikely because of the second factor—the complex intergovernmental relations that it would involve (Kneese 1982:10).

Other problems crop up too. For example, the economic and ecological considerations in interbasin transfers of water would be as complex as the political issues. Second, budget restrictions at the national level make interbasin transfer of water unlikely. Beattie and colleagues found that past interregional income transfers, while large in the aggregate, were small on a per capita basis and did not produce political pressures from the "rest of the nation." However, the political situation has changed substantially. One of the most careful scholars of water in the United States, Emery Castle, has concluded, "Though small raids on the Treasury may be tolerated or made feasible through logrolling, massive transfers of income to particular regions are not likely in times of budget stringency" (1983:9).

The era of regional distributive politics concerning water has come to an end. What is emerging now is an intraregional distributive politics between groups. In short, the urban and industrial use of water is now competing with the historic diversion of water to agriculture. In economic terms, the incremental value of urban and industrial water is higher than the agricultural use of water. The "home on the range" may be the nostalgic way of thinking about life in the West, but the truth is that three out of four people in the West live in metropolitan areas (in California the figure is 95 percent). Urban decision makers now view with considerable skepticism the frequent superabundance of water for agricultural purposes. Cities have taken a number of actions to acquire what they regard as surplus agricultural water. Here is how one observer describes the situation:

> Water is becoming a market commodity in the West....In northern Colorado, the trading of water rights became so active that "water brokers" went into business. And in California's fertile Central Valley,

corporate farming operations have approached San Diego and Los Angeles about selling water rights. San Diego recently acquired an option to buy water from the Upper Colorado Basin from a private company despite opposition from Los Angeles and several states that share the waters of the Colorado River. (Arrandale 1987:1)

Clearly, western water is moving from an era of interregional transfer of income to an era of intraregional competition and conflict. The question now is who in the West will be the winners and who will be the losers. The political economy meaning of this policy problem is that the use of water and the interstate politics of water distribution dramatically affect such things as economic development and outcomes, migration, and social changes in regions.

State Growth Management: The Gauge of Subnational Political Economy. If political economy is defined as the interpenetration of the economy and the polity, then the gauge of the degree of that interaction, particularly at the subnational level, is **economic growth management policy.** In no other policy area is the interpenetration of politics and economics seen more clearly. Economic growth management is government action to stabilize or increase economic growth through industrial policy, deindustrialization policy, and no-growth policy (we will discuss these types of policies shortly). It is clear that the interpenetration of the political and the economic in this area has gone much farther in the states than in the national government. In fact, it has been argued that there is a systemic bias in the political economies of the different levels of government (David and Kantor 1984). This bias exists, it is contended, because developmental policies (one class of growth management policies) dominate in the cities (and states) while national politics is more open to social reform and income redistribution.

The most important reason for this bias, we believe, is found in the interplay of the federalist traditions at the two levels. For example, the historic influence of compound federalism makes difficult the formation of a national industrial policy, even if a number of influential business groups are calling for such a policy. As we saw earlier in this chapter, the federalist culture of the states involved few of the constraints imposed on the national government. The state-centered nature of public policy left each state with the occasion to develop a growth management policy.

But this last fact means that growth management policies vary widely among states. In a very perceptive article, Robert L. Savage (1982) attempted to determine whether those wide differences meant that no patterns could be found in growth policies among the states, or whether there were enough commonalities to permit classification. Savage found "considerable idiosyncratic development among the states" (p. 109). But he also found enough commonalities to identify several basic patterns of growth management among the states. What is most interesting about Savage's findings in a political economy sense is that the degree of commitment to growth management differs among the several. Some states showed a strong agency thrust and public relations dynamic; others offered few if any real incentives for industrial development. Savage's conclusions about the latter group of states are interesting: "The notion that this may be a transitional stage is appealing, but a transition *from* what *to* what is not evident" (p. 108; author's italics).

Growth management, as used here, refers to a jurisdiction's policies about the direction of its economy (toward growth or no growth). As such, growth management includes three policy subsets: industrial policy, deindustrialization policy, and no-growth policy. *Industrial policy* is designed for growth in the economy of a jurisdiction. As such, it involves active strategies such as tax expenditures, credit subsidies, and development grants, as well as "passive" strategies such as deregulation or the reduction of government involvement in the economy. **Deindustrialization policy** is designed to reduce the effects of "runaway" (fugitive) plants in a jurisdiction. And **no-growth policies** are designed either to limit or cap economic growth. Each of these policies has resulted in intense competition among the states. And each has important political economy effects.

In many respects, state and local industrial policies resemble get-rich-quick schemes. In the 1970s, the amounts and kinds of incentives provided by state and local governments to firms began to increase significantly. Savage (1982) identified ninety-four strategies states could use to attract industry. The most prevalent of these were tax breaks, low-interest-rate loans, site improvements, and direct grants. The *Wall Street Journal* reported that such incentives "exploded to unprecedented levels" in the 1980s (September 24, 1986, p. 1). The *Journal* concluded that bidding had gotten out of hand, with Ohio in 1977 offering Honda Motors a $22 million package and Kentucky offering Toyota five times that much in 1985 for the same number of jobs (about 3000).

In considering such actions, we should remember that government intervention has been crucial to the development of the economy since the days of Alexander Hamilton. It has been particularly important to the development of corporate capitalism in the twentieth century (see especially Weinstein 1969).

However, as the *Wall Street Journal* article suggests, there are new elements in current industrial development policy. In the first place, the scope of the incentives offered is unparalleled in American history. But there are growing indications of a backlash. A National Governors Conference study reported that states are now relying more on education, worker retraining, and small business assistance than on the more blatant forms of location incentives (cited in *Wall Street Journal,* September 24, 1986, p. 27).

A second new factor is that states have firmly established themselves as important actors in any national industrial policy that may be developed. As we have noted, the scope of state industrial policy is considerable. A national industrial policy simply could not ignore this policy. State decision makers would certainly mobilize to influence a national policy, if for no other reason than to protect their substantial state and regional commitment (Dubnick and Holt 1985:128).

Much has been written of the nationalization of the states—with regard both to the Fourteenth Amendment and to various policy areas. One of the important contributions of the political economy approach to federalism is that it allows one to see clearly that the effect between levels is two-way. The states and the locals can indeed preempt and localize national problems. We will expand on this idea with a number of other illustrations in Chapter 6 when we discuss the **localization of national policy concerns,** or when locals take control of unresolved issues.

Deindustrialization policy attempts to lessen the effects of plants that have closed or relocated. Again the problem of definition is present, particularly in determining the effects of outmigration of plants. Disagreements center in such issues as the meaning of *outmigration* (firms leaving for other places) and whether only direct job loss should be used as the basis for calculating the unemployment effects of relocating firms. Another issue is whether nonmanufacturing firms damaged by such "industrial flight" should be included in determining unemployment effects. Simply put, some stores and shops close as a result of the outmigration of other firms. Estimates of the effect of outmigration on localities vary substantially, depending on how these issues are resolved. Some authors conclude that the unemployment effect of outmigration is trivial, on the order of 1.5 to 3.0 percent (McKenzie 1981:50). At the other extreme, some analysts see the effect as excessive, with somewhere between 32 and 38 million jobs lost as a result of outmigration during the 1970s (Bluestone and Harrison 1982:8). Thus the evidence on the unemployment effect of outmigration is unclear.

As a result, policy prescriptions for deindustrialization also vary widely. For decision makers who see the effect of outmigration as trivial, the best policy is reliance on the "free marketplace" and minimal state legislation. For those who see the effect of outmigration as significant, the best policy is substantial legislation—usually referred to as *plant-closing legislation.* Advocates of the latter policy view have been moderately successful in getting states to pass such laws, but have been unable thus far to obtain much action at the national level: a 1988 law merely requires 60 days notice to a community of an impending plant closure.

State plant-closing legislation takes two forms. A few states (Maine, Wisconsin, Connecticut, and Massachusetts) have direct plant-closing legislation. This type of legislation attempts to deal specifically with the problem of outmigration. Among the provisions of such legislation are prenotification of workers, severance pay and extended benefits, worker buyout provisions, and compensatory funds for the locality. The second type of legislation, existing in twenty-five states, targets assistance to the employees of the runaway plants. Retraining and job relocation assistance are prominent features of this approach. These states also help employees who wish to purchase a plant (Leary, 1985:114). Just as the evidence on the effect of outmigration is inconclusive, the "evidence on plant closing legislation is scant and inconclusive" (Leary, 1985:118). For our purposes, deindustrialization policy is an area of interstate conflict reflecting clearly the connections between the political and economic spheres. It is also another policy area of state activism and national passivity that demonstrates the potential of the localization of national policy concerns.

No-growth policies are designed to limit or cap growth. The specific instruments to accomplish this purpose are zoning and land-use controls designed to keep the population of a jurisdiction or area from surpassing a maximum figure. Since zoning and land-use controls have historically been local prerogatives, no-growth policies are normally found in local jurisdictions rather than at the state level. A common tactic is for local governments to make it difficult to get, or to ban entirely, building or site permits.

No-growth policies involve the relationship among all three levels of government. For the national government, the issue has been primarily a legal one. The Supreme Court has taken a very narrow view of its role in adjudicating land use control. As Jeffrey Henig has observed, "the federal courts have treated local zoning and growth policies with kid gloves. In this area, perhaps more than any other, the courts have functioned as if the old concept of dual federalism was still in vogue" (1985:238). The federal courts have limited their involvement in several ways. They have consistently taken a very narrow view of who has the standing to bring land-use-control cases to the courts. In short, there is a rather rigid requirement that an individual or group must experience direct harm as a result of a land-use control before the courts will hear the case. In the few instances where standing has been granted (Henig observes that the Supreme Court did not hear a single zoning case between 1928 and 1974), the courts have deferred to state legislatures for remedial action.

The one area that has stirred the Supreme Court's interest is the just compensation of individuals under the Fifth Amendment. In *Penn Central Transportation Co.* v. *New York City*, the Court upheld a historic-landmark designation for Grand Central Station in opposition to Penn Central's desire to construct a multistory office building on the site. The city had permitted the company to transfer its development rights to another site, even though construction on the second site would have violated the city's zoning laws.

Also, state court practice varies widely among the states. The rigid dual federalism perspective that undergirds legislation on land-use control has meant that states are virtual islands unto themselves in this policy area. State courts in some states are very passive, interpreting the standing issue strictly and extending to local jurisdictions the presumption that land-use controls are local prerogatives (Henig 1985:238). In other states, courts are somewhat more assertive on the issue. But even in these more assertive states "there is no real evidence of any judicial assault on localities' discretion to legislate their own development and growth" (Henig 1985:239).

From a political economy perspective, we need to emphasize two effects of no-growth policies. The first is their impact on the poor and on minorities. Henig poses the question squarely when he asks whether no growth-policies are "a guise for exclusion" (1985:230), and he proceeds to ask whether such exclusion is an "unfortunate side effect...or shrewd hustle?" (p. 232). There is little evidence that the goal of exclusion is a "shrewd hustle," although some analysts contend that it is (Frieden 1979; Danielson 1976). But a disproportionate burden is placed on the poor and minorities by land-use control. When limits are placed on the number of housing units that can be built in a particular locale, acquisition costs will rise. Such an increase may be insignificant to upper-income individuals (and in some instances may actually be desired by them), but they do limit the capacity of low-income individuals to acquire housing. Much the same dynamic exists in the rental market as well. As the stock of rental units becomes fixed, landlords will probably raise rents. In both instances, as Henig observes, "the burden can be expected to fall most heavily on minorities and the poor" (1985:232). In this unanticipated consequence, at least, land-use-control policies, which particularly support a no-growth policy, amount to a politics of exclusion.

A second effect of no-growth policy is that along with industrial and deindustrialization policies it represents the localization of national policy concerns. Unless it has a zero-growth population, the nation as a whole simply cannot enforce a no-growth policy. Thus from a national perspective no-growth policy is a strategy for redistributing growth between jurisdictions and regions. Again, Henig's comments are well worth pondering: "Redistribution of growth may be rational for the nation as a whole. It is less likely to be so, however, when the shape of that redistribution is determined by localized politics rather than national goals" (1985:241). We develop this point in Chapter 7.

Interstate conflict between official governments and private interests is clearly a dominant feature of the relations between states. In all areas of interstate conflict, there is a clear intersection of politics and economics. In many areas, the effect of that intersection is the use of government authority to undergird and secure the interest of economic elites. Sometimes this is an unanticipated consequence, as reflected in state-to-state copying of land-use controls. Sometimes this bias is a more overt and intended consequence, as in the choice of sites for storage of hazardous wastes. Even the agreement in the Great Lakes states compact to collect each other's sales taxes is part-ly a consequence of a desire to make up for lost federal revenues, a desire that reflects national conservative elite goals to reduce revenue collection and social spending in the states. So when many interstate policy patterns start to affect who gets what, when, and how, they often fulfill the ancient biblical myth that "to those who have, much shall be given; to those who have not, even that which they have shall be taken away." In this sense, the resolution of interstate policy conflicts is often the politics of redistribution.

Interstate Cooperation

The constitutional obligations discussed earlier in this chapter are a major class of interstate cooperative relations. In addition to the three con-stitutionally mandated obligations, there is a wide range of voluntary forms of cooperation between the states. Much of that cooperation is informal, taking such mundane forms as environmental officials from two states dis-cussing EPA standards over cocktails at a convention. Other forms of volun-tary cooperation are more formal—even to the extent, as with interstate compacts, of requiring congressional consent. Among the most important formal means of cooperation are the **interstate compact, uniform state codes,** and **intergovernmental lobbies** (political cooperation).

Interstate Compacts. The Constitution prescribes that "no State shall, without the consent of Congress,…enter into any agreement or compact with another State" (Article I, Section 10). Consent may be given by Con-gress through either a formal statute or a resolution. In fact, congressional consent has occurred both before and after states have signed an agreement. In a somewhat dated but excellent study of interstate compacts, Marian Ridgeway concluded that "congressional concern with interstate compacts has traditionally been permissive and to some extent casual" (1971:10). Even so, states did not use the device to an appreciable extent before the 1960s.

Today compacts are becoming rather common. As David Nice reports, "the rate of adoption accelerated to more than four compacts a year during the 1960s.…A total of 119 interstate compacts were in force as of 1983, and the typical state now belongs to approximately twenty compacts" (1987b:70). The major types of state compacts concern commerce, correc-tions and crime, society, the environment, and education. Of these five types, the most numerous and historically the most important have been commercial. In recent years, compacts have been "particularly useful for cooperative endeavors involving natural resources, particularly the regula-tion and control of rivers, lakes, and streams" (Kearney and Stucker 1985:213).

The increasing use of interstate compacts in the area of natural resource policy is reflected in the Low Level Nuclear Waste Policy Act of

1980. This act reflects the three basic principles that disposal of low-level nuclear waste is a state responsibility, that states should be encouraged to form interstate compacts to carry out this responsibility, and that compact states could prohibit disposal at their facility of low-level waste generated in noncompact states (Kearney and Stucker 1985:215–16). In the act, as Richard Kearney and John Stucker observe, "the federal government seemed quite agreeable in shifting what had been for it an almost intractable problem to its partners in American federalism" (1985:216). This again illustrates the increasing trend of the preemption of *national* responsibilities by states and locals, an idea we develop in Chapters 7 and 12.

While it is too early to assess the effectiveness of the compact solution to low-level waste, it is apparent that many of the difficulties historically associated with interstate compacts are present in low-level-waste compacts. The most frequently cited problem with compacts is that they are at best "a slow and cumbersome process" (Thursby 1953:140). The Low Level Nuclear Waste Policy Act was passed in 1980, but even by 1986 not all regions had formed compacts. In addition to the problems associated with compacts generally, the low-level compacts are unique. As Kearney and Stucker conclude, "apparently no previous interstate compact has attempted to deal with a public policy problem which requires concentrating adverse consequences in one or several states while distributing benefits to all the other party states" (1985:216). This NIMBY syndrome has placed severe strains on some existing compacts. For example, the Southeast compact was relatively easy to form, in large part because South Carolina already had a facility and volunteered to be the first host state. But when the South Carolina facility was nearing capacity, that state declared that it expected one of the other party states to be the second host state. Needless to say, there has hardly been a scramble among these other states to accept this responsibility. This is not to imply that the compact will break up as a result of this tension, but to emphasize that the newer natural-resource compacts put unique strains on this form of interstate cooperation.

Uniform State Codes. Because of the "islands unto themselves" posture of states, there are substantial differences in state laws on the same subject. These differences produce substantial problems, particularly for businesses attempting to operate in two or more states, and for those seeking to practice certain professions. The latter problem is the subject of the reciprocity legislation discussed in the section on the privileges and immunities clause. In essence, reciprocity legislation is a form of uniform state law having to do with a state-granted privilege.

While uniform state laws have been proposed on a wide range of subjects, the most frequently occurring laws deal with business activity. The Uniform Commercial Code and the Uniform Narcotics Code are the only codes adopted by all fifty states—despite the efforts of a number of groups who sponsor or propose uniform state laws. Among the most active of these groups is the National Conference on Uniform State Laws. This group has proposed uniform laws dealing with such subjects as state taxes, state criminal procedures, state economic development, and the state environment. In those areas of substantial state conflict, such as economic development, the proposals have met with little success. Frequently, proposals for state legislation come from national government agencies. The Environmental Protection Agency, for example, has a number of uniform definitions of hazardous substances and uniform standards for their handling and storage. As we have seen, the Resource Conservation and Recovery Act allows states to adopt the EPA standards with virtually no change. Any variance in state law from EPA definitions and standards must be in the direction of more, not less, stringent regulation. A number of other organizations, including the Advisory Commission on Intergovernmental Relations, suggest uniform legislation for the states.

Intergovernmental Lobbies. By far the most important means of interstate cooperation is the intergovernmental lobby. There are two basic "official" governmental lobby groups. First, there are organizations of various state and local officials or organizations consisting of the jurisdictions themselves but dominated by elected officials. Prominent among this group of lobbies are the National League of Cities, the United States Conference of Mayors, the National Governors' Conference, the National Association of Counties, and the Council of State Governments. An excellent history of these groups was written by Donald A. Haider (1974). Second, there is an almost endless number of groups representing professionals across the entire spectrum of the public bureaucracy. Perhaps the best known of these lobbies is the International City Management Association.

All told, the positions taken by both types of groups cover the full range of policy issues. The student would do well to consult at least two of the many policy summaries of these groups—*National Municipal Policy,* the statement of goals, policies, and program objectives of the National Municipal League, and a similar publication by the National Governors' Conference entitled *Policy Positions.* For the past several years, the latter statement has involved goals and program objectives in the broad policy areas of criminal justice, fiscal affairs, human resources, natural resources and the environment, community and economic development, transportation, technology, and agriculture. The program areas covered are as specific as predator control and as broad as conservation.

In Chapter 9 we will show how intergovernmental lobbies fit into the much bigger picture of intergovernmental power politics. Then in Chapter 10 we will show to what degree these lobbies affect the intergovernmental policy process.

WHAT THE INTERSTATE MODEL EXPLAINS TODAY

We come back, then, to a central question of the book: What does this model best explain in politics and economics?

One of the problems in identifying what the interstate model explains today is that this model and the dualist model are closely related as "structures" affecting policy. One interesting way to sort out this complex relation between the two models is to imagine interstate relations as a sort of economic and social "foreign policy" of "allied" and semisovereign states. These "foreign policies between states" are directed at policy problems, at Washington, and sometimes at other states. This "foreign policy" of various "allied states" is limited, of course, by the Constitution and the compound model.

With this in mind, we now suggest several ways the interstate model best explains significant features of contemporary political and economic life. First, the interstate model helps explain what political scientists refer to as *issue agenda formation*—or how something gets to be a political issue. There are issues raised and issues suppressed that can be explained only by the states' interaction with each other. Daniel Elazar has correctly referred to race relations as the issue that best illustrates this point. But in addition, economic issues—and even the very nature of the American economic system itself—have been a front-burner concern of the interstate model. The states act as pressure points in the regulation of much business activity by intrastate means, which often have *inter*state business consequences. Some of the new interstate compacts function like this. Another effect of interstate politics is the question of whether an essentially unregulated national capitalist economy should be regulated by the national government or by interstate compacts copied from one state to another. Naturally, these issues of who shall regulate business have prompted big business to lobby hard in Washington (against the 1986 tax reform, for example).

Second, the interstate model explains certain features of policy implementation. Whatever policy emerges on the issue agenda at any period of American history, states as states are at the center of implementation. In our view, this is a more powerful explanation of policy variation among states than are socioeconomic differences (some important research shows this too: see Downs 1976). Just as race relations illustrate the importance of the interstate model in determining social life, the interstate patterns of handling the disposal of low-level nuclear waste and chemical toxic waste are key examples of the economic effects of the interstate model and its power to determine policy implementation.

Third, the interstate model is the best explanation for the patterns of regionalism that persist in the United States. A recent study suggests that the most distinctive region in America today is the Southeast (Tucker 1984). Other distinctive regions are New England and the Southwest.

Fourth, the interstate model goes a long way toward explaining many of the power effects of the federal system. We suggested in Chapter 3 that the interstate model helps explain how our federal system fragments power without democratizing it. Also, the model certainly helps explain the regional differences between economic elite, differences discovered by some researchers on power (Sale 1984; Domhoff 1986). In spite of the belief that decentralized federal power is "best" or "more democratic," the fragmented federal system in the United States has sometimes helped elites isolate and "capture" parts of the system. (On federalism and power, see Chapter 9.)

Certainly, this list does not exhaust the effects of the interstate pattern on power, policy, and economics, but it does illustrate the continuing impact of the pattern in the federal system. In Chapters 9 and 11, we will show how the interstate pattern performs other important social functions in American life.

But Some States Are More Equal than Others

The constitutional system of legal equality of the states and "official" interstate relations is not the end of the story. Other factors make some states "more equal" than others. We are not proposing that some states are "superior" or "inferior" from a value perspective. People will always argue that, say, Missouri is "superior" to New York, or vice versa. In this sense, New York and Missouri are never "equal." (Everybody knows you get better barbecue in the Midwest, right?)

More seriously, Thomas Dye (1969; see also Dye 1981) has called attention to the socioeconomic differences among the states and rightly concluded that these variations help explain the differences in state spending on education, welfare, and other policy areas. Similarly, Daniel Elazar (1966) has identified significant differences in the political cultures of states, concluding that those variations go a long way toward explaining the tendencies of the citizens and policy makers in those states to favor one kind of public policy over another. Certainly an understanding of federalism must include these kinds of differences in political behavior and public policies across the states; they make a difference in the quality of life.

But we argue that analyses of federalism must go well beyond identifying such "environmental" differences that explain political behavior and policy differences. They must also concentrate on *policy outcomes*, because federalism affects *people's lives*. It must be made clear what difference federalism makes, and how it affects the great issues of distributive politics: justice, equity, wealth distribution, power distribution, representation, stability, health, and all the rest. How, for example, do the inequalities found among states express themselves in public policies on these issues? And who benefits from these inequities? Who loses? Even in the "rich states," for instance, program failure by government agencies is often explained by "inadequate funds." Such an explanation is unconvincing in a day of gargantuan budgets at all levels of government. The more plausible explanation is that adequate funds are *unequally distributed*. The external socioeconomic well-being of a state may not be as important a policy force as the politics of federalist implementation and redistribution (see Downs 1976). Among the more important federalist forces that make a difference for people are the **regional differences** in policy and social outcomes. Regional policy differences and conflicts are shown in Chapters 10 and 12. These conflicts often dilute the benefits intended by "official" policy in favor of regional preferences or funneling resources to elite projects and goals (see Pressman and Wildavsky 1973). This is one of the numerous ways in which the interstate pattern demonstrates and affects politics and economics. The next three chapters will show the political economy effects of the other subnational patterns of federalism.

SUMMARY

Interstate relations are deeply rooted in the political culture of dualism. This means that constitutionally, the states are separate and equal political entities for all practical purposes. In practice, the dualist culture has meant that for today and for much of American history, much public policy is centered in specific states. However, examples of interstate cooperation can be found in the earliest history of the states.

Not all interstate relationships are rosy. Indeed, the dominant pattern of relationships among the states may very well be one of conflict. The conflict relations discussed in this chapter have had their counterparts throughout American history. (The Civil War is not referred to as the "War between the States" by accident.) Through it all, however, states have cooperated with one another in significant ways. These "cooperative foreign policies between states" are directed at various policy problems, at Washington and the national government, and at other states. These various conflict and cooperative relations make the interstate model the best explanation of several significant features of American political and economic life.

States are parties not only to the interstate model but to two other significant patterns of subnational federalism—the state–local pattern and the interlocal pattern. The state–local pattern is the subject of the next chapter.

KEY CONCEPTS AND THEMES FOR REVIEW

deindustrialization policy
economic growth management policy
extradition

full faith and credit obligation
intergovernmental lobbies
interstate compacts
no-growth policy
privileges and immunities obligation
southern populist movement
state-centered public policy
uniform state codes

NOTES

[1]Judy B. Rosener, "Intergovernmental Tension in Coastal Zone Management," *Coastal Zone Management Journal* 7 (1980): 95–109; Richard C. Kearney and Robert B. Garey, "American Federalism and Management of Radioactive Wastes," *Public Administration Review* 42 (1982): 14–24. John A. Worthy and Richard Torkelson. "Managing the Toxic Waste Problem: Lessons from Love Canal," *Administration and Society,* 13 (1981): 145–60; Ann Bowman, "Intergovernmental and Intersectoral Tensions in Environmental Policy Implementation: The Case of Hazardous Waste," *Policy Studies Review,* 34 (1984): 120–44; cited by Tom Arrandale, "Western Water," in *Editorial Research Reports,* January 30, 1987, p. 2.

Subnational Federalism:

5

The substate pattern

On June 17, 1787, Luther Martin of Maryland made what was described as the longest and most boring speech at the Constitutional Convention, "enhancing a reputation for tiresome bombast with a three-hour speech" (Bowen 1987:33). What made the speech boring? Perhaps it was the weather: it was "hot and muggy" in Philadelphia that day. Perhaps it was Martin's speaking style. Or perhaps it was Martin's subject — the "rights of states." To summarize his long speech, Martin argued that the convention had no legal authority to alter the rights of the states and that reason would dictate that the convention not reduce states' rights.

Whether Martin's speech was dull or not, the ideas he expressed were widely held. In a commonly quoted passage, Patrick Henry was to ask the Virginia ratifying convention, "Who authorized them to speak the language of We the People, instead of We the States?" (quoted in Bowen 1987:43). In short, the states had numerous defenders both at the Philadelphia convention and in the state ratifying conventions. And so did the "necessity of a strong national government" (see the discussion of Madison and Hamilton in Chapter 2). The point is that the relationship between the states and substate governments was determined largely by neglect, in the heat of the battle over how to balance the powers of the national government on the one hand with the rights of the states on the other. Simply put, few if anyone spoke for the localities.

LOCAL GOVERNMENT: THE LEGAL WEAK SISTER

It is interesting to speculate on why there was so much neglect of localities at the Philadelphia convention. Certainly, the neglect ran counter to the popular opinion of the day. There was broad acceptance, almost as a "self-evident truth," of the doctrine of the **inherent right to local self-government.** Roscoe Martin puts the situation nicely:

> The spirit of local independence ran high in America at the time of the Revolution, as indeed it does today. The hard-won fruits of rebellion were considered to be local gains, and any enterprise not associated with the immediate local community was regarded with suspicion. Government in particular was held close to the bosom of the people. They had won the right to control their own affairs, which to the greatest degree possible were to be vested in the seeable, touchable government of the small community. (Martin, 1965:28–29)

But this strong and broad popular opinion was not well represented at the Constitutional Convention of 1787.

In this regard, the Convention consisted of two competing groups. On the one hand, there were those of "centralist" tendencies (to use Patrick Henry's term of derision), who were generally identified under the broad label of *federalists.* This group of delegates was interested, as we have said, in striking a federalist bargain that would protect and extend its economic and social interests in the country's political economy. On the other hand, there were those delegates, generally called *antifederalist,* with strong state or regional interests. Most antifederalists were regional elites. As such, they were also interested in striking a federalist bargain that would protect and extend their region's (if not their state's) economic and social interests.

Neither of these groups was concerned with local elite interests, with the interests of nonelites (the masses), or with what we would today call grass-roots democracy. The federalist position ultimately "won" at the convention through a bargain with the antifederalists that sufficiently protected the latter's interests. This bargain—Madison's compound federalism—was silent on local matters. Thus the Constitution speaks of the nation, the states, and "the people"—but not of local government.

This aspect of localism in the United States has somehow been difficult to see, and has been neglected by observers primarily because the "issues" of those days were those of regional and agrarian economic elites. Some of those regional elites' interests were best protected by centralizing further the power to govern—through the compound model. Others found their interests best protected by retaining states in a dominant power position—through dualism. These latter groups, as we have seen, were primarily agrarian with a strong but secondary "mercantilist interest" reflected by merchants and bankers.

In modern social science terminology, what happened at the convention to define the relationship between the states and local governments may best be described as a *nondecision*. (Actually, there were several important nondecisions, including voting rights and slavery). As we saw in the previous chapter, a nondecision is something like a punt in football— elites or decision makers decide *not* to pursue something, maybe even to take action to keep the concern from coming up or being considered, for fear of the bigger consequences. Neither the federalists nor the antifederalists had any interest in "rousing the rabble" with talk of democracy or of the inherent right to local self-government. To stir up the locals would have endangered the federalist bargain. So the convention simply did not allow local interests to become one of the issues of the day. Tradition has it that one locally minded delegate, reputed to be Patrick Henry, summed up his impressions with the comment "I smell a rat."

To be sure, the bargain did leave local interests intact by preserving the status quo at the local level; to have done otherwise would have excited the locals. But it remained silent on the great political, economic, and social issues of interest to locals, among them the place and role of local units of government in the federal design. Thus the relationship between the states and substate governments was determined by practice and emerging case law.

This evolution resulted in the renunciation of the doctrine of the inherent right of local self-government and the adoption of the doctrine of **state supremacy.** Again Roscoe Martin puts the matter succinctly: "It is worthy to note that this rejection signaled a reversal of the teachings of colonial history: for by it the anterior governments, the local communities, were made secondary and the derivative governments, the states, became primary" (1965:29). The evolution from local self-government to state supremacy was defined by a commentator on the law—Judge John F. Dillon—and a series of U.S. Supreme Court cases. What is generally referred to as Dillon's Rule became the definitive statement of the evolving legal tradition:

> It is a general and undisputed proposition of law that a municipal corporation possesses and can exercise the following powers, and no others: first, those granted in express words; second, those necessarily or fairly implied in or incident to the powers expressly granted; third, those essential to the accomplishment of the declared objects and purposes of the corporations—not simply convenient, but indispensable. Any fair, reasonable, substantial doubt concerning the existence of power is resolved by the courts against the corporation, and the power is denied. (Dillon 1911:48)

Since Dillon's commentary, the United States Supreme Court has consistently followed this interpretation, which is one of the rare instances where case law has been perhaps predominant over politics and economics in determining the activities of government in the political economy. In the best-known of the cases in the law of local units, *Trenton v. New Jersey* (262 U.S. 182), the Supreme Court referred to a municipality as a "political subdivision" of the state, as a "creature of the state," as a "department of the state," and as a "convenient agency" of the state. Deil S. Wright has summarized the legal situation as it has emerged from case law as follows (1982:298):

1. There is no common-law right of local self-government.
2. Local entities are creatures of the state subject to creation and abolition at the unfettered discretion of the state (barring constitutional limits).
3. Localities may exercise only those powers expressly granted.
4. Localities are "mere tenants at the will of the Legislature."

In view of such language, to say that localities are legally subordinate to the states seems to understate the relationship. Therefore, when looked at from a "top-down" perspective, the political culture that dominates the legal tradition of state – local relations is a radical centralism. Indeed, it is possible to refer to the states as "unitary systems" more on the British pattern than on the American federal pattern. When the state as an isolated geographic area is the unit of analysis, all power to govern in that area is ultimately vested in the central state government.

This fact places the states in a unique relationships with their "local creatures." The Advisory Council on Intergovernmental Relations, citing Jeanne and David Walker, summarizes that relationship by referring to **states as the architects of local governments** (ACIR 1982b:151). The quotation from the Walkers by the ACIR is worth repeating: "The states, after all, are the chief architects, through conscious or unconscious action or inaction, of the welter of servicing, financing and institutional arrangements that form the sub-state governance system of this nation" (Walker and Walker 1975:39). Following this theme, the ACIR reported five major categories of relationships between the "chief architects" and their "creatures."

Whatever else the function of chief architect means, it is "a general and undisputed proposition of law," to use Judge Dillon's quaint phrase, that states are decision makers for local governments. States decide which local governments shall exist, including substate regions. The important matter of the assignment of functions is also a decision of the states. As the result of Dillon's Rule, local units simply cannot perform a function in most states without a specific grant of authority from the state. States also determine the internal structure of local units and most of the formal procedures they will use. Whether a city uses the mayor–council or the council–manager form of government depends ultimately on a decision of the state legislature. In most states the salaries of local officials may be raised only by approval of the state legislature (through a "local or special act"). States control and determine in detail the financial options available to local units—which taxes and other revenue sources they may utilize, which expenditures they may make, and certainly how much debt they may incur. And, states determine how local units relate formally to other units of governments—including the state. This factor also extends to state determination of the extent of and procedures for formal local–local cooperation (except for informal political relationships and contacts).

As architects of local governments, states are also the general legal supervisors of local implementation. Although practice varies widely between and within states, all states particularly supervise the local implementation of state functions. The techniques of supervision may be either noncoercive or coercive (Adrian and Press 1977:256–57). Noncoercive devices include attempts at persuasion (a state bureaucrat "buttonholes" a local bureaucrat on a "professional" level), the requirement of reports, and the giving of advice and technical aid. Coercive techniques of supervision include the withholding of grants-in-aid, the issuance of an order, the requirement of prior approval of actions, the provision for review of local decisions, the removal of local officials, and substitute administration. As the ACIR has concluded, "the less coercive appear to be the most effective and most frequently used. The most stringent—substitute administration—rarely occurs and, when it does, it is in crisis situations such as financial, health or disaster emergencies." (ACIR 1985b:289).

As architects of local units, states are enhancers of local technical capability. States make available to local units a number of resources for increasing local capacity and for improving levels of service. As the ACIR has reported, states "offer a wide range of technical assistance in such matters as purchasing, accounting procedures, drafting of charters, and design of personnel systems, not to mention a host of other subjects" (ACIR 1985b:289). It is is worth noting that local governments are not always anxious to avail themselves of such assistance. A General Accounting Office study found that 58 percent of local officials responding to a 1978 survey *never* asked the state for technical assistance. However, those who did seek technical assistance were more willing to turn to state agencies than to federal agencies: "Apparently local officials perceived fewer problems and less paperwork in dealing with state officials than with federal agencies" (ACIR 1985b:289). All fifty states have an agency specifically charged with assisting local governments—as separate departments, as agencies within a department, or as a unit within the Executive Office of the governor.

States are also "sugar daddies" for local governments. Involved here are both funds made available directly to local units in the form of state grants-in-aid and federal funds—called *pass-throughs*—that are distributed through the states to local units. We will examine these two classes of funds in the "nuts and bolts" section of this chapter. The scope and importance of these funds need to be emphasized here. Again according to the ACIR, state aid currently constitutes approximately one third of the funds local governments spend. In addition, states pass through to local units about 27 percent of the federal funds they receive. (ACIR 1985b:289)

Finally, as architects of local governments states ensure "equity, effectiveness, efficiency and accountability" (ACIR 1985b:289). In short, states take a variety of actions to ensure that their creatures are "good" governments. A most important function is that states establish their own systems of representation, fitting local governments into the setup. For example, some states have provided for the use of district rather than "at-large" elections in city councils to help ensure that blacks have a more reasonable chance at representation in city councils and on county commission boards.

In the area of finance, states have mandated property assessment procedures (the use of "boards of equalization" for example) and have set standards for the minimum percentage of market value assessments to ensure fair treatment in the taxing of property. The promotion of local competence through personnel requirements also contributes to efficiency at the local level. And states can contribute to accountability by mandating *sunshine laws* for local units. Sunshine laws require open access and disclosure of records, research, and procedures.

Despite all these legal constraints, however, in practice the states have often been quite lenient with their "creatures." In part, this is due to what we will call **intrastate political intergovernmental relations** (Chapter 9). To put the matter concisely, local units need not, and seldom do, roll over and play dead in the face of attempted positive state action, either coercive or noncoercive. It is important to note that "each state performs differently in these matters, a fact that makes nationwide assessment of their actions difficult. They have ... unique political cultures, economic and social systems, and other characteristics that make for different patterns of response to problems" (ACIR 1985b:290) Daniel Elazar has called the states "civil societies" (1972:10).

Beyond this point, the federalist traditions affect state and local relations in many critical ways. As we have pointed out, it is clear that a radical centralist federal culture dominates state legal traditions, since local units are "legal creatures" of the state. But there is a countervailing tradition— one that modifies and changes the pattern of relationships between states and localities in important ways. This tradition is what we refer to as *substate dualism*.

Substate dualism, or grass-roots democracy, assumes the right of local self-government. It is rooted, as Roscoe Martin observes, in the experience of the early colonists and their struggle for independence: the "hard-won fruits of rebellion were considered to be local gains" (1965:28). Substate dualism was given eloquent intellectual expression by Thomas Jefferson. As almost every schoolchild knows, Jefferson's vision of the only "good life" was that of an agrarian society. Jefferson's ideas, as we demonstrated in Chapter 2, have had a profound influence on the federal system. Their tenacity as a federalist culture is seen most clearly in the state–local model. Substate dualism provides the political culture for the emergence of what we call political intergovernmental relations. The political relationships between states and localities modify, limit, and often nullify the legal exercise of power by the "chief architect."

THE COLLISION OF LAW AND POLITICS:
THE POLITICS OF SUBSTATE DUALISM

The legalistic idea that the states are the chief architects of local units helps explain the five important features of state –local relations just described. However, the idea that local powers over politics and policy are legally determined is only a small part of the story. Legal subservience and political passivity are two different things. The nondecision on local governments at the Constitutional Convention certainly left intact a belief system that assumed that people have a common-law right to local government. This tradition was embodied in the many towns, villages, boroughs, and counties that were already part of the apparatus of government in the new nation. These units did not cease to function, to await either the permission or the requirements of their states for action; they continued to function largely unaffected by the federalist bargain. This situation provided the environment for the evolution of political relations between the states and the locals. While this evolution began in the earliest periods of the new nation, the major forms have cropped up in the twentieth century as state and local governments have reacted to urban growth, "urban decay," the problems of the macroeconomy, and changes in national-level federalism and public policy.

The key aspects of substate political intergovernmental relations have to do with the way state and local government institutions and private elites and interests relate to each other. The vast literatures on substate politics, state legislatures, and community power demonstrate that intrastate political intergovernmental relations make a significant difference in politics, economics, and policy (Dye 1966; Hawley and Wirt 1974; and many others). We identify five key aspects of state–local political relations that have major significance for locals, state officials, and policy outcomes.

First, there is the matter of the effectiveness of state legislatures in making law and supervising enforcement. In the literature on implementation (Williams, 1982; Van Meter and Van Horn, 1976), *effectiveness* is defined as the degree to which law is appropriate to solving the problem it addresses and whether adequate implementation is built into the law. Thus, the simple question is: Does the state legislature have the ability to make "good" law? Considerable attention has been given both to the adequacy of state legislative capacity and to the "reforms" necessary to build capacity (Citizens Conference on State Legislatures 1971; ACIR 1985b). The conclusion of much of this research is that state legislatures have substantial "institutional lag" but have shown a willingness to "catch up" or introduce reforms since the mid 1970s. The ACIR study for example, concluded that "state legislatures are quite different bodies than they were twenty, or even ten years ago. Although the changes have been uneven with some states modifying their structures and practices more than others, all have participated in the adoption of recommended reforms." (ACIR 1985b:122–23)

Local governments are subject both to the general laws of the state, which apply to all local units, and to special or "local" legislation, applicable to a specific unit. The question of state legislative effectiveness, then, is crucial both to general policy and to local specific policy. Since a number of these laws affect the electoral process at the local level, the ultimate outcomes of political battles are also affected by legislative effectiveness.

Second, state–local political intergovernmental relations involve what are sometimes called *functional relationships*. This term refers to the fact that bureaucrats in a program area at the state level oversee the activities of bureaucrats in that program area at the local level. For instance, the bureaucrats in the state department of health oversee the activities of bureaucrats in county health departments.

What makes this aspect of political intergovernmental relation so important is that state departments, local field offices of state agencies, and local agencies have broad discretion in formulating and implementing public policy (Dye 1969; Rourke 1984). To put it simply, state agency personnel may interpret a policy differently than local agency personnel (and both interpretations may be different from that of the state legislature and/or governor). These differences may be minor and go unnoticed. Or they may mean that state and local personnel fight like cats and dogs, simply because they see things differently. Public policy is often determined by the "bureaucratic winners" in these policy battles between local and state agencies. For example, Georgia is attempting to implement a statewide reform of public education, involving school consolidation, beefed-up curricula, formula funding favoring mergers of districts, and teacher competency tests. The carrot to lure local district cooperation is state funding. At least one county in the state (Heard) has indicated that it will not participate in the new program. There are indications that the response by locals will vary substantially among districts as they attempt to come to grips with the new law (*Atlanta Constitution,* July 1, 1987, p. 1). What all this tells us is that life down at the local level, in the classroom, on the street, is "on the receiving end" of what comes out of intergovernmental battles among bureaucrats for control over policy in substate federalism.

The third key factor in substate political intergovernmental relations forces us to switch from a top-down view of things to a bottom-up perspective. This factor is the effectiveness of local government officials. Again, local government capacity has received considerable attention—from determining the degree to which it exists, to prescribing how to build increased capacity. Both the evaluations and the prescriptions vary by type of local jurisdiction. Counties, for example, have been viewed in the political science community as the dark continent of American government. On the other hand, there has been an active effort to "modernize" urban government since the Progressive movement of the early 1900s.

However, for our purposes these viewpoints are not the most important things about political intergovernmental relations. Whether local officials are competent is not strictly the issue. Of course, whether local councils, mayors, school superintendents, judges, and other public officials can make decisions reflecting public demands and responding to technical problems (is the bridge really safe?) is always important. But to what degree local officials are *competent to respond to* state laws, regulations, bureaucratic interactions, gubernatorial policy leadership, and the like is what makes up the intergovernmental aspect of local effectiveness. In this regard, effectiveness can mean altering "stupid" state policy to fit local needs on the one hand, or complying with "good policy" as effective enforcers on the other hand. How locals play this game —facilitators, resisters, or indifferents —determines much about the quality of life and the reality of the outcomes of statewide lawmaking. If "Johnny can't read," for example, this outcome may very well have something to do with the effectiveness of local officials and how they enforce local policy in relation to state law and state regulations.

The fourth factor is what most people think about when they hear the term *political intergovernmental relations.* It is the "who influences whom" among state versus local interest groups and elites. Who is "running" government at different levels has significant consequences for individuals and policy (Dye 1980; Hawley and Wirt 1974; and others). For example, one of this text's authors was recently appointed to the zoning appeals board of the county in which he lives. What appears to many observers to be a dry, mundane, and routine policy process often features great drama (thus while the pay for serving on such boards ranges from low to nonexistent, the entertainment, educational, or "shock" value of such service is high). How property gets zoned and used often involves conflict between local elites as they fight to keep out "undesirables" and big-city developers. In the author's county, a recent conflict involved primarily the mass political action of "white picket fence" homeowners who sought to "zone out" the developers of mobile home parks. This kind of interest group and elite conflict runs through all policy areas. It is certainly the real stuff of state versus local politics. And it is often about big money.

Substate political federalism is about interest group and elite struggle for control over official policy and taxpayer money. We wish we could say that state–local political intergovernmental relations are always about "making democracy work" and "enforcing good law." Sometimes it is about those things. But, as we shall see in Chapter 7, the front-burner issues at the local level are distributive and redistributive issues. State – local political intergovernmental relations are intensely about who gets what, when, and how. Writers of textbooks about federalism have often neglected these heated facts of life in their neat, legal models of federalism. We have described the political economy as the zone of impact between the political and the economic. When the zone is analyzed in the state–local model, it closely resembles a war zone between competing groups and elites.

Finally, there is the matter of local-to-local politics. Recognizing elites and policy conflict in substate politics also forces us to recognize the conflict and cooperation that occur between local elites and between local elites and "official" units of government. Locals dispute or cooperate with one another over such things as state grants, federal grants, land-use control and interlocal service agreements. How locals relate to one another in the local–local model is the subject of Chapter 6. State law and regulation often structure those relationships. Therefore, local–local cooperation or conflict is rooted in the state – local model. For example, states often determine the extent of and procedures for interlocal service agreements. In the land-use area, most states have adopted the model zoning enabling act recommended by the Department of Commerce in 1922. As architects of the substate system, states often determine the structures through which locals cooperate or compete.

In summary, the legal subserviency model is only a limited statement of the limits of local government from a legal point of view. One of the factors in understanding the actions of local governments is to see how the "legal cards" are stacked against them inside the states. This legal card stacking is an important but not always controlling factor, and is rarely seen when one looks at the states and the nation. In a nutshell, the people, following the Jefferson ideal of grass-roots democracy, expect local governments to be able to act in a number of traditional policy areas (fire, roads, crime, water, health, parks, and the like). Local government power to act, however, is often legally constricted or directed by the state. But, even when local powers are legally defined, political relationships can either strengthen or weaken the capacity of local governments to act. It is in the political relationships between states' interests and their local units that we see most clearly the collision of law and politics (for more on this, see Chapters 9 and 10).

SUBSTATE REGIONALISM:
THE ASCENDANCE OF ADHOCRACY

As architects of local governments, states continue to exercise their creative juices by bringing into being numerous forms of substate regions. Those creative juices have flown freely. No standard typology has emerged for these regional units; we divide them into two broad categories. First, there are the single-purpose governments known as **special districts.** Second, there are numerous nationally encouraged districts for program operation and planning. Starting in the 1950s, there was an explosion of both types of substate regionalism. In a comprehensive study, the ACIR reported that special districts increased by 93.6 percent in the period 1952–72, a rate of growth that outstripped that of any other governmental unit (ACIR 1982b:23). The same type of explosion occurred in the nationally encouraged districts (we will discuss these regions in Chapter 7). By 1980, there were around 4000 nationally encouraged single-purpose program regions, more than 600 councils of government, and dozens of nationally encouraged regional planning agencies in all states (ACIR 1976:106 – 7). This avalanche of regional authorities has created a "shadow government" whose structures and functions are not well researched.

Special Districts

For reasons we shall review, the special districts may have more profound political and economic implications than many features of substate relations, yet they have received little serious attention. The very descriptive term *adhocracy* was used by the ACIR in evaluating special districts. Special districts are limited-purpose governments that exist as separate municipal corporations. There are some multipurpose special districts, but most special districts serve a single purpose. The Bureau of Census's *Census of Governments* lists twenty-two categories of single-purpose districts and three categories of multipurpose districts. The single-purpose categories are cemeteries, school buildings, fire protection, health, hospitals, highways, housing, drainage, libraries, natural resources other than those covered by a multipurpose district, parks, recreation, flood control, irrigation, water conservation, sewers, soil conservation, general functions other than those covered by a multipurpose district, water supply, electric power, gas supply, and transit. The multipurpose categories are natural resources and water supply, sewer and water, and other multiple purposes. Each of the functions assigned to special districts is performed in certain instances by multipurpose local governments. Why, then, single these functions out for performance by a new single-purpose government?

Four reasons are commonly given for the creation of special districts (Smith 1964:13–14; ACIR 1973:21). In the first place, special districts make possible certain revenues that rarely affect the public directly. This advantage is normally referred to as "fiscal self-sufficiency" (ACIR 1973:21). We do not think that *self-sufficiency* is the best term. It is not clear (primarily because of the absence of research) whether special-district governments are self-sufficient or not, and if so, by what definition of self-sufficiency. We prefer the term *limited fiscal impact.* Special districts (except for the special case of school districts, which the ACIR rightly concludes should be treated separately) generally obtain their revenues from nontax sources. They finance the service they perform or the projects they build either through the sale of nonguaranteed revenue bonds, by user charges, or by special assessments.

Such arrangements offer a number of advantages. To beleaguered political decision makers they provide the means for financing a service without the glare of "tax increase" or "budget busting" associated with general revenue funding. They do provide a certain flexibility in that they enable state decision makers to escape tax limitations and debt ceilings. The limited fiscal impact of special districts also offers the "advantage" of the careful targeting of benefits; the distributive game is not limited to general-purpose local governments. Along with observing that special districts "do not necessarily eliminate political patronage," Adrian and Press report that "the behind-the-scenes way in which they generally operate helps to make them especially profitable for lawyers, engineers, bonding houses, and sellers of equipment, services, and real estate" (1977:23). Perhaps *fiscal self-sufficiency* is not such a bad term after all. But the important question is *whose* fiscal self-sufficiency special districts serve.

The second reason given for the use of special districts is the claim that they provide the flexibility needed to conform to the service boundaries of a given function. On its face, this justification appears compelling. It is easy to conclude that making an institution's boundaries coincide with the service area is a rational approach to a problem.

But this argument is overly simplistic. Problems don't always recognize boundaries. It is not difficult to convince the average citizen that mosquitoes (and criminals) do not necessarily respect the boundaries of existing general-purpose governments. So the basic question is simply: What is the service area? What is the "natural" service area for a cemetery? Is there an identifiable self-contained service area for health problems? At first glance, it would appear that the "natural resources" functions would be the easiest to link to a service area, by simply organizing them on the basis of "natural systems." Even if such a linking is possible, two additional questions present themselves. Are natural resource districts in fact linked to "natural systems"? Is it desirable to link natural resource districts to "natural systems"? With the possible exception of drainage districts and flood control districts, there is little evidence that natural resource districts are established on the basis of natural systems (Wells 1986). For many such districts, the area is primarily a commercial one, consisting of either users (as with irrigation) or producers (who would use toxic chemical waste-disposal districts) in an artificially defined geographic area. Additionally, some analysts downplay the importance of natural systems as "service delivery areas." After a careful analysis of natural systems, Baste and Blair concluded:

> Experience dictates that it is less important that the boundaries of the region include all of the residuals dischargers and all those affected by

changes in ambient environmental quality than that the boundaries represent some region or area for which there is an institutional arrangement which can be responsible for REQM [Residuals Environmental Quality Management]. It is also extremely important to recognize ... factors ... exogenous to the region.... . (1982:87)

These comments are as pertinent to the "service area" concept as they are to "natural systems." We believe it is important to recognize exogenous factors (external forces) in the concept of service areas. Thus, intergovernmental politics, the struggle of local elites, distributive decisions, and the like are frequently more important external forces in determining the boundaries of special districts than the idea of a somehow self-defining or self-contained service area. To put the matter simply, in most instances the concept of service area is specious, and is more likely to be determined by local conditions.

The third argument for the use of special districts involves the claim that these organizations "can get the job done." Based on a theory of specialized functions, it is claimed that special districts can perform a function more "effectively and expeditiously than can general purpose governments" (ACIR 1973:210). Specialization, along with the ability to pay higher salaries and thus attract more qualified personnel, is supposed to give the special district the technical competence to do a superior job at service delivery.

There is some evidence that special districts have done quality work in the areas of construction and engineering (see Adrian and Press 1977:235). However, the problem with this kind of conclusion is that we simply do not know how far it can be generalized. There has not been adequate analysis of the functioning of special districts to enable us to determine the degree of effectiveness and efficiency. Certainly, some researchers are skeptical on this point. After asking why the average citizen should be concerned with special districts, the ACIR cited money, waste, and overlap: "With ad-hocracy in the ascendancy, functional assignments among state, regional, and local units frequently have been dysfunctional and designed to solve immediate crisis" (1976:107). It is almost a matter of common sense that special districts would duplicate some of the personnel, materials, and facilities of nearby general-purpose governments. Thus, when looked at in isolation, special districts may appear to be efficient. But when compared with existing or alternative delivery systems, the conclusions can be something else entirely.

Finally, it is argued that special districts, compared with the alternative solutions to the "urban problem," offer a less threatening and thus less politically hazardous solution. As the ACIR put the matter, "annexation, consolidation, federation, and intergovernmental service agreements often infringe on ingrained political traditions, which are not as affected with the establishment of a special district" (1973:21). This sounds more like a copout than an advantage. But from a political economy standpoint, the problem is considerably more serious than the lack of political courage. Special districts often take the steam out of an emerging community issue. They can diffuse the effort to mobilize a more comprehensive and long-range solution. They can provide local elites with the mechanism by which mass concern is prevented from developing (this is a nondecision strategy), and at the same time maintain elite control over the function. Special district politics is a very special brand of politics. It is a limited-access, low-visibility politics ripe for elite control and dominance. Special districts, by diffusing mass concern and establishing a politics of special access, can allow local elites to have their cake and eat it too. Again we ask the question: Less threatening to whom?

An examination of special districts suggests very clearly that all is not well with the states' view of these new creatures. The conclusion of an ACIR study is especially appropriate:

> Local officials and citizens groups have begun to realize that a monster has been created as they see...money used in uncoordinated ways by special districts, the loss of public control over the direction of their public services, and the irony of a structure established to fill servicing gaps which in turn produce management gaps and coordination problems (1976:106).

The reference to local districts as "monsters" may be unwarranted hyperbole. However, special districts should be carefully scrutinized for their political and economic impacts. They represent, in the clearest ways in the American government system, the "microagencies" of the political economy. Their structures create a limited-access politics for the few, almost unrivaled among other government agencies. Their services and effects are perhaps the most direct representation of the politics of who gets what, when, and how that is found at the subnational level. Special districts deserve more attention from analysts of the American political economy.

NUTS AND BOLTS

As indicated earlier in this chapter, states are the "architects" of local governments. As such, the states have a myriad of formal and legal relationships with their "creatures." Certainly those relationships—the making of decisions on salaries of local officials, for example —are important parts of the "nuts and bolts" of state –local relations. In this section, we will concentrate on two other areas of formal relations between state and locals — state mandates and fiscal relations.

State Mandates

State mandates are legal requirements — constitutional, statutory, or administrative —that local governments provide a specified service, meet minimum state standards, engage in an activity, or establish certain terms and conditions of local public employment (ACIR 1981b:61). In spite of these noble-sounding purposes, state mandates have become a major friction point between state and local officials.

The ACIR has identified five types of state mandates (1978:6). First, there are "rules of the game." These requirements are for the organization and procedures of local governments. They concern such things as the form of government (mayor– council, council– manager, and so on), election procedures, and provisions of the criminal code. A second type, *spillover mandates,* has to do with state requirements for new programs or enrichment of old programs in areas of "strong state concern." These are most frequently found in education, health, welfare, hospitals, the environment, and transportation. Third, *interlocal equity mandates* require local governments to act or refrain from acting to avoid injury to or conflict with other local governments. This type of mandate is most frequently found in land-use regulations, tax-assessment procedures, and environmental standards. Fourth, *loss-of-tax-base mandates* remove property or selected items from the tax base of local governments. Historically, the exemption of church property is such an example. More recently, a number of states exempt medicine from local sales taxes. Finally, there are *personnel-benefit mandates.* These set salaries, working conditions, and fringe benefits for various local officials. Use of the various mandates varies widely among the states. No comprehensive survey of the use of all types of mandates has been conducted, but a 1976 ACIR survey of seventy-seven possible and specific program areas indicated that twenty-two states had thirty-nine or more such mandates (ACIR 1985b:302).

The primary question that has occupied the attention of those analyzing state mandates is whether states should notify locals of, or reimburse them for, any loss of revenue or mandated expenditures resulting from state mandates. The most frequently used practice among the states is to require the attaching of a "fiscal note" to *legislation* that imposes mandates (few states require the attachment of such notes to *administrative* requirements that involve mandates). The fiscal note would identify the revenue lost by or expenditure required of local jurisdictions as a result of compliance with the mandate. Some states (twelve in 1982) provide for state reimbursement of certain types of mandate costs. Such reimbursement is most likely when the state mandate necessitates an increase in property tax rates. The ACIR recommended partial state reimbursement for state-initiated program or service-level mandates, and full reimbursement for mandates affecting local retirement systems and local employee working conditions (1978:18–19).

State fiscal notes and reimbursements are important topics, particularly for local governments, but a more important question is the political economy effects of state mandates. We mention several effects as illustrations. The most widely agreed upon political economy effect of state mandates is that they provide the occasion for frequent "end runs." An ACIR study put the matter bluntly:

> State mandates can be—and are often—used as a political football by special interest groups, state policy makers, and even local officials. Special interest groups, rebuffed at the local level, may use the state legislature as a hunting ground to capture for themselves or their constituencies a larger slice of local expenditures. Local authorities particularly resent this "end run play" or actions by which local employee representatives, such as police and firemen, successfully obtain from the state legislature more generous personnel benefits on a mandated basis than they could obtain through negotiation with locally elected officials. (1978:5 – 6)

It has always been easy to be free with someone else's money.

Second, states may use mandates to relieve some of the pressures on state revenues. This can be done by shifting the responsibility for a program to local jurisdictions. Georgia recently mandated a "statewide" kindergarten. The governor received the media credit for this "educational reform," but local school districts received the bill for its costs. The ACIR reports that localities can also play the mandate game: "Localities can use mandates as convenient scapegoats to claim that state action was the reason they had to raise taxes" (1978:6). In a period of taxpayer revolt, perhaps local officials have found an "end run" around taxpayers.

We do not mean to imply by this that all the political economy effects of state mandates are negative. State mandates are most common in the area of solid-waste disposal. State regulations have been important in both determining the siting of solid-waste landfills and controlling what can be placed in them. State mandates prohibit the disposal of toxic chemical waste—a practice that was almost routine in the past—in local solid-waste landfills. Such mandates move beyond the domain of equity to that of the police power of the state to provide for the health of persons in neighboring jurisdictions. Additionally, states are increasingly using what are known as *horizontal mandates*. These requirements are much like the crosscutting requirements discussed in Chapter 3 in regard to regulatory federalism. They are constraints, such as nondiscrimination or open-meeting requirements, that cut across all program areas of local jurisdictions. Although it is likely that compliance with horizontal mandates is "mixed" (ACIR 1985b:302), it would be difficult to dispute the worthiness of the objectives behind them.

Fiscal Relations

Many of the state mandates just discussed may be conceptualized as parts of state–local fiscal relationships. Certainly, states impose direct "expenditure mandates" and a number of program mandates require expenditures by local units. In addition to these forms of state – local fiscal relations, three other practices need attention. These are state intergovernmental transfers, tax lids and debt limits, and state monitoring of local expenditures. State intergovernmental transfers, in turn, are most clearly understood in three categories — direct state grants, federal aid pass-throughs, and state revenue sharing. We provide a brief description of each of these fiscal devices.

State Intergovernmental Transfers Direct state grants. States have established grant-in-aid programs for localities that are, for the most part, patterned after the national system of categorical grants. Indeed, one of the most significant developments in state–local relations in the last several decades has been the emergence of the states "as senior partners in state – local expenditures" (ACIR 1985b:307). Among other things, this senior partnership has meant a significant increase in the amounts and purposes of state grants-in-aid to local governments. Table 5-1 shows total state outlay in relation to local own-source revenue by major program area. The table clearly shows that state financial assistance to local governments was a substantial portion of the revenue available to local governments from the mid-1960s to the mid-1980s.

Table 5-1 also shows that the program to which most state financial assistance is distributed is education. An ACIR study is worth quoting at this point:

> The safest generalization that can be made about the distribution of State aid is that this system is best considered in two parts—public education and all other functional areas. Although each public function supported by State financial assistance has unique characteristics, the distribution of State grants among the several non-education functions is more comparable than the distribution formula between any one function and State aid for public education. (1977d:25)

Apart from the amounts of money involved, the primary distinction between the two education and noneducation aids is their underlying objectives. The primary objective in state education aid is to equalize fiscal disparity between schools. (See the discussion of the Supreme Court in Chapter 3 for cases involving this objective.) In the 1970s, more than half of all states changed their public school funding formulas in an effort to achieve intrastate equality in per-pupil expenditures. The change seems to have worked. The ACIR has reported that within-state disparities in per-pupil expenditures decreased in seventeen of the states that changed their formulas over the period; they increased in six, and in New Mexico the formula change had no effect on disparities (1985b:309).

From a political economy perspective, it appeared that state aid would benefit low-income and racial-minority groups by narrowing the gap between high- and low-educational-resource districts. But the equalization movement fast dissipated as a result of several developments in the 1980s. Many states experienced increased educational costs connected with declining enrollments. The education reform movement also resulted in demands for education efficiency measured by scores on competency tests (for both teachers and students). These and other factors meant that the demand for fiscal equality "sometimes got caught in the middle," to use the ACIR's innocuous phrase (1985b:310). We repeat that the most intense issue in local intergovernmental relations is usually the distributive issue —who will actually get what. The "noble" objective of equality of fiscal resources quickly gave way to the realities of the politics of redistribution in the education reforms of the 1980s. As Proposition 13 in California amply demonstrated, voters perceive their self-interest more directly in the property taxes they pay than in the education of children in the "faraway" fiscally restrained districts of their state.

In noneducation grants, the objective of fiscal equalization, though present in some grant programs, is secondary. The most important basis for the distribution of general state grants in program areas other than education is the cost-reimbursement method: States reimburse local governments, on a formula basis, for all or part of local units' past expenditures for aided programs. As a result, the state grant system can be described as "one of relative simplicity. It is based basically on non-equalizing measures—particularly the cost-reimbursement method—and is nearly exclusively formula rather than project ... . Equalization assistance is of major importance, however, in the field of public education ... ." (ACIR 1977b:25)

Federal aid pass-throughs. An important, but unfortunately somewhat technical, feature of the state grant-in-aid system is **federal aid pass-throughs.** This consists of grants that originate at the national government

TABLE 5-1 *State Aid in Relation to Local-Source Revenue by Selected Programs, 1984*

	Amount (millions of $)	As a % of Local Revenue from All Sources
total state aid	106,651	54.3
general local-government support	10,745	10.1
education	67,485	63.3
highways	5,687	5.3
public welfare	11,924	11.2
others	10,810	10.1

Source: ACIR 1986:61.

and are then channeled through the states to local governments. Pass-throughs are a significant and growing factor in intergovernmental aid to local governments. As reflected in Table 5-2, this constitutes 20.1 percent of total state aid to local jurisdictions. Studies have not distinguished between pass-throughs and state "own-source" aid. Thus as the ACIR rightly concluded, "traditional discussions of State and Federal aid to local government, to the extent of pass-through funds, tend to overstate the State aid flows and to understate the Federal aid dimension" (1977b:14). The ACIR found that little effort to influence local policies and practices is exerted in pass-through-aided programs. On the other hand, little research has been done on pass-throughs. For example, it is difficult to obtain reliable data on them. If the scope and levels of pass-throughs are indeterminate, then certainly the effect of states on aided programs is also unknown. Unfortunately, so are the general political economy effects of pass-through funds or the political economy implications of the pass-through technique of intergovernmental fiscal transfers.

TABLE 5-2 *Intergovernmental Aid and the Pass-Through Component, by Function, 1972*

	Total StateAid (millions of $)	*Federal Component (millions of $)*	*Federal Component as % of Total State Aid*
all programs	35,143	7,073	20.1
education	20,677	3,048	14.7
highways	2,510	45	1.8
public welfare	6,823	3637	53.3
health and hospitals	661	56	8.4
all other	4,455	287	6.4

Source: ACIR 1977d:16–17.

State–local revenue sharing is a special form of state –local fiscal relations. The ACIR defines state revenue sharing "as money given to localities … to be spent on purposes determined by the localities themselves" (1980:2). The justification for state revenue sharing funds is said to be found in "state need" for ways to compensate localities for revenue loss they experience as a result of state-mandated property-tax relief usually for low income groups and the elderly. Whatever the justification, state revenue sharing has expanded substantially since the early 1970s. It is now the third largest form of state aid to localities, surpassed only by state aid for education and welfare.

The basis on which states share revenue with localities varies widely among the states. Three methods are frequently used. In the *origin system*, the state functions as the collection agency for a variety of taxes, primarily income or sales. In most, but not all, cases it is the state that determines the rate on such taxes and applies that rate uniformly across all jurisdictions. This practice is an almost certain cure for "tax flight," and has the advantage of minimizing intrastate tax competition. The ACIR has shown that the origin method is utilized in thirty-seven states and accounts for 13 percent of revenue sharing funds (1980:5).

The *reimbursement method* consists of state payment to localities for taxes they lose as a result of state-mandated property-tax exemptions. The idea behind this practice is closely akin to the "federal impact" basis for national payments to states and localities in lieu of taxes. Thus fairness is presumed to require states to reimburse localities burdened by a state facility (say a college or university) that is exempt from local property taxes. The method is used in thirty states and accounts for 21 percent of general revenue sharing funds (ACIR 1980:8).

Finally, *population methods* are politically popular since they spread the aid to every locality in the state. Such methods have the advantage of simplicity, although estimates of midcensus population trends may be somewhat complex. The ACIR reports that population-based state revenue-sharing systems do "provide a limited degree of redistribution..." but that localities "with declining populations may also object that per capita aids penalize them when their need may be steady or rising" (1980:8).

States have experimented with a fourth method for allocating state revenue sharing money. This method attempts to identify the local "need" for such funds. The basis for need-based formulas can be either the different capacities of localities for raising money, or the different need for public expenditures in various program areas.

The attempt of states to find need-based formulas for revenue-sharing systems reflects rather clearly the political economy dimensions of state – local fiscal relations. The ACIR cited a study by Richard E. Nathan that concluded:

> It's not hard to design a formula based on need. There are an infinite number of possibilities but you have to start with an essentially political decision: What dimension of need do you care about? (ACIR 1980:10)

We are not so certain that "it's not hard to design a formula based on need." It seems to us, as it did to the ACIR, that "the dimensions of public expenditure need are indeed complex" (1980:10). But we do think that Nathan is right on the mark with his question about distribution. Probably the more important issue is *whose need you care about*. In Nathan's "physical decay" dimension of need, for example, do we care about inner-city housing stock or housing stock for agriculture migrant workers? In his "socioeconomic distress" category, do we care about unemployment among young black adults or about the frequency of bankruptcies among small businesses? The ACIR concludes that there is too much concern for the "politics of printout," which it claims has resulted from state revenue sharing systems (1980:14). The concern for the "politics of printout" should go beyond the somewhat technically based desire for "accurate measures of needs" voiced by the ACIR (1980).

Perhaps the most important concern in the politics of printout is a distributive concern: *Whose* needs do the formulas recognize and institutionalize? In the terminology of budget analysts, state revenue sharing carries high *rigidification costs* (McKean 1968:154). Once the formulas are set—to someone's advantage —they tend to drive out other choices. This might aptly be called "the law of budgeting bias" in the political economy view of federalism. Thus the initial choice, with a heavy political component, tends to drive out subsequent choices, perhaps potentially based on a more complex understanding and accurate measurement of local need. The advantage to successful participants, who affect the writing of the fiscal formula, then, is obvious.

Tax Lids and Debt Limits. A special form of states' control over "their creatures" is a specific decision that local financial managers would ordinarily be expected to make. On the one hand, states constrain several types of local decision makers in their ability to tax. On the other hand, there are limits, if not outright restrictions, on local jurisdictions' ability to incur debt.

Tax lids are set primarily on the local property tax. The most common such lid is a specific limit on the tax rate (ACIR 1985a:324). However, by 1985 fourteen states had placed a limit on the aggregate tax rate of all local governments, twenty states had imposed limits on property tax levies, and six states had limits on assessment increases. The most publicized tax lid, Proposition 13 in California, specified that no property could be taxed at more than 1 percent of its estimated 1975–76 market value and that no property tax assessment could be increased in any one year by more than 2 percent unless the property was sold.

The use of tax lids has received considerable attention, but measuring their actual impact is somewhat difficult (Shannon and Gabler 1977:7). One of the primary reasons for this is that many states provided for local revenue diversification or for reimbursed lost local revenues at the time the tax lids were imposed. These actions had the effect of providing other sources of revenue for local jurisdictions. The impact of tax lids seems to be most clear in two areas. First, local officials have been encouraged to find sources of revenue other than the property tax. In particular, they have been encouraged to make claims for state revenues. Second, states have begun to rely more on special districts, unaffected by the tax lids, for the delivery of public services. Tax lids, then, may increase both state intergovernmental transfers to localities and the use of special districts (ACIR 1977c:3 – 4).

Just as tax lids apply in most cases to the property tax, **debt limits** primarily limit general-obligation bonds. The security behind the general-obligation bond is the "full faith and credit" of the jurisdiction. It is argued, then, that state restriction of general-obligation debt is a legitimate policy, since states generally have an interest in the integrity of the credit of "their creatures" (ACIR 1985b:327). On the other hand, there are few state restrictions on revenue bonds. The security behind revenue bonds is the earnings of the facility or project financed by the bond (many college dormitories are financed by revenue bonds). Four types of limits are placed on local indebtedness by states: (1) limits on the amount of indebtedness, (2) requirement of a local referendum on the debt, (3) ceilings on the interest rate paid, and (4) limits on the period for which the debt can be outstanding (ACIR 1985b:328).

It is difficult to measure the policy impacts of state debt limits. However, the evidence suggests that such efforts have not been particularly successful in insulating local units from debt difficulties (ACIR 1961b:63). The ACIR (1961b) has implied that there are simply too many "means of circumvention" of state debt limits. Certainly, as we have pointed out, the debt limits placed on general-obligation bonds do not restrict local use of revenue bonds. Thus common sense would indicate that locals have simply shifted from general-obligation bonds to revenue bonds. Ironically, in doing so they have shifted from a bond that normally has the lowest interest rate among municipals to a bond that generally has a higher interest rate. In essence, the states have forced their creatures to pay more.

Further, to the extent that debt limits apply to all local jurisdictions, they have tended to restrict some types of localities more than others. For example, school districts have few opportunities to rely on revenue bonds (except for football stadiums), whereas cities have a wide range of occasions to do so. Finally, the ACIR has concluded that debt limits have affected intergovernmental relations:

> ... debt restrictions complicated various federal programs of public works loans; played a major part in the federal promotion of public housing authorities (which in most states operate as separate units, independent of other local governments); probably contributed to unhappy relationships between urban and rural areas because they have largely affected communities in the process of rapid urbanization; and stimulated pressure for new or enlarged federal and state aid programs (1961b:62).

In a word, one of the effects of debt limitations has been a centralization of functions, not simply in the form of the state picking up some program responsibility but also in the form of more national delivery of the service.

State Monitoring of Local Finances   As we have indicated, states are the legal architects of local government and the senior partners in state – local fiscal relations. States are thus cast in the role of decision makers for local jurisdictions. One of the problems states have faced in carrying out that role is the lack of information on local fiscal conditions. As a result of the increasing involvement of the state in local fiscal decisions, there has emerged a powerful motivation to construct an information system that would produce the information needed by the state. Several states have tried to develop systems for monitoring local fiscal activity. The intent behind these systems is to provide a mechanism that national, state, and local decision makers can use to anticipate and ward off fiscal problems.

A number of "model" monitoring systems have been proposed. Among the best-known of these are the ones proposed by the International City Management Association (Grover 1980) and the Municipal Finance Officers Association (Rosenberg and Stallings 1978). The ACIR has made important studies of the problem of urban fiscal stress (ACIR 1975).

One of the most comprehensive efforts to implement a state monitoring plan was that of New York State (Pillai and Bronner 1984:108). Among the more instructive aspects of this plan—the New York Financial Tracking System—is the effort to put into operation the concept of fiscal health (see Table 5-3). To do this, the FTS used eleven indicators prepared on the basis of guidelines developed by the International City Management Association. Various statistical measures were then developed for each of these indicators (see Pillai and Bronner 1984:110–11). The analysis of the data collected for each of the measures resulted in fiscal profile trends for the localities involved in the FTS.

Since the plan is relatively new, it is difficult to predict how useful the information will be. "The potential benefits of the relatively new types of information and its reliability are unproven. Only a longer period of continuous experimentation with the data can address this problem" (Pillai and Broner 1984:112). Certainly no information system in and of itself would prescribe action for decision makers at any level in the face of impending fiscal stress. All such monitoring systems should be viewed for what they are—an attempt to create an information base for decision making. With the extensive involvement of the state in local fiscal decisions, it would be difficult to dispute the need for such a base.

HOW MUCH CONTROL SHOULD THE ARCHITECT AND SENIOR PARTNER RETAIN?

The discussion in this chapter should have made it clear that this question has been central to the evolving relationship between the states and localities. Should state centralism or substate dualism govern state –local

TABLE 5-3 *Eleven Specific Charcteristics of Fiscal Health as Outlined by New York State's Financial Tracking System*

Revenue Policy

1. reliance on locally generated revenue rather than intergovernmental aid or borrowing
2. existence of balanced revenue mix between elastic and inelastic revenues
3. use of user charges where practical

Expenditure Policy

4. adequate expenditure levels that are funded by current revenues
5. control of fixed costs—such as statutory or contractual obligations in the current and future periods

Financial Management

6. maintenance of adequate fund balances to meet financial emergencies
7. adequate monitoring of approaching tax and debt limitations
8. use of realistic budget practices
9. maintenance of cash solvency
10. adequate fixed asset replacement policy
11. control of long-term debt

Source: Pillai Vel and Kevin M. Bonner (1984). "State Monitoring of Local Finances: An Analysis of New York State's Financial Tracking System." State and Local Government Review, Vol. 16, no. 3, p. 109. Used by permission of the authors and Carl Vinson Institute of Government, University of Georgia.

relations? In truth, both traditions have had enormous influence over time. And both continue to exercise a strong pull on the loyalties of state and local decision makers (ACIR 1985b:394). The result is the simultaneous attraction of two seemingly conflicting sets of policy prescriptions—state dominance and local discretion. This ambivalence is what sets up cycles of experimentation in federalism.

SUMMARY

The position of local governments in the federal system may be the longest-running nondecision in American history. The Constitutional Convention directed its energies to determining the position of the nation and the states in the federal system but left unanswered the status of local governments.

This status was worked out in the operations of the system and articulated in several very important court cases.

The evolutionary bargain struck on the position of locals created legal subservience and political activity, sometimes to the point of dominance by the locals. Legal subservience and political passivity are two quite different things, and local governments and their officials have hardly been politically passive. We speculate in the concluding chapter of this book whether locals are really anyone's creatures.

Locals are active participants in two other major patterns of federal relations—the interlocal pattern and the national–local pattern. The next two chapters treat these patterns.

KEY CONCEPTS AND THEMES FOR REVIEW

federal aid pass-throughs
inherent right to local self-government
intrastate political intergovernmental relations
special districts
state mandates
states as the architects of local government
state supremacy
tax lids
debt limits

Subnational Federalism:

6

The interlocal pattern

City, county, and special district governments have a complex whirlpool of relations with one another, local elites, and interest groups. Part of this interaction is political intergovernmental relations, which are touched upon briefly here and at length in Chapters 9 and 10. The relations that have received the most attention have been legal, administrative, and technical—things such as contracts, compacts, and cooperative agreements between official units of government. As with the patterns of federalism previously discussed, in this chapter we will focus on the roots of the pattern in our political culture and practice, its fate today, the "nuts and bolts" of local–local relations, and the pattern's meaning in politics and economics.

ROOTS: JEFFERSON AND GRASS-ROOTS DEMOCRACY

The political-culture roots of localism are found in the mythology of **grass-roots democracy.** We use the word *mythology* deliberately: grass-roots democracy is a belief about how the political world should be. This myth becomes reality in political thinking and finds expression in public policy. We do not mean by *myth* that grass-roots democracy is a completely fabricated falsehood. Rather we want to emphasize the importance of myths as powerful ideas in people's minds and therefore in their actions. And this power is present whether the myth fits well with reality or not.

Grass-roots democracy was eloquently and intellectually expressed by perhaps the greatest American maker and popularizer of ideas and myths, Thomas Jefferson. We have discussed in Chapter 2 the profound influence Jefferson had over the dualist federal culture. Certainly, his idea of grass-roots democracy has been as pervasive and lasting as any element in that federalist culture. Americans seem forever persistent in the belief that they have an inherent right to local self-government. They are puzzled by such concepts as home-rule city charters because in the popular mind local units have a natural right to exist and to govern themselves subject only to the intervention of "nature's God." As we saw in Chapter 5, this point of view is not quite rooted in reality. Simply put, there is no inherent right to local self-government in the American federal system, thanks to the evolution of state–local relations. The "privilege" of local self-government is derived from the states. Jefferson's ideal never became reality.

Whereas Jefferson imbued localism with powerful symbols and justifications, it was Andrew Jackson who mobilized the interests of locals into a viable political force. Jackson's career is an interesting one from the standpoint of his grass-roots populism. Of "humble" birth, Jackson, on his move to Tennessee, identified closely with elite interests in that state. He married well, cultivated the land and hobnobbed with its gentry, and in his law practice took the side of creditors against debtors and landlords against squatters (some populism!). Most biographers of Jackson argue, however, that Jackson's intellectual sympathies were always Jeffersonian. Once in office, he became a symbol of the power of the masses, transforming the presidency and directing national power, through political parties, in favor of the masses. To be sure, in the process he strengthened national power. But in so doing, he *redirected* its use at least temporarily away from the national, Yankee, and regional elites who were so well served by the initial federalist bargain. This action accomplished, for the first time, policy aimed at benefiting the masses. The outcomes, and a bit of the direction of the political economy, had been redirected in a fundamental way.

The Jackson legacy involved the use of national power in the service of "locals." It is difficult to trace what happened within localities and between localities in the turgid era of the 1820s and the 1830s. The initial federal bargain had left local interests intact in that the status quo was maintained, if not neglected. It is doubtful that Jacksonian "democracy" transformed locals and altered the outcomes for local government policy. Localities probably remained untouched in Jackson's struggle for control over national policy. Thus it is highly probable that local policy outcomes often continued to serve local elites (after all, we didn't see much change in slavery, or the rights of women and others, in this period). Still, Jackson introduced the first "package" of policies at the national level focused on reducing the regressivity of taxation, aiding lower-class homesteaders, and weakening the central bank. In a sense, these actions were sweet revenge on Hamilton.

Another of Jefferson's visions that was politically invigorated by Jackson was that of an agrarian nation meeting agrarian needs. Jefferson's distaste for and distrust of cities is well known. As Jackson demonstrated, his vision could be pursued politically as long as the nation was predominantly rural. But as the nation became increasingly urban, the Jeffersonian political culture was unable to hold the loyalties of all who were committed to government at the grass roots. Thus, the Progressive movement became the attractive alternative for the new urbanite local in the latter 1800s.

EVOLUTION: THE NEW MORALITY OF PROGRESSIVISM IN INTERLOCAL AFFAIRS

Actually, the **Progressive movement** of the late 1800s was an amorphous grouping of seemingly incompatible elements. On the one hand, Progressives came from a distinctly rural background and thus retained a distinctly agrarian perspective. This branch of the Progressive movement owed a lot to populism. As a result, it was definitely "reformist." Its reformist orientation probably was this group's strongest link to the general Progressive movement. The second major segment of the Progressive movement was rooted in the urban areas. This group took its cues from the writings of social critics in the late 1890s and early 1900s. These social critics—Mugwumps, as Theodore Roosevelt called them—were concerned with the concentration of wealth and with **"the urban problem."** Thus they had an extensive reformist agenda, a perspective that linked them to the Progressive banner (Caine 1974:19–34). Although these two groups formed the primary legs of the Progressive movement, they were by no means its only components. The movement came to be an umbrella for nearly every group that desired change.

Richard Hofstadter has argued that "the distinguishing thing about the Progressives was something...which for lack of a better term might be called 'activism': they argued that social evils will not remedy themselves, and that it is wrong to sit by passively and wait for time to take care of them" (1963:4). Progressives connected this moral imperative with an intense optimism: not only should reform be undertaken, but it could be successful.

This strong moral component of progressivism elevated efficiency to the consummate moral imperative of government. As Melvin Holli has written, "the transformation of the high moral emphasis of nineteenth-century good government reformers into a keen concern for municipal efficiency was one of the principal accomplishments of institutional municipal reform" (1974:143). Government moved beyond the era of the "good and honest men" in whom Jackson had so much confidence, to require the "practical and efficient" man of Theodore Roosevelt. Holli quotes a remark of Theodore Roosevelt to the First National Conference for Good City Government in 1894: "There are two gospels I always want to preach to reformers....The first is the gospel of morality; the next is the gospel of efficiency....I don't think I have to tell you to be upright, but I do think I have to tell you to be practical and efficient" (1974:144). Two things about Roosevelt's statement are instructive. First, there is the assertion, widely associated with Progressives, that efficiency is at least equal in moral value to honesty. In Holli's words, "in the palladium of values that informed structural reform, efficiency has won its spurs and edged out good old-fashioned honesty" (1974:147). Second, and not as frequently connected with municipal government, is the highly judgmental nature of Roosevelt's statement. Teddy claimed to believe that he really had to tell municipal officials to be practical and efficient. The Mugwumpers had succeeded. Americans then, as many Americans now, believed that municipal governments were corrupt, wasteful, and uneconomical. And the explanation for this sorry state of affairs for the Mugwumpers was the fact that municipal governments were controlled by the "politicians." Thus the moral value of efficiency came also to include the necessity of ridding city government of politicians.

Structural reform and professional ("businesslike") management became the by-words of the Progressive prescription for urban ills. Thus the reformers advocated nonpartisan elections, abolition of the ward system in favor of citywide elections, and the city–manager system. Again, something more was at stake than simply tinkering with organization charts and election-district lines. What was at stake was political power in American cities. Holli has stated the character of the struggle precisely: "These new urban forms....facilitated a fundamental shift of urban political power. The lower classes invariably lost representatives to the local business classes and their professional auxiliaries who moved into the centers of municipal power" (1974:142). Progressive reforms represented the triumph of the middle class in urban politics. Largely through bureaucratic means, the "new middle class" hoped to create an "urban world that they would control for the benefit of all, a paradise of new-middle-class rationality" (Wiebe 1974:166). Following Charles A. Beard's well-known work on the Constitution, the future definitive history of the Progressive movement should perhaps be entitled *An Economic Interpretation of the Progressive Movement.*

The moralistic, middle-class Progressive movement extended far beyond city limits. As we have indicated, the two primary concerns of the Progressives were the overconcentration of elite wealth and the "squalid urban problem." We have seen in Chapter 3 how the doctrine of laissez faire was read into the Constitution by the federal courts in the late 1800s. The strong moral orientation of the Progressives did not square well with the non-interference requirement at the heart of the laissez faire doctrine. Substantial challenge to laissez faire had developed in the form of the social gospel and what was referred to as a "new school of political economy" (Fine 1956:374). Thus the challenge to laissez faire was both ethical and scientific: "The critics of laissez faire, as Richard T. Ely declared, brought 'science to the aid of Christianity'....The protagonists of these bodies of thought disputed the validity of the tenets of classical economics and social Darwinism and helped to undermine the theoretical foundations upon which the structure of laissez faire had been reared" (Fine 1956:374). This combination of the ethical and the scientific appealed strongly to Progressives.

The Progressives, then, were not afraid to use the power of the central government. They supported substantial national legislation that we would classify today as regulatory. The best known of these activities was the trust-busting of Theodore Roosevelt. But there were many others—public ownership of or regulation of public utilities, regulation of the railroads and other "common carriers," inspection of meat and mines, control of "impure" food and drugs, and increased regulation of the banking system. All of these regulations are quintessentially "middle class." But the Progressives were middle-class individuals with a strong sense of liberal Protestant moral outrage. Particularly in the states, the Progressives pushed through general welfare programs designed to assist the poor. States provided us with the first unemployment insurance, the first slum-housing programs, the first workman's compensation insurance, the first day-care centers, the first-school lunch programs, and the first old-age-pension law. Two states (Illinois and Missouri) almost simultaneously enacted the first aid-to-dependent-children programs (Fine 1974:385). It is well known that Theodore Roosevelt and his more illustrious cousin, Franklin, co-opted these state experiments, linked them into a national program, and made them key features of national-government centralism.

Two important political economy outcomes of the Progressive movement need special emphasis at this point. First, the Progressives fundamentally altered the way Americans viewed the interaction of politics and economics. Fine has expressed this outcome as follows:

> As the mid-point of the twentieth century was reached, Americans would appear to have rejected the admonition that government is best which governs least and to have endorsed the view that in the interests of the general welfare the state should restrain the strong and protect the weak, should provide services to the people as private enterprise is unable or unwilling to supply, should seek to stabilize the economy and to counteract the cycle of boom and bust, and should provide the citizen with some degree of economic security. Thus had the ideological conflict of the late nineteenth century between the advocates of laissez faire and the advocates of the general-welfare state been resolved in theory,

in practice, and in public esteem in favor of the general-welfare state. (1956:399–400)

We do not mean to suggest, and Fine certainly does not, that the Progressives were the only factor in this change in public attitudes. But they were a major force in it, and the consequences of that shift cannot be overexaggerated.

The second political economy effect of the Progressives that is important for our purposes is that they set in motion an ongoing concern for the "urban problem." This concern is very much a part of the contemporary political economy. Indeed, we hear frequently the term *urban crisis* rather than *urban problem*. And the urban crisis perspective has its modern Mugwumpers too. A 1975 "Dunagin's People" cartoon had an Indian chief admonishing two other chiefs, "Watch for tricks in that offer to give the country back to the Indians....They might want us to take the cities, too." (Quoted in ACIR 1976:1) An avalanche of scholars—joined by the Advisory Commission on Intergovernmental Relations—has produced an extensive literature on the urban problem.

It is not our purpose to summarize and evaluate this extensive urban literature. However, several features of it should be stressed. First, some of the literature is well within the Progressive tradition. Building on the suggestions of earlier Progressives, various writers have urged upon urban governments legal reforms as the solution to the urban problem (MacMahon 1955; Zimmerman 1983), structural or reorganization reforms (Pressman and Wildavsky 1973; MacMahon 1955; Zimmerman 1983), decentralization as a way to increase responsiveness (Zimmerman 1983), and fiscal reforms at the local level (Derthick 1974; Pressman and Wildavsky 1973; Farkas 1971; ACIR 1976). But not all scholars share the (Progressive) optimism of these writers. Edward Banfield (1974), in particular, put forth the "conservative" viewpoint that immediate prospects for solution to the urban problem were not as bright as some had assumed. Others, and we think rightly, began to link the problems of urban areas with features in the larger economic and political system of this country (Goodman 1971). Garry Brewer (1973) cast doubt into the soul of the Progressive faith by questioning the usefulness of science applied to urban problems. And the advocates of "neighborhood government" and public choice attacked the other article of the Progressive faith by arguing that large, well-intentioned bureaucratic systems in urban areas could be the major barriers to social change (Kotler 1969; Bish 1971; Bish and Ostrom 1976). Substantial dents had appeared in the Progressive armor.

The ACIR tends to view these developments positively. In a report on the urban problem, it concluded that:

...the climate for the solution of urban problems in the future...is substantially different...than it was only a few years ago. The atmosphere of crisis politics—reflecting the explosive situation in the nation's cities just a few years ago—is giving way to a more measured one of paying heed to the nation's precise urban needs by making and filling specific commitments that can be directly acted upon and funded within currently available budget ceilings to help meet these needs, thereby making life in urban America increasingly (though perhaps modestly) more attractive and productive than it has been. (1976:15)

The Progressives could not have looked at today's divisions among scholars, the loss of faith in planning techniques, the mistrust of bureaucracies, the disaffection with government, the reduction in federal funds to cities, and more, and reached a conclusion of optimism, however.

Two somewhat contradictory elements form the roots of the political culture of optimism, reform, and self-rule in our traditions of localism. These two elements are a mythology of an agrarian society as the only good life, and a commitment to modernize local governments so as to make them equal to the demands of an urban society. As if this built-in contradiction were not enough, one of the major problems with grass-roots democracy is that being involved with or concerned about local government is simply not part of the "weekly time clock" of most Americans. Political participation rates in local politics in this country have historically been low and continue to be so today. Grass-roots democracy as a political phenomenon is weak in America. Thus grass-roots democracy has evolved in ways far different from the Jefferson vision of agrarianism or the popular myth of widespread local control and concern. We will assess the fate and effects of localism and the interlocal pattern in more detail at the end of the chapter. Now we will summarize the practical features of interlocal relations.

NUTS AND BOLTS

Much is made about too much fragmentation of government at the local level. It is true that there are a lot of the "local beasties" around—some 82,000 of them by the latest census of governments. However, we find this view of "too much fragmentation" a bit misleading. If we may borrow from quantum physics, local political units are the equivalent of atomic elements. One of the more interesting issues in physics is whether a bit of subatomic matter should be treated as a wave or as a particle. It depends on how you look at it. In federalism, whether local units appear as overly fragmented units or basic elements in a dynamic system depends on how you look at them.

From the political economy perspective, a "wave theory" of local units is much more appropriate than a "particle theory." Local units are in dynamic interaction with each other, with their creators, the states (see Chapter 5), and with the national government (see Chapter 7). It is difficult to look at this complex system of *interactions* and see much of importance about fragmentation. Of course, many of the fragmentation theories are based on a geographic analysis that attempts to match geographical boundaries with the parameters of the problems confronting local units. But if such a marriage of geographical boundaries and problems is insisted upon, there is virtually no possibility for a full understanding of the "urban problem." The following point illustrates this view. A recent area of study has to do with what Bayless Manning calls "intermestic" affairs (1977:307). Manning uses this term to refer to the interdependence of subnational units in the federal system and other nations. International economic affairs have "interlocal" effects. Manning showed that disruptions of particular international trade flows can cause disproportionate concern and reaction in certain local areas or affected groups. This is best seen with farmers and in markers of the international food and grain trade.

We emphasize this point not only to encourage a more transnational analysis of American federalism but to emphasize that fragmentation theories are a result of a particular way of looking at local units —namely, from a very narrow geographic perspective. A geographical assumption is valuable, but it ignores a number of factors in federalism viewed as a political economy. We suggest that the interrelationships in the federal system are far more important to an understanding of the system than the viewpoint of local fragmentation. (On interrelationships in federalism, see especially Chapter 10.) Also, most interlocal relationships are political: they have to do with the exercise of power and the implementation of public programs in the federal system. We will examine the important questions of the power and policy aspects of the interlocal model in succeeding chapters. Our purpose in this section is to describe the most important formal and functional aspects of that model. We will look at three functional elements of federalism at the interlocal level—interlocal agreements (service contracts, joint service agreements, and service transfers), privatization, and local implementation of nationally encouraged programs.

Interlocal Agreements

Analyzing interlocal agreements has been difficult, in part because of the absence of standard definitions of key terms. The ACIR has monitored interlocal agreements since 1961 (ACIR 1961a; see especially ACIR 1967). In 1983 the ACIR together with the International City Management Association conducted a comprehensive survey of interlocal agreements. This effort resulted in the development of definitions that should serve as the basis for comparative study of these agreements:

> *Intergovernmental Service Contract:* An arrangement between two governmental units in which one pays the other for the delivery of a par-

ticular service to the inhabitants in the jurisdiction of the paying government. Such contracts may be *formal* (written) or *informal* (unwritten).

Joint Service Agreement: An agreement between *two or more* governments
for the joint planning, financing, and delivery of a service to the inhabitants of all jurisdictions participating in the agreement.

Intergovernmental Service Transfer: The permanent transfer of total
responsibility for the *provision* of a service from one governmental unit
to another. (ACIR 1985a:1–2; we have placed these definitions in an
order slightly different from that found in the ACIR publication.)

These definitions should no doubt become a part of standard usage in this
policy area.

All forms of interlocal agreements occur under permissive legislation of the states (even in cooperating with one another, local units are in
many ways still "creatures of the state"). Constitutional and statutory
provisions regarding such agreements vary widely among the states. Indeed, most state constitutions, in spite of their detail, are simply silent on
the matter of interlocal agreements. Thus the legal provisions governing
interlocal agreements are primarily statutory.

Two patterns of such laws are found among the states. In some states,
such statutes are written in broad, general language. These laws simply
authorize certain types of interlocal agreements and provide the most
general procedures for establishing them. In other states, the statutes tend
to be specific, establishing more carefully the details of interlocal agreements. In all states, laws relating to contractual agreements between local
units tend to be more specific, particularly in specifying the approval procedures for such contracts. Given the wide variation in state practice, it is
important to remember that state constitutions and laws establish the
"legal framework" for all forms of interlocal agreements.

Service Contracts. Local units frequently enter into agreements by
which one unit pays another to deliver services. In the ACIR–ICMA survey referred to earlier, 1084 of the over 2000 responding cities and counties had such **service contracts** (or 52 percent of responding jurisdictions).
The total number of such contracts reported was 4328 (ACIR 1985a:29).
The services most frequently purchased by contract were jail and detention home facilities, followed by sewage disposal, animal control, tax assessing, solid-waste disposal, water supply, police and fire
communications (911 emergency communications systems), fire prevention, tax and utility bill processing, and sanitary inspection (ACIR
1985a:28). Among those services less frequently purchased through contract were transportation, health and welfare, parks and recreation, education, culture, and general government and finance. Cities contracted most

frequently with counties to deliver services, while counties divided their contracting almost evenly between other counties and cities.

Joint Service Agreements. The 1985 ACIR–ICMA survey found that slightly more local units used joint service agreements than used contracts. Of the 2039 reporting cities and counties, 1132, or 55 percent, had such agreements with other local jurisdictions (ACIR 1985a:30). The total number of joint agreements was 3319. The services most frequently delivered through joint agreements were libraries and police and fire communications. However, as in the case of contracts, a wide variety of other services were also delivered through joint agreements. The most frequently provided services in addition to those already cited were fire prevention, sewage disposal, jails and detention homes, solid-waste disposal, emergency medical and ambulance service, animal control, recreational facilities, and programs for the elderly. Among services less frequently provided through joint service agreements were water supply, public health clinics, and planning and zoning. Cities entered into joint service agreements most frequently with counties, while county joint service agreements were divided almost evenly between other counties and cities.

Transfers of Services. The ACIR–ICMA survey identified a significant number of **service transfers** from one local jurisdiction to another, or from a local unit to a private firm or nonprofit agency. Of the 1786 local units responding, 710, or 40 percent, had transferred responsibility for a service since 1976 (the survey was conducted in 1982). The total number of such transfers was 1412. The services most frequently transferred were refuse collection and solid-waste disposal. The remainder of the ten most frequently transferred programs were animal control, jails and detention homes, tax assessing, sewage disposal, emergency medical and ambulance service, police and fire communications, computer and data processing, and tax and utility-bill processing. A variety of other services were less frequently transferred, including alcohol and drug rehabilitation, street and bridge construction and maintenance, recreational facilities, mental health services, and hospitals (ACIR 1985a:58). The ACIR describes the pattern of such transfers this way:

> ...private firms tended to take on mechanized and production-type services (refuse collection, solid waste disposal, computer services), nonprofit agencies received human service activities (mental health, alcohol and drug rehabilitation, recreation, and programs for the elderly), and regional units took over services of an areawide nature (water supply, mass transit operation) (ACIR 1985a:59).

Certainly, as the ACIR concluded, this pattern seems logical. Later in this section we will return to the transfer of functions to private firms.

Fruit Basket Turnover: What Guides the Pattern of Interlocal Agreements? The general concept involved in each of these three types of interlocal agreements is what is known as *functional assignment*—the allocation of program (functional) responsibilities among different levels of government. When compared "up close," national, state, and local jurisdictions show little consistency in their functional roles. To put the matter simply, what local unit X does may be significantly different from what local unit Y does in the same state. Variation among locals may be even more pronounced than that among states.

What is even more important, and quite obvious from the data collected in the ACIR–ICMA survey, is that the "pattern" of interlocal functions is not static; it is highly dynamic and ever changing. It is analogous, as our section title indicates, to the child's game of "fruit basket turnover." The problem created by this almost tumultuous situation is that of monitoring who is doing what: Who can say what should be the fruit basket of interlocal responsibilites? And by what criteria do we evaluate the patterns of functional assignment? Who should do what and why? Is delivery of a service by unit X better than delivery of the service by unit Y? Thus the critical questions in evaluating any general scheme of functional assignment are the same ones that can be used to evaluate interlocal service agreements.

Considerable attention has been given recently to the development of normative criteria by which public policy performance can be evaluated. The evaluation of local government performance has been a part of that research. One of the better studies was the ACIR's "normative approach to functional assignment," designed to evaluate what level or unit should do what in the federal system. To this end, the ACIR developed four normative criteria — economic efficiency, fiscal equity, political accountability, and administrative effectiveness (ACIR 1974b:7). The criterion of *economic efficiency* means that functions should be assigned to jurisdictions that can realize economies of scale, that are willing to provide alternative services, and that will adopt pricing policies when appropriate. *Fiscal equity* requires that a jurisdiction compensate other jurisdictions for economic externalities (costs that spill over from one party's actions to another area, such as the costs of pollution). Fiscal equity also means that a jurisdiction can finance its service responsibilities. *Political accountability* means that citizens have access to and control over public problems, and that provisions are made for maximum citizen participation in the performance of the function. Finally, *administrative effectiveness* requires geographic and legal adequacy, management capability, intergovernmental flexibility, and a "general-purpose character." In summary, policy or program functions should be assigned to jurisdictions that can "(1) supply a service at the lowest possible costs; (2) finance a function with the greatest possible fiscal equalization; (3) provide a service with adequate popular political support; and (4) administer a function in an authoritative, technically proficient, and coopera-tive fashion" (ACIR 1974b:7). But how do interlocal agreements stand up when evaluated by these ideal criteria?

The truth is that so little analysis has been done on interlocal agree-ments that we simply do not know the answer to this question. Most of the evidence of how well interlocal agreements meet the ACIR criteria of func-tional assignment is in the form of survey data. We know, in part at least, what people who are parties to the agreements think about them. Again, the ACIR–ICMA survey is the most recent and comprehensive source of such information. Table 6-1 summarizes the responses to that survey.

It is clear that most of the reasons given by local managers have to do with either economic efficiency or administrative effectiveness. Not many of them were motivated by goals of fiscal equity or political accountability; perhaps local managers are not yet sensitive to such criteria in entering into interlocal agreements.

The ACIR–ICMA survey also identified the factors local decision makers thought most "inhibited" interlocal agreements. These factors, in order, were limitations on local independence, inequitable apportionment of costs, adverse public reactions, and restrictions on termination of the agreements (ACIR 1985a:40). Interestingly, only a few officials reported in open-ended questions that interlocal agreements resulted in a reduction of service levels or the quality of service provided. Apparently, local decision makers believe that interlocal agreements work well.

From a political economy perspective, it is always important to ask who benefits and who loses. But unfortunately there is so little research on interlocal agreements that it is virtually impossible to answer these sig-nificant policy questions. The extensive network of interlocal agreements needs a great deal more policy study than it has received to date.

Privatization

Privatization is difficult to define. Some writers (such as Hatry 1983) use the term to refer to a broad range of services delivered by the private sector that were previously or are potentially supplied through government. Other writers define privatization in a dreamy and simplistic way as govern-ment turning over to "its citizens" the responsibility for obtaining and paying for a service previously or potentially supplied by government (Citizens League 1982). As with interlocal agreements, standardized defini-tions would facilitate comparative research on the practice.

However defined, privatization is clearly rooted in the Jeffersonian federalist culture. As Hatry observes, it is particularly appealing to those who believe that less government is better (1983:9). It also contains an ele-ment of the Progressive reformist orientation in that most who argue for privatization also believe that the private sector is inherently more efficient

TABLE 6-1 *Reasons for Entering Interlocal Contracts and Joint Agreements*

	Lack qualified personnel		Lack facilities		Achieve economies of scale		Eliminate duplication		Need larger area		Remove politics		Citizen demand	
	No.	%	No.	%	No.	%	No.	%	No.	%	No.	%	No.	%
contracts (total: 4328)	873	20	1386	32	2257	52	1325	31	1662	38	81	2	179	4
joint agreements (total: 3319)	393	12	732	22	1770	53	1248	38	1539	46	83	2	150	4
transfers of services (1976–1982) (total: 1412)	252	18	289	20	711	50	301	21	393	28	48	3	49	3

Source: Adapted from ACIR 1985a:36–37, 61.

in service delivery than the public sector (for a more balanced view, see Goodsell 1983). In many respects, privatization has in recent years become more of an article of faith than a carefully explored policy option. Combining the two views—less government is bett⁀ and the private sector is more efficient—the advocates of privatization argue for a new role for public sector managers. Instead of functioning as direct service providers, public managers would become overseers, brokers, and facilitators of services however they are delivered (Citizens League 1982:2).

Hatry usefully categorizes eleven *actions of privatization*. First, local governments can contract with private firms to deliver services. In many ways, this form of privatization is quite similar to local units contracting with other local units for service delivery. Second, the local unit may award a franchise to a private firm to provide the service. The most common examples of this practice are solid-waste disposal and ambulance services. Third, the local unit may provide a grant to a private organization to provide a service. The taxi companies in urban transit systems are often privately owned and publicly subsidized. Perhaps the most controversial, and certainly the most discussed, technique is the use of vouchers. By this fourth device, local authorities provide citizens with a voucher or "credit slip" to be used to purchase services from sometimes a public but usually a private provider. Education, day-care centers, and housing are the areas most often suggested for vouchers.

Fifth, volunteers work with public agencies in providing a service. Historically, "volunteer" fire departments are the best example of a public service staffed primarily by volunteer or nonpaid lay personnel. Sixth, the local unit can encourage individuals or groups to undertake services previously provided by government. This self-help method is quite prominent in many states in the form of state-government-promoted "Share a Ride" commuting programs. Seventh, the local unit can use its taxing or regulatory authority to encourage private firms or individuals to provide a public service. Hatry places dog regulation in this category. A local unit's leash law that forces citizens to keep their dogs on leashes serves to reduce the need for public sector dogcatchers, pounds, and so on. So much for our best friend.

Eighth, the local unit may give up responsibility for a service and work with a private firm that has voluntarily accepted delivery responsibility; Hatry refers to this as *service shedding*. Hospitals are a good example of this device.

Ninth, there are various *demarketing* strategies, whereby local units attempt to reduce the demand for a service. Smokey the Bear of the U.S. Forest Service is an excellent example of an attempt to reduce the need for firefighting equipment, personnel, and so on by reducing the incidence of forest fires. Tenth, local units may obtain temporary help from private firms. It is not uncommon for private firms to do free needs-assessment work in such areas as data processing and establishment of information systems. Finally, local units can impose user fees and charges to reduce demand for a government service. State park systems can raise cabin rentals to the point where "demand" stabilizes and no additional cabins are needed.

While we prefer the broader definition of privatization used by Hatry, we think that service shedding, demarketing, obtaining temporary help from private firms, and the use of fees and charges to reduce demand (a form of demarketing, it seems) have limited potential and other problems as privatization devices (a view shared by Valenti and Manchester 1984). We will now review some of the major shortcomings of privatization strategies.

Is Privatization a Shiny Rotten Apple? Reliable data on privatization are very difficult to find. Most of the existing information is in the form of survey data. Unfortunately, the surveys conducted to date do not use standardized definitions and thus produce little comparable information. Also, Valenti and Manchester (1984) report that response rates on these surveys are very low. This is probably not accidental, given the diverse, ad hoc, and decentralized aspects of privatizing. Thus it is difficult to say with any degree of confidence what the extent of privatization is among local units.

Even more important, the policy effects and outcomes are unclear at this time. It is for this and other reasons that skepticism about privatization is probably not unwarranted. Hatry reports, for example, that the assumed superior efficiency of the private sector is offset by a number of negative economic effects of privatization. These include failures to deliver services contracted, productivity declines, a tendency to focus on short-term benefits (profits) as opposed to service quality, increased incidence of service delays, cost overruns, and occasional fraud (Hatry 1983). We like the way an author of an introductory text in public administration put the matter:

> [Privatization] has its disadvantages. Perhaps the most obvious is that too-cozy relationships between business and government contracting personnel might develop. The possible result of such relationships is graft. And some observers, looking ahead, see totalitarian tendencies resulting. Contracting officers and the contractors could simply begin to bypass both the legislative and executive branch, enrich themselves, and build a syndicate state, responsive to hardly anyone. (Starling 1986:522)

Whether privatization would result in a syndicate state would be interesting to speculate about. But there are a number of more common-sense objections to privatization. One simple motive that may explain a great deal of the new advocacy of privatization is that advocates usually stand to make some bucks from it. The vast majority of the "writers" who advocate privatization have come out of business schools or hold positions in the cor-

porate world. If the bandwagon rhetoric in the Reagan years is "less government," why not jump on, especially if you or your firm might end up with
the contract? Potential profit or extra consulting fees are no poor reasons for
writing academic-sounding proposals to "shed government" (a phrase that
reveals a great deal about the bias of privatizers). In the light of this motive,
it may not be such a mystery that there is a lot of advocacy of but little solid
research on privatization.

Second, privatization is another form of adhocracy, one that extends
the adhocracy found in special districts. Again, the survey evaluations of
privatization practices concentrate heavily on measures of management effectiveness and efficiency (ACIR 1986); they virtually ignore political accountability and equity.

We believe that the more important questions to ask about privatization
have to do with the *outcomes* of adhocracy as a service-delivery method. How
does the local unit ensure the *equitable* distribution of services among all
citizens? Or, to turn the question around, is privatization a means to avoid the
demand or need for equal provision of services? Certainly, the demarketing,
self-help, and service-shedding trends seem particularly suitable to instruments for the enjoyment of services by some but not by others.

A similar criticism could be made of vouchers. Does anyone really
suppose that low-income parents will purchase elementary school education for their children at the high-cost academy across town? And, if
vouchers are the instruments for the unequal provision of services, will
the law provide relief from this effect as it is beginning to provide relief
from the unequal provision of services by general-purpose governments?
The idea that jurisdictions will be able to ensure fairness in the delivery
of services through privatization is a pretty big and often unquestioned
assumption. Quality-control is also a big risk. How can those governments
whose resources are presumably being restricted ensure quality control in
hundreds of new providers of privatized services? Georgia contracted
record keeping in medicare programs to a private firm only to discover
increased errors in those records (billings, payment to doctors, and so on),
delays in processing payments, and other problems. It may be true, for example, that the use of private providers is more often than not a bailout
or a sweetheart deal for an inefficient service provider, rather than a way
to raise service levels and achieve service equity.

The lack of accountability inherent in privatization may yet prove to
be the *worst* problem of decentralizing and dispersing services to numerous
private providers. For one thing, private contractors are not famous for
being friendly and open to government audits. More important, the mass
media and the Freedom of Information Act are *less* likely to be used to track
down graft in the many dozens of private firms than in the halls of government. The media have more of an antigovernment nose for news and less of
an inclination to hound numerous businesses, especially when "the beat"

leads away from a few elected officials and government buildings and out into the maze of thousands of private firms. If things become privatized, how will we be told, and by whom, when things are not kosher or not working? And whom does the citizen call in city hall for action when nothing happens? Certainly there must be greater interest and attention to researching the accountability problem of privatization.

In short, a number of highly publicized claims for privatization have been made. Those claims may or may not reflect the actual *outcomes* of privatized services. Solid research is slim today, and may always be difficult to come by given the ad hoc, decentralized aspects of privatizing. If we do not know the extent of privatization, or find the results hard to track down in the maze of numerous new contractors, then it will be difficult to weigh accurately the policy outcomes and effects of privatization. The problems of adhocracy and inequity in service delivery that can result from privatization are major causes for caution and concern.

THE LOCALIZATION OF NATIONAL POLICY CONCERNS: HOW LOCALS TURN THE TABLE ON THE FEDS

As we indicated in Chapter 3, much has been made of "the nationalization of the states," particularly as a result of regulatory federalism (Hanus 1981). Certainly, there is substance to this argument. Partial preemption, perhaps more clearly than other regulatory device, makes it possible for the national government to wrap the cloak of national–state cooperation around a policy clearly dominated by national objectives. But too great an emphasis on this clouds an understanding of the full range of outcomes in the relations between federal levels. In particular, paying too much attention to nation–state relations will result in overlooking the profoundly significant role locals have over policy in the American political economy. Locals influence, mold, and occasionally control what is generally thought to be national policy in pursuit of national objectives.

This **localization of national policy concerns** can be examined on two levels. First, there is the power of locals to influence the implementation of national programs. What is at stake here is the effective implementation of national policy. Second, locals on occasion exercise their own version of preemption, in the political if not the legal sense. In this situation, local political actors seize the issue area. They can take the initiative in forming issue agendas and by and large can control a policy that would normally be thought of as involving national policy. The first factor has been subjected to substantial study; the second, far too little.

In the rest of this chapter we will focus on how locals and interlocal action can influence or even preempt national policy goals. In some policy areas, the localization of national policy concerns involves interlocal cooperation in the clearest and most effective ways that can be found. As we shall see, vacillation between locals is almost zero. But the influence of locals in the *implementation* of national programs—particularly those programs that we will call *nationally encouraged programs* — occurs within the national–local pattern. Thus we will reserve our discussion of this subject to the next chapter.

The localization of national policy concerns may be viewed as a form of *functional preemption,* in that local action takes precedence over or displaces national action. In a sense, functional preemption reverses historic practice in policy innovation. Historically, local or state policy actors would "invent" an approach, such as worker compensation, only to have the feds take it over as national policy. The localization of national concerns works in the opposite direction. The feds "invent" an approach, only to have the locals take it over. Or local policy actors become active in a policy area, seize the issue agenda, and lock out the feds. Often, as with policy on chemical hazardous waste, local takeover is aided by national legislation in the policy area.

The same phenomenon occurs with the localization of state policy. State decision makers "invent" a policy approach to an area only to have it taken over by locals. It is possible, as a result, to refer to all of these actions as the localization of national and state policy concerns.

The policy area in which localization of national and state policy concerns is seen most clearly is that of locally unwanted land uses (referred to by the delightful acronym LULUs). LULUs are an interesting and pervasive phenomenon. Some LULUs are created because of technology. Examples are nuclear power plants and certain high-tech industries (who wants a DNA experiment in their back yard?). Other LULUs are the consequence of the production or delivery of a service. Examples here are sewage-disposal plants, hazardous-waste facilities, and chemical plants. A third type may be referred to as *social LULUs* because they are created by the type of people they draw. This category is undoubtedly the largest. It includes such things as prisons, low-income housing (see the previous section), adult book stores, and military installations.

Public attitudes toward LULUs are complex. A cursory survey of the categories just cited (which are far from exhaustive) shows immediately that the public response to LULUs is highly ideologically and emotionally charged. It is possible to speak of LULUs of the right, such as prisons, military installations, nuclear power plants, and even strip mines. And there are LULUs of the left, such as low-income housing and halfway houses, which are usually supported by liberals. Thus, what really makes public attitudes complex is that every LULU is someone else's wanted land use (should we invent a new acronym—WALU?). The resulting tension between those who want the land use and those who do not creates the issue. To say that consensus exists on only a few LULUs is to understate the problem.

The siting of some of these LULUs is clearly a national objective of immediate importance. The two policy areas that have involved the most national legislation and controversy are sites for hazardous chemical waste and sites for low-level nuclear waste. To provide for the first policy area, Congress passed the Resource Conservation and Recovery Act; for the second, it passed the Low Level Nuclear Waste Act. In both instances, Congress provided for state assumption of major responsibility in the policy area. And, at least in the Resource Conservation and Recovery Act, Congress mandated substantial local and "popular" involvement in the siting of facilities.

What has made the implementation of both acts so difficult is that every specific siting attempt sparks intense local opposition. The reason for this opposition is clear: LULUs concentrate the risk and disperse the benefits of the facility. The risks associated with a facility for chemical waste disposal, for example, are concentrated in the immediate vicinity of the site. Benefits are dispersed among the producing industry, the state and the region through "industrial development" potential, to the general public in the form of a "healthier environment," and the like. As we have seen, this concentration of risk and dispersal of benefits creates a NIMBY syndrome: almost everyone favors the siting of such facilities, but "not in my back yard." When the site is to be nearby, locals will prefer almost any alternative use of the land (Getz and Walker 1980).

Each attempt to site such a facility produces immediate, intense, and protracted local opposition. Local policy actors seize the initiative. They determine the public agenda for the issue. They set the terms of public consideration of the proposal. And they are tactically very imaginative in opposing every phase of the siting effort (Wells 1982:732). Locals are very united in the use of these techniques. Vacillation among affected local units on the use of any obstructionist tactic available is almost zero.

The outcome of the protracted conflict between locals and state or national policy actors is most frequently policy stalemate. Locals have been consistently successful in opposing specific siting efforts. The states have had varied success in implementing general regulations for chemical hazardous waste (Lester et al. 1983), but both national and state institutions lack the capacity to site facilities in the face of local obstruction, even though they are armed with the legal power to issue regulations and guidelines.

This situation, as with the problems created in locally implemented, nationally encouraged program areas, results in proposals for further centralization of policy powers. For example, the National Conference of State Legislatures has speculated that "perhaps the most effective institutional strategy is the establishment of state-owned facilities that provide alternative technologies" (1982:16). This proposal is an interesting variation on the centralist federalist culture, reflecting a type of subnational centralism. There is certainly a lot of that type of centralism going around. As we shall see in the next chapter, proposals for more effective state control are frequently made for what are perceived to be problems in the local implementation of nationally encouraged programs.

What is interesting about both the localization of national policy and the local implementation of nationally encouraged programs is that no "Jeffersonian" proposals have been put forth. From a political economy perspective, it might be worthwhile to speculate on the possibility of creating substate microinstitutions having the formal power and the political legitimacy to carry out policy. For example, why not create microinstitutions having the power to site hazardous-waste facilities? Locals have repeatedly demonstrated a punch adequate to preempt national and state policy on siting. Why not harness that energy to the management of microinstitutions? We suggest this possibility to drive home once again the point that one's policy prescriptions are often determined by the federalist lens one is looking through.

On a less formal level, the vitality of locals in preempting national policy concerns is very high (see Chapter 10). One would have expected the nuclear-freeze debate, for example, to have been most vigorous in the august chambers of the United States Senate. Instead, it had its institutional birth and meteoric rise in the town halls of New England. Recent counts show that around 57 American cities and towns have banned nuclear weapons within their borders. In essence, they have constituted themselves into nuclear-free zones. And they did this while national policy makers continued their long if reluctant affair with the bomb.

LOCALS CAN OVERCOME: WHAT THE INTERLOCAL PATTERN EXPLAINS TODAY

What the preceding discussion indicates is that local governments have three strikes against them: they are legally subservient to states; there is a built-in contradiction in their political culture; and there is widespread political apathy about government at the grass roots. However, unlike in baseball, having three strikes against you in the federal system does not mean that you are out. As we have seen, legal subservience and political passivity are two quite different things. The contradiction in the political culture of local governments may spark the search for new and improved ways of doing things. (For example, the dualistic culture combined with the Progressive drive for modernization may have been the underlying force in the development of direct national–local relations.) And political apathy serves local elites well. Thus the interlocal pattern continues to be a powerful force in the American political economy. It is one of the best explanations of certain important features of the federal system.

One of the most important historical trends explained by the local–local model is the use of the law as the instrument for protecting private property. Hamilton and Madison argued that the primary function of locals was to maintain order, ensuring the loyalty of citizens by protecting both their lives and their property. Whether Hamilton and Madison anticipated the selective use of the law to protect selected property and selected lives is difficult to determine (certainly Hamilton in particular was concerned with the interests of the rich and wellborn). Locals, however, quickly understood the issue to be a question of what property was to be protected. Thus a five-dollar can of gasoline stolen from a store is included in the state definition of what is to be protected. The owner of that store, on the other hand, can steal five dollars or more through excess profits, but the money lost to the customer is not (yet) defined as property to be protected by the law.

The selective enforcement of the law in the protection of life and limb is well known also. Even with the current extensive concern for driving under the influence, it is much more likely that a college student will be given a ticket for it than an influential local businessman.

This selective enforcement has to do with the practical content or meaning of the law. That is, it is the local, "street-level bureaucrat" who determines what the law actually means in a specific situation. For example, one of the cities in which an author of this book once lived had an ordinance prohibiting the discharge of water in such a way as "to produce a nuisance or a health hazard." A local car dealership, owned by an influential member of the city power structure, released its car-wash water in such a way that it flowed directly onto the adjoining lot. The owner of the home on that lot filed a complaint with the local health inspector, who was empowered by the ordinance to issue restraining orders preventing such practices. The health inspector refused to take action, explaining to the complaining property owner that "it all depends on what you mean by a nuisance and health hazard."

Also, it is common knowledge that locals are the most important determiners of *which* laws get enforced. Although there is a general belief that all laws should be strictly enforced, nearly everyone can cite laws that are seldom if ever enforced. Georgia, for example, has a law that makes "cohabitation" illegal. Cohabitation is the living together of unmarried persons of the opposite sex. Obviously, the law is honored more in the breach than in the keeping. The dockets of state courts are hardly overburdened with cohabitation cases.

We like the term *marginal definition of the law* for this phenomenon. It suggests that all law must be given an "added" definition in order to be applied to a specific case. And that definition must include determining the meaning of the law and the level of its enforcement. Marginal definition must be given to all categories of law— criminal, civil, property, regulatory, consumer-protection, and so on—in street-level implementation (Lipsky 1971). The marginal definition of the law is often the occasion for the unequal administration of the law, a function performed most effectively by locals. Interlocal politics and practice must be examined if the unequal administration of the law is to be understood.

The second feature of the American political economy for which the interlocal pattern is important is urban outcomes—who gets what from urban politics. Ample research suggests that the front-burner issue for locals has been the question of who gets what, when, and how (Lineberry 1977; Levy, Meltsner, and Wildavsky 1974). It is possible to interpret the literature on **urban service delivery** in two ways (Hero 1986:666). According to the *dispersed-inequality theory*, urban service delivery varies in unpatterned or dispersed ways. Thus there is little or no pattern of equality or inequality. According to the *underclass hypothesis*, service-delivery patterns reflect a distinct inequality of outcomes for the underclass. This line of interpretation recognizes that there are programs in which equitable service delivery exists. But this equality is seen as a by-product of the concern for efficiency, or as a necessity for the accomplishment of political support:

> It is frankly difficult to say whether such equality as exists is more an accidental or a conscious process of allocation. We would speculate that equality of treatment is a secondary value of urban administrators, one which might emerge from other decisional premises but which is not an overarching value in service allocations. If equality premises are indeed reflected, they are probably reflected more in response to the need for political support than on their own terms. (Lineberry 1977:158)

In Lineberry's view, the concern for equality, where it is part of the decision itself, is important mostly when it is seen as a way to develop broad political support. Others have argued that whatever degree of equality exists is simply a by-product of other concerns, such as a concern for efficiency (Viteritti 1982:64– 47). As administrators pursue the most efficient ways to deliver the service, they produce a certain equality of outcome.

What is to be made of these two somewhat contradictory conclusions? It is clear that the literature on urban services should be accepted with some caution. Hero (1986) has pointed out a number of measurement problems involved in studies of urban delivery systems. Beyond this, however, the conclusion of his review of the literature is difficult to refute: "it is doubtful whether this literature's conclusions concerning 'dispersed inequalities' are accurate and whether the 'underclass' hypothesis can be ignored" (1986:676). It is difficult to read the urban-renewal literature, for example, without concluding that local governments have helped elite developers acquire land that they could not have acquired through normal market transactions. (A cynic could say, "So much for laissez-faire, unless it is for the poor.") Local jurisdictions vie for the "honor" of such economic development.

Certainly this desire of interlocal governments to compete in aiding local elites expresses itself in stark terms on occasion. The media reported widely an incident in 1981 when the city of Detroit worked with General Motors to overcome local opposition to destroy Poletown, an established working-class neighborhood, for the purpose of building a Cadillac plant there (*Washington Post*, March 1, 1981). We have referred to the distributive and redistributive function of locals several times previously, but we emphasize the point again here: how policies are implemented, and for whose benefit (regardless of their origin in other sectors), depend at least as much on the interaction of various local jurisdictions, local officials, local elites, and local interest groups as on federal or state decision makers, laws, or court rulings. We develop this view in Chapter 9.

The third area that shows the importance of interlocal relations is the representation system. Political scientists generally agree that one of the most important features of American politics is the primacy of local interests in national representative institutions (especially Congress). As we pointed out in Chapter 3, this primacy of local interests does not necessarily result in a democratic system. Local interests are by and large isolated, specific interests that find it difficult to unite in purpose or otherwise. And where such coalitions do form, there are sometimes enough compound institutional protections against popular majorities to check the "excesses of democracy." If we are to understand the policy effects of the representation system, we must understand interlocal relations and interests and how they influence jurisdictions to copy one another's policy and election practices and form intergovernmental lobbies to press their views on states and the national government. This process is fully pictured in Chapters 9 and 10.

Finally, we believe that the interlocal pattern perhaps best explains the heavy hand of tradition on American government. The bedrock of that stability is found at the interlocal level. Since the seminal work of Ira Sharkansky (1970), it has been recognized that urban decision makers develop patterns of policy making that are very difficult to change. This same phenomenon occurs among street-level bureaucrats. As these bureaucrats carry out policy they develop "successful" ways of behaving. Secure in their ways, they will continue in them until there are overwhelming environmental pressures to change. Eulau and Prewitt (1973) refer to this tendency as **policy momentum.** Policy momentum is particularly prevalent at the interlocal level. As a study of two local programs in Nebraska concluded, "left undisturbed...we can expect local decision makers to pursue, incrementally, policies consistent with the predominant momentum built up over time" (Mueller 1984:167). All of these things combine with the remarkable durability of the three federalist cultures to ensure, in Madison's terms, the "maintenance of order."

Political scientists also often refer to the *spread of innovation* between units and levels of government. An important finding of innovation studies is the widespread suppression of innovation by the locals who look to each other to help maintain traditional elite rule, policy preferences, and the "lowest common denominator" of public policy. Perhaps the classic example of this suppression was the tactics of white officials who tried to resist the civil rights movement in the 1950s and 1960s.

These and other phenomena suggest that the interlocal pattern continues to be a powerful force in the American political economy. We recognize that there is a problem in sorting out the influences and actions of local governments from their patterns of intergovernmental relations. To some, for example, each of the four important elements just explained by interlocal patterns may be viewed as "solo" functions—a single city engaged in the unequal administration of the law, for example. However, we believe that the patterns just identified are better understood most of the time as the outcomes of borrowed and patterned relations among local governments. No person is an island, and no locality is an island.

SUMMARY

The political-culture roots of the interlocal political-economy pattern are found in the myth of grass-roots democracy—that commitment to extreme decentralization that Thomas Jefferson was so enamoured of. Jefferson believed that extreme decentralization was better in large part because he believed that the people at the grass roots—who at that time lived largely in rural areas and small villages—were better. When disillusionment with the inherent virtue of locals set in, the Progressives became active in the interlocal pattern, pushing reformist proposals that they thought would neutralize whatever evil tendencies might be found in the locals. In this way, moralist, middle-class values combined with the extreme decentralization of Jefferson to form the culture of the interlocal pattern. Most urban-reform proposals even today have their roots in these two traditions.

In a period when much is made of the "nationalization of the states," the vitality of the interlocal pattern needs to be emphasized. It would be hard to identify a more important development in the American federal system than what we have called the localization of national policy concerns. Locals have turned the table on the feds—in spite of all the talk about legal subservience, the "intrusiveness of conditions of aid," and the like.

Thus locals are not powerless victims in the federal system. The vitality of locals is seen in part in their dynamic relationship with national policy actors. These relationships have been called *direct federalism*. They are better described in terms of the national–local pattern—the subject of the next chapter.

KEY CONCEPTS AND THEMES FOR REVIEW

grass-roots democracy
localization of national policy concerns
policy momentum
privatization
Progressive movement
service contracts
service transfers
urban problem
urban service delivery

Subnational Federalism:

7

The national–local pattern

The last pattern of federal relations we will discuss involves the national government and local governments. As we did with the other patterns, we will attempt to clarify this model's roots in the federalist culture of this country and broadly trace its evolution to the present day. Then we will explain the basics of national–local relations in the political economy. Next we will attempt to identify what the national–local pattern explains today by examining its meaning in politics, policy, and economics.

ROOTS AND EVOLUTION: IS THIS PATTERN REALLY
THE NEW KID ON THE BLOCK?

One of the views of the traditional literature on federalism is that direct national–local relations came late to the American system. W. Brooke Graves reported that as recently as 1932, the American delegation to the International Congress of Cities was the only one of more than forty to report no direct administrative relationships between the central government and cities (1964:655). More recent work declares flatly that relations between the national government and local units were minor up to the 1930s and that "direct federalism" was a product of various national fiscal assistance to localities beginning with the **New Deal** (Glendening and Reeves 1984:171).

Thus the national–local pattern is pictured as the new kid on the block, almost an interloper in the American federal system.

It is certainly true that the federalist bargain struck at the Constitutional Convention was silent on the relationship between the nation and local units of government. In Chapter 5, we found that the federalist bargain was also silent on the relationship between the states and locals. This "nondecision" left the relationship between the nation and local units to be worked out in practice, over the years, in much the same manner as the relationship between localities and the states. Thus, what has developed is explainable more by political practice than by constitutional provisions or statutory or institutional arrangements.

This last point is fundamental to an understanding of national–local relations. In the first place, it corrects somewhat the misleading perspective generally found in the literature that national–local relations are somehow outside the "normal" pattern of federalism. We like the perspective of Roscoe Martin in this regard:

> [Federalism] is an evolving arrangement for the division of powers and the distribution of responsibilities among governments of different levels. Far from being rigidly bound by philosophical or ideological conceptions, the federal system is a pragmatic scheme that not only permits but also requires adjustments to meet the varying needs of changing times. American federalism...is a major instrumentality for adjusting the relations among nation, states, and localities so as to make and keep government in its totality abreast of the needs of the people. (1965:41)

Certainly, to date the beginnings of national–local relations with the New Deal is to ignore the important political evolution of this pattern in the American federal system.

A look at this evolution corrects the misunderstanding that this model is the "new kid on the block." To take as definitive the report of the American delegation to the International Congress of Cities in 1932—that the American federal system involves no direct administrative relationships between the central government and local units—is to slight history or to have a very limited definition of administrative relationships. Daniel Elazar (1962) has demonstrated that from the early 1800s cities were practicing partners in many ventures with the nation and/or states. The first major example of such cooperation was the establishment of joint programs of internal improvements. The first known national–local project involved the city of Norfolk, Virginia, and the U.S. Army Engineers in the construction of a canal in 1816. Others in the first half of the 1800s included the provision of appropriate educational facilities, the provision of necessary and acceptable public welfare assistance, and to some extent the development of a sound fiscal system.

These efforts, by any reasonable definition of administrative relationships, involved many of the "normal" devices of federal relations. For example, in the areas of education and internal improvements, the instrument for implementing national–local agreements was the grant-in-aid. The difference was that the grant was in the form of land, not money. Since the national government held all public lands, national–local relations reflected then, as now, the use of the superior resources of the nation in meeting common program needs.

These earlier examples of nation–local cooperation not only used many of the devices but also reflected many of the characteristics of present-day relations:

> The practice of cooperation has combined national standards with state and local responsibility for administration. This has had the effect of placing a floor under performance without destroying local responsibility for what have been, in impact at least, local problems ... the setting of standards has entailed a measure of national supervision in the matters both of fiscal management and of achievement of program goals, and this has raised recurrently the question of centralization. These features suggest the nature of cooperative federalism as it has been practiced almost from the beginning of our history. (Martin 1965:39)

The practice of giving substantial responsibilities to locals for implementing national policy has been a part of American federalist practices from the start. Simply because it is not traceable to direct constitutional prescription or to clear statutory authority does not make the practice of recent vintage. Looking at federalism through institutional lenses has resulted in a too limited view of the dynamic evolution of the American federal system.

Another reason for the difficulty of seeing the important role of cities in the early history of federal relations is that America was then a rural nation by and large (Martin 1965:39). The problems that were the basis for much national–local cooperation involved agriculture and the distribution of goods—matters common to all general subnational governments (including the states). In short, America in the first half of the nineteenth century did not face the highly specialized problems of an urban society. Even so, "the cities were practicing partners in many cooperative programs from the early 1800's, and in some they were signatories...of the agreement on which cooperation rested" (Martin 1965:39).

In addition, there were significant indirect and informal administrative contacts between national and local officials. Such contacts were in the form of "expert advice" and "technical assistance" given by national officials in field or regional offices to their administrative counterparts in local governments. Obviously, such contacts have increased dramatically with the emergence of a differentiated urban society. Thus it is simply not true that pre –New Deal national–local relations involved no "**direct administrative relationships.**"

And certainly it should not be overlooked that there were frequent political relations among all levels of the federal system. As we saw in the last two chapters, local governments, though legally subservient to the states, have hardly assumed a subservient political posture to either the states or the nation. We will see later in this chapter that the political relationships between locals and state and national government actors have become so complex that a viable strategy for locals is to cut the best deal possible with either jurisdiction. In Chapter 9, national–local political relations are described within the bigger picture of the public policy process. The third partner in the federal system, the one of which the Constitution would not speak, has "come a long way, baby."

FDR, Hamilton, and Enlightened Centralism

The preceding discussion is an attempt to place national–local relations in a more accurate perspective. It is not meant to disparage the impact of the New Deal on this pattern. The New Deal transformed both the nature and the scope of national–local relations. There were a number of factors in this transformation (Graves 1964; Martin 1965; Elazar 1984); we emphasize two of them.

The first factor was the economic realities of the Great Depression. Simply put, there was an urgent need to distribute relief funds. State and local governments were experiencing declining revenues. The resulting fiscal stress only dramatized the financial and administrative inability of states to respond to the crisis. The realization of this fact led New Deal policy makers to find ways to short-circuit the states and deal directly with cities. Thus, many of the early New Deal welfare and public works programs— such as the Federal Emergency Relief Administration, the Civil Works Administration, the Works Progress Administration, and the Public Works Administration—provided financial assistance to *both* state and local governments. As a congressional study from the New Deal period suggested, cities almost immediately assumed a prominent role in the implementation of New Deal legislation:

> The Federal Government turned to the local units with the realization that their programs would remain on paper unless communities of all types were receptive and undertook projects, issued bonds, and in other ways carried out measures of relief and the construction or repair of the municipal physical plant. (National Resources Committee 1939:61)

Why the strategy of going directly to local units was adopted over a strategy of building up the capacity of states to deliver programs is a study in itself. An important part of the answer to that question involves the second factor that helps explain the change in national–local relations— Franklin Roosevelt's efforts to forge a nationwide coalition and his relationships in that effort with big-city bosses. In this respect, the conventional wisdom does not seem to be borne out by the facts. Conventional wisdom argues that Roosevelt built a nationwide coalition and destroyed the big-city machines by preempting the basis of machine political power—the giving of services to the poor in the nation's large cities. In essence, the argument goes, big-city bosses had political power because they provided food, shelter, coal, jobs, and other assistance to the poor. Roosevelt's welfare program—social security, direct assistance, minimum-wage requirements, and public-works jobs in particular—supposedly destroyed the need for the bosses and thus the base of their power.

Lyle Dorsett has pointed out several fallacies in that thesis. The most important fallacy for our purposes deserves special attention:

> Actually the distribution function was not preempted by the federal government: under the New Deal many welfare programs were financed in Washington, but they were *directed* at the local level.
>
> The evidence shows that where New Deal welfare legislation had any measurable impact, it was to strengthen individual urban bosses and their political organizations. (1977:113; italics in original)

Dorsett does not argue that all big-city bosses prospered under Roosevelt. Whether an individual boss prospered or suffered depended on whether or not he cooperated with the Roosevelt program. The point is that New Deal welfare programs were *directed at the local level.* The new largesse from Washington could be directed to the individuals whom local decision makers wished to benefit, and withheld from those whom local elites did not want to benefit. Thus the Roosevelt coalition could be forged without necessarily disturbing the status quo at the local level.

From a political economy perspective, what emerged with the New Deal acceleration of national–local relations was a new external source of funding for local elites. The New Deal avalanche of programs put the distributive aspects of national–local relations on the front burner. Since the New Deal, the question has been how far locals can go in distributing benefits and in determining the implementation of "national" goals. The answer is usually "Pretty far." In fact, how the power of locals interacts with national policy is at the core of the national–local model.

In the Roosevelt administration we see a change not only in national–local relations but in that model's political-culture roots as well. It is clear that the roots of the national–local model are found in the Hamiltonian vision of central elite dominance. Ironically, it was Theodore Roosevelt, fifth cousin of Franklin, who best articulated the new enlightened centralist intent that became, under FDR, the cornerstone of the national–local model. In a speech at Osawatomie, Kansas, in 1910 Theodore argued that:

> ... the National Government belongs to the whole American people, and where the whole American people are interested, that interest can be guarded only by the National Government. The betterment which we seek must be accomplished, I believe, mainly through the National

Government. The American people are right in demanding that New Nationalism without which we cannot cope with new problems. The New Nationalism puts national need before sectional or personal advantage. It is impatient of the utter confusion that results from local legislatures attempting to treat national issues as local issues. It is still more impatient of the impotence which springs from over-divisions of governmental powers, the impotence which makes it possible for local selfishness or legal cunning, hired by wealthy special interest, to bring national activities to a deadlock. (quoted in Sherwood 1948:51)

Alexander Hamilton could not have agreed more. Franklin Roosevelt made the views expressed in Teddy's statement the operating code of his new political coalition. And as a result of FDR's efforts, the new goals of centralism had a softer, more populist flavor in the 1930s. Centralism as a federalist culture had experienced substantial mellowing under the influence of Woodrow Wilson and the Progressives. Roosevelt reasserted this **enlightened centralism** as a strategy for change, and it was at the heart of the New Deal throughout the 1930s. One result, as we have seen, was a vastly increased policy role for governments at all levels. Certainly, the new centralism gave a substantial boost to subnational federalist structures, and particularly to the national–local model.

NUTS AND BOLTS

After World War II, national–local relations expanded even more rapidly, taking a number of very important forms. Seven of these forms deserve special attention.

First, and in some ways most important, national–local program relations take two forms—**national general programs** and direct national–local (or **direct federalism) programs.** All general programs have important consequences for and necessitate substantial involvement by local governments. That is what most policy analysts mean when they say that public policy in the United States is intergovernmental. But in addition to the expansion of general intergovernmental programs, there has also occurred an expansion of direct federalism. Among the most important of the postwar direct federalism programs are planning (with the so-called 701 Program), the Community Facilities Program, and the older Urban Renewal Program. The emergence of regulatory federalism and the expansion of direct federalism have been among the most important developments in the federal system since the 1950s.

A second important form of the national–local model is found in fiscal federalism.[1] It consists of **direct national grants** to cities for specified uses. (Our city has conducted a "reduce drunk driving" program for the past three years with money from a direct national grant.) In addition to direct grants there is the pass-through component of national grants. These are the grants that go first to the states, with all or part of the money to be sent on to local units. As we noted in Chapter 5, **pass-throughs** are significant sources of revenue for locals, although the exact dollar amount involved is difficult to determine. Although made defunct in the Reagan years, **general revenue sharing** required the states to distribute two thirds of federal funds to local units and allowed considerable local discretion as to how the money would be spent. The formula to be used by states in that program was very similar to the formula used to determine state allocations. In the mid-1970s, general revenue sharing made up about 12 percent of all local funds. Finally, direct fiscal federalism includes a wide variety of **national–local loans**. The home of one of the authors is served by city water because the small town close to where he lives obtained a Farmers Home Administration loan to expand its water system. These three elements of fiscal federalism—grants (direct and pass-through), the local share of general revenue sharing, and national government loans to local units—are important examples of the national–local model.

A third form of national–local relations is what may be called **nationally encouraged regions**. These are substate creatures, but with a twist. They are "local creatures" of the feds rather than creatures of the states. There are three types of nationally encouraged regions—national program regions, regional planning councils, and councils of government (or COGs, as they are sometimes called). Along with special-district governments, nationally encouraged regions are important parts of that "shadow government" resulting in the adhocracy we evaluated in Chapter 5. We shall see later in this chapter that these nationally encouraged substate creatures have important policy implications.

The fourth and fifth forms of national–local relations often occur simultaneously. The fourth form is the wide array of national advice and assistance to locals. We saw in Chapter 5 that locals are not always quick to avail themselves of either formal advice or informal assistance from state sources. It is probable, although there are little survey data to prove it, that the same situation exists in the relationship between locals and national sources of advice and assistance. Common sense dictates that most such advice would occur in the context of the fifth form of national–local relations—the vast network of informal bureaucratic relations between local professionals and their national counterparts.

One of the most slippery forms of national–local relations consists of **informal policy interactions**. It is well known in the policy literature, for example, that local officials are important actors in the implementation process (Pressman and Wildavsky 1973; also see Chapter 10). What is not as well known, but nevertheless very important, is that locals are important actors in all phases of the policy process — even when national policy is involved. We will discuss this point in much more detail in Chapters 8–10, but it is important here to illustrate several of these phases as representative of the national–local pattern.

In policy formation, locals are important in affecting the national issue agenda. As we have seen, for all practical purposes the nuclear-freeze movement in the United States had its origin in town meetings in New England. Drunk driving, child abuse, and other issues referred to earlier began as essentially local concerns.

The most subtle policy phase that is part of the national–local model is policy enactment. We will use the term *directive enactments* in Chapter 10 for enactments that originate with the feds, often with some coercive features, but that end up dependent on and virtually revised by local negotiation before they take their final form. National regulations concerning solid-waste landfills (regulations that are "fully enacted" as far as the national decision maker is concerned) are not really enacted until local decision makers agree on the siting of a particular facility. Frequently national court cases affecting locals are also directive enactments. To the United States Supreme Court, the *Garcia* v. *San Antonio Mass Transit System* case is fully enacted. But the decision to include local employees under the provisions of the Fair Labor Standard Act as required by *Garcia* is *not* fully enacted until, say, local decision makers determine exactly how to give workers in their water department overtime pay when required by the FLSA. Thus enactment is a process of consensus adjustments in a formal government decision.

The final form of national–local relations that needs mention here is **political intergovernmental relations.** Organizations of local officials, general local interest groups, local elites, and even occasionally individuals with local concerns are active participants in an ongoing effort to influence what the national interests and Washington do. But the process of influencing is a two-way street. The public administration research literature contains careful documentation of the efforts of national agencies to sell their programs and objectives to agencies and individuals at the local level. And certainly no president or member of Congress could afford to turn a completely deaf ear to the needs of locals.

All of these are important forms of the national–local political economy. But in some ways an understanding of the national–local pattern as it functions today is best accomplished by viewing it from the bottom up. As we have indicated, today's national–local pattern is fed by the policies of the enlightened centralism of the New Deal. But at the bottom the model takes on a life separate from that of its enlightened parent, even though its fiscal techniques, regulations, and other devices spring largely from the national level. This new, separate life has come about because local elites, legal systems, officials, and interest groups in the grass-roots political and policy game are *locally determined*. It is a pattern linked to enlightened centralism through the umbilical cord of policy, but its politics, economics, and implementation are *local, local, local.* Much like the big-city bosses of the New Deal period, local policy actors and political decision makers largely direct implementation of public policy. The policy that comes out—who gets what and how they get it—is fashioned and determined largely by locals.

On the political side of the balance between the nation and locals, we have seen that the national–local pattern is a two-edged political sword. It is traditional to note that the problem at the bottom gets fed back to the top through many forms of feedback; policy formulation by national elites and officials does not take place in much of a vacuum. But more is at work here than this. In the previous chapter we labeled the recent policy activism of locals in areas traditionally of national concern the *localization of national policy concerns.* And—a final irony—in many program areas locals not only control implementation but also evaluate effectiveness. It is almost as if the locals are saying, "We will do it, we will say how well we are doing it, and on the basis of our determination of success we will have proved that locals should be given control." This is the political basis of the call from the bottom to "reduce Washington meddling." It is dualist culture recycled with a vengeance.

The expansion of the national–local pattern has raised the unasked question of the convention of 1787: What about the locals? That nondecision has now become a very deliberate decision, thanks to the New Deal, and locals have become, although in extraconstitutional fashion, important partners in the federal system. The national–local relationship is now, if not in FDR's time, a truly two-edged policy and political sword. We'll say more about this in the next section.

THE POLITICAL ECONOMY EFFECTS OF NATIONAL–LOCAL RELATIONS

Our purpose now is to examine the features of national–local federalism that have the most significance for the American political economy. We will discuss the bigger political economy picture of local influence over the implementation of policy, fiscal relations between the nation and local units, and nationally created local organizations. Finally, we will examine the search for a national urban policy. We begin with the political economy view of local influence on policy implementation, if for no other reason than to emphasize that not all important factors in federalism are fiscal. We describe the policy process in federalism more fully in Chapter 10. Here we are interested in the effects of locals on national objectives.

Locals and the Implementation of National Policy

The influence of locals on the implementation of national policy has been the subject of extensive analysis, beginning with the seminal work of

Grodzins (1966), Derthick (1972), and Eulau and Prewitt (1973). These studies primarily described local influence on the implementation of national policy. This early work is probably best represented by Derthick's conclusion that successful implementation requires involvement by national policy actors in local politics. She argued convincingly that national officials "must intervene successfully in local politics" (1972:84). This intervention was necessary because locals significantly influenced the implementation of national policy.

Later work described the characteristics of national–local interaction in policy implementation. The authors of the best known of these studies (Pressman and Wildavsky 1973) found a number of "veto points" among semiautonomous local agencies. Among these were the local offices of national departments and state and city agencies. This situation also meant that many sets of decisions and rules were in effect. For example, seventy separate agreements were necessary in order to implement federally financed public works projects in Oakland.

The problems of coordinating policies in this typically complex local environment led Pressman and Wildavsky (1973) to give their book the rather colorful subtitle *How Great Expectations in Washington Are Dashed in Oakland Or, Why It's Amazing That Federal Programs Work at All*. In most policy areas, the feds and the locals each have a stake in retaining the support and cooperation of the other (Edner 1976). As a result, considerable bargaining typically leads to mutually acceptable positions in most program enforcement.

When viewed from a political economy angle, several studies of locals and the implementation of public policy have reached some very interesting conclusions. In the first place, it is not clear that local dominance of many policy areas results in the accomplishment of national objectives. In a perceptive study, Hall and Mushkatel concluded that:

> ... in the case of the Community Development Block Grant partnership, local government partners have emerged in charge of the program they implement and, in large part, they evaluate it. Dominance of local governments in the current program can be explained as either a policy failure or success. Certainly, enough decentralization has occurred to mark the program successful by that criterion. But what of "national objectives"?...Can local governments be expected to work toward lofty ideals when the national government has abdicated its opportunity to shape program content? Is federalism, "new" or "old," viable when program and accountability become the sole prerogative of the local partner? (1985:88)

These are important points indeed. They certainly reflect a picture that is substantially different from the recent rhetoric of an "intrusive Washington" bureaucracy dominating helpless locals. The "silent partner" to the federal bargain is not so silent or accommodating.

Second, it is even more important from a political economy standpoint to identify the **policy effects** of local dominance of national policy enforcement. In this regard, Margaret Wrightson (1986) conducted an extraordinarily intriguing study of implementation of the Housing and Community Development Act. Wrightson attempted to determine which of two implementation strategies was more effective, direct federal intervention or interlocal cooperation. Although the HCD law provided for federal intervention, the Department of Housing and Urban Development developed a program allowing an alternate implementation mode. This program, the Areawide Housing Opportunity Plan, called for interlocal cooperation to accomplish the policy goal of the deconcentration of housing for low-income individuals.

Wrightson found that interlocal cooperation clearly worked: "Left to their own devices, local governments get things done faster than Washington, even when difficult choices must be made" (1986:272). But she took a close look also at which policy goals were being implemented. She argued correctly that the clear intent of the act was to offer low-income families housing opportunities in areas where housing had not previously been available to them. These areas were to offer better schools, recreation, and so on. In policy terms, the act was redistributional in intent. However, the effect of interlocal implementation was to modify the act to serve distributional aims instead. That is, the locals modified the intent of deconcentration in such a way as to provide low-income housing to those areas that "needed it." As a result, low-income families remained frozen in areas where schools and other services were inadequate. In a word, the intent to get deconcentration was transformed to a result of concentration. In Wrightson's words, interlocal cooperation raised "the potentially damaging issue of *what policy is being implemented*" (1986:272; italics in original).

Wrightson concluded that the problem in the locally run Areawide Housing Opportunity Plan "is unlikely to be resolved by interlocal cooperation" (1986:273). We would modify this conclusion somewhat. The literature on implementation suggests that locals rather effectively resolve policy—in the direction favored by locals. In the case of the intended deconcentration of low-income families, locals used and altered housing policies to accomplish primarily middle-class goals (Henry 1987:478ff.).

This study of housing had to do with an instance of formal cooperation. How much local informal collusion is there about the implementation of national policy? Local policy actors interact in myriad ways—through formal organizations and informal contacts. At this point in the study of the federal system, it is simply impossible to tell how much effect, and in what direction, this interaction has on national objectives in various policy areas. It is certainly a topic worthy of much more study.

Recent scholarship reflects considerable pessimism about the role of locals, formal or informal, in policy implementation. Peterson (1981) began this new line of inquiry, arguing cogently that distributive policies (benefits—for example, a highway—available to all comers) could be implemented effectively by locals since the costs are diffused. On the other hand, redistributive policies (those that take something from one group, such as a corporate tax break, and give it to others) were simply self-defeating for locals. Locals had to pay the price of choosing winners and losers. Wrightson concluded that "insofar as the difficult problems facing urban areas are concerned—the devolution of domestic policy responsibility may need to come to rest on the shoulders of the states. Interlocal cooperation is a less than effective substitute for the involvement of higher levels of government" (1986:273). And the author of a case study of housing policy in Omaha and Lincoln, Nebraska, bluntly asserted that "the need arises from time to time in specific instances for federal administrators to play hardball with local officials....When local officials prove to be recalcitrant because their history of policy implementation is not in tune with national goals and objectives a nonincremental shove in a new direction is required" (Mueller 1984:176–77).

These suggestions may be valid. They certainly reflect the dualist idea that states are the dominant service providers and strongly echo the centralist culture (the feds should shove locals around—at least just a little). But what these prescriptions seem to overlook is what we have found evident in state–local relations—that locals are not passive objects allowing themselves to be willy-nilly shoved anywhere. The shoved can and do become the shovers. And perhaps often the locals shove to get goals not originally intended in laws.

Fiscal Relations: The Name of the Game Is Money, Money, Money

Although we have been careful to portray federalism as a great deal more than just fiscal relations, it is true that the money flows between levels of government are a very important part of federal relations in the United States. In Chapter 3 we discussed how money flows between levels. Local governments are the recipients of all three types of intergovernmental transfers from the national government—categorical grants, block grants, and general revenue sharing. Our objective now is to examine the policy effects of their transfers—that is, what difference all those fiscal details make to local units and people. We are also interested in the factors that produce those outcomes—particularly since one of the more important determinants seems to be the political culture of the local area.

It is instructive to review just briefly the development of transfers from the national government to local governments. We have referred to the significant acceleration of national–local fiscal relations as a result of the New Deal. A similar set of changes occurred during the Johnson administration beginning in 1964. Certainly one of those key changes was a sharp increase in national aid to local governments. In 1960, national revenue to all local governments was $592 million; by 1980 it had increased to $21.1 billion. Expressed in percentage terms, national aid to all local governments increased from 2.6 percent of general revenue from own sources in 1960 to 16.3 percent in 1980.

The numbers are even more impressive when cities alone are the subject of analysis. National transfers to cities increased from $256 million in 1960 to $10.8 billion in 1980. Expressed in percentage terms, such aid increased from 2.8 percent of general revenue from own sources in 1960 to 22.8 percent in 1980. (ACIR 1985c:62) However, this aid was not distributed evenly across cities; smaller and rural cities were late getting in on the act, and benefited less from the dramatic buildup in funding. Federal aid as a percent of own-source revenue of the nation's forty-seven largest cities increased from 2.6 percent in 1957 to 49.7 percent in 1978 (ACIR 1985c:30). We shall see later that this fact may have important consequences for who is hurt and who is not by possible cutbacks in the level of national spending.

The increase in national aid to locals was accompanied by a similar increase in the number of aid programs. In 1960 there were approximately 150 aided programs, in 1980 approximately 500 (ACIR 1981a:30).

What is often overlooked in financial data is the spread of aid among recipient jurisdictions. Aid to cities has expanded to the point where virtually all local units receive national funds. As the ACIR has indicated, this was not the case as recently as the early 1970s (ACIR 1981a:30). The spread of aid also involved funding special-purpose units as well as general-purpose governments. For locals, at least, this spread of aid to special-purpose units complicated their intergovernmental relations:

> Adding to the complexity of the intergovernmental partnership are organizations like Federal Regional Councils, multistate and substate regional planning and development agencies, and neighborhood bodies that have been established to plan for, administer, coordinate or spend federal money. (ACIR 1981a:30)

Obviously, such diversification among recipients increased the problems of coordination. Several major funding departments resorted to a number of gimmicks to accomplish coordination among recipient governments. The best known of these was OMB Circular A-95 (ACIR 1977:216ff.). The circular required areawide review and comment on new grant applications and projects before monies could flow to any state. The goal was to reduce program overlap, redundancy, copying of services, and therefore waste. This procedure was the most serious effort at coordinating federally assisted programs with one another and with state and local plans. The circular was repealed in 1987 as a result of considerable disenchantment with the process among Reagan administration officials.

A second area of significant change during the Johnson administration was in the practical features of aid programs. The most important of these functional changes was the decision to use federal aid to stimulate state and local action in pursuit of national objectives. Previously, aid was designed almost exclusively to support ongoing operations of state and local governments (Sundquist and Davis 1969:7). The ACIR is accurate in saying that there were some programs prior to the 1960s that sought to accomplish national objectives (1977:29). But the Johnson administration sought to use its fiscal muscle in a centralist style to prod state and local governments into new policy areas such as poverty, crime, unemployment, illiteracy, housing, and urban development—programs deemed necessary if the **Great Society goals** for the nation were to be realized.

It was this latter point—the desire to accomplish national objectives through expansion of money flows—that stimulated an increase in the number of controls and conditions attached to grants. These infamous "strings" were discussed in Chapter 3, and that material should be reviewed in this context. Such strings were not as "extensive, expensive, and intrusive" as some have thought (ACIR 1981a:30). Rather, many of the grants were highly *fungible* (they could be used for purposes other than those specified by the granting agency). Also, audit trails were indeterminate, and most federal agencies lacked the staff and resources, if not the will, to vigorously enforce those conditions. It is true, however, that the sheer number of conditions increased during the 1960s and 1970s.

Given the emphasis on national objectives, what are the **policy outcomes** and **effects** of transfers to local units? Does the use of national money result in the accomplishment of national objectives? If so, or if not, what are the determinants of those policy outcomes? With some answers to these questions, we learn a good deal about the dynamics of the national–local model.

Thomas Dye and Thomas Hurley conducted an extremely valuable study of whether federal aid programs responded to urban problems such as housing, poverty, and crime (1978:196ff.). The first two of their research propositions deserve special attention:

(1) whether *total federal outlays* in the cities are correlated with any generally accepted measures of social need in cities—poverty, overcrowding, old age, female-headed households, racial imbalance, mortality rates, segregation, crime, income inequality, or age of cities;

(2) whether *total federal outlays* have a redistributional effect, that is whether they are negatively associated with measures of economic resources—home ownership, property value, median educational level, median family income. (1978:196–97)

The other research propositions included whether federal outlays changed over time, whether federal grants-in-aid were positively associated with need, and whether state grants-in-aid were more responsive to indicators of need than federal grants. The study found that variations in federal spending were only weakly associated with **urban needs.** Dye and Hurley express the results this way:

> These findings lend some empirical support to the notion that aggregate federal spending in cities is not directed at the cities with the greatest recognized needs. Moreover, HEW spending is *not* closely associated with poverty, female-headed households, aged, deathrates, segregation, inequality, or even social dependency. HUD spending is *not* closely related to room crowding, inadequate housing, non-home ownership, or the age of the city. OEO spending in *not* closely related to poverty. And so it goes. (1978:206–7)

Moreover, as a final blow to the egos of the feds, the study found that there is a slight tendency for variations in state spending to be *more* closely associated with urban needs than variations in national grants.

Dye and Hurley are careful to point out that their approach used aggregate data. Thus they emphasize that the situation may be different within a particular city. On the basis of their aggregate analysis, however, they conclude that the national approach has "failed to produce a federal urban policy with concrete goals, clear directions, or distinct priorities" (1978:207). Expressed slightly differently, when locals are placed in control of the implementation of national policy, local objectives and goals will redirect or displace national priorities.

Ironically, recent directions in national fiscal policy have had serious implications for the national objective of meeting "urban needs." The intergovernmental transfer policy of Reagan's New Federalism appears to be having the most damaging impact on those metropolitan areas with the strongest commitments to social goals (reducing poverty, improving housing, and so on). The findings of a recent study are important:

> If one expects the impact of the New Federalism to be neutral in its local government consequences, then these results suggest that many difficulties may face policy makers. It appears the local impact of large-scale, across-the-board cuts has the potential of most affecting those areas which have shown the largest commitments to social goals and those areas undergoing both population and economic decline. These are precisely the areas which will have the most difficulty replacing intergovernmental dollars with locally raised revenues. (Johnson 1985:721)

What the research by Johnson assumes is that present policy favors the continuance of the "social goals" objectives of the past. Many of these goals were redistributive. Thus current national intergovernmental transfer policy may serve, in more effective ways than some have thought, to reverse the Great Society's goals of social redistribution.

There are those who maintain that the New Federalism is an attempt to fundamentally redirect public policy rather than an effort simply to reverse Johnson administration policy. Demetrios Caraley is among the more effective representatives of this group: He concluded that "the 'New Federalism'...has represented a bold and controversial attempt to revise fifty years of American domestic policy by disassembling the constellation of grants to local and state governments that the federal government was using to help poor people and needy jurisdictions" (1986:289). Thus, in political economy terms, the **Reagan New Federalism** will have four effects. First, "the disparities that already exist between rich and poor people and between rich and poor local and state jurisdictions would get larger" (Caraley 1986:296). In essence, Caraley comes to the same conclusion as that of Johnson quoted earlier. Reductions in federal aid flows will have a differential impact on local jurisdictions, and some localities will have more difficulty replacing lost federal dollars with locally raised revenues. Some research conducted by the Urban Institute's series on Reagan public policies has tended to confirm this view (see Palmer and Sawhill, 1985).

Second, "the vast majority of large central cities of metropolitan areas would be hurt" (Caraley 1986:296). Johnson (1985) suggested that these are the very jurisdictions that had made the largest commitment to the Great Society social goals of meeting "urban needs." As we indicated earlier in this section, small and rural cities—those cities less likely to participate in redistributive policy—benefited less from the acceleration of national aid during the Johnson administration. The large central cities gained the most in the 1960s and stood to lose the most in the late 1980s.

Third, "even wealthy jurisdictions will have [an] incentive to not increase or to reduce poverty-related services and benefits" (Caraley 1986:297). To do either of these things, Caraley argued, would be to create a "high-service and benefit-consuming" environment that would serve as a magnet to low-income families. In a period of aid-flow reduction, no jurisdiction would chose to create such an environment.

Fourth, "all of the previous factors in combination will produce a constant 'ratcheting down' of minimum benefits and services for the poor" (Caraley 1986:297). The third factor, Caraley maintained, would mean that other local jurisdictions would have to create a "low tax/high essential services/low poverty services" environment in order to stay competitive. Thus all local jurisdictions would reduce services to the poor.

Much of what Caraley argued could be called "eyeballing the data." But considerable research suggests that his predictions are highly accurate (see Benton 1986; Caputo and Johnson 1986; Caputo, Cole, and Taebel 1986; Palmer and Sawhill 1985). The analysis of the New Federalism's policy effects can tell us a lot about intergovernmental transfer effects in the American political economy (see Caputo, Cole, and Taebel 1986). Certainly, what we know about the effects of intergovernmental transfers tells us that efforts and plans to alter the federalist political economy can serve occasionally to change policy goals. The Reagan administration's policy objectives were different from those of the Johnson administration (if not from those of the previous fifty years of policy history). The structure of intergovernmental transfers, not surprisingly, was changed in the 1980s in pursuit of those changed goals. Certainly, also, the policy effects of intergovernmental transfers reflect the dynamic, interdependent nature of the political economy; official goals and actual outcomes can be two very different things (see more about the fate of the New Federalism in Chapters 9 and 10 and later in this chapter).

Locals also have to function within the constraints of national policy as it shifts from administration to administration. If nothing else, locals should by now know better than to take the feds seriously about keeping up long-range redistributive social objectives. And national policy makers, as long as federal intergovernmental transfers are directed by locals, must function within the constraints of local policy forces and outcomes.

Since locals in the recipient jurisdiction exercise such significant influence over grants, the determinants of local grant behavior are important. Three such determinants deserve special mention. The first is the **fiscal condition** of the recipient jurisdiction. We have mentioned that some jurisdictions are more likely than others to use grant funds for redistributive purposes. The "fiscal variable" is one of the most important factors in this variation. The proposition is best stated this way: "The more fiscally hard pressed a jurisdiction is, the more likely it is to merge federal grant funds with its own resources and use them to pay for the basic services it provides" (Nathan 1983:51). *Basic services* here means much the same thing as *essential services* in the Caraley analysis. That is, fiscally strapped cities will merge grant funds with own-source money to pay for such things as police, fire, sewers, and other "traditionally" local services. Conversely, local jurisdictions "with the luxury to do so prefer to isolate federal aid funds and use them for their prescribed purposes" (Nathan 1983:51).

Nathan argues that the reason more affluent jurisdictions prefer to use federal funds for their prescribed purposes is because such funds are "unstable." Funding unreliability and instability makes political officials in affluent jurisdictions fearful of becoming dependent on federal funds (Nathan 1983:52).

A second important determinant of grant effects is the **federal representation function**. The make-up of a state's congressional delegation is much more statistically significant than an "economic need" factor. The situation is well expressed in a study of who gets grants and why:

> Political considerations are the primary determinants of the allocation
> of Federal grants. The grants examined here were all grants intended to
> be given based upon relative economic need. However, variables
> measuring the percent of the population below the poverty line, per

capita income, percent of population in urban areas, per capita income and population were not statistically significant in explaining the level of per capita grants. Instead, the data showed the grants to be allocated based upon political power. Per capita grants were higher in those states with more seniority in the Senate, with a larger percentage of majority party members in the House, and with members on the influential House and Senate committees. (Holcombe and Zardkoohi 1981:399)

To put it differently, those with political clout, get. And if a jurisdiction has political clout in Congress, it has political clout in the funding agencies. So much for the "metropolitan problem"—just insure that your congressional representatives stay elected!

The third determinant of local grant outcomes, and one of the more interesting ones from our perspective, is the **local political culture.** In a "bottom-up" analysis, Terry Clark examined what he called the rather considerable "resiliency to intergovernmental grants by cities" (1983:63). Clark's point on local resiliency is important: "Intergovernmental grants significantly increased local spending for only 2 of the 4 dependent variables [in the study], and suppressed only 1 of 28 effects of major local variables. Thus, more local initiative remains than many accounts suggest" (1983:61). What Clark found was that local jurisdictions' attitudes towards federal grants reflect their own local dynamics. Clark argued that some localities pursue, while others avoid, intergovernmental grants. He found that the most important factor in local dynamics was the political culture of the area. He developed four categories of local political cultures: New Deal Democrats, New Deal Republicans, ethnic politicians, and new fiscal populists. The urban Republican and fiscal populist leadership and culture generally avoid grants; the others "choose and pick." Others have found less support for urban aid and public services in the southern and Sunbelt states (Yiennakis 1977:116; Lupsha and Siembieda 1977:169–90).

It should come as no surprise that we believe that many of these findings are probably better understood in terms of the historic federalist cultures than by new names. For example, the urban Republicans, fiscal populists, and southerners are very likely strong supporters of dualism (a rose is still a rose by any other name). The point is that differences in local political cultures were found to be among the best explanations for why cities chose particular types of intergovernmental grants and avoided others, as well as for why some cities chose not to pursue any grants. Clark is probably dead right that "political activists and urban analysts could work more effectively if they had a sharper sense of how local political cultures shape urban policy orientations" (1983:63). One of the basic themes of this book is that observers of the federal system generally could work more effectively if they had a sharper sense of how *federalist* cultures shape power and policy in the American political economy.

Nationally Encouraged Regions:
Now You See Them, Now You Don't

The discussion of fiscal relations in the national–local model should have made one point clear. It is not easy for the feds to buy national objectives by routing money through locals. Although changes in national policy preferences do trickle down to affect locals, the determinants of grant policy outcomes are primarily local. And, if we know anything about policy implementation at all, we know that locals can modify or redirect policy in such a way as to displace national policy objectives. Thus an alternative strategy would be to create institutions more directly tied to the national government and more immediately responsive to it. This strategy, although often overlooked in the mainstream literature on federalism, has been tried with a vengeance. It has resulted in a large number of **nationally encouraged regions.** There are three types of these regions: national program regions, regional planning councils, and councils of government.

National program regions—about 4000 of them—have been established by a number of federal agencies and grant programs. Some of these regions are single-purpose program areas. The Department of Agriculture was especially prone to use the single-purpose program region in a number of its New Deal–inspired programs. For example, the most numerous of these regions are the Agricultural Stabilization and Conservation Committees and the Soil Conservation Service districts. The "agricultural democracy" advocated by the department spawned a large number of other regions, including the Extension Service, the Rural Electric Cooperatives, and farm-loan associations. These groups were called *federally engineered local government* by Morton Grodzins (1966:191), an apt term indeed. Other national program regions are policy councils for the administrative department involved. Examples here are the Economic Development Districts of the Department of Commerce and the Rural Area Development Councils of the Department of Agriculture. These policy councils, moreover, exist in some twenty national grant-in-aid programs, including law enforcement, work force, health, economic development, resource conservation, air quality, transportation, environmental protection, social services, and comprehensive planning (ACIR 1976:106).

Regional planning councils are created by the states to serve a wide variety of functions. One of the most important stimuli for such councils was OMB Circular A-95. The A-95 process, mentioned earlier, mandated an areawide clearinghouse for the development and review of grant proposals by substate jurisdictions in the region. The areawide A-95 units (abolished in 1982) were also used as the implementing agency for "a little under half of the Federally encouraged districts in their respective regions" (ACIR 1976:107). For example, they were often the agencies responsible for securing environmental impact statements in the regions they served. The establishment of these units was encouraged also by Section 701 of the Urban Planning Assistance Act of 1954. Section 701 allocated national money to state, regional, and local planning agencies "to promote coordinated planning." The availability of such monies was a powerful stimulus of the states for the creation of these *state planning districts* or *area planning and development districts,* as they are variously called among the states.

Section 701 was also a powerful stimulus for the creation of **councils of government** (COGs), the third type of nationally encouraged region. COGs are voluntary regional associations of local governments (under permissive legislation of the "architect" of local government, obviously). Normally, each local government has one vote, thus diffusing the influence of the central city. Although COGs have no governmental powers or operating authority, their position as the locus of substantial federal funding means that they "wield considerable authority under these programs" (ACIR 1976:106). Their original purpose was to provide a voluntary forum for interlocal communication, planning, and problem solving.

The absence of careful evaluation of nationally encouraged regions makes it difficult to assess their performance in the American political economy. Several things can be said, however. In the first place, the use of national program regions has created a context in which substantial conflict with other jurisdictions can occur. An analysis of the Department of Agriculture's Agriculture Stabilization Committees found that:

> ASC offices in every rural county compete with the county government in attracting leaders, skilled personnel, electorate attention, and in other ways. In many areas, county operations are dwarfed by ASC programs, as measured by dollar expenditures or impact on the resident, or both. This competition has without doubt been deleterious to county government. More important, by not working collaboratively with local governments (or states) the Department of Agriculture had deprived these governments of significant advantages. (ACIR 1966:34)

It is ironic that "agriculture democracy" may have weakened "grass-roots democracy." Some national program regions have become embroiled in conflict with other national departments or agencies. The TVA and the Soil Conservation Service are an example. One study of their conflict reported that its basis was:

> ... deeply rooted in the nature of the programs, the organizational structure of the two agencies, and differences over the approach to be taken in resource development. (Wells 1964:84)

Interagency rivalry and conflict is not an isolated phenomenon in American government, of course. But the adhocracy of nationally encouraged regions seems especially suited for such conflict.

Second, nationally encouraged regions, while using the rhetoric of dualism and participatory democracy, often function in the centralist culture as instruments of national control, as Morton Grodzins pointed out in his study of the Agriculture Stabilization and Conservation Committees:

> What is said to be ideal local democracy is also, *par excellence,* a device of manipulation and control from the top ... Committees are inundated with instruction from Washington and state headquarters, they are jacked up weekly by visits from farmer fieldmen (the name given to regional supervisors) and commodity specialists, and they are urged to greater and more effective action in state and regional meetings. The democratic grass roots committees are spoken of in Washington as "federal instrumentalities." To the extent that Washington officials preserve the committees in order to mask central control, or make it more palatable, they are guilty of using democratic forms in an authoritarian manner. (1966:351–52)

Grodzins certainly was correct in sensing an inconsistency in rhetoric and practice. However, we do not think that what he reports is to be interpreted as a scheme by power-hungry central bureaucrats to use the ideals of democracy as a conspiracy to further their aims. Rather, what is at work in many of these nationally encouraged districts is the clear interplay of two federalist cultures. The dualist federal culture is used largely as a means of gaining acceptance and legitimacy for the activity at the local level. The centralist federal culture is invoked largely as a means of gaining acceptance and legitimacy for the activity at the national level. Both the national purpose (centralist culture) and the local outcomes (dualist culture) of the new device of nationally encouraged districts must be sold to skeptical political decision makers and the affected clientele.

A third factor that needs to be stressed in an assessment of nationally encouraged regions is that they reflect, as clearly as can be found in the American system, what has been referred to as *bureaucratic politics.* A number of years ago G. Homer Durham predicted that "the structure of intergovernmental relations...affords a wider play for administrative politics...than is possible in a direct service...," and that administrative politics may be regarded as "the basis and core of a rising federal politic in which the generic concept of 'administrative politics' threatens to replace the traditional 'politics *and* administrative,' and to embrace the entire process" (1940:4–5). Durham's prediction could not be more descriptive of nationally encouraged regions. These regions reflect a displacement of traditional politics by the politics of bureaucracy. Public policy is made almost entirely by "experts," and policy implementation is almost entirely the domain of professional managers. And all of this from a top-down perspective, with professional bureaucrats in Washington providing the cues that fellow professionals at the service level feel "professionally bound" to follow. In a discussion of inadequate citizen involvement and political accountability, the ACIR described the situation this way:

Present functional assignment patterns frequently neglect the need for citizen access, control, and participation in the delivery of services. Regional special districts are often mandated by the states and fail to develop effective working relationships with general purpose local governments. (1976:111)

It is ironic that a movement whose impetus is found in a desire for "agriculture democracy" not only weakened grass-roots democracy but also displaced traditional politics with bureaucratic politics.

These problems, accelerated by the sometimes purist dualism of the Reagan administration, resulted in a substantial shift in national policy on nationally encouraged regions. Beginning in the early 1980s, Congress, at the president's request, began to reduce grant support for regional agencies, particularly planning commissions. In 1982 the Section 701 program was eliminated altogether by Congress. In that same year, President Reagan revoked the A-95 review process. These rather small changes will affect regional planning councils and COGs, and leave virtually untouched national program regions. This shift in federal policy indicates the problems of and skepticism about nationally encouraged regions as a strategy for accomplishing national objectives. It illustrates again the highly complex but very dynamic character of the national–local pattern.

Can We and Should We Have a National Urban Policy?

Whatever the answer to these two questions, the one point on which urban specialists agree is that the American political economy does not have an urban policy. Not only has national policy making failed to produce an urban policy with "concrete goals, clear directions, or distinct priorities," as Dye and Hurley (1978) maintain, it has failed to produce an urban policy at all. Indeed, there has been wide vacillation in national policy. Several observers have come to a conclusion identical to that of Sweat and Bingham: "National urban policies over the last 40 years have swung wildly from conservative neglect to excessive liberal outpourings of federal concern, dollars and controls" (1987:22). Given such "wild swings," can we really have a national urban policy?

A national urban plan was first proposed by Robert Merriam in 1969 (ACIR 1976:262). Merriam's cogent argument received substantial support from many sources. Even so, "it is not surprising that no national 'urban plan' has ever come forth from the White House...." (ACIR 1976:262). The reason for this, the ACIR concluded, is the nature of the presidency: "How Congress is structured is probably not quite as important as how the presidency is structured to deal with a particular problem....The American Presidency is not well equipped to deal with urban problems....the structure of the institutionalized Presidency does not make urban public policy a central concern" (ACIR 1976:262). But an examination of recent presidencies suggests that urban problems and policy were central concerns.

Urban policy has been a central concern of the American presidency since the administration of Lyndon Johnson. We have referred to the significant expansion in the number and scope of grants-in-aid in that administration. These grants were designed to pursue "national objectives" over a wide range of social welfare problems. This new approach involved new legislation, such as the Economic Opportunity Act of 1964. The Office of Economic Opportunity declared "war on poverty" by creating new institutions empowered to implement innovations that the established bureaucracies were too conservative to attempt. Among the most controversial of the OEO features was the provision that the poor themselves should participate through community action programs in the design and implementation of programs to fight poverty. Other new provisions were attached to established federal programs. For example, the Elementary and Secondary Education Act of 1965 moved national involvement in funding education in the new direction of earmarking certain funds for schools with large numbers of economically disadvantaged students. Along with changing fiscal relations, the Johnson administration elevated urban concerns to cabinet-level status. The Department of Housing and Urban Development was created in 1965 and vested with the responsibility for coordinating a wide range of national urban programs.

The Nixon administration attempted to modify the Johnson approach. Substantial evidence suggests that the purpose behind the Nixon approach was political—namely, the reorienting of urban policy to serve more traditionally Republican constituencies and to attempt to use urban policy to broaden the appeal of the Nixon administration. On the first point, John Harrigan has concluded that "even granting President Nixon the best of intentions, many of his proposals seemed biased toward Republican-oriented constituencies, perhaps in reaction to the Great Society's bias toward Democratic constituencies" (1981:363). On the second point, Paul Dommel concludes that under Nixon "increasing amounts of aid are coming under the influence of a new 'something for everyone' distribution politics" (1975:370). These are important points and we will return to them shortly.

The Nixon urban policy, then, was a two-dimensional one. On the one hand, it did include a substantial assault on the key features of Great Society urban policy. For example, Nixon emasculated the Office of Economic Opportunity by impounding several hundred million dollars of its funds. And he selectively impounded funds for such programs as urban renewal, housing, and the Model Cities program (a centerpiece of the Johnson urban policy). On the other hand, Nixon proposed a "New Federalism" with its key policy of general revenue sharing. Nixon argued that general revenue sharing would strengthen state and local governments. Others observed that it would place substantial federal funds at the discretion of locals—with the local political culture being the environment for spending decisions (see Reagan 1972:102ff.). Certainly, local discretion created a policy environment in which the "something for everyone" policy would be more likely to dominate.

Carter made the most serious attempt until then to develop a comprehensive urban policy. First, he appointed a cabinet-level Urban and Regional Policy Group with the charge to develop an urban policy. The group's proposals (in the form of seventy-odd "options") quickly ran into a buzzsaw of bureaucratic turf-guarding. The resultant **Carter New Partnership** was more a pragmatic compromise among these factions than a coherent urban policy (Harrigan 1981:368). Key features of the policy faced stiff opposition in Congress, even from members of the president's party. The National Development Bank (originally called the National Urban Development Bank), for example, was never approved by Congress, although it was a key element in the New Partnership package.

When the key features of the Carter urban policy are examined, it is clear that, as with the Johnson and Nixon policies, political factors were predominant. Carter called for the economic revitalization of inner cities—largely through various incentives to private corporations to invest in them. The allocation of federal funds was to be targeted to the most distressed cities. And there were to be new forms of fiscal relief for city governments. In a word, the Carter urban policy was designed to move national action back into the service of Democratic constituencies.

The New Federalism of the Reagan administration has been subjected to substantial analysis (Conlan 1986; McKay 1985; Caraley and Schlussel 1986; Caputo and Johnson 1986). The key elements in the New Federalism were (1) a proposed swap of welfare programs, with the states taking over Aid for Families with Dependent Children and food stamps and the national government assuming total responsibility for medicaid; (2) a proposed turnback to the states of over forty social programs with revenues adequate to pay for them; (3) a reduction in overall federal aid flows to state and local jurisdictions; (4) the rewriting of eligibility rules for social services to restrict the number of recipients; and (5) the virtual abolishment of national public development, jobs, housing, energy, and mass-transit programs. From an urban policy perspective, the key actors in federalism, from the New Federalism perspective, were the states, not localities. In this respect, the Reagan administration is the most extreme example in this century of a dual federalist administration.

A strong case can be made that the driving objective behind the New Federalism was political—a concern for reducing the budget deficit largely through social program cuts. As a participant in the development of New Federalism acknowledged, "we allowed ourselves as an administration to be trapped into an obsession over short-term budget considerations" (Williamson 1983:31). The Reagan proposals ran into a buzzsaw of opposition by governors. Some observers believe that it was possible for the administration to strike a deal with the governors. Such a compromise would have involved commitment by the administration of more funds to meet some of the urgent problems the governors felt their states faced. Reagan was unwilling to compromise on that point, and as a result the New Federalism proposals were implemented in a rather piecemeal fashion, and primarily in the area of reducing federal aid flows to states and localities.

This sketchy review of recent administrations shows that urban policy has been a central concern of the presidency at least since Lyndon Johnson. What we see are presidents playing out their own political culture beliefs about the federal system (see Chapter 3). Franklin Roosevelt's enlightened centralism and Ronald Reagan's rhetorical dual federalism are perhaps the most cohesive such belief systems. And we see extraordinary efforts made to mobilize political forces to change the output of the American political economy in directions favored by the president. Of course, Lyndon Johnson sought to have national policy serve Democratic constituencies, Richard Nixon Republican constituencies. Federalism from the beginning has been about the intersection of politics and economics.

Although we do not have a single national urban policy that endures from president to president, it is not true that no urban policy exists. In the American political economy, urban policy unfolds in large part through the interplay of national–local forces. What varies between presidents is not their desire to redirect the output of the policy economy in directions they favor, but their effectiveness in achieving that redirection.

SUMMARY

National–local relations accelerated in the twentieth century as a result of efforts to cope with the problems of urbanization, and because of the redirection of the national political economy under the Progressives and during the New Deal and the post–World War II years.

Although national–local relations have little basis in the constitutional period or design, they do have roots in the earliest national grant and economic development programs. Also, the patterns of national–local relations are generally guided by the three national traditions of federalism. However, since the mid-twentieth century, the locals have had more say in the creation, direction, and outcomes of what originally were national grants and programs that served national political powers and purposes. In fact, the national–local relations of the 1880s to the 1930s accelerated the modern patterns of interlocal and substate federalism in the latter two thirds of the twentieth century, as we have seen in earlier chapters. Today, national–local relations involve complex two-way avenues of political influence, economics, and policy control, which in turn still largely involve national and local elites and government agencies. How federalism arbitrates the power struggle among these and many other interests is the subject of the next several chapters.

KEY CONCEPTS AND THEMES FOR REVIEW

Carter New Partnership
councils of government
direct administrative relationships
direct federalism programs
direct national grants (catagorical and block)
enlightened centralism
federal representation function
general revenue sharing
Great Society goals
informal policy interactions
local political culture
national general programs
national–local loans
nationally encouraged regions
national program regions
New Deal
pass-throughs
policy effects and policy outcomes
political intergovernmental relations
Reagan New Federalism
regional planning councils
urban needs

NOTES

[1]We know that tables of financial data do not make for the most exciting reading. But certainly every student of federalism should be aware of an annual publication of the Advisory Commission on Intergovernmental Relations that records financial trends both within and among all three levels of government. This annual publication—*Significant Features of Fiscal Federalism*—contains much valuable data on public-sector fiscal affairs.

The Power-System Environment of Federalism:

8

Who has the power and how they use it

This chapter and the next one introduce the topic of federalism and power politics in America. In particular, this chapter is about how power systems operate in the intergovernmental context. The next chapter summarizes how federalism alters the best-laid plans of power elites and interests and how this alteration affects policy outcomes. Part of the discussion, then, has to do with the thorny subject of what **power** is, who has it, and how much of it they have. But the central concern is federalism—how those who are powerful attempt to cope with federalism and how federalism regulates the powerful and affects policy results. As these two chapters will show, federalism is perhaps the most important regulator of power in American politics.

Our exploration of federalism and power will start with the question "What is power?" Then we will summarize who are the powerful groups in America and how they exercise their power. We will then examine how political power is forced across intergovernmental battle lines. This foundation will enable us in the next chapter to summarize the most important issue — how federalism affects power and policy outcomes in America. We believe that the major challenge posed by power research to the study of federalism is not merely that writers on federalism have largely ignored power research (which they have), but is rather the issue of whether federalism successfully thwarts elite power or not. Thus we are interested in exploring how federalism has widely underestimated but extremely strong regulatory effects on power elites and powerful interest groups.

IDEAS OF INTERGOVERNMENTAL POLITICAL POWER

The Study of Power

The study of power is complex and tricky. There is a long history of careful investigations of power structures in America. These studies cut across both sociology and political science. In brief, the sociological tradition in power studies is guided by **elite theory.** Research on elites involves the investigation of *power elites* as a social class and the identification of their means of controlling major decisions and institutions in society. Therefore, elite theory is the theory that a ruling class controls most of the important decisions in public life most of the time. Political scientists have taken sides both for and against the idea of ruling elites, but the dominant approach in political science through the later 1960s was **pluralism.** Pluralists agree that elites are more powerful than other interests, but they see no convincing evidence of a ruling class. They recognize that the power of elites is a fact of politics and economics, but emphasize that power is at least partially fragmented some of the time and is often dispersed among competing groups in public and private life.

What can we make of these conflicting views? In the first place, there is substantial truth in both. Elite research provides considerable evidence that elites either largely control, or have what might be called competitive hegemony, over major policy decisions. For example, policies that seem particularly amenable to elite influence are international economics, trade, defense strategy, labor relations, macroeconomics, and regulation of banking and finance. Elite influence in government is said to penetrate the judiciary and the executive branch and to a lesser extent Congress. On the other hand, pluralists provide considerable evidence that elite power is limited and at least partly fragmented among competing groups. Good examples of areas where nonelites control policy are race relations, some features of government regulation, social life, law enforcement, and education. The highly visible tactics of nonelite groups—lobbying, protest, civil suits, media campaigns, and the like — are what pluralists insist counterbalance the tactics of elite interests.

As we have noted, some pluralists have argued that the existence of many competing groups using myriad pressure tactics has produced policy stalemate more often than decision success in government. This leaves governments impotent to achieve vital objectives (Lowi 1969). Thus the impressive bodies of evidence for both the elite and pluralist views make it difficult to write off either interpretation. It is difficult to say which side is right about the concentration and use of power in America.

Fortunately, the two traditions are not altogether incompatible. It is possible to combine the two perspectives into a concept of **pluralistic elitism.**[1] Certainly such a view would lack the theoretical clarity that both pluralism and elitism now hold. But such a synthesis may actually be a more accurate view of power in America than the antagonistic traditions of pluralism and elitism. Proponents of a pluralistic-elite view would hold that power in America is exercised by somewhat diverse, occasionally competing, and limited-access elites. They would reject the proposition that there is a single dominant elite in the United States. They would argue that elites occasionally compete with one another but would recognize that at other times they substantially agree. They would also accept the idea that pluralist groups sometimes "win."

More important, though, virtually all studies of power have largely ignored federalism. Any complete view of power must take into account federalism's influence. For example, in elite research there is significant evidence on how often elites "win" in various government decisions (Greenberg 1974; Dye and Domhoff 1984). But elite research has virtually ignored the question of whether federalism thwarts elite power. Similarly, pluralist research has only vaguely recognized how federalism fragments power on many significant issues. Indeed, pluralists show a rather marked tendency to concentrate on local community power structure. Therefore, the bigger federalist system as an arbiter of power plays second fiddle among pluralists.

To explain how federalism's cultures, system of representation, and influence on implementation increase the degree to which power is regulated in American politics, it is necessary to explain the patterns of power in the United States and to describe how power is transferred by the powerful across intergovernmental lines. That is the subject of this chapter. Only after this picture is drawn will we be able to explain in Chapter 9 how federalism's seven political economies specifically regulate each kind of power. Next, we will summarize our argument about federalism and power. Then we will explain how power operates in the context of federal relations.

Federalism and Power

In our view, power in politics can be defined as substantial control over time of three facets of politics: (1) political ideologies and belief systems, (2) government decision making and institutions, and (3) intergovernmental policy implementation. This chapter describes how that happens. Federalism in America regulates **political power** in these areas in three parallel ways—federalist political cultures, federalism's representation system and its influence on government decision making and institutions at different levels, and, perhaps most important, the complex intergovernmental process of implementing public policy decisions (see Chapter 9).

Our basic theme in this and the next chapter is thus threefold. First, those who have or seek power over political ideologies and beliefs are at least partly thwarted by federalist political cultures. These cultures limit the kinds of political, policy, and economic changes that can take place among public institutions, jurisdictions, and regions. Limits are set by cultural influences on intergovernmental law, policy, and government roles in society and economics. Thus it is possible to have cultural extremes in federalism that allow quite a range of human behavior but at the same time severely limit it in local ways. We see legalized prostitution and "extreme" pornographic literature in Nevada, yet such books as *The Wizard of Oz* and *The Catcher in the Rye* are banned from public school libraries in some religiously fundamentalist areas of Alabama and South Carolina.

Second, those who have or seek power by influencing government decision making (through lobbying and other means) are often thwarted by **federalism's representation systems** (dual elections, parties, and separation of powers, to mention a few). The federalist representation system is derived from both national and state constitutions. The main way in which representation systems thwart private power is by setting up publicly elected or indirectly regulated representative institutions (legislatures, governors, and so on). These bodies act in part on the basis of institutional roles (governors initiate budgets, legislatures mainly write laws and try to supervise government agencies, and so forth). Also, power is thwarted on the basis of whom or what these officials see themselves as representing (voters, particular interests, their own judgment, or combinations thereof). These representational interests often compete with private interests (why else do business interest groups spend so much on lobbyists?).

The third theme is that those who seek to influence intergovernmental policy enforcement have a hard time winning policy on their terms. This is because lobbying and other means of influence may have to start with Congress, but efforts must proceed through numerous layers of governors, state agencies, city managers, local interest groups, and others in order to get things to come out in the end as they were decided in the beginning. For example, industrial polluters and other interest groups that try to weaken environmental regulations or cut enforcement budgets through the White House or Congress may have to turn to federal and state bureaucracies to influence environmental policy. If they fail at the national level, they may win at the state or local level. Or if they "win" at the national level, as they did in the early Reagan years with the EPA scandal (see Lash 1985), they may lose later because of lower-level resistance and complaints to Congress. Either way, the overall federal system is a maze of governmental, private, and public-interest obstacles to private influence. As scholars have noted recently, policy enforcement is *intergovernmental*, reflecting a labyrinth of representational and private forces on public decisions.

All this thwarts both policy-maker control as well as private power. The federal policy maze in effect becomes a power "meat grinder"; to some extent, Madison and Hamilton intended this as well (see *The Federalist*, Nos. 10 and 39, for example). But before we detail how the seven political economies of federalism regulate power through culture, representation, and implementation, we need to look a little more closely at what power is and at who attempts to use it in the intergovernmental system.

More about Power

There is a significant academic literature that has attempted to conceptualize power. Some theorists argue that power is the exercise of preponderant influence or the capacity to produce intended and foreseen effects on others (Wrong 1978), in an environment in which no one form of power is more basic than others (Russell, cited in Domhoff 1983:9). Robert Dahl, who has written probably more than anyone about the nature of power, adds that it is the ability of person A to influence person B to change a behavior that he or she would not otherwise change (Dahl 1961). This is the beginning point of most modern ideas about power. G. David Garson (1977) has reviewed much of the classic philosophical and sociological theory of power, and insists that it is useful to understand power as having "two faces"—an obvious or visible aspect (overt power) and a more subtle aspect (covert power). We agree that power is overwhelming influence, overt or covert, that gets people to change their behavior in an intended direction. But we need to convert this general idea of power into an idea of political power. Garson's ideas can help us out.

Garson pointed out that earlier theorists (Max Weber, for example) thought of overt power as involving such means as coercion, legitimate authority (religious, political, and otherwise), use or manipulation of socially desired benefits (money, contacts, status, jobs, and so on), and that mysterious, extremely rare quality of charisma (a magnetic personality combined with leadership qualities). But Garson has also distinguished more subtle means of power. One of these is the manipulation of mass belief systems or political ideologies. In American politics, elite groups attempt such manipulation through several tactics. Two familiar ones are paying for mass political advertising disguised as "public service announcements" and forming "political action committees," which screen candidates for major political office and support those who are sympathetic to elite policy goals. A second form of covert power is the manipulating or influencing of temporary issue agendas. An issue agenda is the major set of "current issues" being debated either in public forums and the media (public agendas) or among government decision makers (government agendas). A third form is the control of policy enactment and implementation. (These processes are described fully in relation to federalism in Chapter 10.) Unfortunately, none of these forms of covert power is easy to see, and to explore them requires subtle and sophisticated research methods. Even so, throughout the discussion that follows, it will be important to keep in mind these three covert forms of political power.

Political power requires *maintaining* influence over time in public policy decision making. This idea of seeing power over time is the most complete way of understanding how power is exercised. For one thing, it is clear that public policy evolves in phases. In political science, policy is widely understood as being "transphase" and intergovernmental. **Power strategies** are not yet fully understood this way, but they are transphase and intergovernmental too. The major phases of political power that can reveal its exercise over time are (1) power over policy initiation, (2) power over government decision making or enactments (intergovernmental lawmaking, regulations, court decisions, executive orders, and so on), (3) power over the implementation of policy, and (4) power over the outcomes of policy.[2]

If we can show who has substantial control over these phases of intergovernmental policy evolution, we will understand much about power, especially since policy develops across levels of federalism in the United States.[3] Certainly it is important to know what the concept of power means in each of these phases. In the **policy-formation phase,** power is held by those who successfully initiate policy issues or agendas, and who modify or veto policy alternatives in the beginning stages of consideration of "problems" in government decision centers. Power in the **policy-enactment phase** is held by those who successfully influence initial government commitments to policies. **Policy-implementation power** is held by those who influence on an intergovernmental basis the administrative and political battles that take place in enforcing enactments and service delivery. It is in this phase that those with power can dramatically alter "official" policies. Finally, **policy-outcomes power** is enjoyed by those who benefit from government decisions as they are ultimately enforced or implemented (do the rich get richer? and so on). Control of the first three phases of policy will largely determine who gets what in the federal system. Policy outcomes are the last indicators of power — of who exercises it and how much of it they wield.

How Intergovernmental Power Works

Groups that seek power must be able to manipulate political ideology or mass political beliefs, and temporary public opinion on issues, in order to support their policies. Furthermore, they must force change the way they want it across intergovernmental lines, since intergovernmental jurisdictions and players can resist and alter in Douglasville, Georgia, what seems to be "decided" in Washington. (Recently, for example, Douglasville citizens won a form of modified prayer at high school football games, through the intervention of a locally influenced judge, despite years of bans on school prayer by higher courts.) The basic goal of power in federalism is to influence policy "your way" over time. Since policy can change dramatically from formation through enactment to enforcement, power-seeking groups must fight to maintain policy "their way" over time through each of these phases. To control policy while it is being discussed and formed, a group must manipulate either mass belief systems (to ensure topics come up its way, in terms it can accept) or public opinion and issue agendas (focusing on single issues through mass-media campaigns, for example— an easier task than affecting the entire belief system of an era).

Several examples of manipulating mass belief systems have occurred in recent years. The first was the effort of the Business Roundtable to re-create a "probusiness" climate in the United States over the last dozen years. This effort involved a complex strategy of grants to schools and universities, mass public advertising campaigns, congressional lobbying, and support of the Ronald Reagan candidacies of 1976 and 1980 (for a description, see Domhoff 1983). A second example, and perhaps the most famous, was the civil rights movement of the 1950s and 1960s, led largely by Martin Luther King, Jr., and later by Lyndon Johnson. This movement was designed to change America's conscience and culture about race relations, and it substantially succeeded.

A much more common tactic is to target specific decisions. Sometimes the goal is to kill a specific decision (as business groups killed the proposed Consumer Protection Department in 1978). Also, specific issues can be targeted in such a way as to build up favorable public opinion over time. The huge, wealthy American oil companies, for example, spent millions on self-serving advertisements in the late 1970s, depicting themselves as proenvironment, hunting for new energy resources, and spending money on responsible public projects. The purpose behind these large outlays was to counter negative public images associated with the mid-1970s scandals in which the industry avoided taxes, raked in windfall profits by exploiting the Arab oil crisis, bought up coal companies, food-store chains, and Montgomery Ward, and fought the Nixon and Carter administrations' energy conservation proposals.

In addition to influencing mass belief systems, political ideology, and public opinion on specific issues, successful power seekers sustain their exercise of power over time, through the various policy phases, and across intergovernmental lines. Manipulation of ideology or opinion greatly raises the chances that a group can control policy formation. Even so, these strategies do not result in control of *all* of policy formation, because government officials may have their own agendas, arising out of the representational pressures of federalism, their own backgrounds, their professional perspectives, and so forth (see Gerston 1983).

It is necessary not only to get public and decision-maker attention but also to get government enactments "decided your way." Thus, groups cannot stop merely after influencing ideology and beliefs to get policy formed their way; they must continue the fight in the halls of government to get decision makers to avoid compromising too much when various governments make law, regulations, executive orders, or court decisions. The fight must be continued through the enactment phase of policy.

If too much compromise comes out of official decisions, the fight must be carried to administrative agencies and to lower governmental levels, where policies are enforced or implemented. Changing the minds of regulators, governors, or local officials about where and how to spend money, who gets it, how strictly regulations are enforced, and against whom, or even whether lower levels and agencies can be maneuvered to "fight back against those Washington idiots to change this before it's too late"—all of this characterizes the exercise of power across the enactment and implementation phases. *Failure to exercise power here means that you lose* — since other groups or levels of government will preempt policy their way, not your way. Therefore, powerful elites and interests must exercise power in spite of the obstacles set up by the various levels of the federal system. In a word, the federal system enormously complicates the implementation phase, and this in turn enormously complicates the exercise of power.

WHO ARE THE POWERFUL GROUPS IN AMERICAN FEDERALISM?

Political power is control over time of political ideology, government decisions, and intergovernmental implementation. We will now use these concepts of intergovernmental power to describe the major power groups in American federalism.

Research indicates that there are a least seven major power groups in American federalism (Dye and Domhoff 1986; Dye 1984; Domhoff 1983; Gerston 1983). These groups are the so-called Reagan coalition, Yankee capitalists, intergovernmental public interest groups, political parties, the mass media, governmental agents and officials, and official intergovernmental lobbies. The first two groups are converted elites. The others exhibit more pluralistic characteristics.

The Reagan Coalition

The most interesting of the elite groups, **the Reagan coalition** began emerging clearly around the 1976 presidential election. It came together because of disenchantment among conservative business and political elites who perceived the emergence of "too many radical and antibusiness trends" in America. Political trends in the early 1970s that many saw as the "radicalizing of America" seemed to these elites to be endless and ominous. These fears had little basis in fact. There was precious little evidence of a swing to the left in the population. Indeed, the literature on parties and voting behavior indicated a trend in the opposite direction, with a breaking up of the New Deal coalition and a weakening of liberalism as early as 1968.

The political result of these perceived threats to business power and conservative values was the rise of an initially uncoordinated collection of right-wing business and popular interests in the mid-1970s. These included the political New Right, the Reagan candidacy, the promilitary Committee on the Present Danger, the anti-ERA and antiabortion movement, the Moral Majority and Christian fundamentalism, and the populist tax-cut and tax-reform movement. Most important of all, however, was the formation of the Business Roundtable and associated business lobbies and political action committees openly dedicated "to restoring a probusiness environment in America."

By 1980, these groups had fully coalesced to support the second Reagan presidential campaign. Thus, the Reagan coalition was actually a somewhat loose alliance of various Republican and Democratic factions, industrialists, and ideologically focused conservative interest groups drawn from across the country. But the elite core of the alliance is said by Dye (1986) to be made up of "new wealth" western and southern industrialists and developers, corporations heavily dependent on military contracts, wealthy patriotic or militaristic elements in the population, the defense and intelligence communities, and the business representatives of mostly middle-sized-to-huge multinational corporations not linked tightly to old-line Yankee capitalist elites. The National Association of Manufacturers, associations of real estate developers, smaller banks, industry trade associations, and the Chamber of Commerce are the business interests most often identified. Thomas Dye and others have referred to these new economic power elites as "Cowboy capitalists" because of the dominance of southern and western elements in the bigger Reagan coalition.

The popular basis of support for the programs and preferences of these economic elite groups, faithfully articulated in the Reagan administration, is fairly widespread. It constitutes 25 to 30 percent of the eligible electorate, if the estimates are based on President Reagan's popular-vote victory margins in 1980 and 1984. Public support for this elite group is spread among the New Right and thus is rooted largely in southern states, the conservative wings of the Democratic and Republican parties, the newly active fundamentalist and "televangelist" religious groups mostly of the South and Midwest, the Mormon church, blue-collar labor disenchanted with the Democratic platforms of the 1970s, and prosperous western developers and farmers. The political gravity of the Reagan coalition is substantially invigorated by the personal force of Reagan. All of this support has been interpreted by some as the basis for an emerging Republican majority (Phillips 1969). But the preponderance of the evidence suggests that a general shift to the right in public opinion or a conservative party realignment has not happened (Ferguson and Rogers 1986; Burnham 1982). Certainly, public support for the Reagan coalition has decreased in the mid-1980s, for numerous reasons (public opposition to many of the president's policies, the peace and arms control movements, Democrat gains in Congress in 1982, 1984, and 1986, the Irangate scandal, and more). Even so, the Reagan coalition remains a potent actor in the intergovernmental power game and will undoubtedly outlast the Reagan presidency.

Yankee Capitalists

Most power theorists have argued that this "**Yankee capitalist**" elite group is traditionally, and perhaps even today, more dominant as a power elite. Said to be made up of older, superwealthy industrialist families (the Rockefellers, Carnegies, duPonts, and others) of the Northeast, and their corporate and banking connections and extensions, this group has had a profound influence on international and domestic economic policy and foreign policy since at least the era of FDR. The roots of their power probably go back to Alexander Hamilton. Today this superelite social class is generally viewed as somewhat more liberal, and as having a high-society social-class identity complete with insider boarding schools, Ivy League colleges, think tanks, secret societies, and discussion clubs. Yankee capitalists generally supported the New Deal under FDR, civil rights under LBJ, and the American military buildup, arms control, and detente under JFK and Nixon. Currently, they most prominently support the arts, arms control, enlightened government regulation, Keynesian macro-economic management, and industrial policy planning that favors economic elite interests (Dolbeare 1984).

The main power resources of this group are found in access to high government offices, social status, and extreme concentration of wealth, ownership, and/or management of banking, finance, insurance, and multinational corporations in America (Dye 1984). Dye has shown that Yankee capitalist corporations and banks and insurance companies hold about 25 percent of all personal wealth and income and control about 50 percent of all industrial and capital assets in the United States through direct ownership, partial stock ownership, or interlocking corporate directors. How these raw power assets are converted into political clout has been the subject of several contemporary power studies (see Domhoff 1984). These studies provide substantial evidence that Yankee capitalists are among the most important, if not the dominant, power group in the intergovernmental game.

Public Interest Groups

It has not been possible to develop a common definition of "the public interest" or a "public interest group" (see Bozeman and Straussman 1984 and Cigler and Loomis 1983). Any group will try to portray itself as promoting the public interest (the Ku Klux Klan and the NAACP both do, for example). Still, it is possible to weed out some of this confusion with a little common sense. We can do this by distinguishing public interest groups by two general tests: (1) they support goals not primarily for their own benefit but for the benefit of others, and (2) their goals are oriented primarily towards furthering democratic requirements and the democratic process in America (informing the public, increasing public choice over power, protecting civil liberties and equality, and so on).

Many public interest groups are active in intergovernmental affairs. They can generally be divided today into traditionally liberal reformist groups and more conservative or New Right groups. In the first class are the ACLU, the NAACP, Common Cause, environmental and consumer protection groups, the majority of organizations in the women's movement, abortion rights organizations, and the League of Women Voters. The second class would probably include the Moral Majority and related Christian fundamentalists who are active in politics, the antiabortion movement, and the National Rifle Association. To be sure, some public interest groups cannot be classified neatly by, nor are they motivated by, political ideology or partisan concerns. These groups include public interests such as Parents Anonymous, Mothers Against Drunk Driving, and Alcoholics Anonymous. There is nothing Republican or Democrat, liberal or conservative, about stopping child abuse or alcoholism.

In general, public interest groups only occasionally have enough political power to obtain their preferences in public policy on the national, state, or local level. Sometimes they target one level at the expense of the others (the NRA works on Congress; the child abuse lobby has focused most successfully on state legislatures). Success is more likely if they are aided by such advantages as huge memberships (the NRA), elaborate and extensive lobbying networks (Common Cause), and the ever-helpful broad media exposure. For example, the new child abuse prevention organizations, and subsequent state laws and regulations designed to detect and treat child abuse, were dramatically strengthened by the sensationalized reporting of a number of child sexual abuse incidents in a few day-care centers in 1985.

Political Parties and the Mass Media

Two other centers of power in politics are political parties and the mass media. We treated the intergovernmental character of political parties in Chapter 3 and suggest a review of that discussion. As for the mass media, particularly television and television news, a growing number of studies suggest that they are increasingly influencing candidate nominations, elections, public opinion formation, and opinions about prominent issues. These studies further suggest that the media have at least contributed to a consistent decline in the general level of political information and popular attachment to political parties since the late 1960s (Graber 1980). Because of these influences, the mass media are said to have increasingly come to replace political parties as a major force in voting, public opinion, and elections. Some analysts charge that the media have other negative social effects, including decreasing the amount and quality of information, overemphasizing conflicts, sensationalizing and oversimplifying issues, neglecting important events, and contributing to losses in reading and creativity among children.

Some earlier studies have contended that the mass media have a "liberal bias" (see Dye 1980); others have noted that the mass media gave disproportionately favorable attention to conservative Cowboy and New Right issues in the 1980s even though the population had not swung right, and failed to target many of President Reagan's shortcomings in contrast with the treatment accorded his predecessors (Ferguson and Rogers 1986). Whether the media are biased one way or the other at any point in time, they certainly have a powerful quasi-governmental role along with political parties. On the one hand, political parties and the media operate "outside" government to transmit and create public pressures and perceptions of issues to decision makers within government. On the other hand, they are part of "official government" as well (the press enjoys a special protection from intrusive government censorship thanks to the First Amendment, and parties nominate candidates, choose congressional and state legislative leadership, guide the operations of legislatures, and more).

Neither the mass media (with their vast power to reach vast numbers) nor the party system has significant roots in the creation of federalism. They were essentially not significant mass social forces in the late eighteenth century. Yet today both serve in various ways to create and form public issue discussion, to make or break candidates (recall Gary Hart's womanizing scandals of 1987), to guide voting behavior (through "dramatic" presidential debates), to influence decision making in government through public pressure, or to influence committee or party leadership attention to the issues. Thus both political parties and the media are potent intergovernmental actors.

Government Agents

This group, whose significance was also discussed in Chapter 3, includes state and local officials, federal and state courts, and national, state, and local bureaucracies.

If one is to understand federalism and power fully, one must recognize that decision making, policy influence, and the like simply are not concentrated merely in governmental hands. This is the unfortunate effect of the term "inter*governmental* relations." Power is shared and fought over at all levels of federalism between private groups (elites and interests) and public groups (government decision makers). Government decision makers often have their own perspectives, partly because they serve different levels of government and populations, partly because they have their own professional interests.

Having broadly outlined how the intergovernmental power game is played, we can examine some of the evidence on who wins on what, *across* the policy phases and *across* the patterns of federalism. Thus we now look at the intergovernmental power patterns of the major groups and how they influence the key intergovernmental policy phases. This will mean examining how groups influence ideology and opinion, how they affect policy formation, how they affect intergovernmental enactments, and how they attempt to influence intergovernmental policy implementation.

THE POWER ELITE PATTERNS OF INTERGOVERNMENTAL POWER IN THE 1980s

Cowboy Capitalists and the Reagan Coalition

The issues that came to media prominence in the 1980s, and that formed the basis of Ronald Reagan's campaign against Jimmy Carter in 1980, were the ones said to have made up "the Reagan agenda" of priorities. The Reagan coalition was able to change the issue agenda in the 1980s—that is, to determine what was most talked about in the media, and what prominent government figures, newsmakers, and journalists talked about as "today's issues" (Maddox and Little 1984).

Methods of Influencing Issue Agendas and Ideology. The conservative agenda of issues in the 1980s had to do with scaling back government, except for defense spending, and placing more emphasis on the states in federalism. These priorities included the following issues:

- cutting social spending, scaling back sharply on government, in conjunction with lowering taxes;
- "restoring" the balance between Washington and state government power (the Reagan version of New Federalism);
- returning to "family values" (banning pornography, putting prayer back in schools, abolishing abortion, and so on);

- reducing the emphasis on affirmative action and government enforcement of civil rights in favor of "market-based" solutions to inequality;
- deregulating (reducing the number and power of regulations enforced by regulatory agencies) and privatizing (contracting to private corporations) government services;
- rebuilding military strength and shifting public monies to the military sector while emphasizing the alleged failure of arms control. The coalition also prefers to move away from detente with the Soviet Union and compliance with arms control treaties. It argues for the "need" to pursue "Star Wars," or space-based defense.

The Reagan coalition was quite successful in making these the issues of public discussion in the 1980s. Yet quite a bit of evidence suggests that this vision of "what's important" in politics did not square with what the public thought was important. The Reagan coalition's "policies" are not very popular (Ferguson and Rogers 1986) even though the president was returned to office in a 1984 electoral landslide. Strong research (Burnham 1982) reinforces the view that voters were not giving anybody a "mandate" in the 1980 elections. Instead more than half the voters in about 40 percent of the states were expressing combinations of doubts about both Reagan's and Carter's image and disenchantment with inflation. The off-year elections of 1982 and 1986 were also influenced by more local and federalistic concerns, and Democrats were returned to congressional power.

However unpopular many of the administration's ideas were, they came to dominate media and congressional discussion. This indicates the Reagan coalition's exercise of power over public issue agendas through the manipulation of ideology and conservative symbols. Perhaps the best evidence for this success is the dominance of this set of issues among campaign consultants, newspaper editorials, and prominent journalists. An additional indicator is the emergence of college students who were loyal supporters of President Reagan and who may have, at least temporarily, constituted a "new political generation" (Burnham 1982). However, all of these are special interest groups. Issue popularity among them does not necessarily translate into issue popularity in the general population. The long-term appeal of the Reagan issue agenda was in question as new issues emerged in the 1988 campaigns.

How did the Reagan coalition achieve its partial success in controlling the public, if not the governmental, issue agenda? Its influence over opinion and ideology in the 1980s was accomplished largely through the use and appeal of symbols and slogans of conservative ideology, and secondarily through a vast and partly coordinated business lobby. For example, one of the most effective of Reagan's "appealing slogans" was the statement "Go ahead, make my day"—borrowed from tough guy Clint Eastwood.

These issues must be seen as a blend of popular conservative symbols and the political culture of dualism. The combination of the appeal of these ideas and the personal appeal of Reagan helps explain the rise of these issues in the media and government agendas.

Methods of Influencing Decision Making. The influence over issue agendas was transmitted into influence over public decision making. The Reagan coalition achieved almost unprecedented levels of influence in government bureaucracies, through the prominent tactic of *bureaucracy packing.* In its first term alone the administration appointed about 5000 people to top government positions; these personnel were largely loyal (and sometimes computer-screened for ideological purity) to the president's new agenda. This strategy was also pursued by the president in appointing members of federal appeals courts and nominating Supreme Court justices. This strategy of bureaucracy and court packing as an element of presidential control over public policy was developed by President Nixon, as described in *The Plot that Failed* (1975) by Richard Nathan. In the case of the Reagan coalition, this strategy was much more successful.

For this group, power over ideology was accompanied by the fairly successful use of decision-making power at least until about 1983, through three successful tactics: bureaucracy packing, court packing, and congressional changes in national budget and tax priorities in the early 1980s. The policy results slowed social spending, increased military spending, began a new foreign policy and arms control agenda, and, most dramatically, lowered the taxing strength of the national government (through a variety of tax-law changes—see Palmer and Sawhill 1984). This partly successful transformation of the ideology power of the Reagan coalition into decision-making power both highlights that power and illustrates the continuing appeal of antifederalist and dualist traditions in American conservatism and public cultures.

Influence on Intergovernmental Implementation. As resistance to its priorities grew through the mid-1980s, the Reagan coalition also used the symbols of dual federalism to influence politics and public policy. Resistance grew as the Reagan policies worked their way through the intergovernmental system, and through the reactions of the public, formed in an environment of local conditions, local cultures, and federalist ideas. Therefore resistance has grown at least in part out of different public views of federalism. Thus the continuing resistance by cities to the New Federalism, the general unpopularity of the drastic scaling back of government services and their transfer to the states, and the reestablishment of a power balance in Congress after the midterm elections all showed the erosion of Cowboy elite power as policy was implemented over time.

Among those policies that were altered dramatically or forestalled entirely by growing resistance in the intergovernmental system were radical scale-backs in social security and welfare programs, scale-backs in environmental regulation, and reductions in affirmative action and civil rights as defined by earlier court rulings and presidential directives. These changes illustrate the overall functioning of federalist cultures and representation systems in the national government in balancing the power of the Reagan coalition. This kind of power balancing, whether it works against the Reagan coalition or any other power group, is a very important feature of American federalism. More evidence on *how* federalism's patterns alter policy-implementation power and the other kinds of power appears in Chapter 9.

We do not mean to imply that the Reagan coalition was totally unsuccessful in exercising power over policy implementation. Among the policy areas in which this elite enjoyed some success were the buildup in the military budget, the elimination of revenue sharing along with significant changes in the intergovernmental revenue system, and a slowdown in general regulatory enforcement. However, these successes did not match either the level of change expected by the Reagan coalition or the coalition's control over the issue agenda. Power, to be successful, must control the implementation process. Federalism is the major contributor to the implementation difficulties of the Reagan agenda.

Yankee Capitalists

Although this group is said to be in competition with the goals of the Reagan coalition, the two should not be viewed as antagonists. The Yankees have sometimes sided with the Reagan coalition, notably in support of the 1981 tax laws, business deregulation, and the weakening of labor power on the National Labor Relations Board.

Methods of Influencing Issue Agendas and Ideology. One of the primary tactics Yankee capitalists use to influence the issue agenda is getting their views voiced by "experts." These experts are located in think tanks, universities, and informal elite associations. This sophisticated body of expert opinion is linked to or sponsored by Yankee capitalist elite networks, according to Dye and Domhoff. In their publications, lobbying, and discussion networks, the Yankees consistently opposed many of the goals and programs of the Reagan coalition. For instance, they supported an increase in conventional arms and a "no first use" NATO nuclear weapons policy, they supported arms limitation treaties, they opposed Star Wars, they advocated "industrial policy planning," and they supported Federal Reserve Board monetarism rather than supply-side Reaganomics.

Yankee capitalists also seemed suspicious of Reagan's New Federalism initiatives, his severe proposals to cut social security benefits, the international "laissez-faire" economic trade positions of the administration, and related proposals to withdraw or reduce funding for the United Nations, the World Bank, and other multilateral economic or transnational public policy agencies. They appeared skeptical of what were said to be administration "rollbacks" in civil rights, and they did not favor the new "social agenda" of the Christian fundamentalist right. However, the organizations, think tanks, and publications sponsored by the Yankees did not take strong lobbying positions against the administration on most of these issues, perhaps saving their resources for greater policy concerns and leaving social regulation questions to the courts and to dual federalism and local conditions. One exception has been education reforms (which we will touch on momentarily).

There is little doubt that the issue agenda influence of Yankee power elites waned as the Reagan coalition's issues became adopted widely in the mass media. Nevertheless, the Yankees have had substantial success in gaining attention in leading newspapers and journals, academic forums, public television and radio, and newsmagazines with their issues of tax reform, industrial planning, selective trade protections, nuclear arms control, and East–West tension-reduction proposals. Yankees have also been attempting to redirect the foreign policy thrust of the Cowboys. They have helped fund centers in American universities for the study of conflict resolution, of East–West tensions, and of the Soviet system. They have supported the establishment of the United States Institute for Peace and the activities of the Carter Center in Atlanta relative to the Middle East, North–South issues, and peaceful resolution of the Central American tensions. Yankees have also pushed for deep cuts in the nuclear arsenals of the superpowers as part of a larger basket of East–West tension-reduction strategies. This idea may have been adopted personally by Reagan in the late 1980s in the "European weapons" negotiations with the USSR. This irked some of the old coalition, who may have been surprised that Reagan picked up on an idea of the Yankees that had been in circulation at least since the mid-1960s.

In intergovernmental domestic policy issues, Yankees have perhaps most notably been prominent in developing and promoting reform proposals for American secondary and higher education (Useem 1987:152–68). These proposals have received substantial media attention and helped stir widespread reforms of public education laws at the state level in the mid-1980s.

Methods of Influencing Decision Making.   However influential the Yankees have been in academic, bureaucratic, and intellectual circles, their agenda did not often dominate the public agenda in the 1980s. Nor in the Reagan years did this power elite have much influence in the mid- and lower-level administrative appointments, especially to federal regulatory agencies. Still, Yankee influence on issue agendas and public opinion has generated for the coalition significant decision-making influence, especially in Congress, on business-tax and arms issues, and in state houses most notably on educational policy. In short, the Yankee agenda of issues has made more headway in top legislative and bureaucratic circles than in the public eye, and has been at least partly transformed into decision-making power. In evidence of this, Domhoff (1984) maintains that a large percentage of Reagan appointees were members of Yankee elite insider clubs, such as the Council of Foreign Relations (although most key appointees were not, especially those in Reagan's second term).

Influence on Intergovernmental Implementation. There is no evidence that Yankees get much involved in following policy through the intergovernmental system. Instead, they seem to rely on affecting Washington, especially Congress, the State Department, and departments involved in international development issues, such as Treasury and Commerce. An example of the Yankees' concern with intergovernmental policy implementation, however, has been their key role in initiating the public debate over the poor quality of American public education. They have been active in developing proposals for national teacher training and certification and improvements for higher education. These policy areas are largely under the control of states and localities.

Also, Yankee business lobbies, especially the Business Roundtable, have fought the introduction of economic protectionist legislation in Congress, a policy that originated in dispersed, populist state concerns with foreign imports, declining industrial strength, and regional unemployment. These ideas have often been promoted by populist Democratic and Republican members of Congress alike. Fighting the formation and enactment of this policy in Congress has been a priority of *both* the Yankee and the Reagan coalitions. Their goal is to maintain free trade, avoid foreign-trade wars, and keep protectionism from being enacted and implemented. Generally, the Yankee elite also stays out of intergovernmental policy enactment or implementation battles over the federal or state courts, civil rights, social-issue and civil-liberties lobbying, or intrastate business or social regulation.

NONELITE INTERGOVERNMENTAL POWER IN THE 1980s

Public Interest Groups

Public interest groups had come to prominence at least by the 1920s, through the civil rights movement, labor, and women's movements. Since World War II they have had even more influence (Lowi 1969). They experienced great turmoil and competition from newer groups in the 1970s and 1980s. All of these groups attempt to influence public issues, decision making, and intergovernmental implementation.

Methods of Influencing Issue Agendas and Ideology. The issue agenda of the 1960s and 1970s was largely that favored by the first wave of politically active interests, which arose in the late 1950s and the 1960s. These prominent issues involved the generally perceived need to strengthen civil rights, to put teeth in environmental regulations, to increase consumer rights through consumer protection laws and regulations, and to increase social welfare for the disadvantaged and minorities.

In the 1980s these issues virtually disappeared, to be replaced by the issues of the Reagan coalition. The meaning of this replacement for the power of the "reformist" public interest groups was that their hold on the public and governmental issue agendas was eclipsed. However, their lobbying power—that is, their power to obtain congressional and federal court attention to their issues—did not decline as drastically. Through the use of civil suits and congressional lobbying, the environmental, civil rights, women's, and consumer protection interests were able to at least fight back against the Reagan coalition. Among the more dramatic examples of their issue power was the defeat of the nomination of Robert Bork to the Supreme Court in 1987—perhaps the most intensive public interest lobbying of Congress since the Civil Rights movement.

Methods of Influencing Decision Making. The intergovernmental lobbies representing cities, mayors, and governors successfully prevented the congressional enactment of most of the proposals of the New Federalism to "swap" responsibilities with the federal government. These lobbies were also able to restore some funding through congressional lobbying and sympathetic congressional committees, although often under drastically restricted programs and regulations by 1983.

Similarly, the EPA and the combined environmental lobby ousted the controversial EPA leadership and diverted the programmatic character of the EPA and the Department of the Interior after the Super Fund and related scandals of 1982–83. So it was with the American Association of Retired Persons, which helped restore lost disability benefits and beat down administration suggestions for decreases in social security benefits, and with the civil rights lobbies, which fought Justice Department attempts to alter virtually the entire range of affirmative action cases and which helped defeat the Bork nomination.

Other "reformist" lobbies, and their closely associated bureaucratic agencies, did not fare so well in the 1980s, however. Accident rates rose in apparent association with lax enforcement and reduced budgets for workplace safety and mine safety. Dramatic reductions occurred in social welfare intergovernmental grant programs, including AFDC, CETA public employment training, federal job-retraining programs, public housing, energy resource and development grants, public transit, and eventually general revenue sharing. The apparent weakening of intergovernmental regulatory enforcement in the 1980s also seemed to extend most strongly, because of Cowboy capitalist appointees, to the easing of Federal Communications Commission regulations on false advertising, the Federal Trade Commission's bite on dangerous or unsafe products, the Department of Agriculture's poultry and meat inspection standards and enforcement, the inspection and regulatory powers of the Federal Savings and Loan Insurance Corporation, and certain other "independent regulatory commissions."

Influence on Intergovernmental Implementation. Lacking strong, organized group constituencies or media attention, the public bureaucracies and interests suffered declines in power and loss of control over their programs. This was due largely to the bureaucracy packing of the Reagan administration, which targeted certain agencies perceived as too burdensome to business for either "deregulation" or elimination. The most prominent advocate of this strategy was the first Reagan secretary of energy, a dentist and former governor of South Carolina who declared his goal to be the elimination of the Department of Energy. As time wore on, it became clear that Congress was not to seek significant restorations of the budget or the regulatory structure of that and many other agencies, unless some sort of "public crisis" in regulatory responsibility became apparent in the news or through oversight hearings (as did the dramatic scandals involving the EPA under Ann Burford Gorsuch in 1982). As a result of the new agenda of conservative concerns in Washington, most public "reformist" interest groups and bureaucratic agencies lost not only issue agenda power but programmatic and policy power as well.

At the same time, a different group of public interests, more closely aligned with the Reagan coalition, gained not only issue agenda control but also decision-making and policy influence. Among the most prominent of these were the conservative, business-oriented Republican candidates in the early 1980s. The often interrelated Christian right, Republican New Right, anti-ERA and prolife women's movements, and obscure policy analysts suddenly said to be "leading economists" (such as the irrepressible California business administration professor Arthur Laffer, the New Right's new guru of supply-side economics[4]) became celebrated in the nightly media as representatives of America's "swing to the right."

As these ideas swept the media in the early 1980s, they seemed to permeate Congress as well: senators and representatives were frequently asked what they thought about the Soviet threat, prayer in schools, a ban on abortion, a constitutional amendment to balance the budget, and (did they dare?) new taxes. This pressure environment, favorable to these groups who but a scant two or three years earlier were largely ignored by the media, or were even scorned as "throwbacks," greatly aided the Reagan coalition in getting congressional approval for new policy and budget priorities in the early

1980s. First the discussion and then the grim reality of decision making and budgets sank into the professional meetings, journals, and daily decisions of municipalities, states, and intergovernmental associations.

These New Right interest groups employed substantial influence. As a result of the rise of the issue and decision power of the Reagan coalition, virtually the entire intergovernmental budget and fiscal relations system turned to such issues as how to cope with cutback management, how to live with fewer grants, what services to cut without political repercussions, and whether states and cities could afford a major "swap" or delegation of program responsibilities from the feds. These new issues hit states and locals just as the grant spigots were being turned off; they stirred closed-door deliberations in localities and many a state over how these jurisdictions could force themselves to judiciously raise taxes (most of them did by 1984). Thus the issue agenda power of the new interest groups of the Reagan coalition became decision-making power in national budgets, and came eventually to dominate the intergovernmental grants and tax agendas of cities and states.

Besides congressional politics, federally rooted concerns and intergovernmental lobbies helped block the implementation of many of these programs. Another obstructionist force was the federal courts. Despite appointing more nominees to federal courts than the last three presidents combined (and conservative nominees at that), and despite three Supreme Court appointments, the Reagan administration and coalition were consistently frustrated by federal court rulings upholding precedents and in some cases expanding them. This occurred in the areas of voting rights enforcement, civil liberties, affirmative action, and the generalized prohibition against school prayer. The federal courts remained a formidable intergovernmental barrier to the policy implementation goals of the Justice Department, and to the Reagan coalition's interests in civil liberties and civil rights.

Offsetting this "trend of protection" somewhat was the failure of the Equal Rights Amendment. The federal system's difficult hurdles to ratifying new amendments (three fourths of state legislatures must approve) made it easier for the New Right "antifeminist" lobby to defeat the amendment despite public approval ratings of roughly 70 percent for nearly a decade. The enactment and implementation of the ERA were effectively stalled.

These new, conservative interest groups thus achieved a mixed record. Still, not since LBJ had relatively weak public interests been catapulted into the national policy arena to so strongly affect intergovernmental issues, implementation, and federal policy outcomes. The issue and decision power of these interest groups had begun to wane somewhat by 1982 (as Congress began restoring some funding cuts and Democrats regained twenty-six seats in the House). Their influence seemed to decline most prominently in 1986, as the Senate came under Democratic control, the Irangate scandal rocked the administration, and the media began to turn the issue agenda to what 1988 presidential candidates were saying were public priorities.

Subnational and National Groups and the Public Bureaucracies

National private elites have significant control over national agendas but their influence is not exclusive, and it certainly fades somewhat in the lower levels of federalism. Other forces, of a more "pluralistic" nature, also influence agenda formation, government decision making and implementation in the federal system. Among these are forces from subnational federalism, Congress, and the public bureaucracies.

Influence on Ideology and Issue Agendas. In subnational federalism, the strongest influences on public and government agendas of issues at the state and local level are particularistic and local. They include local elites, state-level business interests, government officials, state bureaucratic agencies, and the local news media. The structure of dual federalism, both nation–state dualism and substate dualism, creates the official arenas and influences the local cultures that foster the rise of these powerful interests.

The issues that predominate in subnational federalism are the issues of local- and state-government-dominated public policies. Henig (1985) argues that these are the issues of crime, education, welfare, basic local services, economic development, urban policy on taxes, zoning, and other services, and, of course, who gets to participate and win in politics (electoral party politics, legislative politics, city council politics, and so on).

Larry Gerston (1983) and other theorists of the policy process in the United States have argued that issues involving vast sums of public monies and acrimonious battles are triggered especially at the subnational level by how these localistic groups see priorities. Thus the levels and directions of spending for major policies are subject mostly to subnational forces. Two of the biggest policy areas in terms of spending and social impact are public education and welfare services. The spending and policy patterns for these areas are an "intergovernmental bargain" worked out primarily between state legislatures and national and state bureaucracies, amid pressures from above in the form of federal regulations and pressures from below by local education and welfare lobbies.

In the 1980s governors played an increasing role in directing spending through gubernatorial bureaucratic management, budget politics, and public relations strategies. In Georgia, for example, in the mid-1980s a political coalition of business people, Atlanta news media, and the governor attempted to bring school reform to the public and legislative agendas. This effort went forward despite intensive resistance by local communities and school interests, who sought to retain unconsolidated schools and local curricula control. At stake were hundreds of millions of dollars, the national scholastic standing of Georgia public school students, and long-cherished traditions of local versus state control of education. These issues are hardly small potatoes.

What was determined by state and local interests, as is most often the case, was the particular direction the political and budget battles took and thus the ultimate decisions made and the policy results. Although the issue agenda of school reform originated with national elites, through the elite-funded *A Nation at Risk,* the state and local response is what controlled these significant developments. State and local groups in the states thus determined how monies were spent, what formulas were used to balance "poor" versus "rich" school districts, which schools got consolidated, what were the specifics of teacher competency tests and statewide curricular policy, and so forth. Thus even if locals sometimes seem merely to react to private and national forces and elites, they still more often than not *control* how issues develop and arise, and how they turn out at the state and local levels.

On the other hand, even if local cultures and locally powerful interests predominate in setting the terms of discussion about policies, the subnational system still responds to higher-level intergovernmental pressures. National private elites, the courts, the national media, and the president seem to have gained much influence since the Kennedy years on subnational issues (civil rights, urban development, and welfare, for example). Congressional and bureaucratic influence on public opinion are, on the whole, weaker than these national forces and the subnational forces in determining local issue agendas.

Influence on Decision Making and Implementation. On the issues mentioned above, decision making in the official government institutions of subnational federalism is largely handled between states and localities, unless federal courts intervene. Official lawmaking is a function divided between state legislatures on the one hand and municipalities on the other. Most certainly, what legislatures decide affects municipal decisions more often than the other way around (see Chapter 5). Intergovernmental facilitation of, say, grants administration and compliance with regulations is aided by the system of intergovernmental agencies, councils of governments, planning commissions, and others, which are thought to have weakened in the Reagan years.

As a decade of research has shown (Williams 1982; Sharp and Palumbo 1980), implementation can dramatically alter policy at local levels, despite federal guidelines or elite intentions. In fact, local and/or state implementation can so dramatically change policy that elite and national intentions are substantially changed. Nevertheless, many programs thought to "fail" or "falter" actually turn out to be better administered, with the intended results, because of intergovernmental bargaining, learning, and fine-tuning of programs initially started in public housing, welfare, and transportation (Henig 1984; Peterson, Rabe, and Wong 1987).

In the 1980s, the influence of most interest groups on congressional budgets and laws generally declined in favor of the policy preferences of the Reagan coalition and national business elites, at least until about 1985. Apparently, by the mid-1980s, congressional laws and budgets were turning back towards the preferences of cities, public interests, small business, nonmilitary sector bureaucracies, and the official intergovernmental lobbies. This influence on decision making can probably best be seen in congressional budgets, which began to reflect in the 1980s more constituent and interest group concerns, rather than presidential budget priorities. The president's use of the veto increased in 1987 and 1988—an indication of the rising power of these groups in Congress.

Interest groups and bureaucracies usually use a multifaceted strategy of lobbying, litigation, "iron triangle" relations with congressional committees, whistle blowing, and "news making." In the late 1980s, their objectives were to avoid reductions in intergovernmental aid to cities, to prevent reduced regulation of certain industries and services, and to revise the tax code in the "populist" tax reform of 1986. The representative influence from federalism on the election system essentially helped create the congressional versus executive budget and policy stalemate of the mid-1980s. Republican presidential prospects in the electoral college gained in the federal system (as the population base shifted to the South and West), while federalism paradoxically helped to return Democratic majorities to the House and Senate in all off-year elections after 1980. The "switch-voters" who elected President Reagan still vote largely along Democratic party lines in congressional elections.

Beyond the general role of Congress in the federal system as discussed in Chapter 3, there are two main views about Congress's specific role in intergovernmental decision making. The first is that Congress has become increasingly independent of the executive branch in lawmaking, budget making, and bureaucratic oversight, because of numerous reforms in the 1970s. This independence is reflected in the War Powers Act, the loss of presidential impoundment powers, the weakening of the seniority system in congressional committees and the resultant "decentralization of power" to subcommittees, the professional staffing of committees, the policy analysis power brought to Congress by the Congressional Budget Office, and the revised budget system in Congress, which has seen yearly budget targets and balanced-budget planning reforms installed in 1974, 1978, and 1986.

A second view, however, is that Congress has simultaneously become increasingly dependent on cues from the mass media, big business lobbies, and political action committees, which have increasingly influenced individual members' campaigns and policy perceptions. The evidence for this view is a little less substantial (Ginsberg and Green 1979).

On balance, the long-term trend in Congressional decision making has been to be fairly sensitive since the mid-1960s to the demands of national elites, intergovernmental lobbies, and the president more than to other outside interests, but the overall assertiveness and independence of Congress has grown slightly over these years. The policy stalemate of the mid-1980s between the administration and Congress may therefore be put in a better light by this view of congressional oversight, budgeting, and responsiveness to intergovernmental lobbies as a slow growth trend despite periods of "subservience" to elites or to presidential agendas (as may have been the case in the LBJ and Reagan years).

As regards public bureaucracies, their influence is not large on public agendas but is much more important in decision making and implementation. In the first place, bureaucracies may sometimes successfully resist elite administration goals, as the "comeback" of the Environmental Protection Agency illustrates. In the midst of budget cuts and hostile appointments, the EPA was able largely to defend itself by mobilizing outside support, media attention, bureaucratic leaks, and whistle blowing. Still, the pattern of influence has favored the administration, with its strategy of partisan appointments and deregulation.

Public administration studies over three decades report that public bureaucracies are strongest in affecting regulatory discretion (who gets fined, for example), revising presidential budgets, lobbying congressional committees, and defending budgets. Bureaucratic agencies have at their disposal a fairly effective arsenal of intergovernmental "power tools." These include the power to write regulations without much lower-level input, public relations offices and lobbyists to obtain congressional and administration favor, legal discretion and independence often granted by law and the reluctance of federal courts to intervene in regulatory decisions, and, not least, the ability to mobilize outside agency help among contractors, sympathetic interest groups, and members of Congress.

Still, they are perhaps least influential in affecting lower-level implementation, for here it is the states and cities that are responsible for administering programs under the law. Federal bureaucracies are probably most influential in the regulatory area, though they came under increasing presidential control in the 1980s. Conflict over bureaucratic power in decision making is highest (and therefore bureaucratic independent power is weakest) under several conditions. One is when there is conflict between Congress and the president on policy and oversight (the CIA weakened in the mid-1970s and the 1980s as congressional committees fought presidents for control of the agency, for example). A second condition is when local needs and constituencies differ greatly on perspectives and goals, as with the notoriously controversial public works, housing, and urban development programs of the 1960s and 1970s. These agencies and programs ultimately were canceled or dramatically altered. A third condition is when programs are "young" and developing a basis of expertise, experience, and learning through trial and error. Henig argues that 1970s housing, poverty, economic development, and health maintenance organizations (HMOs) achieved their objectives as they gained program experience and as intergovernmental resistance abated. A cycle of "intergovernmental learning" may be typical of initially controversial programs, just as in the private sector, where "the bugs" have to be worked out when new product lines are introduced (see Peterson, Rabe, and Wong 1986).

On the whole, however, public bureaucracies, and their control over programs and implementation, are quite unstable in American politics because of intergovernmental opportunities to intervene, alter regulations, and so on through politics. Bureaucratic power in public decision making is a kind of twilight zone of partial independence from private elites, lobbies, and congressional and administrative oversight. The primary outcomes are intergovernmental battle zones and a mixture of program successes and failures.

SUMMARY

Power is inherent in the federal design, politics, and socioeconomic outcomes. To exercise power in federalism, interest groups must acquire substantial control over public beliefs, decision-making institutions, and policy implementation across the seven patterns of federalism. This is quite difficult to achieve and sustain, for reasons directly related to federalism that we will present in the next chapter.

Although elites exercise significant and often dominant power over issue formation, government decision making, and implementation, it is clear that not all goes well with elite goals in federalism. Local elite traditions and issues can have significant clout. In government decision making, federalism makes it possible for pluralistic interests to vie for control of decisions. This is true largely because of federalism's representation features and the influence of local cultures on Congress. Certainly in the implementation phase it is possible for local interests, even relatively powerless ones, to dramatically alter the policy directions of the elite. The courts and intergovernmental lobbies can also alter elite preferences during implementation, if not earlier.

But political power in federalism, to be fully understood, must take into account the "rest of the story"—how the seven patterns of federalism alter national and local power, and with what effects. These are the subjects of the next chapter.

KEY CONCEPTS AND THEMES FOR REVIEW

agenda of issues
elite theory
federalism's representation systems
pluralism
pluralistic elitism
policy formation power
policy implementation power
policy outcomes powers
political power
power
power-enactment phase
power strategies
public interest groups
the Reagan coalition
Yankee capitalists

NOTES

[1]Grover Starling suggested this view as the best approach to linking the study of power with the study of policy. See Starling 1979:126ff.

[2]The most important contemporary scholars of power, such as Thomas Dye and G. William Domhoff, have neglected to study power across these phases, and across intergovernmental lines.

[3]Domhoff (1984) suggests that the policy phases are "comprehensive indicators" of the use of power.

[4]Laffer was a professor of business economics at the University of Southern California at the time of the 1980 election. He holds an M.B.A. and a Ph.D. in international economics. In the 1970s, his unusual and untested ideas on the negative economic effects of taxing had been rejected by prominent economists of various schools. Even Martin Feldstein, President Reagan's first chairman of the Council of Economic Advisors, claimed that the Laffer curve gave "absolutely no indication" that it would work in the way Laffer suggested (see *Current Biography* 1982:213). For almost a decade, such outstanding economists as Arthur Burns (Nixon's Federal Reserve chairman), Alan Greenspan (President Reagan's nominee for Federal Reserve Chairman in 1987) and even Nobel Laureates Milton Friedman, Paul Samuelson, and John Kenneth Galbraith had assailed Laffer's ideas as professionally unsupported and unsupportable. Yet the Laffer curve and Laffer himself gained celebrity status as the centerpiece of and salesman for what came to be called *supply-side economics*. David Stockman, President Reagan's first Director of the Office of Management and Budget, also attacked the idea after leaving office. See *Scientific American*, 245 (December 1981):18–31; and Esther Gesik, "A Critical Evaluation of Supplyside Economics," *Economic Forum*, 12 (Winter 1981–82):103–11.

The Invisible Hand:

9

How federalism is the arbiter of power and policy

In the preceding chapter, we outlined the federalist environment of political power in America. This chapter will summarize the profound effects of federalism on power and public outcomes in America. Our basic thesis is reflected in the title to the chapter: federalism is the great arbiter of power and policy in the American political system.

INTRODUCTION

How does federalism "fight back" and influence public and private power? The answer to this important question—our basic theme concerning federalism and power—has several dimensions. We will briefly summarize them and then turn to federalism as the arbiter of power in the American system.

The first aspect of the answer involves federalism's seven political economy patterns. Each pattern has its own culture, design, roots, and operational characteristics. These four features, in each of the seven patterns, are the independent variables or basic forces that influence power. Essentially, federalism's various cultures are the main forces that serve to counter the efforts of private actors to manipulate political ideology and agendas.

Another part of the answer is that federalism sets up various representation systems by which officials of government are either elected or appointed to institutions. These officials are then influenced by the traditions and politics of the office they hold. The "big picture" result of this is that different interests are represented officially in government offices. These interests operate in a pattern in federalism. Civil rights policy, for example, is subject to Supreme Court views at the top, presidential preferences and the represented views of Congress in the middle, and the inclinations of local officials and people at the bottom. Civil rights outcomes (do elections give minorities a fair chance to elect officials? is there really equal pay for equal work for women? and so on) depend largely on whether these various folk think it is "right" for central or local government to be in the business of enforcing civil rights regulations. This, in turn, is largely controlled by prevailing federalist cultures, the *interaction* of government decision making at different levels, and the interests that get represented in the decision-making institutions at different levels. To look only at how *single* institutions at one level (courts, for example) affect power over civil rights policy is to obscure how policy and power actually come out over time, and what difference it makes for people. Instead, the story of federalism's influence must put together all these "little pictures" into a big picture.

The third part of our answer is that power is fragmented by federalism's influence on intergovernmental implementation. Federalism's seven patterns influence the attempt by power-seeking groups to manage the implementation and outcomes of policy, largely through what we call *power buffering* and channeling. This means that the private effort to control implementation must cross governmental jurisdictions and encounter various mazes of institutions and various local federalist cultures.

The essential causes of this implementation complexity are federalism's design features. In other words, because there are seven patterns, there are seven sets of political traditions and institutional networks that those who would control the implementation of policy must fight through. To get government to make a decision is only the first step; it does not mean that what really happens with policy will follow the preferences of the groups that initiated the pressures for reform. In short, intergovernmental policy implementation is a nightmare of obstacles. These structural features of federalism were once called the noncentralized character of federal design and policy making (Elazar 1966).

In summary, federalism regulates power through seven patterns. These seven patterns feature cultures, representation systems, and power-buffering obstacles and institutions through which policy and power must filter. The various patterns of federalist cultures help control the efforts by private actors to manipulate public ideologies and agendas, by competing with elite visions of what is needed or proper policy action. Local people, and therefore local government, may not want and may not accept what elites or other governments and forces have "decided" for them.

Federalist representation systems contain institutions to which people are publicly placed. These people tend over time to adopt the traditions of the institutions along with the preferences of those who appoint or elect them. Supreme Court justices, for example, are notorious for forgetting what the presidents who appointed them want, and come to think like the unruly legal minds that they are. These institutional traditions help guide government decision making, because legislators cannot wholly ignore constituents, judges just will not ignore legal precedent, and presidents cannot completely ignore public opinion or congressional representation and power. Government decision making is influenced by federalist representation systems. Thus representation competes with private power seekers and with other governmental jurisdictions under federalism.

Finally, private control of policy implementation is challenged by structural complexity in the federal system. This occurs because elites who "win" issue attention, or get laws and budgets their way somewhere in government, afterwards have trouble persuading the myriad officials and publics in the other levels of federalism to act their way. These "other people" or jurisdictions have partial, sometimes substantial, control over how policies are enforced—who really gets the grants, who gets housed, what regulations are followed, and so on.

Having sketched the basic picture of how federalism regulates power, we will now fill in the details about how it does so within the seven political economy patterns.

HOW FEDERALISM AFFECTS THE CONTROL OF IDEOLOGY AND ISSUE AGENDAS

The Effects of National Federalism

The three national patterns of federalism—centralism, compound federalism, and dualism—were described in Chapters 1 and 2. These patterns are among the controlling aspects of federalism which compete with private actors for power. The overall effects of national federalist cultures have at least three variations. First, centralist culture can legitimize the placement of elite personnel in top government posts, a factor that favors elite preferences over public preferences. Second, compound federalist culture balances private preferences against such things as separation of powers, congressional primacy in interstate commerce and lawmaking and subsidy of the market economy, and congressional guidance in stabilizing macroeconomic fiscal policy and intergovernmental regulation of business. Third, the politics and federalist culture of decentralized governmental power (dualism and its legal systems, election systems, local cultures, and the rest) can dramatically alter the achievement of elite or national goals. We will examine these effects for each of the national federal cultures.

The federalist culture of centralism always aids elites. It does so by facilitating and justifying their efforts to place their members in top posts, to persuade the public to accept elite and business-oriented policies, to limit government and public power in politics, and to stabilize and subsidize the private economy at public expense. Business culture, its values, and its life-style permeate the beliefs and practices of centralism. Both business culture and centralism have a long tradition of influence in political parties, constitutional economic powers, and the economic development policies laid out as part of the federal and political approach of Alexander Hamilton (see Chapter 2).

The major effect of centralist culture is that Yankee capitalist elites expect to have power in top government posts, and have developed accepted means of promoting their business elites to Cabinet-level appointments, whether Democrats or Republicans are presidents (Dye 1980). The emergence of a business "high society" culture and how it rationalizes such things as elite power and ostentatious American consumption are best described in the brilliant writings of the great American economist Thorstein Veblin (1964). The result is that the "appropriateness" of the dominant influence of business people and the business culture over federalism and public policy is often not questioned.

This dominance converts into ideology and agenda control in several ways which were covered in Chapters 8 and 9. One way is that the policy preferences of top elite Cabinet appointees usually became the "talked-about" governmental agenda of issues, which often influences executive budget proposals or proposals for legislation from the administration to Congress. Second, these ideas, which get media attention, are the ideas of elites, often with a big-business flavor. This amounts to disproportionate influence on "top-down" issue agendas, which originate in government agendas. Public issues, which tend to originate in public interest lobbies, environmental groups, intergovernmental lobbies, the media, and so forth, must compete with the "top-down" issues, usually on less-than-favorable terms. For example, Dolbeare argues that the dominant economic-renewal ideas of the 1980s, such as industrial policy and supply-side economics, are traceable to (what we call) centralist federalism, through the appointment of top elite Yankee capitalist or Cowboy capitalist members of socioeconomic elites to the Reagan administration. Their ideas have become the ideas of attention in the media and Congress, and are less prominent in public opinion (Ferguson and Rogers 1986). Thus the ideas of economic Democrats, for example, receive little media attention (Dolbeare 1984).

Economic Democrats are those who advocate public means of direct influence over economic finance, banking, federal monetary policy, corporate location, and labor policy decisions. They generally advocate public planning agencies, referenda, plant closing legislation, and locally elected boards who administer these reforms.

Through the Reagan coalition (including Dolbeare's Cowboy capitalists) the new agenda of right-wing social and business issues, has received much attention. Through this brand of centralist federalism, the "ideas of the president," and the platform of the Republican party, the mass media and thus the general public were exposed to the issue preferences espoused by this political coalition in the 1980s (see Chapter 8). We also show in Chapter 8 how public opinion in the mid-1980s neither substantially mirrored these ideas nor strongly shifted to the right. Thus the control of ideology and agendas by elites may or may not result in changes of public opinion on issues of public policy or federalism (Ferguson and Rogers 1986). Nevertheless, the appeal of centralism aids the formation of government issue agendas, determining somewhat how Congress responds to administration proposals, what issues the national media focus on, and how elites and their representatives in government get attention.

Compound federalism has three basic elements that are important in a discussion of federalism and power—(1) the acceptance of separation of powers and roles of institutions, (2) acceptance that the power of the national government is legitimate to monopolize or manage certain central functions of life, and (3) the view that a revised dualism is "necessary and proper" to politics and social development. In particular, compound federalism supports the belief that states and localities have a proper role in regulating social life, localistic business interests, provision of basic services and education, and control of crime and civil order. (See Chapter 2.)

The effect of this culture on public opinion and private power is to create a national public consensus about several aspects of public policy, a consensus that mitigates against the successful use of private power to control agendas and public opinion. One of the more important examples of this consensus is the widespread belief that it is appropriate for the government to regulate the hazards of business, predatory market practices, and unsafe spinoffs of industry such as pollution. This makes it difficult for elites to convince the public that only elite values ought to prevail in politics and economics. The basis of widespread libertarian and populist ideas can be traced not only to Jeffersonian civil liberties and egalitarianism, but also to the Madisonian compound culture, which is suspicious of power concentrations, including wealth and big-business interests. Compound federalist culture has always promoted the ideas of a limited representative republic (McCoy 1980). Thus it is one of the historical bases of libertarian and populist preferences for both limited government power and the use of government power to limit private or big-business power by giving limited voice, representation, and public benefits directly to lower levels of government and society. See Chapters 2 and 3 on these themes.

It is also part of the general consensus that the equality and civil liberties amendments to the Constitution should enjoy active court protection (although Americans typically have ambiguous feelings about equality, and how far it can or should be carried in America). The idea that civil liberties and egalitarian values should be *rights* is derived more from Jefferson's ideals in the Declaration of Independence, but the idea that it should be *enforceable* through *national* action is a compound or Madisonian belief, which the general population supports. The effect of this on private power has been to loosen the hold of Jim Crow on the South, to equalize opportunity in services, especially education, and to expand the rights of labor, minorities, and women. The effects of these beliefs are to reduce at least somewhat the tenacity of sexism and racism among localistic elites, at least through official public policy and public opinion.

Compound culture, which recognizes and transmits state and local demands on central government through representation, means that at least some public issues and pressures rise up the policy ladder from *representational* sources (individual members of Congress and Senators, city officials, intergovernmental lobbies, media attention to problems and policies at the grass-roots levels, and more). Demands that rise from lower-level public interest groups, intergovernmental lobbies, governors, and other subnational officials are given attention in the media and in Congress. These *linkage institutions* not only operate in local environments with legitimacy (dualism), but also have credibility across governmental levels (compound culture). Also, federal court decisions usually make big news in the national media, and this in turn makes a big impression on the general public.

The total effect of this for private power is that compound federal culture strongly affects public opinion and the public and governmental issue agendas. This, in turn, means that private issues must compete with those arising from layers, cultures, and interests rooted in the compound federal system. The Cowboy capitalist elites in the Reagan coalition, for example, wanted extensive rollbacks on taxation and social welfare spending. But pressures from intergovernmental lobbies, which are ultimately traceable to the widespread influence of compound culture, led to the alteration of the issue agenda in the mid-1980s, which once again came to stress the problems of poverty, the cities, the homeless, affirmative action, and so forth. Thus *representational* forces, in addition to what presidents or public elites want, are present in government decision making.

Dualist culture has three main effects on power. The first is to encourage the vastly decentralized and varied system of local political cultures that thrive in federalism. These cultures exhibit great variety on such issues as who should participate in politics, who ought to have power, what government functions should be, and what role governments should play in local economics. Additionally, local cultures adopt or accept elements of the national cultures. That is to say, some localities and national regions favor centralism (the northern Midwest), some dualism (the southern states), and some compound culture (the Pacific Northwest and the farm-belt states). Regardless of the political and federalist-culture variations among states and localities, the essential power effect of dualism is that elite and/or national government policy agendas and proposals collide head on with localistic preferences (see Chapter 7).

The appeal of national or elite policy in different regions varies tremendously as a result. For example, northern and midwestern states strongly resisted President Reagan's "New Federalism" initiatives in 1982, particularly the proposed dramatic "swap" of national responsibilities to states. As we see in Chapter 8, northern and midwestern governors and cities were extremely resistant to the swap, not only because of their perceived adverse fiscal and socioeconomic effects on urban life, but also because the New Federalism violated long-held beliefs about what was proper for the national government to "handle" and what national responsibility should involve (environmental protection, welfare standards, protection of income and health security for the elderly and the poor, and so forth). Objections were raised not only on the basis of "winners and losers" (would some states lose benefits to others?), but also on the basis of which government level should provide guarantees and services—essentially a point of view about federalism itself. The persistence of dualist-inspired cultures, which allow for much variation among localities and regions, means that elite and national policies are all the more controversial when they are deemed "improper" in the federalist design or considered to "intrude" upon local prerogatives and preferences.

The second effect of dualist culture on power is that state and local functions (such as education, crime control, provision of basic services, and local economic growth) are influenced more by state and local elites, cultures, and interest groups than by national or private elites. Dualism thus often prevails over compound federalism at the local level—for example, when southerners refuse to give up practices banned by the federal courts, such as distributing Bibles on school property, conducting prayers at sports events, and placing huge lighted crosses on school-board property at Christmas.

The third effect of dualist culture is often noticed by federal scholars —namely, that dualism fosters decentralized *linkage institutions*, such as political parties and grass-roots interest groups. For example, the nuclear-freeze movement, the New Right, and the Christian fundamentalists all originated at the local level in recent years. These pluralistic forces had their greatest influence over candidate selection, choice of legislative leadership, voter behavior, and political reforms and participation roughly from the 1950s through the 1970s (the labor, feminist, and populist progressive interests go back to the late nineteenth century, however). To the extent that these groups and institutions exercise power over local governmental and public-issue agendas, they can affect policy options and compete with national private elite ideas and proposals.

The Effects of Subnational Federalism

Dualism has allowed subnational federalism to thrive and grow. The essential effect of subnational federalist cultures is to disperse the power of elites over public opinion in various ways, as has been mentioned, through the complex blend of local and nationally shared values about politics.

State and local issues arise from a myriad of political cultures and conflicts. State –local conflicts are greatest, according to surveys, over grant formulas, state legislative mandates from cities, and the perceived insensitivity of state bureaucracies to local conditions and needs. Often, local media and local political and social elites vie with state officials and interests to control issues. But perhaps more preeminent as "issue setters" are governors and mayors, especially big-city mayors. Often activist governors and mayors are "policy entrepreneurs." These entrepreneurs are innovators in local programs or budgets who have an eye partly on "public service" but who are also motivated by personal political success and their careers. As we have mentioned, local and state political cultures determine responses to national issues (civil rights was always the classic example). Finally, because of substate dualism (legislatures and municipal councils, mayors and governors as executive, cities versus state agencies, and so on), many conflicts arise within states, especially between governors and legislatures and between state and cities over grants, policies, and taxation. School reform or severance taxes may be good for a governor's political career, but they often create local pressures and antagonisms that are registered most often with local officials who tend to side with local views. City managers and mayors may also side with city planners for or against "developers," or for or against state economic development or the governor's economic priorities for economic growth.

As for interlocal federalism, there is virtually no "cultural" basis for consensus. However, there are *conflicts of interlocal perspectives,* based on regional differences *within* states. The most famous of these differences include upstate/downstate differences (Illinois and Georgia), which shade into big/rich/city-versus-poor/farm/rural conflicts (Georgia, Alabama, Missouri). Sometimes big-city rivalries dominate state legislative politics and policy making: St. Louis versus Kansas City, Pittsburgh versus Philadelphia, and Minneapolis versus St. Paul are three of the most famous. These rivalries are often over services, highways, taxation, grants, and other primarily redistributive issues. Interlocal cooperation is popular within some states and communities in the form of sharing fire fighting, police protection, and other services (St. Louis has a lot of this), and interlocal cooperation against "the statehouse" sometimes occurs. These various interlocal patterns derive mostly from historic state divisions, intercity rivalries and images, grass-roots twentieth-century competition for federal and state grants for urban services, and features of the intergovernmental grants system, which have increased urban rivalry and competition for grants, highways, public funds for housing, and so forth.

As for interstate cultures, there is a longer and deeper historic basis, growing largely out of **regionalism.** Today regionalism is best seen in regional differences in the benefits of federal grants. One of the most prominent examples of this is the "second war between the states," pitting the South and West against the North and Midwest for grants and tax policy influence and benefits (see Chapter 4). Regionalism also means patterns of identity and association, whereby states in a region share cultural traits, economic, historical, and religious developments, similar ethnic composition, and identities as a political region. The most coherent regions are the Southeast, the Yankee "original colonies," New England, and to a lesser extent the Midwest and northern Midwest, the Pacific Northwest, and the Southwest. The regional basis of identity and culture specifically means that states within regions tend to copy one another's laws and policy innovations, to stick together in governors' associations and municipal associations, and to lobby Washington based on consensus views pounded out between their governors, bureaucrats, and cities.

As for the national–local pattern, cities largely see the national government as an adversary. This is a switch in roles and perceptions from the 1960s and 1970s, when city, county, and other municipal officials generally viewed the national government as a partner in grants, regulation, urban development, and other policy areas. National–local relations generally soured in the 1980s as cities were forced to take the brunt of budget and social program cuts. Cuts in housing, employment, mass transit, and economic development programs were particularly galling. Cities, in turn, had to respond with "cut-back" services, which often brought local discontent. Their other choice was to rely either on raising local revenues (when city tax bases were broad enough) or on state government tax subsidies and increases. This was not a comfortable burden for cities to bear in the mid-1980s. The general climate of adversarial intergovernmental relations has grown for city and municipal officials, with special animosity on the rise against Washington (and sometimes the "stingy statehouses"). This climate may represent a shift in national–local relations for the foreseeable future.

The influence of mayors on the public opinion of city residents, especially in regard to federal policy, is relatively unresearched. As mayors grew increasingly critical of Washington in the late 1980s, and as local news media often highlighted the losses of federal funds and the local economic impact of national policies, public opposition or disenchantment with specific national policies showed a potential for increase. Adversarial national–local relations may have contributed to policy stalemate in the 1980s as local interests resisted federal priorities for cities in budgets and lawmaking in Washington. In any event, national–local relations are yet another source of public opinion formation about policy and power in the federal system that may have the eventual effect of stifling or altering national decisions.

HOW FEDERALISM AFFECTS DECISION-MAKING POWER

The Effects of National Federalism

Centralism. The effect of centralism on decision making is to strongly legitimize the *representation* of private elites in top government posts. This effect occurs, as we saw in Chapter 8, largely through presidential bureaucratic appointees, elite-sponsored research, lobbying and discussion networks, and think tanks and other elite-connected university programs. A substantial body of research has detailed these influence networks (see the various works cited in the References section by Dye; Domhoff; Rose; McConnell).

The particular "targets" for appointments are the Treasury, the Federal Reserve, State, Defense, the White House Office, and the Office of Management and Budget, as well as representatives to multinational institutions such as the United Nations, the IMF, and the World Bank. According to Domhoff, members of the Yankee elite combined with members of the Reagan coalition in the 1980s to get top appointments, and they jointly supported the reduction of the welfare state, intergovernmental and direct business regulation, and the reduction of corporate income taxes in the early Reagan years (Domhoff 1986). This has meant that centralist federalism legitimizes the role of elite power in top government posts, responsible for macroeconomic stabilization and subsidy, government regulation, international trade, and tax policy. These are decision-making areas where economic elites have had governmental power since Hamilton and the ratification of the Constitution.

Compound Federalism. The *representative* features of compound federalism have a different and balancing influence on decision-making. In essence, the design of compound federalism features separation of powers and the recognition of dualism. The most important representative feature of national government design lies in the separation of powers. As we have seen, Madison and the Framers intended to "divide power concentrations" and thereby thwart potentially dangerous majorities or factions, especially economic ones (*The Federalist*, No. 10). But the separation of powers also was a certain scheme of representing different social interests in the three branches. In this respect, the Senate was to represent more elite, educated interests and was to be more insulated from direct electoral and constituent pressures; the House was to represent the more frequently changing opinion of the slightly more common person; the presidency was a weakly constructed office, intended to have some military command, foreign policy, and administrative functions. Obviously, the presidency today has evolved into the center of national popular consensus and leadership. In the process it has become the perceived organizer of national political coalitions and the perceived center of national symbols and policy initiation, especially in foreign policy. Finally, the role of the courts was to represent the interests that Hamilton originally wanted—a sort of guardian class of legal philosopher-kings who intervene in crucial disputes and settle social order principles primarily on the basis of "received legal wisdom." Thus the separation of powers is also a system of representing competing social interests.

The compound federal system, then, creates tension between different competitive represented interests (territorial, social-class elites versus populist pressure and aspirations). These social interests were to compete and to achieve minimum consensus through *creative institutional tension.* Thus in the federal system the separation of powers has three decision-making effects—*social representation, creative institutional tension,* and *a minimum consensus* in American national politics. (See Chapters 2 and 3.)

An important secondary effect of **tension-balanced representation** is the fragmentation of private influence. The key point about the fragmentation that grows out of the compound design is that all power, whether public, private, or elite, must face *four branches* (executives, legislatures, courts, and bureaucracies) over *three general political levels* in America (Washington, states, localities) in order to influence decision making at all levels. The problem for elites trying to influence implementation at the lower levels is even greater, since enforcement is so widely dispersed among various agencies (whereas decision making, at least, is institutionally concentrated).

In the final analysis, what makes the influence game in decision making so difficult to play are the traditions, roles, and cultures associated with dispersed institutions and local communities. Legislative, executive, and bureaucratic institutions, not to mention the media, have their own self-defined "roles in politics." Public as well as private pressure can penetrate these "mind sets" only with time and effort. Institutional consensus and conflict accelerate the already existing divisiveness of private views between outside interest groups. Adding to all this are the federal courts, which remain relatively isolated from executive and public pressures, and the semiindependent and "entrepreneurial" public agencies that are only partially controlled by legislatures, presidents, or governors (Glendening and Reeves 1986:30). All of this adds up to policy-making fragmentation among institutions, an effect of the design of compound federalism on the representation system. Therefore, compound federalism produces *representation fragmentation* and *decision-making fragmentation*. In so doing, it tends to produce *power fragmentation* among elites and other interests in decision making. These features of federalism are generally neglected by power research.

Dualism. The effect of the traditions of dualism on decision making in America is to isolate official power and policy making into two main national and state levels. Dual levels of courts, legal systems, bureaucracies, and legislatures are the most prominent features of this tendency. These layers (which certainly have intergovernmental links and overlaps), are a set of twin hazards for those who wish to exercise private power over public decision making. Elites tend to concentrate on the Washington layer. States, meanwhile, have been the leaders in introducing "progressive" or "populist democratic reforms," such as the referendum, the recall, open primaries, and elected judiciaries. Also the fact that parties are more state-centered and powerful at local levels tends to take formal power away from national elites and government. This means that in many one-party states, local elite, business, or party interests often dominate politics to the detriment of public interests and reforms (party machines and Jim Crow are just two examples). These effects may not be "more democratic" or in line with guaranteed civil liberties, but they are power-dispersing effects.

The core aspects of dualism are two powerful main layers of political cultures and institutions. These cultures and institutions inhibit different national elites and even many locally powerful interests in getting what they want all the time in official decision making.

The Effects of Subnational Federalism

Of the four political economy patterns of subnational federalism, the substate, interlocal, and nation–local patterns are more complex, highly developed systems that fragment decision-making power.

There are a number of basic forces in substate federalism that affect decision-making power. One is the predominance of local legislative and bureaucratic policy making (as affected, of course, by culture, opinion, and private lobbies). Legislatures and bureaucracies are regarded as the main centers of official decision-making powers (Henry 1987). A second main force is substate pluralism, or "outside" interest groups, which represent localistic and nonelite groups. There are a number of such nonelite groups, including colleges and universities and teachers. These forces are arrayed against traditional elites within states. Usually, for big-city interests, the dominant groups are convenient alliances among developers, big-city banks, and businesses; they often align with "city hall" elected officials.

Often aligned against them within cities are public advocacy lobbies, city departments, city managers, and social service interests. At the state level, there are usually links between big state business interests (farming, oil, banks, finance, developers, or industrial firms, depending on regional economies), the governor's office, and state bureaucracies.

The political focus of substate interest groups is the state legislature and litigation. But the focus of political lobbying for substate elites is more often a potent blend of strategies — bureaucratic lobbying, "courtin' the governor," financing the party system, and legislative lobbying (Dye 1986:103).

It is the combination of these power systems that guides the major policy areas influenced by substate federalism. Policy preferences decided here, plus substate implementation of bureaucratic and national policies, produce what can be called **local preemption of national functions** (see Chapters 4 and 12). Crucial here are the patterns of substate intergovernmental politics in the writing and administration of grant formulas, substate revenue sharing, and the state constitutional and legal effects over city functions (see Chapter 4).

The main decision-making effects of all these factors are threefold. First, conflict is common between levels and institutions (cities versus counties, or the statehouse; legislatures versus bureaucracies or governors). But much of this conflict masks what is going on behind the scenes. Thus the second effect is the fragmentation of power within states and among elites and pluralist groups as they try to influence government decision making. Finally, fragmentation of power and of decision making often means local preemption of national or elite goals and programs (see Chapter 12).

As for interstate federalism, the political and economic forces and interactions are less developed. There are three main forces affecting power and decision making. One is the **official intergovernmental lobbies** and contacts (the National Governors Conference and the National Conference of State Legislatures are the most prominent). A second is the **interstate networks and alliances** between state and local bureaucracies. Through these networks, common views and lobbying positions on reforms and issues are pounded out. These have strong effects on states and cities, and on congressional and presidential "federalism programs and proposals" in Washington, as discussed. Bureaucratic and professional associations reach common agreements on programs, standards, and regulations, leading to interstate "copycatting" of these outcomes. Although intergovernmental communication was reduced in the 1980s by the OMB's virtual elimination of federal regional councils and the A-95 grant review process, these private networks in interaction with regional planning agencies still provide the basis of intergovernmental communication, idea exchange, and lobbying consensus. The decision-making result is an increase in common approaches to interstate programs and common lobbying positions in Washington.

The third interstate force, ultimately traceable to the compound federal design, is federal court rulings on interstate relations. In Chapter 4 we reviewed the impact of federal courts on interstate business, state powers over cities, and interstate reciprocity and compacts. The point is that interstate patterns are largely official ones, although some corporations and national business lobbies take common approaches in pressuring states and planning the location of their operations. States respond by competing for business locations through advertising, governor's programs, and a "business climate" of easy tax and investment packages. The overall decision-making effects of interstate patterns heavily favor adopting probusiness decisions on the part of state governments, but there is occasional resistance by official interstate lobbies to national and big-business policies.

Interstate lobbies also complicate the job of lobbying Congress for national elites, since elite and corporate views must compete with lower-level official expressions about the effects of policies (see Chapter 8). In the 1980s interstate official lobbies took positions opposite those of elites and business interests on tax cuts, grant policies, the New Federalism, social spending cuts, decreases in regulation of the environment, toxic waste, and nuclear power and waste management, to mention only a few issues.

Interlocal federalism is also a major force in decision making. Four main features of interlocal federalism have influence. The first is the close link between city officials and business elites in communities. This link tends to emphasize economic development and growth as the foremost community goal (as many writers have noticed—see Henig 1986; Molotch 1976:311). This is centralist culture, but at the local level. Other important private influences on city decision making and interlocal issues are said to be power companies, construction lobbies, and real estate and mall developers.

Interlocal planning networks also influence decision making. These include city, state, and regional planning agencies, local planning, and city manager planning. These agencies develop varied relationships in pursuit of federal grants, sharing information about developing regulations and the like. They supply vital information to elected and executive decision makers about a vast range of economic development, grant, and service issues. The intergovernmental and bureaucratic origins of these influences emphasize career, technical, regulatory, and professional goals somewhat more than raw "economic development" needs.

A third feature of interlocal federalism that influences decision making is state and local public advocacy interest groups. These include community planners, social workers, civil libertarians, local units of national groups such as labor unions and environmental groups, the League of Womens

Voters, state municipal leagues, and public employees' unions. The urban mass media should also be included here. These power interests simply represent local political pluralism. Considered singly, the groups might not have local elite status or clout in government and interlocal issues. But they are active and influential in myriad ways and on myriad issues, especially in their spheres of interest. The effect of these interests in persuading local city officials to take positions contrasting with the goals of the New Federalism in the 1980s, for example, was considerable (Palmer and Sawhill 1985).

The fourth important, but weakening, influence in interlocal power politics is political parties. Party identification and party organizations still retain considerable influence over voting behavior, recruitment of local and state politicians, and media issue agendas. But the days of strong party machines influenced by consistent voter loyalty and participation have virtually disappeared in America. Interlocal party connections and influence between municipalities affecting state legislatures are even less important. At the local level, political party influence has drifted to prominent mayors and political figures, even including prominent blacks, such as Mayor Young of Atlanta and former mayor Washington of Chicago. Even prominent party officials, such as speakers of the house in one-party states, have more influence in the legislature and in the local media than they have in interlocal power politics.

The effects of interlocal federalism on power and decision making lie, first of all, in the practical aspects of intercity or city–county services (such as police protection and 911 emergency numbers). Second, interlocal politics also tends to slightly favor local business elite priorities—but not exclusively, for the various public advocacy groups, bureaucratic planners, and prominent single politicians have come to be more important in power politics. Some of what happens in local and interlocal decision making is so strongly influenced by the statehouse and by federal grants that it is difficult not to conclude that power struggles at the local and interlocal level are somewhere between one third and one half of the time reactions to higher-level pressures. Nevertheless, many "decisions" are fueled mostly by local reactions, interlocal problems (pollution or traffic from nearby communities), interlocal service needs (schools, water, housing, sewer development, zoning, and growth regulation), or interlocal power struggles. Interlocal decision making is thus greatly influenced by higher national and elite power through federal grants and Congress, but it is also greatly affected by interlocal issues and power struggles.

As for national–local federalism, the effect on decision making cuts two ways. One dimension is the effect of locals on national decision making and on private, nationally powerful elites. The flip side is the effect of national interests and elites on local government decision making (see Chapter 12 on this too).

As for the first dimension, local influence is felt up in Washington and the state capitols as well as within local communities through the effects of representative forces in politics and the lobbying effects of local officials at national levels. Representation forces that give voice or power to public forces in various ways include state and local elections, which determine political leaders who in turn often lobby Washington for local needs. Second, local party organizations do help recruit persons for national conventions, activists in presidential primaries and caucuses, and for elections for all levels of legislatures. Of course, the territorial basis of Senate elections (two per state) and the proportional-population basis of electing House members send local representatives to Congress with at least some local and/or statewide concerns. Research demonstrates that the district-oriented role perception is a powerful one in Congress, particularly in the House (Fenno 1978). Thus the representational aspects of national–local relations push local needs upwards. Some of these pressures are derived from compound federalism (the election system) and some from political conditions (local parties, state and local officials, delegations).

Not all power flows from the bottom up in national–local federalism; much flows from the top down. Certainly, the majority of writing and analysis in recent years has focused on the influence of "national preemption" of local government decisions, through administrative and bureaucratic grant requirements, crosscutting requirements, and other devices. Chapter 7 showed that local preemption of national or elite goals is largely performed through local influences on policy implementation (more on this shortly). The more important point about administrative and bureaucratic intergovernmental "regulation" is that elite and official national policy preferences and local policy preferences *alter each other* on many issues. Federal requirements, grantsmanship rules and games, and federal monies provide tempting reasons for locals to make decisions along centralistic lines sometimes. Conversely, locals lobby Washington with significant effects. This is done through daily, pragmatic feedback about bureaucratic regulations, what problems they pose below, and how they should be altered. Often, national regulators listen and adjust accordingly (Peterson, Rabe, and Wong, 1986).

In addition to this informal daily feedback, locals engage in more direct congressional lobbying, through the powerful intergovernmental lobbies mentioned earlier. As suggested in the preceding chapter, the pattern of the 1980s seemed to be that cities and local interests battled the feds and national elites to readjust federal policies. States have not been bypassed in this battle, but they have taken a role of weaker opposition to federal and elite policies than cities. This is probably because states have the fiscal resources to adjust somewhat to federal cuts whereas cities and local interests can only "battle back" with political, media, and administrative lobbying. This is producing a transformation of intergovernmental power issues and perceptions, which are starkly different from those of the 1960s and 1970s, when states were often said to be "bypassed" by categorical grants and intergovernmental regulation on behalf of either urban or minority interests, and where cities and the feds were characterized as "allies" (Derthick 1970; Haider 1972).

If we strip aside the common polemics about elites, national preemption, and so forth, we find that the amount and quality of research on power do not allow much generalization about the overall degree to which one pattern or another (national versus local) exercises more "power." There is simply mixed evidence today on whether national power or elites influence locals more than vice versa, or whether official government lobbies carry more weight than private elites in Congress on issues important to locals themselves. This is something of a testament to the power-buffering aspects of national–local representation and complexity.

To summarize, due to the complexity of the patterns of subnational federalism, national private elites probably exercise little direct control over local decision making. Their influence comes more indirectly, through their weight in national issue agendas, national or federal grants, budgets, and laws. Still, it is the power of subnational federalism to alter intergovernmental policy enforcement that may well be the strongest way in which federalism alters power. That is the topic we turn to now.

HOW FEDERALISM AFFECTS POWER
OVER INTERGOVERNMENTAL IMPLEMENTATION

The Effects of National Federalism

The essential effect of federalism's political economy patterns on those who attempt to control policy implementation is to channel power and policy through a maze of institutions and varied cultures, and thereby buffer different levels and institutions from the exercise of private power. Again, the exceptional pattern is national centralist federalism, which has institutions and a political culture that implant and legitimize elite power in government and economics. As Chapter 8 showed, the 1980s saw elite representatives (mostly of the Reagan coalition, but apparently also some Yankee capitalists) attempting in a variety of ways to get their policy decisions *implemented* through lower levels of resistance. Five main techniques were used. The first was bureaucracy packing, mentioned before as the Nixon-developed strategy of appointing as many partisans (even zealots) to top positions. This strategy emphasized administrative enforcement and regulatory change, not only in intergovernmental programs and budgeting, but through regulatory agencies of direct federal power as well. The implementation of conservative policy priorities was a prime goal, and was accelerated by various means of strengthening the OMB's oversight of regulations and by legislative and budgeting proposals, including regulatory clearance mechanisms (Reagan 1987:162–77).

A second method was the switching of priorities to different forms of **intrusive regulation** (officially, the policy for regulatory agencies was deregulation). For example, much more federal control was exercised over welfare eligibility regulations. Restrictions were placed on state and local capabilities to fund local developments through bonding. And Secretary of Education Bennett suggested a national accreditation agency to assure tighter control over colleges and universities. In other areas, intrusion was reduced only when it meant returning to more laissez-faire conditions. This is seen in FTC control over unsafe products, deemphasis on enforcement in the EPA and OSHA, the easing of savings and loan regulations, and FCC controls over violence levels in children's broadcasting and advertising, among others. The effort here was to implement, through either regulatory tightening up or "de-enforcement," the goals of a more free-market regulatory environment for business, with less government involvement in economic decisions.

A third area of intrusive regulation was the imposition of *strict monetarism* (tight money, high interest rates) on the economy by the Federal Reserve. Representing most clearly the views of Yankee capitalist bankers and insurance and stock-brokerage firms, the Fed adopted policies that accelerated the recession of 1981 into a minidepression by intentionally wringing out inflation with tight money and high unemployment. One of the most careful and certainly nonpartisan econometric analyses of the effect of this was presented by economists Isabel Sawhill and Charles Stone in *The Reagan Record* (1984). The Fed's tight-money policies began in 1979 and accelerated the 1981– 83 recession. They eventually succeeded in wringing out about 50 percent of total inflation through very high unemployment caused by tight-money policies: unemployment rose to a record 10 percent (from 7 percent). Without the Fed's policies, unemployment would have changed little and inflation would have fallen more gently through 1983 – 84. (See Table 9-1 and Figure 9-1.) From the political economy angle on federalism, all this shows that Yankee centralists were enjoying influence through the tight money of the kind that only Hamilton dreamed of 200 years earlier. This was despite the initially loud protests of the Reagan administration and certain core industries such as Detroit automakers. Even the popular industrial wizard Lee Iaccoca, chairman of Chrysler, opposed the Fed's policies, but without effect.

The final form of new experimentation, fairly intrusive in its fiscal consequences for states and cities, was the administration's early strategy of "Reaganomics." This legislative strategy was controlled almost entirely from the top, and was at first almost self-implementing. It produced

TABLE 9-1 *Why Fed Policies Overkilled Inflation through High Unemployment and Recession*

Isabel Sawhill and Charles F. Stone have estimated that fully 50 percent of the "economic slack" (that is, recession) and the decline in inflation was caused by tight-money monetary policies adopted deliberately by the Federal Reserve as early as 1979. By fighting inflation through tight money the Fed created deliberately higher unemployment and a more severe recession than would otherwise have occurred. Sawhill and Stone estimated that without the Fed's policies, unemployment would not have risen much above the baseline of 7 percent prevalent in the country in 1980 and 1981. Instead, unemployment rose to historic levels in a recession (higher than any levels since the Great Depression of the 1930s). Inflation would have fallen more slowly through 1983–84. (See Figure 9-1. 1984:80–85.)

The other 50 percent drop in inflation came from very different factors. Sawhill and Stone estimated that 20 percent of the drop in inflation in the mid-1980s (often claimed by the administration as a victory of their budget and supply-side tax policies) came about instead by adjusting for measurement errors in the Consumer Price Index, which had overestimated the inflation rate by overstating housing-costs effects on inflation. In 1983, corrections were introduced that more properly discounted housing costs in government calculations.

More than a third of the drop in inflation came from fortunate drops in the prices of food, oil, and other imports in 1980 and 1981, factors that came about through international and bumper harvests and were not traceable to either official supply-side or Fed policies or the recession some eighteen months later.

Sawhill and Stone conclude; "We found that if the Fed had reversed course and increased the supply of money beginning in 1981, there would have been some economic slack, but not recession (see Figure 9-1). *Unemployment would have risen hardly at all* (our italics) from its 1981 base of just over 7 percent. *Inflation would have fallen,* but more slowly and not quite so far (to 6.6 percent in 1984 versus the actual 4.9 percent)." The "supply-side" tax and social budget cut program of the administration had little actual effect on anything (Sawhill and Stone 95–99), not even on business investments (p. 99).

Source: Isabel Sawhill and Charles Stone, in *The Reagan Record,* John Palmer and Isabel Sawhill eds. (Washington, D.C.: The Urban Institute, 1984), Chapter 3. Reprinted by permission of Ballinger Publishing Company.

dramatic, mostly high-income and corporate-tax reductions, across-the-board "indexing" designed to cut increased tax collections during inflation, reductions in social spending and intergovernmental transfers, and increases in military spending. The implementation of Reaganomics was effective for the first three years, and it was a potent brew of tax and budget adjustments. This overall strategy certainly seemed intrusive to cities,

Figure 9-1 *Estimated Impact of an Easier Monetary Policy,*
1981–1988

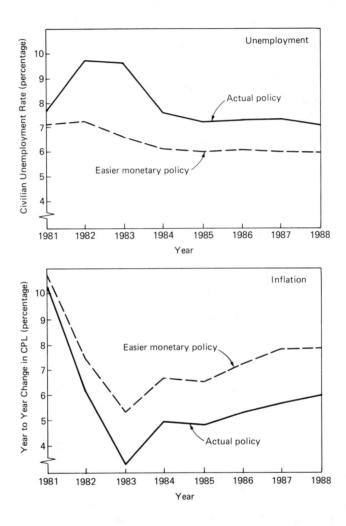

Source: Isabel Sawhill and Charles Stone, in *The Reagan Record,* John Palmer and Isabel Sawhill eds. (Washington, D.C.: The Urban Institute, 1984), Chapter 3. Reprinted by permission of Ballinger Publishing Company.

minorities, the poor, and declining industries in the Midwest and Northeast. See Chapter 8.

In some respects, the strategy worked to keep the Treasury somewhat dry and to focus government and media attention on budget cuts, budget balancing, and lower taxes. In short, the implementation strategies of elites in the 1980s achieved some success in redirecting macroeconomics, reducing some of the government regulation of business (sometimes with adverse health consequences, such as rising mine fatalities), shrinking intergovernmental transfers and declining rates of growth of services, and limited success in packing federal district and appeals courts with the "strict constructionists" preferred by President Reagan (Palmer and Sawhill 1985).

On the other hand, compound federalism (and dualism) had fairly strong influences in preventing the full advance of policy implementation preferred by centralist elites in the 1980s. First of all, compound federalism is so complex in its institutions and cultures that it tends to focus elite attention on national or Washington-based bureaucratic and executive-branch agencies. Among the modern presidents, President Reagan had the most success in penetrating federal courts with "partisan" appointees. The permanence and effectiveness of this implementation strategy are questionable, as federal judges (not Supreme Court justices) have fairly short tenure and tend to follow precedents more than the transitory policy preferences of public officials. The overall effect of compound federalism, then, is to buffer the attempt to control policy implementation through varied institutions, especially through the relatively intractable federal courts. Elite power over enforcement tends to dissipate as efforts are made to *maintain* bureaucratic and executive-branch consistency in implementing policy goals, while congressional oversight of implementation gets rather more swamped by representative, pluralistic, and bureaucratic interests.

Dualism has this effect even more dramatically at lower levels. Both national decisions and even elite issues get bounced around a lot and significantly altered between layers of lower-level administrators, interests, and public cultures. Layers of bureaucracies, differing legislative requirements, and the sheer number of significant local enforcers produce distortion in the implementation of national or elite policies over time. Market functions and powers of lower levels of jurisdictions, including courts, strongly affect local economies. Tax strategies and farm subsidy reductions popular among big-business interests in Washington, and pushed by the Business Roundtable, may not be all that popular among members of the Farm Bureau or among local bankers in the farm-belt recession town of Belleville, Kansas, for example.

Dualism gives rise not only to different regionally based economic perspectives, but to their expression in Congress, in state legislatures, in intergovernmental and subnational patterns of lobbying, and in state and local officials. All of these folks directly influence how policies play and are administered in their jurisdictions. But the *particular* character these things take is affected most by subnational federalism.

The Effects of Subnational Federalism

Subnational federalism has several features that complicate policy implementation, especially for power and national elites. First, substate federalism features a variety of state and local institutions that often conflict. Such conflicts occur because officials in these institutions frequently have differing perspectives on how national or state policies should be administered. For the most part, the administration of grant programs is truly intergovernmental, especially at the state-to-municipal level, where at least two sets of bureaucracies must interact fairly frequently. Education, welfare, social services, and economic development are frequently administered by both state and local bureaucracies, making the pattern of program implementation very complex. Policy simply changes character as it passes from federal offices to *street-level bureaucrats* (Lipsky 1971). More often than not, research suggests, state or local interests come to take over program content. The power of locals (be they officials, public interests, or local elites) to alter or block policy implementation is in fact the power to *redecide* policy effects.

In interlocal and interstate federalism, the prime force in policy implementation is probably public bureaucracies. State legislatures (the main force in official enactments) and to some extent city officials spend less time on interlocal or interstate issues than on "domestic" lawmaking and budgeting. Again, such joint actions as "copycatting" each other's programs, developing interagency communication networks, and using interlocal and interagency lobbies in Washington are the prime ways in which public bureaucracies not only "administer" grants but actually seek to change the rules and procedures they cannot change at their own individual discretion.

Finally, the success of locals in resisting national and elite implementation strategies (discussed previously) has been considerable. Local responses have been guided within the framework of substate and interstate political interests and intergovernmental lobbies. Not only have locals come to see nationals as "enemies" in the 1980s, as we mentioned, but they have been rather successful at blocking the newer implementation strategies. This has been accomplished through the variety of mechanisms, previously described (interstate lobbying, media strategies, representation mechanisms in Congress, and so forth).

The important point about national–local implementation seems to be that when cooperative alliances are built between the two levels, the priorities of policy can be implemented (as with the grants systems of the 1960s and 1970s). But the experience of the 1980s suggests that when national–local issues are divisive, and when local state jurisdictions and agencies come to resent national policy priorities, then implementation usually fails. Contemporary conditions in national–local federalism can be characterized best as **local preemption of national goals** (state- and local-led educational reform, industrial, and reemployment policy, for example) and *implementation stalemate* (the defeat of New Federalism and the partial restoration of taxes, services, and social programs following federal scale-backs). We will discuss the implications of these trends more in Chapter 12.

Finally, implementation is so complex in America—largely because of subnational federal structures, interests, and cultures—that powerful elites shy away from the lower levels of bureaucratic implementation. Generally, elite hopes for implementation control are tied to adjusting the enforcement strategies and ideologies of those in top positions. The implied objective is that these "top-level" enforcers will be able to carry policy through the lower levels of enforcement and the thicket of lower-level interest groups and officials. Policy failure can result from lower-level resistance. But policy failure, so exaggerated in the 1970s, is actually much more characteristic of the 1980s. This is largely due to implementation resistance at lower levels. Evidence exists that where there is some consensus among levels about goals and priorities, and where there is time to bargain priorities, learn from program experience, and fine-tune mechanisms of intergovernmental cooperation, then locals will not block the implementation of national goals (Peterson, Rabe, and Wong 1986). But where, as in the 1980s, local and to some extent state interests and officials resist national and elite priorities, then policy failure will be more likely. Federalism may be the key factor in both program success and policy implementation (see Chapter 9).

HOW FEDERALISM AFFECTS PUBLIC POLICY OUTCOMES IN AMERICA

Power is not exercised in the abstract. It has *effects* on people and places. The effects of power in the federal system can be described as *policy outcomes.* Policy outcomes have to do with "who gets what, and what difference it makes" for people and politics (Lineberry 1982). The private power system *and* federalism interact to produce policy outcomes (since to some extent they work against each other, as just described). We have just described how federalism alters power. Now we'll describe how federalism affects public policy outcomes in the context of the power system. The key question to keep in mind from this angle is: How does federalism affect public policy outcomes, and what difference does it make for people and politics? In discussing this question, we will concentrate on the several major effects of each of the seven political economies. Here a caution is in order. Our goal will be to illustrate the major policy effects of federalism, not provide an exhaustive list of effects.

The policy consequences of federalism have only recently received limited direct research (Henig 1985, Peterson 1986), although there has been substantial research since the 1960s on small pieces of the federal system. Since federalism *as a system* has been neglected as a policy force, it is necessary to pull together these strands of research to see the bigger picture more clearly.

The Policy Consequences of National Political Economies

Centralism. The practices and features of centralism have several powerful policy effects. Perhaps their major effect is in guiding government macroeconomic policy. Centralized economic powers were granted to Congress by the Constitution. Hamilton strengthened both centralist powers and the centralist political culture through a variety of pragmatic policy developments (see Chapter 3). Today centralism means that it is the national government's role to control macroeconomic fiscal and monetary policy, most major aspects of national government regulation of business, and economic development priorities. Centralist culture and elite power legitimize the control of the nation's monetary policies by key representatives of the big banking establishments in the Federal Reserve's top committees, for example. Few persons outside of big banking and Wall Street circles or apart from sympathetic academic economists occupy important posts in the Federal Reserve. As a result, monetarism in its strictest terms has been the dominant philosophy of the nation's central bankers in recent years. In the 1980s centralist monetarism dominated both the executive branch's supply-side Reaganomics and congressional fiscal policy.

Another major policy effect is the exercise of centralism by power elites in national political institutions (see Chapter 8), which in turn has implications for public decisions, macroeconomic policy, budgeting, and the like.

A third major policy effect is that centralist practice, through the making of regulations and grants policies, has produced the operational complexity of intergovernmental grants. Modern centralism emerged out of Franklin Roosevelt's attempts to cope with the Depression. This "enlightened and collaborative" centralism of the New Deal took many new forms. These included new grants, new relief programs, and new methods of stabilizing the economy (pump priming, labor arbitration, regulation of banks and securities, new farm programs, and housing programs). A considerable number of the policy and grant programs operated on a new nation-to-local basis. Almost all of the policies operated explicitly with elite direction and goals but with state and local implementation. They were formulated by FDR with many mixed intentions: to stabilize state and local governments, curry favor among state and city politicians and machines, improve working, health, and family conditions, and boost regional and economic development (through schemes such as the TVA, economic development grants, and planning, see Chapter 7).

By the end of the 1930s, this new centralist approach in the political economy ended up *legitimizing* in the public's eyes (eventually in the Supreme Court's also) the kinds of political and economic interventions judged suspicious if not heretical in earlier eras. It legitimized vastly increased government regulation, encouraged congressional control over interstate commerce, sanctioned social welfare and social security, and empowered public bureaucracies at all intergovernmental levels.

In the 1950s and 1960s, as interest group activity increased and as the postwar economy grew and urbanized, this general pattern of enlightened centralism grew. Especially by the mid-1960s, the increased complexity of centralism spawned many new efforts at categorical grants, intervention in civil rights, and increases in social welfare (medicare, AFDC, disability income, and jobs programs, to mention a few).

The apparently widespread political consensus that supported enlightened centralism rested partly on the slowly declining dominance of New Deal liberalism and the Democratic party, and on the activism of the Kennedy and Johnson years. All of this helped develop an atmosphere of pluralism in politics that in turn encouraged the rise of many of the modern public interest group movements: civil rights, women's equality, environmentalism, consumer protection, and indeed ultimately their counterparts (today's New Right, Christian fundamentalists, antiabortionists, and the rest).

In essence, as we argued in Chapter 2, the new centralism was not merely the filtering down of some new practical "Keynesianism," but instead involved a shift in the very definition of the role of federalism in the overall political economy. Thus, intergovernmental programs throughout the 1960s and 1970s increasingly guaranteed civil rights, housed the poor, experimented in fighting poverty, extended economic regulation to drugs, mining safety, consumer products, and air and water quality, dramatically expanded food production, and expanded many other policy areas. With the exception of macroeconomic policy, most policy expansion was pursued through subnational federalism in the form of collaborative grants, bureaucratic agreements across jurisdictions, court orders affecting local life and politics, and state and local grantsmanship. This was centralist policy making with intergovernmental collaboration.

The new centralism was especially important in expanding the regulatory powers of federal agencies over business operations and hazards to the public. It usually meant a process of national elite assistance, under congressional laws, to neglected urban, agricultural, and regional economic sectors. By the mid-1970s, the new centralism meant that economic and development capital and resources were shifted to the South and the West. Finally, the new centralist federalism gradually aided the rise of subnational federalism and intergovernmental lobbies. It also expanded the representative basis of power of urban, southern, and western interests in congressional, presidential, and state-legislative elections. Thus these regions disproportionately gained from early government urban, development, and social regulation policies.

Despite recent rhetoric against intergovernmental regulation, grants, and programs, considerable evidence indicates that these policies—all outgrowths of enlightened centralism—had numerous salutary effects. Air and water quality deterioration was partly arrested, voting rights dramatically increased, women's positions in management enhanced, farm and family incomes increased, elderly poverty and health conditions significantly stabilized, and even some inroads against poverty made (Schwarz 1983; Peterson et al., 1986).

Compound Federalism. One effect of compound federalism's institutional arrangements is the frequent degree of **policy consensus** achieved between positions advocated by Congress, the executive branch, and the courts. On an intergovernmental basis, compound federalism's widely shared cultural consensus means widespread general support for civil rights, environmental protection, and voting rights. Today, for instance, police forces in the South protect civil rights marchers—a profound difference from twenty-five years ago.

However, another effect of compound federalism's complex arrangements of institutions in the federal system is what some call **hyperpluralism** (Lowi 1969). By trying to achieve policy consensus over time, through complex power balancing between institutions at the same level and between levels, policies sometimes get nowhere fast. For example, federal housing policy, job training, urban development, grants for energy, and mass transit all seemed to swing back and forth in the 1970s and 1980s between "market solutions" (vouchers, rent subsidies, and big-ticket spending for such things as nuclear power and workfare) and "government programs" (youth job corps, CETA, government housing, nonnuclear alternative energy incentives, and direct or in-kind assistance to the poor, for example).

Advocates of hyperpluralism take a rather cynical position on the effects of intergovernmental programs over time. Their argument goes about like this: No sooner is one program in place and seemingly gaining some ground or developing program expertise than some political sector cries out "waste, mismanagement," only to replace the program often with previously tried or worn-out programs. This *policy-cycle stalemate* seems to follow irregular cycles of government activism versus "market solutions" implemented as soon as political opposition to current programs crystallizes. In this light, the Reagan domestic policies—housing, job training, and the rest—appear to be mere repetitions, for the most part, of approaches tried before in the states and discarded.

Yet another policy effect of compound federalism has been felt profoundly in the area of social regulation. Primacy here must be attributed to the courts. From civil rights to pornography, peaceful protest rights, representation, privacy, women's pay and benefits, school prayer, integration and curricula, and numerous other areas, the federal courts have increasingly controlled both enactment and enforcement (see Chapter 3).

Thus, the compound system (from courts to state laws to changes in state constitutions) is the controlling factor in the basics of political participation in America. This includes voting rights, redistricting, apportionment, rights of assembly and protest, labor–management arbitration, expression of views in the media, campaign finance, and the Freedom of Information Act (regulated through federal court decisions and congressional laws). Meanwhile state laws have governed and generally expanded recall, referendum, and petition procedures, and sunshine laws, in the majority of these cases "preempting" or substituting for historical federal inaction with new state innovations. That state laws are sometimes passed to rectify federal inaction demonstrates the compound nature of policy making.

Perhaps the major policy effect of the compound system is its balancing of power, especially between institutions, described earlier. That compound federalist culture and institutional process strongly affect power struggles means in a de facto sense that policy decisions or enactments strongly reflect who "wins." We have reviewed the details and *policy effects* of this in the 1980s in Chapters 2 and 8.

Finally, it is the institutional complexity of compound federalism that sometimes produces **fragmented macroeconomic and regulatory policy.** Quite often, for example, congressional preferences in budgets, fiscal stimuli (such as unemployment compensation), and social entitlements (medicare, social security, and so on) are predominant over White House preferences. Regulatory policy is severely fragmented when presidents disagree with congressional views on economic regulation. The fragmented character of regulation policy grows out of presidential versus congressional control of regulation, and out of intergovernmental agreements that allow state-level substitution of federal regulation (as with air and water quality). Thus, intergovernmental relations, filtered through compound levels and institutions, help explain diversity in shared federal programs. This is especially true in energy, welfare, urban services, air and environmental quality, and other "intergovernmentally bargained" policies.

Dualism. Even a quick summary of the policy consequences of dualism will reveal possibly the most profound of all of federalism's effects.

Policy effects, especially from intergovernmental grants and regulation, end up even more complex because of dualism.

Dualism allows for the **semisovereign status of states.** This status is probably the best explanation of profound policy outcome differences between the states. Levels of spending by states and communities on education, environment, and welfare, to mention just a few major areas, vary tremendously. Reflecting even more variation are the conditions or regulations under which recipients can receive benefits from apparently similar programs, especially in welfare and education. The variations among states in the outcomes of education, welfare, and health care are traceable mostly to differences in the nature and quality of programs provided by different states.

Because of dualism, social regulation is even more profoundly different between states and communities, in hundreds of significant areas of life. Such areas of tremendous variety in life-style and regulation include how people and jurisdictions practice and regulate gambling, drinking, divorce and marriage, child abuse and custody, family planning and crisis intervention, prostitution, school curricula, professions, religion in schools and public places, and women's role in managerial positions in the private and public sectors. All these policy areas are dramatically affected by state and local conditions. All of this variety is an outgrowth of dualism, which places local social life and the regulation of it significantly in the hands of states and communities, unless national constitutional questions are involved.

Even when national constitutional questions are involved, court decisions can be one thing and community compliance another if local resistance is high. Regular school prayers, the passing out of Bibles on school time, the teaching of creationism, the banning of books, discrimination in lending, illegal union-busting tactics, and government job placement without advertising are still prominent in many local areas, despite "federal regulations" to the contrary. As a result, too much is too often made of "intrusive federal regulations" in social life.

Yet, the traditions and cultures of dualism can help explain both the "progressive" and the "backward" aspects of policy outcomes in America. Dualism probably explains "inequitable" and variable social policy outcomes about as much, or as often, as it explains the rise of "progressive" state-led policy experiments in such areas as criminal justice and education reform.

In similar fashion, dualism explains significant political differences between states in parties, constitutions, elections, business tax environments, urban fiscal conditions, and referenda and other populist political mechanisms (see Chapter 4). Finally, it is the cause of policy and legal dualism in America, where some traditions of law and policy (education policies and criminal and family law, for example) are under decisive local or state dominance (or local power systems. See Chapter 5).

The Policy Consequences of Subnational Political Economies

The Interstate Model. The most important policy effect of the interstate model is to produce similarities within and differences bewteen
regions of the country in policy outcomes. *Regionalism* has long been recognized as one of the prime aspects of federalism (Elazar 1966). Regionalism
means that geographic groups of states have shared political cultures, traditions, and historical identities, as well as common patterns of associations,
"copycat" networks of relations and policies, and political lobbying of
Washington.

Differences in political cultures have been shown by Daniel Elazar and
others to significantly influence policy approaches in many areas. These include taxes, sex and class roles in politics, typical patterns of reform, the degree to which politics is affected by strong parties, ideas of public service,
corruption, and other styles of political decision making. Political cultures
help determine the pattern of social spending and economic regulation, affecting whether spending levels are high and redistributive or low and
"pork-barrel." They also strongly affect whether laws and regulations
promote business through lower taxes and easy regulations or whether they
control economic development.

Traditions and historical identities explain some features of policy.
Southern states have always been recognized as somewhat distinctive,
through historical patterns of race conflict, religious fundamentalism, Jim
Crow discrimination tendencies, and similar congressional delegation positions on social welfare, economic development grants, civil rights, and so
forth. The New England States, as the earliest colonies and as "bastions of
liberty" and grass-roots democracy, also have similar historical identities,
rooted in antiurban ideas. Today, those states take similar positions in
public policy on health care, criminal justice reform, drunk driving, nuclear
power plant siting, waste storage, interstate transmission of wastes, acid
rain, and many other areas. In the late 1970s, many Western states adopted
similar "tax reduction" laws and similar positions on wilderness area
protection and later on the leasing of federal lands for development, drill-
ing, and other purposes.

Regionalism is one of the strongest explanations of several kinds of
public policy features of the American system. One is that some redistributive and regulatory policies (the Equal Rights Amendment, religion in
schools, race, environmentalism, taxes, and "right-to-work" or other legal
approaches to unions) often have great similarities *within* regions. Another
difference between regions is their adoption and similarity of new policy
patterns. Similarities within and differences between regions have emerged
in education reforms, welfare, criminal justice, and lobbying of Washington
on environmental issues or shared economic troubles or needs, for example.

A third regional factor is differences between regions in political system style and function (one-partyism, party machine politics, sex roles in politics, and so on). This difference, in turn, affects social welfare, social life regulation, and reformism within and between regions.

A fourth regional factor is common approaches to economic regulation and development issues. Some regions are more concerned than others in getting national subsidies, labor arbitration, macroeconomic intervention, and development grants, and fighting cuts in public grants and welfare, as their economies decline. The "rustbelt"—the declining industrial states of the Northeast and upper Midwest—and the farm-belt states pursue these goals in common. Such common lobbying approaches can have a dramatic impact on national budget and tax policies, as was the case in the 1980s with some of these states, and with cities opposing further cuts and changes in IGR transfers and programs (Caraley 1986; Benton 1986).

The Substate Model.   Forces within the substate pattern are what most affect the choice of local executives (mayors, county commissioners, city engineers, managers, and the rest). Local executives and bureaucracies, in turn, largely determine the nature, quality, and effectiveness of public management and programs. Chapter 4 describes **effectiveness** as the degree to which laws, grants, and so on, are considered appropriate to solving local problems, and whether adequate implementation measures are built into policies. Thus, from one angle, effectiveness depends on whether local units can live with intergovernmental policies and programs, whether they want them, and whether they can comply. On the other hand, effectiveness can depend on whether locals plan to resist regulations, ignore program grants, and so on. These considerations apply whether policy sources are national or state-level.

For example, more than 40 states in the 1980s have tried out statewide reforms of public education. These reforms involve school consolidation, beefed up curricula, formula funding favoring mergers and benefiting poorer schools, and teacher competency tests. What will be the political response of locals to efforts to implement laws embodying these reforms? The answer will determine the fate of these efforts. Obviously, the **policy consequences** of local executive responses—for example, their effectiveness in terms of balancing intergovernmental needs, legal requirements, and program resources—can really make a difference in the **ultimate local outcomes.** These outcomes are as specific as whether the locality gets new roads, whether Johnny learns to read better, whether businesses are attracted to a better-trained and -motivated labor force, and the like.

Another major effect of the forces at work in the substate model is significant differences in socioeconomic conditions within states. Things such as urban zoning, growth, quality of life, and criminal prosecution and enforcement are affected by substate politics, state funding of cities, and constitutional restrictions on city powers (see Chapter 3). The conditions of rural areas are affected by numerous policies, not the least of which are public funding for education, agricultural extension services and similar assistance, roads and highways, electrification, and water resource and other economic development policies of states. All of these, as mentioned, are affected by political cultures, party systems, and to some extent regionalism.

Another prime factor in the substate model is state versus local interest groups and elites. Who is "running government" and enacting policies at different levels can make for big policy differences, and often features great, even tragic public drama (see Hawley and Wirt 1974). It may determine "who gets what," depending on resistance to implementation (see Chapter 10).

In Manhattan, Kansas, for example, one of the last big federal urban development grants (amounting to a total of $17 million from various sources by 1984) built a huge downtown mall, primarily for big chain marketers such as Sears, while tearing down and "compensating" 50 percent of main street businesses and relocating numerous residences and streets. The ensuing rancorous dispute over local economic development drastically split the local city council. Additionally, it resulted in a fierce battle between promall local elites and big state-level mall developers allied with grant agencies on one side, and an alliance of most of the local business people (many of whom lost third- and fourth-generation and centrally located family businesses to the mall), the local Chamber of Commerce, Kansas State University economists, and the local news media on the opposing side. The issues at play were not only who would win but who would benefit economically. Ultimately, the issues involved the overall direction and stability of the local economy. For example, unanticipated costs for sewers, land clearance, civil engineering to avoid a high water table, insurance, and other hidden items soared well beyond the forecast, while the farm-based economy sank to depressed levels unforeseen in the initial developer-led impact statement. In Manhattan, as elsewhere, who "runs government" determines substantially what happens to people's economic lives, family businesses, local trade, tax bills, monies for other vital services such as schools, and "the downtown."

The Interlocal Model.   The policy effects of interlocal federalism are significant. Recognizing elites in substate politics also forces one to recognize both the power disputes *between* "official" local units of government and their "cooperative" features. Local governments and politically active elites and other groups dispute or cooperate with each other over such mundane things as state grants, federal grants, zoning, and interlocal services and agreements. To return to the Manhattan case, the hot issue of interlocal concern is what will happen to property taxes, housing, and business relocation because of the new giant mall. Uprooted individuals, and those wishing to escape property taxes (which were forced upward to pay for city-supplied mall services and development costs), were beginning to relocate housing construction, businesses, and mobile-home sites across the nearby county line, where taxes were lower but city access was still easy. County officials welcomed these taxable businesses and property displaced by the mall, but Manhattan city officials and mall supporters were not happy with this threat to the city tax base and thus to continued mall development.[1]

As the Manhattan situation and countless others demonstrate, whether you get dispute or cooperation between elites and jurisdictions depends on interlocal politics and power. And what happens determines, for example, whose tax bill goes up and which jurisdiction gets revenue for schools. Local outcomes depend on interlocal power. This means that the major differences between localities in social life, economic conditions, and schools and other vital services depend not only on macroeconomic conditions and higher-level intergovernmental forces; they are also affected by interlocal relations, disputes, and attitudes toward culture and development (Friedland and Palmer 1984).

The National–Local Model.   As happened in Manhattan, the growth of local services results in part from the effect of national intergovernmental programs on local markets and politics. We pointed out in Chapter 7 that national-local relations were greatly accelerated by the New Deal. Since the 1930s, the political and social conditions of local life have been more and more affected by national-level initiatives and policy enactments. Court decisions have affected local election systems, local interest groups have arisen in response to federal grants, and national policy has changed many aspects of local life, from school curricula to racial integration of public services.

But it is also the case that local styles of adjustment to national social regulation determine actual compliance with federal regulations and court orders (see the discussion of dualism earlier in this chapter). In fact, many programs administered at the local level (medicare, social security, family services) are quite effective, despite the problems of policy consistency in other areas (public housing, for example).

In the 1960s and 1970s, communication from locals to Washington and federal agencies based on such things as lobbying, intergovernmental contacts, and city managers' grantsmanship had generally less conflict than state–national relations, at least until the budget and social spending reductions of 1981–82. The 1980s featured less reliance and cooperation between locals and Washington, and more "go-it-alone" city- and community-provided and -funded services, coupled with locally rising taxes and service cuts, and growing local political opposition to Washington's policies.

Although the total picture is not yet clear, the *net policy effects* of the most recent developments in the national–local model can be glimpsed

(Palmer and Sawhill 1985). Some of these effects have been negative—increased poverty, redistribution of wealth to the wealthier, slight reductions in spendable income among the poor and the working class, and reductions in the quality and availability of day-care services, for example. Such negative local effects are primary factors in the increasing anti-Washington attitude of cities and localities (Benton 1986; Caputo and Johnson 1986).

SUMMARY

Discussions of power and policy—the subjects of this and the previous chapter—are virtually new to federalism studies. In Chapter 8 we focused on power—what it is and how it is exercised in the federal system. In particular, we sought to show how the exercise of power affects political opinion and issue agendas, government decision making, and policy implementation. In the present chapter we discussed how the interaction of federalism and power has certain outcomes. We believe that outcomes are an important indicator of power. But power does not clearly determine outcomes. The main reason for this is that federalism buffers and alters the effects of power.

In this chapter we examined two important aspects of federalism and power. The first was the degree to which federalism in its seven patterns "fights back," functioning as the great arbiter of power and the invisible hand of the American political system. We outlined how federalism in its seven patterns regulates power. The seven patterns feature cultures, representation systems, and other power-buffering obstacles and institutions through which power and ultimately policy outcomes must filter.

The second major theme is how federalism interacts with power to produce public policy outcomes. Power is not exercised without effects on people and places. We described these policy outcomes, identifying who benefits and what difference the interaction of federalism and power makes for people. In short, the interaction of federalism and power makes a significant difference in the lives of people. But even the vast picture of federalism and power is only part of the total picture or public policy. We need to turn to the even bigger question of how federalism's seven patterns affect the larger public policy process in America.

KEY CONCEPTS AND THEMES FOR REVIEW

effectiveness
fragmented macroeconomic and regulatory policy
hyperpluralism
interlocal planning networks

interstate networks and alliances
intrusive regulation
local preemption of national goals
official intergovernmental lobbies
policy consensus
policy consequences and ultimate local outcomes
regionalism
policy outcomes
semisovereign status of states
tension-balanced representation
the Federal Reserve

NOTES

[1]The most important theorist of the dominance of the business culture in America is Thorstein Veblin (1908).

Federalism and the Public Policy Process:

10

The paths of change

As we pointed out in the last chapter, it makes no sense to summarize social power systems without talking about how power has policy effects. Power makes a significant difference in the lives of people. But how federalism and the powerful affect policy outcomes is only a part of the story. The bigger picture involves a description of how the policy process works in the federal system and how federalism influences that process. Such a description necessarily includes some very important questions. How do issues arise and spread in federalism? What are the contentious issues at stake in the federal policy process? How do formulation, enactment, and implementation take place within federal political economies? And finally, how is the policy process affected by federalism's seven political economy patterns? To be sure, this is relatively unexplored territory: few writers on federalism have attempted to describe how federalism affects the policy process. But it is that topic, and the attempt to answer the important questions just raised, that animate this chapter.

The phrase *policy process* reflects the understanding in political science that public policies are not decisions that fall like manna from the skies. The common understanding that "decisions are made, and things happen" has been replaced in political science by the more sophisticated view that *policies evolve in phases, over time*. This chapter will describe how policy evolves over

259

time within and because of federalism. But first, we have to start with a few ideas about what a public policy is.

WHAT IS A PUBLIC POLICY?

There are different ideas about what a public policy is, but we will stick with the definition that public policies are *standing but evolving decisions to either do something or avoid doing something, which are made and enforced on behalf of various interests, through government offices and authority* (see Greenberg et al. 1977 for the origin of this definition). This definition of public policy incorporates many important ideas. One is that policies are government decisions, but ones that evolve because of power pressures (see Chapters 8 and 9). Another is that public policies reflect a mixture of both public elements (voters, government officials, and others) and the wishes of private interests that sometimes get government to do their bidding. A third is that *public* does not mean just "government official action." It can also mean that government sometimes represents the interests of duly elected officials and voters and at other times acts on behalf of private, interest group, elite, or narrow bureaucratic interests. Thus our definition captures the many lively meanings of what is public about public policies. (For more about the idea of public policy, see the readings at the end of the chapter.)

The notion of policy evolution is illustrated in Figure 10-1, which draws on the ideas of Charles Jones, one of the first to suggest that public policy evolves through phases. The very important theoretical contribution of Jones and others is that policies are at least a little like people — sometimes stable, sometimes changing in response to external and internal forces, and going through stages. Jones's basic idea is that policies are a long time coming. They spend years in a formulation stage, where government merely begins to listen to public and private interest-group pressures about an issue. This stage leads to an enactment phase, where laws, regulations, and other formal decisions are initially made. Then, policy must be enforced or implemented over the years, despite various kinds of resistance at different levels. Formulation, enactment, and implementation—these are the three basic phases in the policy process. Of course, along the way, policy makes a difference—that is, people are affected by the outcomes. We will use these key ideas in discussing the policy process in the federal system. We will add the idea that federalism not only complicates what public policy is (a commonplace observation to anyone who has gone to different schools in different states, for example), but also alters public policies.

A quick example of what we mean by **public policy phases** is civil rights policy. Today's civil rights policies started with 1930s Supreme Court decisions about the rights of minorities to higher education, handed down in response to litigation by the NAACP. But whereas the Court slowly ex-

Figure 10-1 *How public policy evolves through phases*

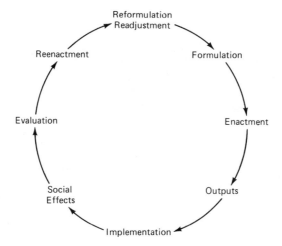

Source: Charles O. Jones, An Introduction to the Study of Public Policy (Belmont, Cal.: Wadsworth Publishers, 1970). Used by permission.

panded civil rights from the 1930s on, the states, Congress, and presidents were less responsive until the 1960s. Public interest groups were not silent, however, as the civil rights movement picked up steam in the 1950s. With all this public and private activity, it took longer than a decade to achieve civil rights laws that had teeth. Then, of course, it has taken over twenty years for the federal government and the states to respond; enforcement has taken an uneven course, varying across state and community lines. And since civil rights affects many groups—blacks, Hispanics, women, Indians, and others—there is no easy way to summarize how civil rights public policy has turned out over the years.

It is possible to see the bigger picture of this and other issues by looking at policy in phases in the federal system, and that is what we will do in this chapter. At the end of the chapter we will concentrate on the effects of federalism's political economies on the policy process. We begin our discussion of the policy process where policy begins, with formulation.

POLICY FORMULATION

Contentious Issues and Bureaucratic Games

Interest group conflict and consensus are focused across intergovernmental lines on several things. We will look first at the kinds of contentious issues at stake in the seven federal systems.

One of the most important contentious issues is the proper level of government to exercise control over a policy. For example, should we have a national public school curriculum to increase our international economic competitiveness and our cultural literacy? Federalism's traditions are ripe with conflicts of this kind. As we have seen, conflicts between centralization advocates and decentralization advocates recur in federalism.

A second area of contention is over whose goals should prevail in a community or the nation. For example, if we have a national curriculum, how do we incorporate local preferences in moral education, teacher preferences, and the like? Simply put, whose interest will the federal structures represent? The people's? Interest groups'? Elites'? As you can readily see, this question is a perennial source of group conflict.

A third contentious issue is what to do about social welfare, social life regulation, economics, and other vital areas that affect people's lives. Example: what alternatives exist for teacher training, curricula, and student competency testing?

A fourth issue is who should have representation or other forms of influence in government circles, and at which level. Example: who should make the decisions about curricula? Congress? State legislatures? Local school boards? What about concerned parents' organizations? Students themselves? How do you set up public input into the notoriously intransigent state education departments? Without doubt, these issues motivate interest groups to get active across intergovernmental lines.

Another entity that acts across intergovernmental lines to influence the formulation of policies is the public bureaucracies. Issues that are typically contentious in bureaucratic politics drive public bureaucracies to "play games" to win allies for their goals at different levels of the federal system. Thus **bureaucratic games and goals** are a common source of intergovernmental conflict and cooperation and an important trigger for **intergovernmental policy formulation.** Here is a list of some bureaucratic intergovernmental games:

> fighting and converting executive appointees
> generating intergovernmental interest in new programs
> getting intergovernmental input into policy alternatives
> tracking and publicizing prior program effectiveness
> building alliances and defending turfs
> accommodating and adjusting to executive controls
> cultivating legislatures and legislators
> coping with formal lawmaker oversight
> coping with intergovernmental interest groups
> diverting or fighting subnational policy battles: defending the administering

agencies, whistle blowing, "marrying the natives," defending the helpless recipients

Fighting and converting executive appointees to agency points of view are perennial goals attached to the four-year election cycle of governors and presidents. In the national government in the 1980s, federal agencies were deeply entrenched in resisting or attempting to divert various presidential initiatives, including most of the objectives of the New Federalism. Defending themselves from these and other Reagan era changes has been a major preoccupation of federal, state, and local public agencies, especially in intergovernmental programs. Usually, however, public agencies pursue, simultaneously and across jurisdictional levels, several if not most of the strategies just listed. Using these strategies, bureaucratic agencies fought many policy battles in the Reagan years, mostly with success. Bureaucracies may fight these battles for numerous reasons: as "protectors" of helpless citizens, because of external interest pressures, because of interdepartmental squabbles, because agencies serve external scientific standards, professions, and goals, or simply because agencies do not wish to see programs (and their benefits to themselves and to clientele) cut back (Rourke 1984).

Bureaucratic Intergovernmental Formulation

A lot of policy formulation takes place between levels of bureaucracies as they work out the details of new policy proposals. But probably the majority of bureaucratic formulation takes place in negotiations between agencies at one level. The issue then spills over into the intergovernmental arena. It is important, then, to know which level more or less controls the formulation of a policy.

Intergovernmental formulation takes place when officials or interests at one level object to or cooperate with policy being formulated at another level. It is at the intergovernmental level that issues accelerate from behind closed doors and onto the public stage, particularly as the media pick up on policy battles between levels.

A good example in the 1980s was the attempted use of the National Guard for training of the Nicaraguan contras in Central America, especially in Honduras. Originally the policy was formulated and pursued behind closed doors and between the bureaucracies of the White House office, the National Security Council, the CIA, and the State and Defense Departments. But several state governors objected publicly to this use of the National Guard and threatened to use their traditional role of commander-in-chief of the National Guard to block their states' participation in Central American adventures. Here we see clearly how intergovernmental conflict boosts policy formation from behind closed bureaucratic doors and onto the public stage.

Intergovernmental Policy Formulation and the Mass Media

A major finding of studies of the mass media in the 1970s was that the media had become increasingly "nationalized" in their coverage. And with fewer and fewer really independent news sources, the media increased their control over issues and policy proposals (ACIR 1986:205). But by the mid-1980s, with increased competition from cable TV, alternative networks, and prominent journalism programs (such as "20/20," "60 Minutes," and the MacNeil–Lehrer report), the media were increasingly accelerating intergovernmental issues "up from the local view." The three major networks, seeing their audiences dwindle, began responding by giving a "lower-down" slant to news. A prominent example was the special-focus reports on the "NBC Nightly News."

Earlier studies of the mass media had emphasized the effects and role of the "big three" television networks. These studies showed that the mass media had considerable power to make, accelerate, and oversimplify issues. The media were shown to sensationalize personalities and conflicts, to over-emphasize presidential power and agendas to the exclusion of other national actors and subnational officials and concerns, to develop attitudes of distrust in government by reporting in a watchdog fashion. The media especially chose to dramatize sex, corruption, or malperformance (more in government than in the business world or, especially, in the media themselves). The ACIR noted studies showing how the growing power of the "big three" networks had accelerated the decline in voting, reduced the power of parties by emphasizing personality factors in campaigns, stimulated the explosion in campaign marketing and advertising, and eroded the general level of information in the population by tempting people away from newspapers and other major print news sources (ACIR 1986).

A major effect of such media policies has been the "presidentialization" of national nightly news. Presidents, in turn, have focused more and more on media relations, especially since the Kennedy presidency. They have attempted not only to countermanipulate media reporting but to use the media as a mass podium for their reelection campaigns, budget proposals, foreign policy proposals, and so on. The presidency has thus emerged in its own right as the major agenda force in American politics. However, presidential effectiveness depends on many factors (style, media sophistication, White House "PR people," opposition in Congress). Presidents thus seem to have more influence on media coverage of budget issues, foreign policy issues, and other Washington-centered political issues. They seem to have less effect on formulating policy agendas and proposals in the intergovernmental system, especially on war-making issues and on civil rights and liberties issues. This is partly because the media and other governmental actors find these issues so controversial, and partly because intergovernmental lobbies take such strong public stances on these issues.

Despite intergovernmental resistance to presidential attempts to dominate policy formulation, the president remains one of the major initiators of ideas and programs about federalism. Of the presidential programs that affected federalism, those of Lyndon Johnson, Franklin Roosevelt, Richard Nixon, and Ronald Reagan gained the most attention. These programs also generated (with the exception of Reagan's) the most change in public policy, including some in federalist cultures. For more on presidents and the limits of "official federalism policies," see the last chapter.

Secondary influences on formulating issues and setting the terms of issue consideration in American federalism include, at the national level, the courts, general bureaucracies, and regulatory agencies. Certainly the Federal Reserve chair, sometimes referred to as the second most powerful person in U.S. government, and the Fed have strong influence in setting public discussions about fiscal and monetary affairs, not to mention their power to unilaterally enact interest-rate and monetary policy. At the subnational level, governors have the lead role in policy formulation, even gaining in influence on legislatures in recent years. Other significant trend and issue setters include the state and local media, prominent mayors of big cities, and city council members. Less important are state legislatures, courts, and local bureaucracies, although local courts are quite prominent in formulating (and enacting) policy. The ACIR has noted (1986:165) that members of Congress are more independent of parties. They are taking on more of a "policy entrepreneurial role," creating public discussion and awareness of issues of the day and thus reducing constituent pressures, including those of parties, in the federal system.

The role of elites in federalism was covered extensively earlier. In brief, local private elites still have considerable influence on the formulation of policies on economic growth and redevelopment and taxation issues, particularly at their level of government (Molotch 1976). National elites, due to reasons previously described, have major mechanisms of influence over policy formulation. These include the manipulation of ideologies and public opinion through mass advertising and indoctrination, research and development funding, institutional control through placement of their people in strategic positions, and massive lobbying. These strategies ensure that elite issues "float to the top" faster than other alternatives.

Intergovernmental Networks and Interlevel Issue Formation

Some theories of organization have proposed that much of what comes out of organizations is a result of interorganizational pressures in the form of such things as bureaucratic alliances, exchange of information, and reliance on expertise and clout (Sales and Chandler 1971; Perrow 1983). Many organizational outcomes result from what are called *interorganization transactions, dependencies,* and *networks.*

Although there is little direct research on IGR networks, there are some very similar concepts. One is *picket-fence federalisms.* Another is *subgovernments*—"circles" of bureaucracies, interests, and officials across government levels. However, these ideas focus on functional relations within specific programs. The concept of IGR networks is more encompassing. Its proponents attempt to identify organizations across levels that interact or depend on one another to a significant degree. And they attempt to describe the power and significance of such organizations. IGR networks should be a more important focus of federalism studies, especially considering the rise of so-called rapid policy diffusion in the mid-1980s (Savage 1986). The new intergovernmental lobbies—multiple-issue groups such as the environmentalists, the ERA lobby, and the New Right groups—are becoming increasingly important in policy formulation. They pursue comprehensive interstate lobbying strategies designed specifically to get the states to do what might or might not be done in Washington. Also, the older intergovernmental lobbies have not faded at all. Instead their presence makes IGR networks that much more complex. The issues of "peace, justice, and jobs" brought together in the 1980s such disparate IGR lobbies as the civil rights groups, environmentalists, and peace and religious activists into a complex network. This network supports such things as deep arms cuts, demilitarization, and economic reconstruction programs favoring labor and farmers. However, these groups and the issues of interest to them have not yet constituted a stable basis for electoral realignment or party discipline on an intergovernmental basis (Dolbeare 1986; Chapter 9).

Another element of the new IGR networks is the alliances, however temporary, between business lobbies and political action committees. The first issue on which business PACs developed an interstate lobbying stance was state "right-to-work" laws. Recently, considerable effort has been expended on tort reform designed to place ceilings on insurance liabilities in medical and other liability suits.

Developments in the mass media have aided the rapid rise of interstate policy diffusion and networks. These developments include the previously mentioned nationalization of the mass media and the media's increasing attention to policy innovation at the subnational level. National media attention to new local issues increases the rapidity with which issues spread in the federal system. Examples in the early 1980s included the formation of the missing-children movement, the spread of joint-custody laws, and the adoption of no-fault divorce laws. However, policy innovation spread rapidly between states in response to factors other than the media. Some of the spread was simply in response to federal inaction or institutional gridlock in Washington, but some was due to the new IGR networks and to the nationalization of issue agendas pertaining to state–local issues. Thus stiffer drunk-driving laws, "lemon-aid" laws covering used cars and new "lemons," educational reform, child-abuse laws and reforms, the rejection of workfare experiments, and plant-closing laws were among the new wave of interstate reforms being adopted by the majority of states within merely a year or two of their initial exposure in the media in the mid-1980s.

It is not clear just how much such IGR networks, both private and institutional, are resulting in "better, healthier states and intergovernmental policy administration." It is certain that they are speeding up the response of states to perceived policy problems. And the new information about IGR networks hints that the health and adaptability of states, the speedy innovativeness of interstate lobbies, and the rise of state–local preemption of federal policy roles bring into serious question the broad claims made about "overload" in a federal system shot through with ineffective intergovernmental regulation, welfare programs, and so on. In fact, the evidence in the mid-1980s seemed to indicate that programs were a little better administered, and administered with their intended effects (Peterson, Rabe, and Wong 1986), and that states not only are increasingly responding to federal cutbacks but are developing innovative solutions to problems that Washington institutions perceive but cannot seem to act on. These developments explain much of why policy formulation in the federal system in the mid- to late 1980s was stalemated in Washington but increasingly innovative and effective in the states (see Chapter 12).

Interstate innovation through the new IGR networks is producing significant effects on policy formulation and also on enactment. It may be a bit too early to assess the policy effects of these developments on society, but their potential for social and economic change is large.

The Politics of Formulation: How Interests Get Issues Started and Accelerated across Intergovernmental Lines

Intergovernmental Interest Groups. In the previous section, we described the many actors in intergovernmental policy formulation. Now we focus on what these actors do to get policy formulated their way in federalism.

Figure 10-2 shows the many-splendored range of **intergovernmental interest group tactics** to get favored issues considered in the public and governmental eye. The most important determinant of the tactics interests use is their power. As Figure 10-2 shows, the more powerful intergovernmental interests use the sophisticated tactics of personal placement in top government posts, funding of scientific research, massive attempts to manipulate ideology and public issues through media blitzes, and educational program funding. Weaker groups are forced into using institutional

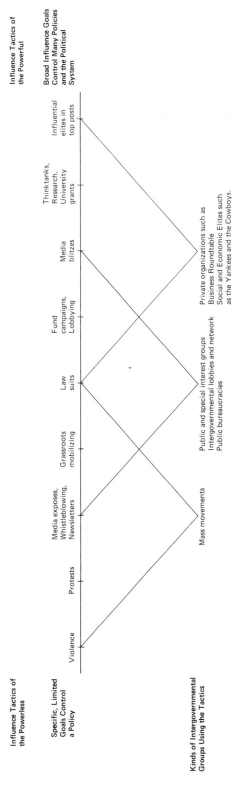

Figure 10-2 *A continuum of the intergovernmental interest groups*

tactics (lobbying, litigation), the tactics of mass peaceful protest, or, as a last resort, violence to obtain issue consideration. Weaker interests are usually "outside of government," whereas more powerful groups have made inroads into government (indeed may consistently have representatives sitting in top positions). The various intergovernmental tactics that interest groups use to get policy formulated their way can be summarized in eight patterns:

1. react to national government policy
2. react to elite or other interest group stances
3. gain public attention (through peaceful protest and other means)
4. sue
5. lobby Washington (both bureaucracies and Congress)
6. lobby other states
7. form IGR networks
8. exercise sophisticated tactics of power (media blitzes and so on)

Most intergovernmental interests active today probably respond to or attempt to influence policy formulation roughly in the sequence of these patterns.

Not a lot is known about how groups start promoting their goals at one level versus another. But it may be safe to say that groups that fail to influence policy at one level of government will shift their strategy to another level. Research from the 1980s (ACIR 1986; Savage 1986) indicates that nationally powerful interests are becoming more sophisticated and spending more time lobbying states rather than Washington, perhaps because of the prevalent national policy stalemate. This pattern is certainly an effect of compound federalism's design of institutional structures (especially the separation of powers).

Public Bureaucracies. Public agencies use a variety of methods to get issues started and accelerated across intergovernmental lines. To keep things in perspective, however, we should remember that bureaucracies are only semiindependent of supervisory (executive and legislative) and interest group influence. However, a good deal of the literature on public administration has emphasized how public bureaucracies—the targets of representative and private influence—are nevertheless sometimes entrepreneurs unto themselves. In short, formulation tactics may be used to further the interests and programs of agencies themselves, of supervising government branches, or of private, usually business interests that heavily influence agency priorities and operations.

Table 10-1 shows most of the important tactics used by public agencies to get issues started and accelerated with a view to influencing policy formulation.

TABLE 10-1 *Tactics Used by Public Agencies to Formulate Issues*

leak information to the media	mobilize advisory groups
alarm constituencies	hold big conferences
feed legislators information	target benefits to localities
commission research	testify before legislative committees
smile for the camera (use public relations methods)	build relations with IGR lobbies
give notice for public hearings and regulations	

Any or all of these tactics will be used to build sympathetic audiences among interest groups and other bureaucracies that have program functions bearing directly or indirectly on issues central to an agency (as in budgeting; see Wildavsky 1985). These tactics are pursued across intergovernmental lines, as many public administration case studies have demonstrated. However, these patterns have not been systematized into generalizations about which IGR bureaucracies form networks and which tactics they pursue.

In the 1980s, public bureaucracies at the national level used formulation tactics to build support for their views on budget cuts and priorities. They vigorously sought intergovernmental alliances in pursuit of policy formulation more favorable to agency goals or in resistance to proposed initiatives. These policy tactics were particularly intensive in natural resources and the environment, intergovernmental grants, urban services, civil rights, social security and medicare, student loans, and other programs that have benefited public interests and agencies (Palmer and Sawhill 1986).

At the top of the chart of bureaucracies that strongly pursued these strategies in the 1980s were the U.S. Navy (defending the 600-ship budget), the EPA, the Department of Agriculture, Amtrak, the Small Business Administration, the U.S. Civil Rights Commission, the General Services Administration, the General Accounting Office, the Office of Technology Assessment, and the Congressional Budget Office. Most of these agencies were motivated to avoid administration budget or program cuts, to reduce OMB regulatory interference in the 1980s, to avoid deregulation, or to analyze controversial policy initiatives, such as Star Wars and the unusual tax proposals of the administration.

Also, whistle blowers and others in some regulatory agencies that have claimed nonenforcement of hazards have used these strategies somewhat effectively for agency self-defense. At least occasionally successful have been the OSHA, the FAA, meat and chicken inspectors of the Department of Agriculture, and certain divisions of the Department of the Interior. Individuals or groups within these agencies went public in the 1980s, affecting policy formulation or attempting to reformulate policy decisions made at the top. The same strategies were used by certain figures in the security and defense establishment to leak information about the Irangate scandal as congressional committee investigations unfolded in the summer of 1987. In almost all these cases, bureaucracies were successful in focusing "public heat" through media attention, leaking to legislators or committees, or alerting and mobilizing external support groups to do the same.

Agencies had considerable success in the 1980s in getting policy formulated their way, or in resisting policy formulations being developed in Congress or by the administration. It appears that the frequency and intensity level of public bureaucracies in these tactics, especially in mobilizing across intergovernmental lines the resources needed to support their goals, were at the highest levels in recent decades. Intergovernmental lobbies served as major allies of public bureaucracies in these tactics, especially in the civil rights, environmental, and economic regulation areas. However, not all of this activity came from the new intergovernmental bureaucracies and interest groups. Some public agencies developed highly sophisticated public relations and program cultivation strategies and services over the decades, to ensure a high degree of success in affecting policy formulation across intergovernmental lines. Especially successful, as certain classic studies of public administration have shown, have been the Army Corps of Engineers, the navy, the Forest and National Park services, the Department of Labor, the Department of Commerce and the Small Business Administration, and the Department of the Interior. Perhaps less successful have been the departments of Health and Human Services, HUD, Energy, and Education and the Bureau of Indian Affairs.

POLICY ENACTMENTS

Policy formulation politics and battles can have several results. One is policy stalemate or inaction: one level of government simply cannot resolve the question of the direction of policy. A recent example was the Reagan administration policy toward Nicaragua. Another policy result may be fragmented decision making, where some elements of government are able to formulate policy into enactments while other branches or levels experience policy stalemate or resist the enacted policy. A good example here is the Supreme Court's enactment of civil rights policy in the 1950s while Congress and the president remained essentially inactive and states in many parts of the country resisted. In any case, something or nothing can come out of policy formulation battles. If something does happen, it means that government—or parts of it, anyway—has decided to take either a unilateral or a cooperative path toward enactment. In today's federalism, enactments happen both within and between levels of government.

The Transition from Formulation to Enactments

That policy enactments are more often than not made practically simultaneously or in quick sequence among as well as between levels and branches of government is an idea whose time has come. The notion of **intergovernmental policy enactment** is somewhat neglected, in that most political science literature treats decision making as if single institutions make single enactment decisions somehow in isolation from other branches and levels. This simply is not the case. Most policy enactment is *inherently* intergovernmental. In essence, enactment is what eventually comes out of a process of institutional bargaining and readjustment, over time and among levels of government. An enactment is not a single decision made once by one agency; it is a process.

Enactments are inherently intergovernmental for a variety of reasons. One is that institutions often make decisions in anticipation of responses made by other branches and levels. This may occur for psychological reasons (professionals do want peers to think well of them), for programmatic reasons (what states do in water quality must certainly take into account what the feds are doing), or for fear of retaliation (if we impose the sales tax, neighboring cities will boycott our stores). Another reason is that decisions more often than not are compromises among levels, branches, or interests. The budget process, considered as a whole, is an excellent illustration of such compromise. The budget process has long been characterized as a system of "partisan mutual adjustment" (Braybooke and Lindblom 1963). But as is apparent in even the most cursory examination of intergovernmental lobbies, budget enactment is also an intergovernmentally driven system of adjustments.

A third reason that enactment is inherently intergovernmental is that various officials, branches, and levels do learn from one another in the process of policy innovation. Enactments are borrowed and adapted with increasing rapidity throughout the intergovernmental system. Finally, enactments are inherently intergovernmental because of the continued persistence of regional patterns of enactments in interstate federalism. (See Chapter 8 for a discussion of this point.) Innovation spread is quickest among, and most likely to take on similar characteristics within, regional groupings of states. For all these reasons, it makes no sense to characterize enactments as something individual officials or institutions do individually.

The Forms of Intergovernmental Enactments

Enactments have traditionally been classified into legislation, regulations, executive decisions ("orders"), and court decisions. This classification scheme suggests that enactments are single decisions made once by one agency. In order to avoid this implication and to give a clearer view of the intergovernmental nature of enactments, we suggest a four-group classification. We believe enactments can better be understood as directive enactments, bargained enactments, influenced (learned) enactments, or process enactments. In each of these categories can be found legislation, regulations, executive orders, and court decisions.

Directive enactments are decisions made by one institution or level in response to an "order" from an external institution and under threat of a sanction. The sanction can be more or less coercive, ranging from a court order to the threat of withholding grant monies. The best example of directive enactments with strong coercive power is court-ordered busing in school desegregation cases. If not for the powerful sanction of legal coercion, a number of school districts simply would not have adopted cross-district busing to achieve integration. But enactment direction may take less coercive and intrusive forms, through indirect incentive or disincentive sanctions. Clear examples here are crosscutting requirements and crossover sanctions (discussed in Chapter 3). Each carries the "threat" of denying funds unless states and localities adopt rules in related programs. But as we saw, state and local officials are hardly passive pawns in the process, and the presence of several other factors means that there is less coercion than might be expected from the threat of loss of funds. The same situation exists in another area of directive enactments—state mandates to local governments. State mandates tend to be more controlling than crosscutting requirements, but local mandates are not nearly as rigid and coercive as some of the literature has characterized them.

Bargained enactments are decisions by one institution or level resulting from negotiation with an external institution. Like directive enactments, bargained enactments occur in all of the structural models of federalism. The best example of bargained enactments in the national–state model is partial preemption. Long touted as a form of the nationalization of the states, partial preemption allows states to substitute their programs if they can convince the feds that they are equal to the federal requirements and standards. Rather than having a directive and centralizing effect, partial preemption allows states and localities to bargain a great deal of elbow room. This flexibility means that programs can go in two quite different directions. In the more frequent instance, program activity and regulations fall far below federal regulations and standards for long periods, with national sanctions slow in coming if they ever do. Less frequently, states go beyond national program requirements and regulations. Thus there is wide variation in state response and in policy outcomes in bargained enactments. Certainly, bargained enactments in the national–state model have not been as rigid and centralizing as the literature initially characterized them.

Obviously, we cannot describe every bargained enactment; in our opinion, they occur more frequently than the literature has suggested. But we can illustrate enactments in other structural models. In the state–local model, bargained enactments occur when state-level agencies negotiate standards, regulations, program features, and the like with local offices. This process occurs in virtually the entire range of local services. In most instances, the process is capped off with a system of reports from locals to their state-agency counterparts. One of the most interesting and innovative forms of bargained enactments occurs in the national–local model. This involves the relationship of specially appointed members of national courts to local units. At issue are such things as redistricting, apportionment, and other civil rights cases. Substantial bargaining takes place between locals and the court in resolving such issues—a radical departure indeed from the posture of the detached court issuing injunctions.

Influenced enactments are decisions by one institution or level in voluntary response to actions by another institution or level. One traditional type of influenced enactments is model legislation and its companion, uniform state laws. But more important recently is the adoption of rapid innovation, as with the previously mentioned educational reforms, child seat belt laws, and a plethora of other reformist enactments. Influenced enactments usually happen in quick sequence and can be made in anticipation of interbranch or interlevel responses. These kinds of enactments are sometimes "too good or too dangerous to refuse" for partisan, electoral, or policy-crisis reasons. Thus they can often involve risks, and in that sense (particularly if the risks are political) can be thought of as somewhat coercive. However, this type of enactment is usually cooperative rather than conflictual; the consultation that takes place is usually friendly and in the best interest of all. The essential point is that these enactments take place not so much in response to constituent, supervisory, or even political preferences as they do with an eye to the responses of other institutions or levels.

Finally, **process enactments** are the outcomes of the administrative or programmatic functioning of an institution in relationship with other institutions or levels. Some of the literature on federalism refers to informal and personal contacts between officials throughout the intergovernmental system (Wright 1982). In these contacts, officials simply talk with one another, often on matters of policy and professional concerns. Most professionals consider it a part of their job to stay in touch with the field, which for all practical purposes means that in their jobs they will consult with and adopt from the ideas of others. Enactments are the result of many such personal interactions. In such instances, it is often difficult if not impossible to trace where the idea came from in the first place. But in any case the process of enactment is certainly interinstitutional and intergovernmental.

Process enactments can also be more formal—for example, when there are interlocal consultation and agreement on such things as contracts, joint service agreements, and interlocal planning councils. These process enactments are found frequently in service delivery decisions. A city–county helicopter service for airlifting emergency patients to more specialized hospitals, for example, is an enactment that is inherently interinstitutional and intergovernmental. In the state–local model, a "circling and adjustment" maneuver is made when legislators size up the demands, responses, and opposition of lower or higher levels of government. We have already mentioned that budgets inherently involve this sort of enactment, not only in a psychological sense but in a process sense as well. Examples of process enactments in legislatures are almost endless. Certainly a highly visible example was the national congressional response to state and local concerns for the New Federalism initiatives of the Reagan administration. But process enactments also occur frequently in state legislatures, as when they pass tax reform laws affecting city revenue capacities and make substantial adjustments in response to interactions with locals.

In summary, governmental enactment is a process occurring over time. Most enactments are inherently interinstitutional and intergovernmental. Even so, there is unfortunately a lack of research on this phenomenon. Writers on federalism need to investigate how much intergovernmental enactment has displaced "solo enactment" in American politics. We suspect that scholars would be surprised at the extent of that displacement.

POLICY IMPLEMENTATION

Intergovernmental implementation of policy began to get attention in the mid-1970s, usually with a focus on how social programs of the federal government had worked out. Initial studies, perhaps done too soon after programs were initiated, seemed to reveal program failures, stalemates, and the like. Later studies pointed out that many of the newer national–state experiments in environmental regulation, safety regulation, and medical care for the elderly, for example, had performed quite well in alleviating problems and fulfilling legal intent (Peterson, Rabe, and Wong 1986). Although the picture is still not very complete on intergovernmental implementation, some information has emerged.

For one thing, implementation carries at least two meanings. The first is the political evolution of program application and enforcement. The second meaning is the degree of program alteration and variance from initial enactment, across levels and participants. Implementation breeds results. At the end of enforcement, political, economic, and social effects begin showing up. For example, more people are or are not housed, or health indicators show or do not show improvement. What happens during implementation breeds political and administrative results too. Probably most governmental programs have some intergovernmental implementation, although it is still useful to distinguish the effects of dualism in determining which programs are still performed largely at or by one level of government (see Table 3-1 p. 59).

Factors in Intergovernmental Program Implementation

A number of case studies have developed a good base of information about the **forces affecting policy implementation.** Intergovernmental factors are shown in Table 10-2.

As the table shows, these factors fall largely into four major categories. First, *national* factors have to do mostly with whether there is national policy administration that is competent, technically adequate, and sensitive to local demands. If not, lower-level resistance to implementation will probably grow and policies will be altered or fail. *Subnational* factors have to do

TABLE 10-2 *Forces Affecting Intergovernmental Program Implementation*

Subnational factors:
- street-level discretion
- state legislature oversight
- government enforcement capabilities
- compatibility with local cultures, elites, interests, legal system
- state and local agency discretion
- gubernatorial management

National factors:
- technical and scientific adequacy of original legislation
- provision of valid indicators, milestones, timetables, and so forth
- sufficient funding for enforcement personnel
- discretion, competency, and devotion of top bureaucratic officials
- subgovernment politics
- national legal feasibility
- volatility among national interest groups

Policy-content factors:
- *most resistance:* redistributive policies, direct intergovernmental regulations, intergovernmental grant or program cuts, programs that encroach on local traditions, cultures, or elites
- *scope of policy:* the more people a policy affects, the greater the likelihood of controversy (example: proposed cuts in social security benefits)
- *intensity:* the stronger certain isolated groups feel about the policy, the greater the controversy (example: environmentalist resistance to threats to endangered species)
- *the cultural-compatibility factor:*
- Are policies within the value limits of the majority of Americans?
- Are policies within the value limits of those who live in various regions and locales?

mostly with the degree to which local agencies or interests like or dislike national policy enactments and regulations, and how they use their discretion to cooperate or resist. *Policy-content* factors mostly determine whether certain kinds of policies are likely, because of their inherent features, to meet with controversy or acceptance. Here, for example, are such factors as whether the most effective political symbols are used to characterize policy problems and solutions (cut taxes to get government off people's backs in the Reagan rhetoric, for example). Certain policies, especially directive regulatory policies and redistributive ones, are almost always controversial (examples: social welfare, intrusive court orders).

Cultural compatibility ultimately determines (regardless of content) whether some policies are acceptable in some places but not others. Thus it will determine the degree of implementation *resistance.* Obviously, school prayers, pornography, and other moralistic issues engage different degrees of resistance or acceptance in different areas of the country. Federal cultures and religious and political cultures are among the cultural belief systems that affect how policies are received and implemented in the United States. When people resist federal regulations, court orders, and so on simply because they violate their cherished beliefs about federalism, local government, women, or other issues, implementation resistance increases (see Chapters 2–7 on the effects of federal cultures in America).

The Effects of Federalism's Political Economies

Compound Federalism. Major theorists such as Lowi (1969) argue that America is unable to quickly progress on issues of importance, primarily because federalism's complex and noncentralized designs facilitate the development of much influence that is essentially competitive. The compound design intended this to happen (*The Federalist*, Nos. 10 and 39, by Madison, are the most famous arguments underlying the constitutional design). As a result of Madison and Hamilton's arguments, the Framers of the Constitution intended to *slow down* the policy process through the various balance-of-power features of the federal structure. These features were copied at the state and even local levels. Thus the compound design helps explain why government supervision of policy (as well as enactment) is so fragmented and often at cross-purposes. One had only to view the Herculean struggle between Congress and the administration over Nicaraguan policy in the summer of 1987 to understand the idea of competitive supervision of policy. This competition helps explain why either institutional or private interest monopoly of policy enforcement (or enactments, for that matter) is tough to accomplish in the federal system.

There are two keys to understanding this effect of the compound model. The first is the different *representation basis* of the various institutions in government. The second is the institutional competition and overlapping jealousies in the supervision of policy. The infinite, perennial rivalries between Congress and the president in foreign policy and bureaucratic supervision are reinforced by the jealousy between the national government and the states. The ultimate determinant of this fragmentation, jealousy, and competition over policy supervision is the compound design. Further, the revised dual federalism in the intergovernmental system gave veto power to the national government as well as dominance over national representation, foreign policy and trade, government economics, and the social order (see Chapter 3).

The compound model most directly affects the struggle for supervision over the national bureaucracy. But because the compound design was copied in state constitutions, a similar struggle between governors and legislatures is mirrored in state politics. The general implementation effect of this fragmentation and competition for policy enforcement is that public policy gets variously enforced by different levels of state and local governments, and is affected by the varying power of interest groups and bureaucracies. For more on this, see Chapter 9.

Dualism. Dualism predates the compound design in American political practice. Thus dualism is the historic cause of implementation *at the local level.* What dualism ultimately explains is the fantastic variation in policy enforcement and outcomes of seemingly uniform national regulations or laws.

This is not only because there is much policy dualism, but also because policy is implemented among the three rather separate national, state, and local layers of diverse bureaucracies, elected representatives, and officials. National and substate *dual levels* have produced fifty states, 82,000 municipalities, numerous Indian nations, and several protectorates (Puerto Rico, for example). The structural dualism of this system in turn produces layers of cultures and legal and bureaucratic systems. As Chapter 9 showed, this means that competitive interests, private and governmental, are channeled into either "higher" or "lower" public institutions. The enforcement that results from this "coopfederalism" or "marble-cake federalism" at any level is bargained and represents numerous compromises. Thus, dual federalism is really the great creator of the many "local veto points" in policy implementation.

Centralism. Enlightened centralism and cooperative federalism became the basic approach of federal–state relations in the mid-twentieth century (see Chapter 3). Until the 1980s, the federal role in intergovernmental affairs occurred in the context of increasing policy roles for all levels of governments. This in turn increased the complexity of operational federalism (new grants, bureaucracies), laying the basis for new interest group involvement in politics (labor unions, intergovernmental lobbies). All this made up the new enlightened centralism, which itself spawned many efforts at both grant reforms and bureaucratic-management reforms targeted at improving intergovernmental performance, responsiveness, and efficiency. These reforms in turn affected state and local political administration, and by the 1970s had led to many state-level executive–bureaucratic reforms and state legislative strengthening (both involved mostly reforms of methods of staffing, planning, budgeting, and bureaucratic management and supervision).

All of these developments vastly increased the complexity of intergovernmental administration of grants, resulting in something of a two-headed problem. On the one hand, by the late 1960s most of the new grants and programs operated under elite or congressional policy direction. On the other hand, grants were operated increasingly with state and local discretion in implementation, as we indicated in our summary of conditions of aid in Chapter 3. The first factor meant that centralism was the instrument for pursuing national policy goals. Centralism at all levels of government gave attention to promoting labor security, macrostabilizing the economy, subsidizing regional and local economic development, building or subsidizing public housing and urban growth, and accomplishing the social and safety goals of regulation. But the second factor meant that the implementation of these national goals was heavily influenced by locals. The result was a highly complex and uneven set of outcomes between jurisdictions. For the policy outcomes of this implementation of these voluminous 1960s and 1970s programs, see Chapter 9.

To implement these new programs, the states were either directly prodded or indirectly inspired by federal regulation to increase the intensity and scope of their own regulatory apparatus in the 1960s and 1970s. Not only was policy implementation power at the state and local level strengthened, but new policy enactment roles were being generated in subnational federalism. It is not surprising that the general trend of state and local responses to national intergovernmental grants and regulations had turned by the late 1970s toward criticizing national supervision and advocating more discretion in the states.

The implementation discretion and grants experience of earlier years, coupled with increased demands and reforms of state and local governments, convinced many at the lower intergovernmental levels that program discretion in implementation should be expanded even more. Ironically, as many federal experiments were on the verge of succeeding, they were being attacked as too centralist, and failing by the late 1970s.

In the 1980s, states and locals faced a "triple whammy" and it looked like their discretion would be strongly diminished. This "triple whammy" was described as a combination of (1) national program cuts in most, and restrictions in some, intergovernmental grants and regulation areas, (2) reductions of tax and fiscal options through the reduction of grants, the elimination of revenue sharing, and restrictions on bonding imposed from above, and (3) increased welfare and labor needs due to higher unemployment in the mid-1980s recession (Palmer and Sawhill 1985). But as Chapter 12 will show, the states had a few policy surprises in store for Washington.

Interstate Federalism. Interstate federalism's effects on implementation are not very great, primarily because it is the least formally structured of the political economies of federalism. However, there are two main effects.

In Chapter 9 we pointed out how regionalism produces fragmented policy and economic approaches across the U.S., as well as common political lobbying viewpoints. Thus, one issue arising from the policy fragmentation of interstate politics is whether the essentially national and weakly regulated capitalist economy should be regulated by common and increasingly similar interstate approaches copied from one state to another. Interstate business regulation patterns often force big business to lobby hard in Washington. For example, the 1986 tax reform started with populist and interstate pressures to control the federal deficit and reduce foreign import competition with basic industries, such as textiles, shoes, and steel. Business also pays close attention to states that market themselves as probusiness states with programs the feds or other states or regions may not have—right-to-work laws, low tax rates, business planning and relocation services, job-retraining programs, and the like.

Interstate patterns of policy innovation also determine the prevailing interstate bureaucratic regulation patterns. Interstate variations are reflected in such policies as "lemon-aid" laws, plant-closing legislation, job-retraining legislation, repeal of the fifty-five-mile-per-hour speed limit, and educational reform packages. Also, many states and locals borrow and copy regulatory enforcement patterns in labor safety, environmental protection, insurance regulation reform, and many other areas affecting safety conditions and business operations. These regulatory patterns can be "standardized" or varied. They represent the tension between regional traditions and legislative and business pressures to stabilize or reduce subnational business regulation.

Substate Federalism. State-to-local federalism is one of the most important agents in policy implementation in America. While dualism channels the implementation of programs into dual levels of institutions and politics, it is the politics of substate environments that most affects the specific aspects of how policies are or are not implemented. There are four elements of substate intergovernmental affairs that make big differences for policy implementation.

The first element is the effectiveness of state legislatures in supervising enforcement. Can state legislatures make, and supervise the enforcement of, "good" laws? From the local point of view, can locals live with laws and state enforcement mechanisms? The quality and effectiveness of legislative oversight can make a difference in the ultimate implementation of policies and ultimately the quality of life at state and local levels.

The second element is the enforcement discretion held by state and local agencies, especially, for example, in school districts, criminal justice regulations, welfare rules, and universities. Real policy outcomes are determined largely by the "bureaucratic winners."

A third element is the degree of local executive effectiveness. The issue here is the very personal one of whether locally elected officials are competent. Whether local officials can make decisions adequately reflecting public demands and respond well to technical problems with appropriate skills is always important. But how they respond to state regulations— whether they enforce or resist them—is the intergovernmental aspect of local implementation. Effectiveness can mean ignoring, altering, or complying with state policy. How local executives play the various sides of this game determines much about the local quality of life and the implementation of statewide lawmaking.

Finally, there is the element of the state and local interest groups and elites who target bureaucratic enforcement. Implementation at the substate level determines who wins out after higher decisions are made. Thus, the implementation issues that affect us all include such things as how property really does get zoned and used, whether local bankers will seek to keep out mobile homes, and whether city leaders will fight to get the local junior college raised to university status by the state legislature. These kinds of things are the real stuff of substate implementation battles, which, after all, are interest group and elite struggles for control of policy enforcement. These battles focus on changing the minds and actions of *bureaucratic* administrators; they are not just means of "making democracy work" or "enforcing those good laws under the good governor."

Interlocal Federalism. The struggles over policy enforcement between official local units of government sometimes also feature wild struggles among elites, interests, and officials. Often, interlocal administration is conflictual as well as cooperative. Locals, and the politicos in their environments, dispute or agree with one another over many grass-roots issues, such as state grants, zoning, and interlocal services (ambulances, police, fire, city–county consolidation, and so on). Again, the political battle usually determines the course of enforcement, the degree of bureaucratic discretion, the clout the mayor has, and other political factors. These last-minute political skirmishes actually determine program outcome, such as whether and how fast the ambulance gets to your house. Local implementation outcomes, that is, determine most immediately and most finally how government services actually serve people.

National–Local Federalism. Two main political effects on implementation come out of national–local relations (see Chapter 7). The first is the distributive efficiency or inefficiency of this model. The second is that a bottom-up view of national–local relations that focuses on implementation shows a varied picture of program success in federalism. Even today, as during the New Deal, the federal largesse is largely distributed *through* local units of government. This puts program and implementation discretion, despite conditions of aid and intergovernmental regulations, substantially in the hands of local officials and interests.

The discussion about federalism in scholarly circles in the 1980s by and large characterized federalism as suffering from "overload," as "impossibly mired down in over-directive federal controls," and in other images of failure (Walker 1981). More recent, sober, research-based inquiries have indicated much the opposite—that federal programs often work (Peterson, Rabe, and Wong 1986). Yet there is no doubt that the spirit if not the reality of the criticism of federal grants and regulation is well placed. Federalism is a complex system that does not lend itself to simple explanations of either program failure or program success.

One possible explanation of program success or failure may lie in the extraordinarily complex picture national–local relations give of the distribution and program discretion exercised by locals in the implementation of national grants. Many case studies show that grants that succeed in one locality may not succeed at all in another—it depends mostly on the implementation and distribution freedom locals have. For example, some research indicates that urban housing and welfare programs have very different rates of success, recipients, degree of corruption, and speed of implementation, depending on local political machine styles and local political cultures.

There is no reason to assume that "we must look only to Washington for an explanation" of intergovernmental programs. This is not a very good picture of federalism at all. The tremendously varied local patterns of carrying out grants, designing programs for housing, and so forth offer at least as good an explanation for the success or failure of national federal grant and regulatory programs. Program research and case studies suggest a much richer picture of national-to-local relations and outcomes.

Locals have most of the cards in determining how national policies will actually be administered—who gets the construction contracts, how quickly a policy is enforced, and other factors critical to implementation. These effects are accelerated by the shortage of Washington personnel, their lack of familiarity with the local scene, and their "arm's-length" administration of grants through such things as grant requirements, which are even in the strictest of circumstances clouded by vague meanings and the infrequency of federal audits and reviews.

Thus a bottom-up view of the administration of national or elite programs by locals usually shows that the changes the locals produce in their implementation of such programs are not under the control of national forces.

SUMMARY

This chapter has presented a unique picture of how the policy process works in federalism's seven patterns. It concentrated on how policy formulation, enactment, and implementation in federalism are inherently intergovernmental. Some of the more interesting aspects of the complex federal policy process are how issues arise and spread among the seven patterns, what kinds of contentious issues recur, and how interests get issues started and accelerated across federal lines. We stressed that policies are transphase, which led us to the revealing conclusion that policy evolution is more completely understood in America as evolving across levels and within the framework of the seven patterns of federalism.

A larger question about the federalist policy process is what differences it makes for society. That is the subject of the next chapter.

KEY CONCEPTS AND THEMES FOR REVIEW

bargained enactments
bureaucratic games and goals
directive enactments
forces affecting intergovernmental implementation
influenced enactments
intergovernmental interest group tactics
intergovernmental policy enactments
intergovernmental policy formulation
process enactments
public policy phases

The Social Significance of Federalism

11

What difference it makes

The massive and complex federal system has a tremendous influence on life in America. The purpose of this chapter is to sketch the bigger picture of this influence. Perhaps we can start by illustrating the great drama of how race relations are changing in the South under the federal system.

THE DIFFERENCE FEDERALISM MAKES:
SOUTHERN RACE RELATIONS

In the early 1960s southern politics and society were aflame with race conflict as the civil rights movement strove to awaken the public conscience to national discrimination. The Klan and wily southern sheriffs and police conspired to fight, terrorize, and jail civil rights marchers. But in the spring of 1987, the nation watched as the same local authorities joined willingly with the FBI to protect thousands of civil rights marchers against the Klan in a race-unity march in virtually all-white Forsyth County, Georgia. The great drama of the **civil rights reform** struggle in federalism between national power and constitutionally guaranteed freedoms on one side, and state traditions on the other, is finding its resolution. Lincoln's "great house" is finally less divided. Federalism is slowly working. As a result, the face of social and political life is changing in the South.

To be sure, some of the changes have to do with changes in demographics and economics, and not just with federalism. Demographic changes have meant waves of people from other regions of the country entering the South. Mostly they have come because of economics: the southern states have experienced greater economic growth and stability over the last few decades than the older northern and eastern "rustbelt" states. These newcomers have entered schools and the labor force, bringing with them new languages and new attitudes about race relations, women, and other issues. A major poll commissioned by the *Atlanta Journal* and *Constitution* in March 1987 showed that due to these changes over the last two decades, the "typical" southerner now exhibits attitudes and social values very similar to those of the nation at large.

Still, most changes are a result of the federal system's layers of governments and cultures and the varieties of policies administered by the many government agencies seeking to heal the social and economic scars of racism. The effects of the federal system on race relations in the South are attributable not only to what the various government sectors in federalism do, but also to what they do *not* do, and to *why* inaction is sometimes government policy. For example, in Rome, Georgia, over 1200 people—about 70 percent of them women or black—have lost their jobs in a large textile mill. Meanwhile, in Washington, trade policy designed to give some protection to the textile industry from foreign competition has been stalled for several years because of the inability of Congress to override presidential vetos in August 1985 and because of threats of vetoes on other bills pending. State legislatures and governors have not stepped in to provide public policy relief in any major way. In other words, what is *not* happening in the federal system, as much as other factors, explains economic conditions such as loss of jobs, especially for minorities, in the important textile industry. This is like a medical emergency where the ambulance gets lost. What fails to happen counts too.

But often, it is what is deliberately decided or what *does* happen in public policy in the federal system that explains changes in life. Some twenty years after the passage of the Voting Rights Act of 1965, a federal court suit was brought against Carrollton, Georgia, by civil rights activists. The suit maintained that the city's districting system split up the black vote in the city in such a way as to almost certainly prevent the election of blacks to the city council. The threat of Justice Department intervention and of federal court orders forced the city to revise its election system in the fall of 1985. That it took twenty years after the Voting Rights Act for "public policy" to produce a racially equitable election system in Carrollton means not only that change is sometimes slow but that change is inevitably sweeping the South as policies filter through the federal system.

On the positive side, the black share in politics has improved through such things as increased black representation in local political offices and slightly increased levels of voting. Blacks also enjoy increased status and respect, unsegregated public and social services, and decreased discrimination in banking, personal financial services, and business development. And some black educational opportunities have improved, especially in higher education.

But other improvements are slow. While secondary and elementary schools are usually partially integrated, outlying and rural school districts and central-city districts are often disproportionately black and typically have less qualified teachers, less developed curricula, poorer facilities, and lower SAT averages than the mostly white suburban schools. There remains in the South (an apparently growing) pattern of white middle-class flight to private schools (some of them fundamentalist Christian) to avoid public school integration and conditions (*Atlanta Constitution,* October 16, 1987, p. 1). Also, black health, housing, and job conditions have simply not improved much since the 1960s, in spite of higher education improvements. In other words, conditions for minorities have a mixed record in the South after more than twenty years of policy intervention in the federal system on behalf of minorities.

Nevertheless, without this policy intervention from various directions in the federal system over the last three decades, the culture, politics, and socioeconomic conditions of minorities in the South no doubt would not have shown the *degree* of change and evolutionary improvement that has occurred. In short, federalism had major significance for evolutionary social change in the important matter of racial equality in the South. But in what major ways does the complex federal system produce social change in America? The rest of this chapter will sketch an answer, showing how federalism has profound socioeconomic and political significance.

Current Views of the Significance of Federalism

On occasion, scholars and textbooks on federalism discuss its larger social significance. Many of the comments about federalism reflect several major themes. It has been traditional to notice that dualism is a continuing feature of federalism. This means that states and communities enjoy semiautonomous control over political, social, and economic life, regardless of the plans and policies of Washington. The joke about the Yankee driving through Texas who is stopped by the Texas State Patrol for some minor infraction and hears in melodious tones, "Yo' in Tay-ux-us now, Boy," pretty well summarizes the image of how life is very different from state to state in federalism.

Scholars often point out that federalism means not only that states and communities have their "semiseparate ways" but also that virtually all communities share to some extent in national identities, loyalties, laws, and other features of national political life in federalism. Although Americans typically identify with their town and county, and sometimes strongly with their state or region, they still share in national identities and federal cultures. We have talked about this melding of cultures in our discussions about federalism's various cultures. Daniel Elazar (1966) argued that federalism in America serves to create and maintain a mosaic of compound civil societies and cultures with their overlapping legal, cultural, and public policy systems. Despite a current tendency to romanticize a "return of power to the states," a trend reflecting the pull of Jeffersonian political culture, the national constitutional government retains a potential supremacy over economic sectarian or personal power concentrations in political life. But this supremacy, especially in the social life and diverse conditions that prevail in public policy and local communities, is often exaggerated.

Scholars have often taken sides about the theoretical advantages or disadvantages of the American version of federalism— **the costs and benefits of centralization and decentralization.** Those who represent or favor a decentralist position had more attention in the 1980s, as even the positions and publications of the nonpartisan Advisory Commission on Intergovernmental Relations reflect. Much of the critique of federalism by those holding this perspective is based on the view that decentralized federalism is best because it allows regional and local "needs" to be met. An extension of this point is that decentralization is supposed to allow more flexible response to "needs."

The second typical view, not in vogue in the 1980s, is derived from a Madisonian position. This is the belief that the complex balance of needs and demands between the local and national levels is best handled by a semicentralized federal system in which the national government does not displace the states but rather takes a lead role in tackling problems for which there is at least a substantial consensus. The public policy "attacks" on environmental pollution and historical sex and race discrimination are the best examples of this modern version of compound federalism.

The essential critique of the "decentralists" by people who advocate either compound or centralized federalism is that decentralizing may "feel nice" and meet some isolated local needs but that it inevitably leads to violations of civil liberties or unequal social and economic conditions. According to this view, decentralized federalism historically favored private power and local elite control over politics, and that this gave rise to slavery, Jim Crow, machine politics, corruption in local politics, big-city bosses, and such. Thus too much decentralization, it is said, inevitably fosters inequality of conditions and uneven public policy responses. One state may allow squalid poverty worsened by stingy, debilitating, and self-defeating welfare programs, while others have much more effective delivery of and equity in welfare services. Some states allow gross violations of pollution regulations;

others end up paying the costs as they attempt to tighten up on violations. An extension of this basic objection is that decentralization slows down responses to true national problems (such as discrimination and industrial pollution), because localities can drag their feet on policy enforcement through a variety of legal, legislative, or bureaucratic means. One need only remember that the 1954 Supreme Court ruling ordering "all deliberate speed" in the integration of the nation's public schools took more than twenty-five years to achieve substantial implementation. Even now, the trend is to resegregate (see Chapter 12). Critics of decentralization essentially argue that with speed like that, who needs decentralization?

In the long run, federalism seems to involve a great trade-off. The federal system's virtually inherent noncentralization (or rather its complexity given it by its seven political economy patterns) means that Americans inevitably trade off some of the benefits of decentralization for some of the costs. We get some flexible response and some "local needs met"—*while* in some circumstances and locales we get inequality of conditions and public policy, unequal civil liberties, and slow national policy response.

Some studies indicate that the slight, long-run centralizing trend in attempting to cope with discrimination, environmental pollution, and poverty has slightly reduced unequal conditions and dangerous public hazards since the mid-1960s (Schwarz 1983). Other studies have emphasized that at various stages in the effort, some local needs have suffered as a result of inept policy design or administration, especially in the early years of new public programs as experience is gained (Peterson, Rabe, and Wong 1986). Other recent research has indicated that the trade-off sometimes works a different way, lending some credence to the critique of decentralization. This research stresses that in comparison with the public education systems of other nations, our largely decentralized system is failing to deliver adequate content, cultural literacy and history, world perspectives, or even math competency. Diverse control and curriculum preferences have inevitably led to uneven training, skills, and competency, within and between states, regions, and even municipalities. This suggests that too much decentralization is sometimes a luxury that cannot be afforded in the great federalism trade-off.

When public preferences are for more centralization of the federal system, as during the 1930s, 1960s, and 1970s, the trade-off seems to sacrifice, at least for a while, local skills, prerogatives, and traditions of governance. When public preferences shift to Jeffersonian experiments with decentralization, as during the 1980s, something else happens: the trade-off seems to sacrifice, at least for a while, equity in civil rights and economics for the poor and minorities (as civil rights and poverty programs are cut or decentralized), and equal conditions of regulatory enforcement (work safety, for example).

Federal cultures do not allow too long or too drastic experimentation in either decentralizing or centralizing federalism. This regulating function of federal cultures and public opinion suggests a few other ideas about the federal system's overall performance. First, the literature from the last three decades on federalism and public policy reveals that within these tensions between centralizing and decentralizing, the federal system has allowed some change in social and political conditions to take place in America—equal rights for women and minorities, business regulation, and so on. But these changes have been slow and sometimes uneven from locale to locale. Second, the "competitive tension" between centralizing and decentralizing trends makes national control of hazardous business practices difficult and largely dependent on getting massive, consistent pressure from Congress or the courts. The control of toxic wastes is an example of an area where policy has largely failed; water-quality regulation is an area that has seen greater success.

MACROECONOMICS AND FEDERALISM

An area generally regarded as quite centralized that yet has come under attack for being less than effective is **national macroeconomic regulation.** Since the courts generally avoid much interference in monetary policy and fiscal policy, it is Congress and the Federal Reserve that mainly direct the macroeconomy. Certainly the Federal Reserve had more influence on the economy in the 1980s than all the much-trumpeted presidential and congressional budgeting and tax programs of that decade (Palmer and Sawhill 1985).

The ways in which the Federal Reserve controls the course of the economy were increasingly questioned from academic, partisan, and other quarters in the 1980s. Numerous programs for both centralized and decentralized "reforms" in the control of the macroeconomy were advanced (see Dolbeare 1984 for the best summary). All involved substantial revisions in the federal system's balance of who controls what among states, localities, and the nation, and between private elites and public opinion in directing the economy.

The Reagan-style Cowboy capitalist proposals for New Federalism "turnbacks" of policy roles to the states usually denied the states the fiscal tools for accomplishing this goal. But "turnback" is but one idea about federalism and macroeconomics. Yankees on Wall Street and some related business think tanks and investment firms advocate "industrial policy"—a potent blend of proposed new centralized economic institutions with new kinds of economic clout. Among the most important of these institutions are industrial development banks, which would make nonpublicly controlled but crucial decisions about where monies and investment should go in the economy—a power worthy of the wildest dreams of Alexander Hamilton. Such economic proposals would drastically centralize the balance of federalism in macroeconomics. These Yankee ideas compete with the "decentralized" reindustrialization proposals of the AFL – CIO and others (Harrington 1987; Bluestone and Harrison 1982) for more state- and locally controlled economic development. Central to these proposals are such policies as state- and locally controlled strategic job-training, plant-closing laws, new taxes to promote labor, and tax-productive public works programs in mass transit and energy. If these become adopted as national policy, they would decentralize significantly the balance of federalism and macroeconomics. Thus, there are currently several competing sets of prominent ideas about readjusting macroeconomics, ideas that could also significantly change federalism. But it was not at all clear, in the midst of the general policy stalemate in Washington, where macroeconomic policy and federalism were to go in the post-Reagan era.

THE BIGGER PICTURE: FEDERALISM'S SOCIAL FUNCTIONS

The social significance of federalism's seven political economies is much bigger than the issues of macroeconomics or the centralization or decentralization of the society. If the literature on federalism, society, and economics is viewed as a whole from the perspective of social and policy theory, a more profound and patterned picture of federalism emerges.

The complex federal system has, as sociologists like to say, profound functions in society. In simple terms, federalism "does things" in politics and economics; it generally regulates or governs the development of a number of typical trends. For example, federalism's cultures guide public opinion while its institutions, public policy, and economic practices largely determine policy and economic outcomes. This is what we mean by saying that federalism has functions in society.

In the broadest sense, federalism performs **eight major social functions** (Table 11-1). We will discuss each of these functions in turn, relating it to the various parts of federalism that have the most influence on it.

1. Federalism Fragments Power and Limits Majorities.

The various federalist patterns influence elite and other powerful groups' attempts to occupy government institutions and manipulate opinion and ideology. Federalism also places significant policy functions and institutional powers into the hands of local elites, which makes the enforcement of national elite decisions difficult. Moreover, federalism places considerable policy decision and implementation power in the hands of multifaceted public bureaucracies, which enormously complicates the efforts of elites to control outcomes.

The various ways the federal design, especially as shaped by Madison and Hamilton, limits majorities and public opinion can also be mentioned here

TABLE 11-1 *Federalism's Social Functions*

1. Federalism fragments elite power while limiting majority democracy in politics (see Chapters 8 and 9).
2. Federalism, especially federal cultures, channels issue debates in American politics and helps set common issue agendas (see Chapter 10).
3. Federalism channels social conflict and policy implementation. Implementation and conflict are filtered through federalist cultures and noncentralized representation systems, including government institutions (see Chapter 10).
4. Federalism cultivates bureaucratic and subelite power at different levels of government and society (see Chapter 9).
5. Federalism softens, regulates, and sometimes even replaces the "economic free market" in creating institutions that produce and distribute goods and services. This is one of the most important but least emphasized functions of federalism. (See the description that follows in this chapter.)
6. Federalism structures political representation while determining the general character of the powers of government institutions (see Chapters 3 and 4).
7. Subnational federalism's cultures and polities create and maintain public or political system legitimacy and foster political socialization (the learning of political beliefs and values) and political behaviors in local community and family settings. (See the description that follows in this chapter.)
8. Subnational federalism allows major public policy innovations to spread and to penetrate national policy agendas and politics (see Chapters 10 and 12).

(they are discussed in detail in earlier chapters). They include the fact that political representation in America is limited largely to territorial units in elections. Representation has been expanded in the twentieth century by granting the vote to virtually all adults, and it has been "equalized" and strengthened through Supreme Court–ordered apportionment and state constitutional reforms that include such direct-democracy features as referendum and recall systems. The separation-of-powers system, existing in all states, serves to limit both institutional strength and public opinion as well.

Public opinion in the national government structure is partly limited by such things as keeping the higher courts "out of reach" of direct election, placing most civil rights and constitutional questions in the hands of the courts and the legal profession they predominantly represent, and by virtually keeping "populist" democratic reforms (recall, referenda, and the rest) out of national government practice. Representation and public opinion in the federal system are not done away with by any means; they simply are not as democratized as they might be. And this effect grows out of the constitutional design and traditions.

2. Federalism Influences Public Issues.

Federalism guides issues in two major ways. First, federalism's various cultures guide the emergence of and debate about issues, influencing what people think and do. But the federalist *design* (various institutions in layers) also affects governmental and issue agendas. How do federalist institutions affect issues? For one thing, many "market decisions" are at least influenced by national or state regulation of business, the threat of such regulation, the existence of interstate tax compacts, or the character of state and regional patterns of policy on taxes, unions, and other economic issues. Business tends to locate where business climates are considered favorable — at least this is one of the many "business" factors that firms use to determine the location of plants, home offices, and other facilities.

Second, all legislative, public agency, executive, and legal systems become the target of powerful businesses, economic elites, or lesser power interests. This is because what government people and institutions do and say "makes issues" for business. Finally, since the federal system organizes so many jurisdictions, bureaucracies, local media, and other entities, the emergence of issues on the media and public agendas is very difficult to control. Local news media respond to many sorts of cues, not just the ones arising from elites. The very existence of noncentralized jurisdictions, interests, judges, elected officials, and so forth means that issues start up like weeds, arising largely from local cultures, interests, political figures, and the like. Interstate innovations in divorce laws, child-abuse prevention, and the like can quickly become national trends. Such trends can quickly and dramatically alter life-styles, change private business practices, and affect public agency policy with little or no stimulation or effective resistance by national elites or institutions.

3. Federalism Helps Resolve Social Conflict.

Institutional federalism does not merely affect how policies and issues develop; it also affects how policy and social conflicts are resolved. In the first place, federal cultures force most public debate or conflict into "open" legislatures, courts, or bureaucracies for decision, enforcement, or conflict resolution. Second, and more important, because of federal cultures, these institutions "get respect." At the very least, this means that official public decisions (laws, regulations, court rulings, and the like) must be taken seriously, even by power elites. Any resistance must usually take semilegitimate forms, such as lobbying, campaign funding, and public relations opposition. Outright noncompliance, even by (perhaps especially by) big businesses or elites can threaten their very survival in the marketplace.

Thus in their most extreme forms civil strife, market rivalries, rivalries between individuals and groups, and such are usually resolved by legislative or court action at one or another level of the federal system, and not often by violence, subterfuge, or similar means. Conflict resolution is handled symbolically, and institutionally, because of federal cultures and institutions. Furthermore, the semiindependent and quasi-governmental role of the media, public bureaucracies, and the legal profession often threatens the private power of elites, interests, or abusive public officials at all levels of federalism. Their countervailing influences can help resolve conflicts with the powerful.

This is best illustrated at the individual level. In Carrollton, Georgia, for instance, a new resident claimed she was harassed by local sheriff's deputies. The deputies had cited her for driving seventy in a fifty-five zone, then cited her for carrying a deadly weapon (a cane under her seat, necessitated by a recent severe auto accident) after she tongue-lashed them. The woman was jailed overnight, allowed one phone call, and required to post a hefty bail ($750, later cut to the costs of the fines and ultimately waived by a local judge). At the time, she had few acquaintances in town, three dependent children, and a traveling-salesman husband who was on the road. Out on bond twenty-four hours after her arrest, the woman carried the evidence of harassment to the locally elected sheriff. She threatened to write a letter to the local paper, place the harassment charge in the hands of a local district attorney, and place the information on the case in the hands of the sheriff's next election opponent. Conflicts such as this can sometimes be resolved by enlisting or threatening to use the semiindependent power of competing bureaucracies and the media. Because of federal cultures and institutions in America, even the relatively powerless may be able to resolve conflict through something resembling due process or some other concept of just treatment.

4. Federalism Cultivates Bureaucratic and Subelite Power.

The following are examples of the powerful public bureaucracies and subelite interests that arise directly from federalism's noncentralized state political systems and civil societies:

- state and local elected officials
- state bureaucracies
- picket-fence relations between state and national agencies and governors' offices
- scientific and public interest groups (examples that are typically quite powerful in the states: welfare advocacy groups, religious organizations, environmental organizations, farm lobbies, universities)
- local bureaucracies

Two points were raised in earlier chapters about local elite and bureaucratic power in the states and in national politics. The first was that studies of power have generally not traced the exercise of power in policy implementation at lower levels of government. Meanwhile, many public administration case studies have shown that subelites, local officials, and bureaucracies can strongly affect policy change (see the discussion in Chapter 8 on the power of decentralized bureaucracies). The second point was that national elites and other private powerful interests do not bother much with local policy formation or implementation, because federalism's complex structures give them incentive to focus on attempting to control the national government. In short, powerful elites are usually busy enough just in Washington.

A few further points will demonstrate the larger significance of the bureaucracies and subelites created by federalism. One is that the federalist political cultures, which have encouraged distinctive elite, policy, bureaucratic, and legal traditions, are strong influences on policy making at the state and local levels (as we've shown in Chapters 3 and 4). In practical terms, local elites and interests usually control, or strongly influence, education curricula, local elections, race discrimination policies and community practices, employment practices, and other features of social life. National elites or national agencies can have little actual control or influence, except in the relatively rare court cases. In many small and medium-size communities across the nation, for example, it is common not to advertise in papers for most of the administrative and professional positions in local government and public services — despite federal regulations and court cases requiring open notice. Instead, most such jobs are distributed on the basis of whom one knows in the local power structure, in parties or public bureaucracies, or through personal or family contacts. It is certainly of great social significance that most of these jobs come to men through male-oriented social and work-related networks.

Another important effect of subelite power is the decentralized, state-oriented party system, especially in strong or modified one-party states. Although the ACIR (1986) and others have noted the decline of parties in public decision making and elections, parties still have some influence, particularly on leadership selection, public appointments in state bureaucracies, and policy and legislation control in statehouses.

Elsewhere we mentioned the significance of the rise of "reform governors" in the 1970s, who increasingly attempted to control more of the budget, policy, and bureaucratic issues in state politics. We also mentioned that some governors are mavericks who may resist federal policy controls. These trends show that decentralized party leaders can still affect public policy.

Furthermore, the recent challenge to the mainstream of the Democratic party from the liberal activist groups of the 1970s and, more recently, the New Right and Christian fundamentalist challenge to the Republican party mainstream show the power of decentralized party systems to affect national elites, political agendas, elections, and policy making. A few scholars (such as Maddox and Little 1984) have explored the rise of the "new populists" and the "new libertarians" and their links to new southern and western power elites as part of the continuing dealignment and weakening of the old New Deal coalition.

In short, all of these various manifestations of local elite power in national politics and economics have been propelled by the noncentralized structures and cultures of federalism. These structures and cultures encourage decentralized party and social elites, religious activism, maverick governors, locally inspired interest movements, and the like to spread their ideas to the larger national society. The cultivation of subelite power, which is largely a result of substate and interstate federalism, is an important social function of federalism, one that frequently has national political and economic consequences.

5. Federalism Regulates and Sometimes Replaces the Market.

We are considering here the function or effect of federalism's patterns as a whole on economic markets rather than taking the usual approach of examining the regulatory functions of single government agencies. Single institutions, such as legislatures and regulatory agencies, are, after all, merely parts of a larger federal system, and are subject to the politics of intergovernmental affairs. One of the primary effects of federalism on markets is that the economic powers of the national government, and to some extent of the states also, function largely to maintain economic stability and the profitability of business. This not only benefits internal commerce but also promotes external trade, the regulation of imports when necessary, and the market penetration and operations of American businesses in foreign countries.

Most of these public policies find their legal roots in compound federalism and the constitutional powers of governments to regulate commerce, levy taxes, and the like. Some scholars have argued that promoting commerce was a central purpose of the Constitution from the beginning (Dye and Zeigler 1983). Today, however, the activities and programs of many national and state agencies perform many services. These range from market analysis to loan guarantees, direct and indirect subsidies, road maintenance, training of future employees in public schools and universities in business-related skills at public cost, and provision of numerous other services important to business operations. These business stabilization policies are shared by both the national and the state governments, although by far the larger share of them are performed by national agencies (among the most important are macroeconomic stabilization, business regulation, and industry stabilization by means such as farm programs).

To a certain extent, the provision of some of these services, at direct so-cialized cost to the taxpayer, also serve the secondary purpose of promot-ing political stability in America. The most important of these services are social security, unemployment compensation, public education, com-munity colleges, and state-run job retraining and relocation. Not only are unemployed, uneducated, or poverty-stricken persons, economic liabilities, especially if they constitute large percentages of the population; their con-ditions are also incompatible with a stable democratic social and political system founded on the principles of equal opportunity, equity, and justice. Persons under such pressures simply cannot become the kinds of informed, active, and concerned citizens that democracy requires. In other words, per-sons suffering from inequality and economic and educational deprivation do not have the time, money, resources, and socialization to participate as citizens in a democracy. In this sense, the maintenance of economic stability and production is simultaneously the maintenance of the **preconditions of the political stability** necessary for the continuance of democratic govern-ment and social values. That these functions were designed into compound federalism, or revised and updated through legislation or state-constitution revision, merely underscores this often overlooked political economy fea-ture of federalism.

At a more mundane level, many national–state programs, reflecting compound federalist culture, provide payment for private services, regulate business fees, and structure the distribution of services in the population. Among these are medicare and health-services planning (location of hospi-tals, establishment of health maintenance organizations, and so forth under various national laws).

Other shared social programs in federalism provide direct services consumed by individuals. Some redistribute services or money to the un-employed, disadvantaged, and disabled, with the primary intent of en-couraging eventual reentry into the marketplace (as with unemployment compensation or job services). Others compensate the unemployable or elderly (as with social security and disability and veterans' benefits) so that economic justice or macroeconomic market stability is enhanced. Also, governments own and control basic resources, especially land and minerals of value (offshore oil shelves, for example), which they usually lease or sell for economic purposes. Governments at all levels are also owners and stewards of lands of primarily environmental or aesthetic value, such as national or state wilderness areas and protected parklands. Stewardship and conservation of land and resources are economic func-tions shared by governments, and are best performed, it is generally recog-nized, by governments for primarily nonexploitive economic reasons. Such functions and interests are not, socially speaking, better performed by profit-seeking businesses, which are compelled by market forces to think more of profit and competition and less of conservation, aesthetic, or environmental values. That such program and economic functions are performed by all governments is a reflection of the compound federal design and traditions.

Usually a discussion of federalism and regulation focuses on the types of economic regulatory policies carried out by different kinds of government agencies. For our brief purposes here, *economic regulatory federalism* takes place in the context of court decisions interpreting the balance between national and state regulation of interstate or intrastate business. Legislatures, however, have the primary role in determining the programs and functions of government agencies, as well as their operating budgets and specific regulatory tasks.

Intergovernmental regulation of business, for all the recent attention devoted to it, is probably no different from the previously discussed forms of government regulation of business. The intergovernmental aspect of regulation illustrates that regulation is a compound, cooperative enterprise, often undertaken by government agencies at different levels that bargain their regulatory territory among themselves. Whether regulation is done by law or by bargained agreement is not as important as the recognition that the regulation of business is, and probably always has been, intergovernmental and cross-jurisdictional. The legal concepts distinguishing interstate regulation (a national matter, legally speaking) and intrastate regulation (supposedly a primary sphere of states) have tended to blind most of us to the slippery and overlapping boundaries among state, national, and political aspects of intergovernmental regulation. Government regulation of business is, with few clear exceptions, inherently intergovernmental.

On an intergovernmental basis, regulation of business usually means one of several things. It may mean that business operations are "regulated" according to standards, requirements, or economic incentives established by law or regulatory discretion. Good examples are the late-1970s energy conservation laws that granted tax incentives for energy conservation measures pursued by businesses or individuals. A more stringent example is the "regulations" devised by the Occupational Safety and Health Administration or the Environmental Protection Agency, which can be enforced either by federal officials or by state agencies that meet federal standards.

Sometimes regulation means that detailed operational requirements are imposed either by federal agencies alone (as with the safety requirements for nuclear power plant construction enforced by the Nuclear Regulatory Commission) or by federal and state agencies working in tandem (as with air traffic flow, noise control, customs, and safety at airports). Sometimes regulation means macroeconomic stabilization policies of different agencies and levels of governments, as discussed earlier. In this case, the compound federal tradition probably plays the largest role, since the major macroeconomic stabilization policies of government are national (control of the money supply, interest rates, and fiscal policy, for example).

Certain other specific economic functions performed by governments in federalism are worth singling out, simply because of their social or economic significance. First, transportation regulation and the provision of roads are either subsidized directly at public cost (note the national construction of the interstate highway system since the 1950s) or regulated by rules and agencies. Everything from the transport of nuclear waste to the speed of highway traffic, the tonnage of trucks, water-shipping traffic loads, and the dredging and maintenance of riverways are provided by governments. Interstate aspects of these matters are usually handled by some combination of federal agencies, although the socialization of the costs and the regulation of traffic and transport are largely state burdens. Another area of socialization of economic costs that benefits the private market involves taxpayer support of education, job services, job retraining, and business location and other services (such as the provision of planning and city services to mall developers). The costs of these benefits are borne for the private market by the taxpayer and provided directly by governments. The provision of skilled services and the socialization of the costs of education constitute the largest budget expenditures for state and local governments and represent the influence largely of the dualist tradition in federalism.

Some scholars emphasize direct or indirect financial subsidies and relief to private businesses through such things as contracted services (anything from trash services to the building of multi-billion-dollar naval carriers and the construction of the space shuttles), tax relief, low-tax enterprise zones, federal and state tax write-offs, the leasing of federal property or equipment, and the use of government forecasting services for market planning. Few studies of direct and indirect business subsidies exist, although some congressional studies in the mid-1970s indicated annual levels of over $100 billion. By 1986, significant changes in the tax laws had reduced the tax breaks of large corporations, but also simultaneously lowered the effective corporate income-tax rates to less than 30 percent. Actual corporate tax rates have been reduced four times by legislation since the mid-1970s. These economic policies represent largely the influence of private power, big business, and centralism in federalism.

Yet another example of the economic significance of federalism is the pattern, at various levels, of government corporations and other kinds of publicly owned and operated businesses. Such "government businesses" provide goods or services in the absence of, or instead of, market or business services. In one sense, social security and medicare provide almost universal social substitutes for private insurance in America, and are examples of market displacement. Other examples include the generation of electric power by governments, the Rural Electric Cooperatives, the Postal

Service, and Amtrak at the national level. At the local level, there are many such services, including municipal power generation, trash services, family planning, and public transit authorities.

"Economic justifications" are usually presented for the establishment of such government "businesses," which in effect are near monopolies of services. Economic justifications for using the government rather than the market are rather arbitrarily assumed to be necessary, because the market is arbitrarily assumed to be somehow more efficient by the literature on American welfare and public sector economics. Some economic rationales are arbitrary because there is little hard research to justify their validity (as with privatization). Others embody the assumption that government should step in only when the market has failed. The various "rationales" for public enterprise include the unprofitability of the service in the private sector, the historic lack of private business operations, the inability of private businesses to cover the service area with equitable fees, or simply the desire of governments to introduce competition in a narrow market (as with trash services).

Looking at federalism as something that sometimes replaces the market requires one to scan the federal system to see how patterns are adopted from city to city (mass transit and trash and recycling services, for example) or are borrowed across levels (power generation, provision of mass transit services). Ideas of market replacement are often developed at one level of government and adopted elsewhere in the intergovernmental system. Thus, the replacement of the market is not a "one-spot thing" by one government institution; instead it becomes a pattern of federal and intergovernmental borrowing. The *pattern* of municipal or governmental power generation, government mass transit, and so on is a characteristic of *federalism*. Thus the interstate, interlocal, and national–local models have all contributed to market replacement, through patterns of market replacement in power generation, basic service provision, and economic welfare and insurance programs, for example. A political economy function of federalism mentioned earlier is the maintenance of the preconditions of social stability, democracy, and political survival, all of which are important for market stability, labor continuity and production, and ultimately profit and markets. The federal system, especially through dualism and compound federalism, places the primary roles for criminal justice and social-order maintenance in the hands of states and localities, while defense and immigration are largely national matters. All of these social regulatory functions of federal governments at different levels have to do with protecting property and lives, maintaining social cohesion (sometimes denying civil liberties and equality at the expense of majoritarian or elite values), and controlling labor-force composition and cost.

These economic functions of federalism are broad and profound, even if they are generally overlooked or oversimplified as the single programs of single government agencies. The broader picture of federalism's influence in economics needs more recognition.

6. Federalism Structures Representation and Government Powers.

Focusing on federalism's structures is the traditional, institutionalist way to describe the significance of federalism. Information about which government does what, and how election systems and representation within the separation-of-powers system operate in American federalism can be found in Chapters 3–7, along with a discussion that places the knowledge of institutions in a political economy context. Here we will merely say that the election system, the way representatives are elected to "houses" in legislatures versus "senates," and what kinds of social groups were meant to receive what kind of influence in different branches and levels of governments all reflect the influence of the federal design on public representation in America. Of course, this influence is largely traceable to the Constitution, court cases, and amendments to the Constitution. Our essential point in earlier chapters was that the separation-of-powers scheme, virtually universally adopted, was meant to function within a compound federal context as a limit to institutional as well as elite and majoritarian power. At the same time, as Madison intended, the various branches represent different social groups' desires in politics. The Senate was intended to reflect the presumed knowledge and compassion of the wealthy and the rough equality of state interests. It thus received a greater hand in executive supervision and foreign policy and less public accountability through less frequent elections. The House was to be more of a barometer of "public opinion," although *the public* meant white propertied males in Madison's days. The executive was vaguely endowed with enforcement functions. The courts were largely left untreated, although Hamilton had strong ideas about judicial review that came to prevail to some extent. At least the courts were left more or less isolated from public opinion or direct electoral accountability in the original design. They still are today, except for state court systems. All of this, as we argued earlier, constituted a specific set of ideas and compromises about who should be represented when and how on which issues in the new political economy. The representation system still casts a long shadow in American federalism and public policy making at both the state and national levels.

7. Subnational Federalism Fosters Legitimacy and Political Behavior.

Federalism's influence at the "micro" or individual level is sometimes not appreciated. Subnational federalism, as previous chapters have shown, often allows local cultures and preferences to predominate over national goals or elite priorities. More important, localistic cultures of federalism and politics inculcate, largely through family and community political socialization, ideas that are localistic or regionally typical. Furthermore, local political traditions allow public control and selection of significant public and governmental officials to take place in line with value preferences, through party mechanisms, and sometimes through populist direct-democratic features. The latter include the election, typical in most southern and some midwestern states, of school superintendents, local judges, and state court judges. They also include the recall of public officials and the placing of referenda and constitutional amendments on public ballots.

These cultural and localistic features of federalism create a large degree of local control over important features of local life, such as crime and education. More than this, they are inculcated into people over their lifetimes, creating the basic fabric of political behavior in national politics as well. How people learn what they do about politics and how to "act" in politics is a significant feature of life in America (and of lots of study in political science too).

8. Subnational Federalism Allows Political Pressures and Policy Innovations to Spread Within the Federal System.

The politics of subnational federalism, especially at the interstate and interlocal levels, influences national policy agendas and institutions (see Chapter 10). Among its more important "spreading effects" are the diffusion of new policy and legislative ideas among states and municipalities, the existence of political and bureaucratic networks of interests that communicate regularly with each other and develop common national positions, the rise of the occasional interstate compact, and the ever-changing scene of private lobbies and interests and new social movements that seek not only to influence single states but also to develop national strategies and approaches (see Chapter 9).

These subnational and interstate influences have led to major changes in the national parties and often in national laws and bureaucratic enforcement as well. They help explain major changes in urban policy patterns, state legislature and governor's office reforms, and the way that national business, public interest, and elite responses to issues arise from the states. Businesses and corporations may be encouraged to locate, or discouraged from doing so, in particular states or urban areas, depending on what is happening in a region of the country or a particular location. The spread of policy innovations through subnational federal systems might not explain such macrotrends as the economic growth of the South, the stagnation of northeastern industrial states, or the entry of women into the labor force. But it can explain the micropicture. It can explain why big firms set up plants in the South, or in one city versus another, or why schools improve their standardized test scores in some states but not in others, or how some urban centers become economically revitalized through locally conceived development plans (Indianapolis and Detroit are recent examples). And these in turn explain quite a lot of what happens to people who live in the various locales where such policy changes are spreading.

SUMMARY

Federalism is more than simply a legal arrangement of government powers or some kind of intricate representation scheme. Rather, as a complex pattern of political economies in America, it has major social significance, not only for fiscal affairs between governments or for representation schemes in elections, but also for economic life, for socioeconomic policies, for local power and national power systems, for public representation, and for economic outcomes in America. We have identified eight main social functions of federalism, which have significant, patterned impacts on American life. These effects illustrate the bigger picture of federalism's profound social significance, something that deserves more attention from scholars of federalism.

KEY CONCEPTS AND THEMES FOR REVIEW

civil rights reform
cost and benefits of centralization and decentralization
eight major social functions of federalism
national macroeconomic regulation
preconditions of political stability

The Winds of Change:

12

Cycles, trends, and directions in federalism

In the preceding chapters we have suggested that there is more to federalism than many have realized. The evidence is strong that federalism is the primary arbiter of policy and power in America and a major force in both economics and politics. In this chapter we will reflect on this point and use the political economy perspective to interpret some of the more important recent trends in federalism. Finally, we will indicate some possible directions for future studies of federalism.

CHANGE AND CONTINUITY IN NATIONAL FEDERALISM

One of the things that impresses an observer of American politics is the dynamic tension between forces for change and forces for continuity. In the case of federalism, the forces for continuity are on balance more impressive. American national federal traditions show remarkable stability and durability over time. In the long run, federalism has been one of the more powerful forces for conservatism and stability in the United States. It produces beliefs and formal systems for the resolution of conflict while allowing for policy developments. Federalism is thus both a fairly stable system and an arbiter of power and policy changes in America.

But what are the **elements of stability and continuity** that have enabled federalism to function as the arbiter and regulator of power and policy? And, perhaps of special interest at the bicentennial of the system, is there anything that may be altering federalism or its capacity to continue as arbiter and regulator?

First, what are the forces for continuity? One of the most powerful social science ideas about change and continuity is the concept of *system capacities.* By this we mean the various ways in which political and economic systems satisfy universal human needs. In the United States, the cultures and traditions of federalism have system capacities in a number of ways. The federalist cultures provide Americans with a sense of identity with the system, which gives stability to policy issues whenever a particular policy debate takes place. The federalist cultures also help routinize political competition and conflict. They structure who has acceptable access to and representation in government and who does not. And the stability of American federalism is attributable in part to the remarkable effectiveness of federal structures to resolve issues, at least partially, in one or another of the federal patterns. Thus the federalist traditions provide different institutions and formal pathways that work in certain stable ways but that can respond to changing policies and the occasional major social crises in our society.

To be sure, we have oscillated between **cycles of federalism** from one tradition and culture to another at various times in American history. See Figure 2-1 on page 36 which shows **the historical dominance of different federal traditions.** Some of the historical oscillations were in response to changing American perceptions of what government should do and which government should do it. The switch, in less than fifteen years, from Lyndon Johnson's enlightened centralism to Ronald Reagan's conservative policies and dualist New Federalism is an example. But the national federalist cultures and traditions themselves have shown a remarkable stability over time. They have been remarkably effective in providing citizens with identities, ideas, political legitimacy, and governmental stability.

The various institutions of federalism are a second major factor in political stability. Organization theorists know that the very existence of institutions demonstrates a social commitment to one set of policy objectives rather than another (Gordon 1986:74). The key word to an understanding of the institutions of American federalism is *differentiated.* American federalism provides differentiated structures of institutions and decision styles — our seven federalist patterns. Previous chapters have demonstrated how each of these patterns *more or less* performs certain policy functions. In this way, policy preferences are institutionalized—but in such a way that allows for local, regional, and national variations (in the three national patterns). These variations reflect the particular federal tastes of a period, government, or public jurisdiction. To some extent, this means that peoples and governments can use structure and culture to "do their own thing" in the overall federal scheme. Also, we have tried to show how federal structure helps to set political and economic priorities. Structure is the capacity for agenda setting. Thus if a particular level or institution in federalism cannot accomplish a policy objective that the "restless natives" want, the issue can be forced on the agenda of a different level or institution that can respond. Finally, some federal structures can provide greater access to some and less to others. In these three ways—*policy preference setting, agenda setting, and access*—the differentiated federal patterns have a lot of system capacities.

Another way of looking at federalism is in terms of the significant social functions it performs (see the preceding chapter). The effectiveness of the federalist patterns in performing those functions is another reason the patterns have such vitality; people implicitly accept the services provided by federalism.

But there are also stress points in the political economy patterns of federalism. These stress points sometimes change the system, despite the stability of the three national traditions. Without question, the most important of these stresses have been **major social crises.** In our opinion, there have been only two such crises, and both produced substantial change in the federal system. The first was the Civil War. Ultimately, this crisis was beyond the system capacities of American federalism. In the quaint phrase of conflict theorists, the Civil War was settled by the "arbitration of violence." And some violence it was: there were over 500,000 casualties, and about 9 percent of the country's population perished. Once the terrible conflict was settled, the system capacities of American federalism worked impressively again. As we have indicated, two rather rigid forms of federalism were reestablished — centralist federalism in the North and West and interstate federalism in the South. This permitted the Bourbon leadership of the South to reestablish its political control of the region and institutionalize a way of life unknown in the South even before the war (Woodward 1966). National elites also had their way as the Supreme Court found in the rhetoric of dualism a rigid constitutional basis for centralist laissez-faire economics (see Chapter 4). Thus as in the founding period, federal traditions provided the system with capacities to work effectively for the goals of both regional and national elites. Though inadequate to handle the crisis of the Civil War, those capacities were certainly adequate for the stresses of Reconstruction and industrialization from 1870 to 1932.

The second major crisis was the Great Depression of the 1930s. Unlike the Civil War, this crisis was resolved by the "arbitration of politics." We have already discussed how Franklin Roosevelt used the Depression as the occasion to forge a new and powerful political coalition. But what is most interesting from the standpoint of federalism is that in the process Roosevelt redefined the centralism of Alexander Hamilton into the enlightened centralism of the modern period. A **major crisis and presidential leadership** combined to produce a shift in the very definition of federalism, albeit largely within a single federalist culture. Although this crisis also helped alter the subnational patterns, especially national–local relations, it did not significantly redefine the essential elements of the other federalist cultures. It changed relations within the patterns, but it did not weaken the vitality and appeal of the other patterns, especially in the case of dualism and compound federalism.

But what of lesser crises? Certainly there have been significant **mini-crises** that have severely strained the federal system. One of the most powerful, and certainly one of the most socially significant, was the civil rights crisis of the 1960s. What is impressive here is that the cultures and structures of federalism functioned to prevent this crisis from taking on major proportions (and surely the struggle for equality had that potential). For minorities, enlightened centralism meant that in spite of extreme frustration in their attempts to acquire equal treatment from state and local authorities and societies, national compound institutions provided relief (unfortunately very slowly and reluctantly). For whites, enlightened federalist policy and institutions meant that national civil rights policies required substantial state and local acquiescence and enforcement to become reality. This provided, relunctant whites a forum for "blowing off steam" (a social safety valve) and a means of seeming to win something through the interminable local delays in integration. In fact, white society has given ground to minorities especially in voting rights, lower-level political offices, social services, and to some extent higher-education access and affirmative action employment enforcement. But segregationist attitudes and inequalities remain in American society in religion, public schools, income, health, housing, and jobs (especially management positions) despite the pressure of the civil rights laws and regulatory apparatus. Obviously, these are not the only social functions performed by the federalist patterns for the civil rights movement. But they illustrate both the effectiveness of federalist cultures and traditions in averting a system-threatening crisis and their slowness in the enforcement of the civil rights laws.

A third category of stresses on the federal system is what might be called **major social trends.** Examples of such trends are the 1970s baby boom labor market "flood", rising divorce, health care costs, and the rise of the Sunbelt, referred to as the *power shift,* (Sale 1985). Various studies in political science have documented the effect of socioeconomic variables on politics, policy, and economics. When applied to federalism, major social trends produce what we have called the **cycles of federalism.** The federal system has sometimes swung from one national federalist tradition to another in response to such changing issues. These cycles have certain typical emphases, such as centralization versus decentralization and the excessive nationalization of the states versus today's localization of national concerns. Thus there is great volatility within the national patterns, and in how public policy is pressed through the federal systems.

A fourth stress in the federal system is political leadership, particularly in the form of the modern active presidency. The president has moved to center stage in the American political system, especially since Wilson and FDR—at least from the standpoint of media visibility. Most modern presidents have had a federalism agenda (we have had two New Federalisms in twenty years). Since we can learn a great deal about federalism from an examination of the role of the president, we will explore this subject in a bit more detail.

OLD WINE IN NEW BOTTLES: THE STRANGE CASE OF PRESIDENTIAL FEDERALISM

In Chapter 3 we emphasized three things about federalism and the presidency. First, federalism both shapes presidential priorities and is affected by them. Second, the president's personal preferences are powerful forces in the federalist issue agenda. Third, the record of presidents as managers of the federal system is mixed. It is the third point that we wish to explore further. How effective can presidents be in directing the federal system's capacities toward their preferred goals? In other words, how amenable is federalism to presidential influence? If leadership can produce stress in the federal system, how powerful is that factor for change?

Our basic point of view is that presidential federalism policies echo the past and recycle the cultures of federalism in policy experiments. Thus presidential federalism policies are, for the most part, old wine packaged in the new bottles of the sitting president's rhetoric. Actually, this idea is not very radical at all. Political science generally recognizes that presidents are not as awesomely powerful as the massive attention to presidential federalism policies would lead us to think (see Cronin 1975). Certainly, the president is not much in control of the bureaucracy of the national executive branch. In fact, many presidents have decried their inability to control the bureaucracy. Presidents are simply one actor in the federal system, just as they are simply one actor, with varied degrees of clout, in their own executive branch.

Several points need to be made to demonstrate our view. In the first place, presidential federalist policies since **Lyndon Johnson** show rather clearly the recycling of federalist cultures. Johnson was as pure a centralist as we have had since Franklin Roosevelt. The explosion of categorical grants and regulatory federalism in the Johnson administration was an attempt to set national objectives and entice, even sometimes coerce, the states and locals into accepting them. Richard Nixon resurrected compound federalism and attempted to reinvigorate the states with his general revenue sharing, block grant, and coordinative plans. Jimmy Carter's New Partnership, even with its strong concern for the health of America's cities, was a continuation of compound federalism. And with the exception of his advocacy of the New Right moral agenda, Ronald Reagan was as pure a dualist as we have seen since President Jefferson.

In examining official presidential federalism programs, we cannot find very much that has significantly affected the federal system itself. Consider the evidence: the categoricals of LBJ have been strongly deemphasized, the general revenue sharing and coordination reforms of Nixon are for all practical purposes defunct, the urban programs of Carter never got off the ground, and Reagan's proposed "turnbacks" are still stuck in the icebox and rarely mentioned today. What remains is the Johnson regulatory federalism and civil rights, the block grant style of Nixon, and the substantial effort by Reagan to ease the enforcement of federal regulations of business. The great majority of most "official" presidential federalism programs, although highly touted by each administration, appear to be very transitory indeed. The only enduring exceptions seem to be Lyndon Johnson and Franklin Roosevelt. One wonders why studies of federalism have devoted so much space to presidential federalism.

To get a feel for the **limited significance of presidential federalism programs,** examine Table 12-1. Listed there are the major intergovernmental programs of six of the major postwar presidents (Presidents Kennedy and Truman, who proposed few intergovernmental programs, are omitted.) The table shows the major intergovernmental programs that were proposed, which of these were substantially enacted, and, most important, which survive today. The approximate percentages of surviving programs allow a rough ranking of the influence of these presidents. The programs considered are intergovernmental programs that either were proposed as official federalism policy or had major implications or consequences for intergovernmental policy, structure, process, or effects.

As you can see, **Franklin Delano Roosevelt** and Lyndon Johnson were probably the two most powerful domestic presidents in terms of program innovation. Not only did they propose more sweeping changes than anyone (except President Reagan), but, more important, they had more of their programs enacted and more of these programs survive today. Roosevelt proposed at least six broad reforms that dramatically altered intergovernmental affairs, and virtually all of them survive today in one or another form. Lyndon Johnson also got sweeping changes enacted, and about 60 percent of his programs remain in funding and operation.

Virtually tied for third place, but with much less influence, are Jimmy Carter and Ronald Reagan. About 33 percent of the programs of each survive. Although President Reagan probably proposed more changes in the federal system than any modern president (by this count, no less than twelve

TABLE 12-1 *The Fate of Presidential Federalism Programs*

Presidents and their proposals	Were proposals enacted	Does much remain today?	Percentage of major programs surviving
Franklin D. Roosevelt			
• social security (New Deal)	Yes	Yes—social security and social welfare legacy	90%-plus
• first significant national-to-local grants	Yes	Yes—national–local relations	
• national regulation of labor and macroeconomics	Yes	Yes	
• accelerated regulation of industries	Yes	Yes	
• national economic development	Yes	Yes—TVA, business loans, farm programs	
• change of court and elite attitudes for increased public economies and welfare	Yes	Yes	
Dwight D. Eisenhower			
• vast decentralization of social and grant programs	No	Nothing	25%
• Interstate Highway System	Yes	Yes	
• "Atoms for Peace" (commercial development of nuclear power)	Yes	Probably no—industry in decline	
• increased state responsibilities	No	Nothing	
Lyndon B. Johnson			
• civil rights, affirmative action	Yes	Yes	60%
• model cities for minorities	Yes	No	
• vast increased categorical grants for mass transit, urban education	Yes	Yes, but reduced significantly	
• medicare, public health planning	Yes	Yes	
• increased public housing, jobs	Yes	No—virtually abolished	

TABLE 12-1 *(Continued)*

Presidents and their proposals	Were proposals enacted	Does much remain today?	Percentage of major programs surviving
Richard M. Nixon			
• revenue sharing	Yes	No—virtually abolished	25%
• block-grant approach	Yes	Yes, but altered	
• regional planning and coordination	Yes	No—virtually abolished	
• environmental regulation	Yes	Yes	
• other New Federalism programs	In part	No	
Jimmy Carter			
• New Partnership urban grants	No	No	33%
• national grants for alternate energy development	Yes	No—virtually abolished	
• oil shale and energy trust fund	Yes	No—virtually abolished	
• mine safety and toxic waste regulation	Yes	Yes	
• Consumer Protection Department	No	No	
• targeted deregulation (airlines)	Yes	Yes	
Ronald Reagan			
• decentralization of federal roles	No	No	33%
• swap of national-state functions	No	No	
• decentralization and cuts of grants	Yes	Yes, but substantially restored	
• block-grant consoli-dation	Yes	Yes	
• deregulation and and rewriting of regulations except for social welfare	Yes	No—blocked by Congress	

TABLE 12-1 *(Continued)*

Presidents and their proposals	Were proposals enacted	Does much remain today?	Percentage of major programs surviving
Ronald Reagan			
• redefinition of civil rights	Yes, through Justice Department rules	No—mostly blocked by federal courts	
• abolishment of socio-economic development grants	Yes—most	Yes—especially urban, social, energy grants	
• centralization of morality regulation (school prayer, porno control)	No	No	
• "packing" of appeals and federal district courts	Yes	Yes, but uncertain	
• balanced budget amenD-ment and line-item veto	No	No	
• ban or restriction on abortion	No	No (some funding restrictions)	
• dramatic tax and social cuts with defense increases	Yes	Major alterations, in decline	

major program changes), virtually the entire package of proposals failed to pass Congress or to get past federal court and interest group resistance even in the "honeymoon" years of his presidency. More important, by his second term in 1988 only about 33 percent (four of twelve) of his proposals for intergovernmental affairs survived. In last place are Presidents Nixon and Eisenhower, with only about 25 percent of their programs surviving today.

The evidence shows that in the end, President Carter had just as much influence as President Reagan in the federal system (although not for proposed alterations, or for initial changes in fiscal relations). For Jimmy Carter also, about 33 percent (two of six major proposals) survive (these are his significant environmental and labor safety reforms and airline deregulation). As far as intergovernmental changes go, the originally breathtaking Reagan agenda is pretty much limited to two areas of achievement: (1) cuts in grants and the rate of social spending (especially affecting urban and social welfare and administrative restrictions) and (2) the packing of appeals and federal district courts with legal conservatives (but even this attempt was partially offset by the fact that Jimmy Carter had appointed about 60 percent as many liberals and minorities). Even the budgetary and macroeconomic changes of the president (important for intergovernmental effects) were drastically altered during Reagan's eight years. Most important, none of his major "swaps," few of his deregulation proposals, and none of his decentralization proposals were ever approved by Congress.

In summary, of the six major modern presidents who have wanted major changes in intergovernmental policy or process, only FDR and LBJ got most of what they wanted (better than 60% of their programs survive). Of the remaining presidents, between 65 to 75% of their official federalism programs are virtually or completely extinct.

Thus the forces in the federal system often thwart the best-laid plans of even politically popular presidents (see Chapters 1 and 9 for the case of President Reagan). Most presidents with high-sounding federal program goals really do not change the federal system very much. Their actions and statements are primarily symbolic. The cultures or structures of the **evolution of federalism** in the United States seem to require a major crisis, such as the Civil War or the Great Depression in combination with effective leadership (FDR). Otherwise, presidential plans for federalism seem best described by Shakespeare: "full of sound and fury, signifying nothing."

DOES FEDERALISM REALLY WORK?

Presidents are not the only ones with pronouncements on federalism. The rhetoric on federalism is quite widespread. Some of the recent rhetoric, including that of the White House, the ACIR, and some of the more prominent writers on federalism, tends to declare flatly that federalism does not work. The literature on federalism from the 1980s is chock full of rhetorical phrases describing a nonworking system: "a system in disarray," "system overload," "dysfunctional federalism," and the like. Consider the idea voiced by Grover Starling:

> If Nobel Prizes are ever awarded in political science, the person who discovers why modern governments do not work any better than they do would surely deserve to be mentioned in the same breath as Francis Crick and James Watson. After all, the importance of unlocking that secret is not less than the importance of discovering the structure of DNA. (1979:20)

Such a view has almost dominated the study of federalism since the mid-1970s. But the unstated assumption behind such broad indictments is that federalism is supposed to work for somebody's idea of a public interest. And thus the unasked question in such rhetoric is: For whom or what does federalism work? Or for which interests is it ineffective? Without attempting to answer these questions squarely, it is easy to fall back into the rhetoric of failure. Our hunch is that the myth of federal failure is an idea tailored by those who wish to benefit from a changed federalism. The federal wheel squeaks for those for whom it isn't turning.

The clamor about failure in recent years has accelerated a rather strong federalist issue cycle over a relatively short period. In the 1960s and 1970s the agenda of the left dominated "official federalism." As a result, there was an emphasis on social planning, social indicators, a preference for enlightened centralism, and a commitment to regulation to accomplish redistributive social goals. Thus the national government was expected to deliver social and economic policy goals through central planning and regulation of lower levels of government and the private sector. But there was an issues shift in the 1980s: the agenda of the right came to dominate "official federalism." As a result, there was an emphasis on private sector solutions to social problems, a preference for dual federalism, a commitment to deregulation, and an almost self-serving plea for privatizing. Thus the government was expected to "get off our backs" while the private sector was to be "unleashed" to deliver a promised cornucopia of goods and services previously held in check.

The political economy approach to federalism demonstrates that what occurred in the 1970s and 1980s was simply a cycle of federalism. Many such cycles have occurred before, as the federal system oscillated between federalist cultures in an attempt to change its policy outcomes and social functions. And such cycles will occur again. Federal cycles are almost never permanent. The most enduring elements in the federal political economy are its cultures and national patterns. Issues, presidents, and even elites change—but federalist traditions and cultures mostly do not.

Still there is the rhetoric: do these traditions "really work"? There is some evidence that policies that cut across all levels of the federal system *do work* in accomplishing social and economic objectives. Several major evaluations of poverty programs, agreed that the current complex array of programs is more efficient and more politically acceptable to fight poverty than a single comprehensive program such as the negative income tax (Danzinger and Weinberg 1986; Schwarz 1983). Recent research shows substantial "success" in many federal programs (Peterson et al. 1986, Schwarz 1983). The studies suggest continued adjustment of existing programs. We have noted throughout the text that federalist structures are sometimes used to produce outcomes favored by elites. Yet federalism can also work to frustrate elite goals. Again, we must see clearly the implications of whom federalism is to work for.

Finally, as we have seen, federalism's cultures and structures perform profound functions in American society. A review of the social significance of federalism (Chapter 11) hardly leads to the view that federalism does not work. It may simply not work for some people but may work quite well for others. In fact, it "works" in different ways (see Chapter 11).

TWO MAJOR TRENDS IN SUBNATIONAL FEDERALISM

The preceding sections concern primarily national federalism. In this section, we take a look at two of the more important trends at the subnational level.

Subnational Policy Momentum: The Slumbering Giant

Many observers have documented the recent "rapid policy diffusion" among state and local levels. The source of such diffusion is the substantial policy innovation in subnational politics and institutions (see Chapter 11). An explanation of this **subnational policy momentum** can highlight one of the most important trends in federalism today. A number of factors—some cultural, some institutional, some political—have resulted in this diffusion. We'll start first with the institutional factors.

The resurrection of dualism in the 1980s altered only somewhat the relationship between national-level institutions and subnational ones (in spite of little long-range effect, presidents can have temporary effects on federal institutions and policy). Actually, national-level institutions experienced a form of policy paralysis in the 1980s. We do not wish to overstate the situation and thus become guilty ourselves of rhetoric. Probably the alleged stalemate is more a matter of which level or pattern of federalism has more policy momentum. But however we label the situation, national institutions have become more timid, more inclined to inaction, and less able to act, as a result of several forces. One of those forces, as we mentioned earlier, is the well-know effect of hyperpluralism suggested by Lowi (1969, 1984). Hyperpluralism has been especially evident in the the policy tug of war between the administration and Congress. But what is often overlooked is its effect on the public bureaucracies as well. The dualism of the Reagan agenda and the national policy stalemate stimulated regional and state policy momentum. In essence, it invited regional and state forces to either block or support the White House (witness the western "grazing lands" controversy, for example). This situation placed severe strains on the president's capacity as a broker of elite interests, especially in the increasingly Democratic Congress. In Lowi's terms, so many elite interests were competing for White House action, so many counterinterests were swamping Congress, that the national institutions could respond effectively to none of them. Because of such forces, national-level institutions lost the policy momentum of the Johnson years of centralist federalism, and even the momentum of the Nixon and Carter years of compound federalism.

Looking at the situation from the bottom up, we find that two factors are especially important. As we have noted, state and local decision makers and interests may be legally subservient, but they are *not* politically inactive. There is a great deal of life at the subnational level. This activity has resulted in substantial institution and alliance building at the state and local levels as states have attempted reforms to increase their policy and fiscal capacities. However effective the urban reform movement was, it certainly suggested a desire to increase capacity among governments. And the energy in local policy momentum has not dissipated. A very interesting variation of local innovation has been noted by Ronald Oakerson, who described "a new consensus...around a simple but powerful idea—that multiple local governments together constitute a 'local public economy' " (1987:20). This local public economy arrangement has resulted in a rich variety of new modes for the delivery of public services at the local level. This is real policy-innovation capacity. National stalemate has stimulated subnational momentum, even though some of it involves the localization or regionalization of national goals. The second factor to be noted is almost a bald fact: social, economic, and environmental problems have not gone away during the reduction of national policy momentum. These problems are the occasion for specific and tangible responses by locals, since someone must mind the shop of policy problems. The "deadlock of democracy" in Washington (a phrase coined by James McGregor Burns in a book of the same title) only made more possible an infinite variety of policy responses by states and locals in the 1980s. And in fact they responded, even preempting previously national responsibilities in the climate of national stalemate in education, economics, job training, and a host of other areas.

This last fact may produce one of the sharpest constrasts between the responses of federalist patterns. This contrast is seen most clearly in the environmental policy area. When looked at from the top by national policy makers, the environment presents a complex array of problems. These are usually described in very generalized terms — clean air, clean water, and so on. But as we have noted, one person's clean air may be another person's intrusive federal regulation. As a result, national decision makers must find a general compromise for a very complex and diffused problem. Thus we see the "strange case of Presidential federalism," in which the posture of the president is largely rhetorical. Or we see mostly the flipflops of the Supreme Court on intergovernmental regulation as it moves in its own world in response to pressures or perceptions from one federalist culture or another. Or what we see is the "symbolic actions" of Congress in such legislation as the Resource Conservation and Recovery Act.

But for subnational institutions, the problems are *much more specific*. For example, in the Resource Conservation and Recovery Act, the problem for Congress was a "chemically free environment." But the problem for the states was that of finding environmentally safe disposal places. And the nasty specific problems just won't go away.

So we come face to face with an interesting federal possibility. What if state policy momentum, in a specific case, opposes national rhetoric or action? Consider this scenario. Today's national policy clearly favors nuclear power plants for the production of electric power. Several state governors have strongly opposed the siting of nuclear power plants in their states. What if these governors simply say that nuclear power plants will *not* be sited in their states, national license to the contrary? At the least, we would have a federal shoot-out at high noon. And what if a governor called out the state national guard to block the operation of a nuclear plant? The state of Washington has investigated what options it has to stop or divert the nationally licensed transportation of high-level nuclear waste across its borders. The frequency of nation–state conflict may increase significantly as a result of recent developments in American federalism.

Are Locals Really Anyone's Creatures?

Looking at the newer policy effects of subnational federalism leads us also to reopen the historically unanswered question about the position of locals in the federal system. Perhaps one of the more important questions facing contemporary federalism is this: What should be the role and function of locals in the nation's political economy? Remember that this issue was a nondecision at the Constitutional Convention of 1787. The position in federalism of the many active and viable local governments and interests existing at the time was simply not determined. As we saw, political practice and court decisions ultimately worked out the ambiguous position of local levels. It was clear eventually that while subservience may be the legal status of locals, they are far from politically submissive. In fact, locals are major actors in the recent subnational policy momentum. This development has extremely important implications. It may portend a shift in federalism to the extent that subnational patterns rise to policy dominance. The interstate, interlocal, and national–local patterns are themselves changing the most, and are leading most of the overall changes—rapid diffusion and state–local preemption of national responsibilities included. Also important are the new trends in the localization and regionalization of national policy goals, to be discussed shortly.

Thus locals are now unquestionably a major political and economic force in the federal system. They are parties to three of the major structural patterns of federal relations—the state–local, interlocal, and national–local. And local governments and private interests are far from passive partners in each of these relationships. This local activism, particularly in the national–local model, forces one to reexamine the position of local governments and local forces.

The expansion of national–local relations has placed on the agenda of federalist issues the question of who should be responsible for local government problems—the nation or the states? The ACIR framed the issue this way: "To what extent should state governments be given future responsibility for those local problems that up to now have been addressed by direct federal-to-local grants?" (1982a:16). But this way of posing the question is to look at the issue from the top down. When looked at from the bottom up, the issue becomes something else again and strikes at the very heart of one of the enduring federalist questions: does the ambivalence in relationships created by national–local relations and the independence and political activism of locals mean that local officials should "cut the best deal possible" (the ACIR's phrase) with the states, Washington, or whomever? Or, more precisely, should locals change their work or modify their structures such that they go their own way in policy areas of state and national interest?

This question offers a contrasting view with the probably overstated case for national "intrusiveness." Our examination of the history of the national–local model suggested a great deal about the occasional capacity of national elites (FDR, Lyndon Johnson) to accomplish their objectives through "extrasystem" means or through creative manipulation of federal traditions. Some saw this adaptability as the means by which federalism keeps government "in its totality abreast of the needs of the people" (Martin 1965:41). But perhaps too often, the national–local model has served as a means of elite control and manipulation of the system for the interest of a few much more effectively than it has served as a means for meeting the needs of all. But present patterns are turning the "fruit basket" upside down. Such developments are profoundly meaningful in federalism. We have emphasized throughout the text the necessity of focusing on policy effects. What are the long-term policy results if locals can cut deals with others largely on their own terms, even to the point of going their own way in policy matters of state and national interest?

One of the most important policy trends today is a growing **localization and regionalization** of what were intended to be **national policy goals**. This trend illustrates how states and locals increasingly cut deals on their terms. The best example is public education and the integration of schools. Recent media attention has been directed to what analysts are calling *resegregation* (see, for example, the eight-part series in the *Atlanta Constitution*, starting October 27, 1987). School resegregation is apparently increasing nationwide. Resegregation occurs when previously integrated schools revert to all-white or all-black status. Important census data on increasing resegregation in the 1980s have so far emphasized the *localized* nature of resegregation. School districts within the same state or within the same region of a state (rural versus urban, for example) are differing in terms of either making continued progress toward total integration or backsliding toward resegregation. Most of the data indicate that those districts tending to resegregate are doing so as a matter of deliberate local decision. Certainly the argument can be made that the *enforcement* momentum of national government authorities responsible for civil rights in education slowed considerably in the 1980s, and that this is probably a factor in increased resegregation (see the *Atlanta Constitution* series). But the *official* policy of both the national government and the states is integration of the public school systems. And clearly the national interest is in equal educational opportunity for all.

What is occurring in resegregation is happening also in a number of other heretofore "national" policy areas. The trend is for either the localization or the regionalization of major policies that affect the states and nation. This is apparent in the case of civil rights; only some localities and regions are pressing vigorously toward the provision of equal opportunity for all persons. The regionalization of effects is also apparent in environmental programs. The Great Lakes region, for example, has allowed the lakes to become "troubled waters," exposing the 40 million people living in the region to more toxic chemicals than those in any comparable segment of North America (*National Geographic*, July 1987:5). Oregon, on the other hand, has pursued environmental policies vigorously, even to the point of accepting the trade-offs (if they exist) between a clean environment and economic growth. This regionalization of effects apparently comes about as locals or states copy each other. A question well worth pursuing in studies of federalism is which policies in America are increasingly becoming localized or regionalized in their effects?

The problem is, of course, that there is a strong national and state policy interest in many areas. But the idea that states and even localities can achieve such influence as to preempt some national policy responsibilities, or regionalize or localize other policies on their own terms, suggests an answer to the question of whose creatures the locals are. The answer is that local governments and interests increasingly are nobody's creatures. Instead, they are a dynamic force in the American political economy and may sometimes end up more master than creature. After 200 years of non-decision, the question of their role and status in the American political economy should be faced squarely.

THE MANY UNASKED QUESTIONS ABOUT FEDERALISM

The question of the role and function of local interests in the American political economy is merely one of a host of unanswered questions about federalism in the United States. We wish to raise four other questions to suggest where the study of federalism might go from here.

The most important question for federalism studies perhaps is this: How can the study of federalism be moved from the back streets into the mainstream of social science theory and concern? We emphasized in the first chapter that what you see when you look at anything (including federalism) depends a great deal on the conceptual lenses through which you look. Thus where you end up in conclusions depends a great deal on the theoretical road map that you take to get there. We have tried to budge the study of federalism away from the legal, institutional, and pluralist perspectives of the past, using the general light of a political economy approach. But is the political economy angle the best approach to the study of federalism? Does some other perspective offer a more productive route to the development of more general theories of federalism rooted specifically in mainstream social science? There must be a continued effort to bring the newer social science approaches to the study of federalism.

A related question has to do with the social significance and policy outcomes of federalism. There should be substantial effort to identify and trace more completely the social functions of federalism. We have illustrated repeatedly that federalism does not consist simply of official relations between levels of government, or money flows or pluralist politics between levels (although that is part of the picture). Federalism is really the performance of vital and necessary social functions in our society—the things we explored in Chapter 11. Further, federalism is really about policy outcomes. In the good fashion of Harold Lasswell, federalism is about who gets what and how. In our opinion, the marriage of federalism and policy theory is long overdue, and promises real fruit. There should be much analysis of this question: What difference does federalism make in politics and economics?

Third, future studies of federalism should concentrate on the question of federalism and power. It is difficult to explain the absence of a concern for the question of power in existing federalism studies. This mystery is even more inexplicable given the views of James Madison and his influence on federalism. Power, after all, was foremost in the minds of Madison, Hamilton, and Jefferson. It has been amply shown that these Framers had the channeling and regulation of power as a prime objective to be realized through the federal system (see Epstein 1984). To ignore the question of power is to ignore the designers and formulators and some of the very essence of federalism.

Finally, perhaps it is the nostalgia associated with the bicentennial of American federalism's founding, but we believe federalism studies should take a fresh look at the question of continuity and change in the federal system. We have stressed that federalism can adapt to social crises, major trends, and political leaders. There is much in the rich mosaic called federalism.

KEY CONCEPTS AND THEMES FOR REVIEW

cycles of federalism
elements of stability and continuity in federalism
Franklin Delano Roosevelt and federalism
limited significance of presidential federalism programs

References

ABNEY, GLENN and THOMAS HENDERSON (1983). "Federal and State Impact on Local Governments: A Research Note on the Views of Local Chief Executives," *Administration and Society,* 14:4 (February): 469–80.

ACIR (1961a). *Governmental Structure, Organization and Planning in the Metropolitan Areas.* Washington: U.S. Government Printing Office.

ACIR (1961b). *State Constitutional and Statutory Restrictions on Local Government Debt.* Washington: U.S. Government Printing Office.

ACIR (1966). *Intergovernmental Relations in the Poverty Programs.* Washington: U.S. Government Printing Office.

ACIR (1967). *A Handbook for Interlocal Agreements and Contracts.* Washington: U.S. Government Printing Office.

ACIR (1973). *Substate Regionalism in the United States.* Washington: U.S. Government Printing Office.

ACIR (1974a). *Governmental Functions and Processes: Local and Area Wide.* Washington: U.S. Government Printing Office.

ACIR (1974b). *Improving Urban America.* Washington: U.S. Government Printing Office.

ACIR (1975). "Urban Fiscal Stress," in *Intergovernmental Perspective.* Washington: U.S. Government Printing Office.

ACIR (1976). *Improving Urban America: A Challenge to Federalism.* Washington: U.S. Government Printing Office.

ACIR (1977a). *Categorical Grants: Their Role and Design.* Washington: U.S. Government Printing Office.

ACIR (1977b). *Improving Federal Grants Management.* Washington: U.S. Government Printing Office.

ACIR (1977c). *State Limitations on Local Taxes and Expenditures.* Washington: U.S. Government Printing Office.

ACIR (1977d). *The States and Intergovernmental Aids.* Washington: U.S. Government Printing Office.

ACIR (1978). *In Brief: State Mandating of Local Expenditures.* Washington: U.S. Government Printing Office.

ACIR (1980). *The State of State–Local Revenue Sharing.* Washington: U.S. Government Printing Office.

ACIR (1981a). *The Future of Federalism in the 1980s.* Washington: U.S. Government Printing Office.

ACIR (1981b). *Measuring Local Discretionary Authority.* Washington: U.S. Government Printing Office.

ACIR (1982a). *Intergovernmental Perspective*, vol. 8, no. 2. Washington: U.S. Government Printing Office.

ACIR (1982b). *State and Local Roles in the Federal System*. Washington: U.S. Government Printing Office.

ACIR (1984a). *Regulatory Federalism: Policy, Process, Impact and Reform*. Washington: U.S. Government Printing Office.

ACIR (1984b). *Strengthening the Federal Revenue System*. Washington: U.S. Government Printing Office.

ACIR (1985a). *Intergovernmental Service Arrangements for Delivering Local Public Services: Update 1983*. Washington: U.S. Government Printing Office.

ACIR (1985b). *The Question of State Government Capability*. Washington: U.S. Government Printing Office.

ACIR (1985c). *Significant Features of Fiscal Federalism 1985 – 86*. Washington: U.S. Government Printing Office.

ACIR (1986). *The Transformation in American Politics: Implications for Federalism*. Washington: U.S. Government Printing Office.

ADRIAN, CHARLES R. and CHARLES PRESS (1977). *Governing Urban America* (5th ed.). New York: McGraw-Hill.

ALLISON, GRAHAM (1971). *Essence of Decision: Explaining the Cuban Missile Crisis*. Boston: Little, Brown.

ALMOND, GABRIEL and G. BINGHAM POWELL (1966). *Comparative Politics: A Developmental Approach*. Boston: Little, Brown.

ALPEROVITZ, GAR and JEFF FAUX (1984). *Rebuilding America*. Pantheon.

ANTON, THOMAS J. (1982). *Intergovernmental Change in the United States: Myth and Reality*. Ann Arbor: Institute of Public Policy, University of Michigan.

ARRANDALE, TOM (1987). "Western Water," *Editorial Research Reports*, January 30, 1987, p. 2.

BACHARACH, PETER and MORTON S. BARATZ (1970). *Poverty*. New York: Holt, Rinehart and Winston.

BANFIELD, EDWARD (1974). *The Unheavenly City Revisited*. Boston: Little, Brown.

BASTE, DANIEL J. and T. BOWER BLAIR (1982). *Analyzing Natural Systems*. Washington: Resources for the Future.

BEAM, DAVID R. (1981). "Washington's Regulation of States and Localities," in ACIR, *Intergovernmental Perspective*, 7:3: 8 – 19.

BEARD, CHARLES A. (1959). *An Economic Interpretation of the Constitution of the United States*. New York: Macmillan.

BEATTIE, BRUCE R., EMERY CASTLE, WILLIAM BROWN, and WADE GRIFFIN (1971). *Economic Consequences of Interbasin Water Transfer*, Technical Bulletin 116. Corvallis: Oregon State University Agriculture Experiment Station.

BEER, SAMUEL (1978). "Federalism, Nationalism, and Democracy in America," *American Political Science Review*, 72: 9–21.

BENDER, LEWIS G. and JAMES A. STEVER (1986). *Administering the New Federalism*. Boulder, Colo.: Westview Press.

BENTON, J. EDWIN (1986). "Economic Considerations and Reagan's New Federalism Swap Proposals," *Publius*, 16:2 (Spring): 17–32.

BERMAN, PAUL (1980). "Thinking about Programmed and Adaptive Implementation: Matching Strategies to Situations," in Helen Ingram and Dean Mann (eds.), *Why Policies Succeed or Fail*. Beverly Hills, Calif.: Sage Publications, Inc.

BISH, ROBERT L. (1971). *The Political Economy of Metropolitan Areas.* Chicago: Rand McNally.

BISH, ROBERT L. and VINCENT OSTROM (1976). *Understanding Urban Government.* Washington: American Enterprise Institute.

BLUESTONE, BARRY and BENNET HARRISON (1982). *Deindustrialization of America.* New York: Basic Books.

BOWEN, EZRA (1987). "Constitutional Convention, Philadelphia, 1787," *Smithsonian,* 18:4: 32–48.

BOWMAN, ANN (1984). "Intergovernmental and Intersectional Tensions in Environmental Policy Implementation: The Case of Hazardous Waste," *Policy Studies Review,* 34: 120–44.

BOZEMAN, BARRY (1979). *Public Management and Policy Analysis.* New York: St. Martins Press.

BOZEMAN, BARRY and JEFFREY STRAUSSMAN (1984). *New Directions in Public Administration.* Monterey, Calif.: Brooks-Cole.

BRANT, IRVING (1961). *James Madison.* 6 vols. Indianapolis: Bobbs-Merrill.

BRAYBROOKE, DAVID and CHARLES LINDBLOM (1963). *A Strategy of Decision: Policy Evaluation as a Social Process.* New York: Free Press.

BREAK, GEORGE (1981). "Fiscal Federalism in the United States: The First 200 Years," in ACIR, *The Future of Federalism in the 1980s.* Washington: U.S. Government Printing Office.

BREWER, GARRY (1973). *Politicians, Bureaucrats, and the Consultant: A Critique of Urban Problem Solving.* New York: Basic Books.

BURNHAM, WALTER D. (1982). *The Current Crisis in American Politics.* New York: Oxford University Press.

BURNS, MCGREGOR (1956). *Roosevelt: The Lion and the Fox.* New York: Harcourt, Brace, Jovanovich, Inc.

BURNS, MCGREGOR (1970). *Roosevelt: The Soldier of Freedom.* New York: Harcourt, Brace, Jovanovich, Inc.

CAINE, MICHAEL P. (1974). "Origins of Progressivism," in Lewis L. Gould (ed.), *The Progressive Era.* Syracuse, N.Y.: Syracuse University Press.

CAPUTO, DAVID A., RICHARD COLE, and DELBERT TAEBEL (1986). "Assessing the New Federalism," a special issue of *Publius,* 16:1 (winter).

CAPUTO, DAVID A. and STEVEN C. JOHNSON (1986). "The New Federalism and Midwest Cities," *Publius,* 16: 81–95.

CARALEY, DEMETRIOS (1986). "Changing Conceptions of Federalism," *Political Science Quarterly,* 101:2: 289–306.

CARALEY, DEMETRIOS and YVETTE R. SCHUSSEL (1986). "Congress and Reagan's New Federalism," *Publius,* 16: 49–79.

CASTLE, EMERY (1983). "Water Availability: The Crisis of the Eighties?" *Resources,* no. 73, pp. 8–10.

CIGLER, ALLAN and BURDETT LOOMIS (1983). *Interest Group Politics.* Washington: CQ, Inc.

CINGRANELLI, DAVID L. (1983). "State Government Lobbies in the National Political Process," *State Government,* 56:4 122–27.

CITIZENS CONFERENCE ON STATE LEGISLATURES (1971). *State Legislatures: An Evaluation of Their Effectiveness.* New York: Praeger.

CITIZENS LEAGUE (1982). *A Positive Alternative: Redesigning Public Service Delivery.* Minneapolis: Citizens League.

CLARK, TERRY N. (1983). "Local Fiscal Dynamics under Old and New Federalism," *Urban Affairs Quarterly,* 19:1: 55–74.

COBB, ROGER W. and CHARLES D. ELDER (1972). *Participation in American Politics: The Dynamics of Agenda-Building.* Boston: Allyn & Bacon.

COLELLA, CYNTHIA CATES (1986). "The Supreme Court and Intergovernmental Relations," in Robert J. Dilger (ed.), *American Intergovernmental Relations Today.* Englewood Cliffs, N.J.: Prentice-Hall.

CONLAN, TIM (1986). "Federalism and Competing Values in the Reagan Administration," *Publius,* 16: 29–48.

CRONIN, THOMAS E. (1975). *The State of the Presidency.* Boston: Little, Brown.

DAHL, ROBERT (1958). "A Critique of the Ruling Elite Model," *American Political Science Review,* 52: 463 – 69.

DAHL, ROBERT (1961). *Who Governs?* New Haven: Yale University Press.

DAHL, ROBERT A. and CHARLES E. LINDBLOM (1953). *Politics, Economics and Welfare.* New York: Harper.

DANIELSON, MICHAEL (1976). *The Politics of Exclusion.* New York: Columbia University Press.

DANZINGER, SHELDON H. and DANIEL H. WEINBERG (eds.) (1986). *Fighting Poverty: What Works and What Doesn't.* Cambridge: Harvard University Press.

DAVID, STEPHEN and PAUL KANTOR (1984). "Urban Policy in the Federal System: A Reconsideration," *Polity,* 16: 284–303.

DEGLER, CARL (1984). *Out of Our Past: The Forces which Shaped Modern America.* New York: Harper & Row, Pub.

DERTHICK, MARTHA (1972). *New Towns In-Town: Why a Federal Program Failed.* Washington: Urban Institute.

DERTHICK, MARTHA (1974). *Between State and Nation.* Washington: Brookings Institution.

DIAMOND, MARTIN (1973). "The Ends of Federalism," *Publius,* 3: 129–52.

DIAMOND, MARTIN (1974). "What the Framers Meant by Federalism," in Robert Goldwin (ed.), *A Nation of States.* Chicago: Rand McNally.

DILGER, ROBERT J. (ed.) (1986). *American Intergovernmental Relations Today.* Englewood Cliffs, N.J.: Prentice-Hall.

DILLON, JOHN F. (1911). *Commentaries on the Law of Municipal Corporations.* Boston: Little, Brown.

DOLBEARE, KENNETH (1986). *Democracy at Risk: The Politics of Economic Renewal.* Chatham, N.J.: Chatham House Publishers.

DOMHOFF, G. WILLIAM (1978). *The Powers That Be: Processes of Ruling Class Domination in America.* New York: Random House.

DOMHOFF, G. WILLIAM (1983). *Who Rules America Now? A View for the '80s.* Englewood Cliffs, N.J.: Prentice-Hall.

DOMHOFF, G. WILLIAM and THOMAS R. DYE (eds.) (1987). *Power Elites and Organizations.* Beverly Hills, Calif.: Sage Publications, Inc.

DOMMEL, PAUL R. (1975). "Distribution Politics and Urban Policy," *Policy Studies Journal,* 3:4: 370–74.

DORSETT, LYLE W. (1977). *Franklin D. Roosevelt and the City Bosses.* Port Washington, N.Y.: Kennikat Press.

DOWNS, GEORGE W., JR. (1976). *Bureaucracy, Innovation and Public*

Policy. Lexington, Mass.: Heath, Lexington Books.

DROR, YEHEZKEL (1968). *Public Policy-making Reexamined.* San Francisco: Chandler.

DUBNICK, MEL and LYNNE HOLT (1985). " Industrial Policy and the States," *Publius,* 15: 113–39.

DUBNICK, MELVIN (1981). "Nationalizing State Policies," in Jerome J. Hanus (ed.), *The Nationalization of State Government.* Lexington, Mass. Heath.

DURHAM, G. HOMER (1940). "Politics and Administration in Intergovernmental Relations," *Annals of the American Academy of Political and Social Science,* 207: 2–19.

DYE, THOMAS R. (1966). *Politics, Economics and Public Policy: Policy Outcomes in the American States.* Chicago: Rand McNally.

DYE, THOMAS (1980). *Who's Running America? Institutional Leadership in the United States.* Englewood Cliffs, N.J.: Prentice-Hall.

DYE, THOMAS (1981). *Politics in States and Communities.* Englewood Cliffs, N.J.: Prentice-Hall.

DYE, THOMAS (1984). *Who's Running America Now? Institutional Leadership in the United States.* Englewood Cliffs, N.J.: Prentice-Hall.

DYE, THOMAS (1986). *Who's Running America? The Conservative Years.* Englewood Cliffs, N.J.: Prentice-Hall.

DYE, THOMAS (1987). *Power, Elites and Organization.* Beverly Hills, Calif.: Sage Publications, Inc.

DYE, THOMAS R. and THOMAS L. HURLEY (1978). "The Responsiveness of Federal and State Governments to Urban Problems," *Journal of Politics,* 40: 196–207.

DYE, THOMAS and HARMON ZEIGLER (1983). *The Irony of Democracy* (5th ed.). North Scituate, Mass.: Duxbury Press.

EDNER, SHELDON (1976). "Intergovernmental Policy Development: The Importance of Problem Definition," in Charles O. Jones and Robert D. Thomas (eds.), *Public Policy Making in a Federal System.* Beverly Hills, Calif.: Sage Publications Inc.

ELAZAR, DANIEL (1962). *The American Partnership.* Chicago: University of Chicago Press.

ELAZAR, DANIEL J. (1966; second ed. 1972). *American Federalism: A View from the States.* New York: Thomas Y. Crowell.

ELAZAR, DANIEL (1984). *American Federalism.* New York: Harper & Row, Pub.

ELMORE, RICHARD F. (1982). "Backward Mapping: Implementation Research and Policy Decisions," in Walter Williams (ed.), *Studying Implementation: Methodological and Administrative Issues.* Chatham, N.J.: Chatham House Publishers.

EPSTEIN, DAVID (1984). *The Political Theory of the Federalist.* Chicago: University of Chicago Press.

EULAU, HEINZ and KENNETH PREWITT (1973). *Labyrinths of Democracy: Adaptations, Linkages, Representations and Policies in Urban Politics.* Indianapolis: Bobbs-Merrill.

FARBER, STEPHEN B. (1983). "The 1982 New Federalism Negotiations: A View from the States," *Publius,* 13:2: 33–38.

FARKAS, SUZANNE (1971). *Urban Lobbying.* New York: New York University Press.

FARRAND, MAX (ed.). (1966) *The Records of the Constitutional Convention of 1787.* New Haven: Yale University Press.

THE FEDERALIST PAPERS, ed. Clinton Rossiter (1961). New York: Mentor Books.

FENNO, RICHARD (1978). *Home Style: House Members and Their Districts.* Boston: Little, Brown.

FERGUSON, THOMAS and JOEL ROGERS (1986). *Right Turn: The Decline of the Democrats and the Future of American Politics.* New York: Hill & Wang.

FINE, SIDNEY (1956). *Laissez Faire and the General Welfare State.* Ann Arbor: University of Michigan Press.

FOSHEE, ANDREW (1985). "Jeffersonian Political Economy and the Classical Republican Tradition: Jefferson, Taylor and the Agrarian Republic," *History of Political Economy,* 17:4: 523–50.

FRANKFURTER, FELIX (1961). *Mr. Justice Holmes and the Supreme Court.* Cambridge: Harvard University Press.

FREY, BRUNO (1978). *Modern Political Economy.* New York: John Wiley and Sons.

FRIEDEN, GUNNARD (1979). *The Environmental Protection Hustle.* Cambridge: MIT Press.

FRIEDLAND, ROGER and DONALD PALMER (1984). "Park Place and Main Street: Business and the Urban Power Structure," *Annual Review of Sociology* 10: 393–416.

GARSON, G. DAVID (1977). *Power and Politics in the United States: A Political Economy Approach.* Lexington, Mass.: D. C. Heath.

GERSTON, LARRY N. (1983). *Making Public Policy: From Conflict to Resolution.* Glenview, Ill.: Scott, Foresman.

GETZ, M. and B. WALKER (1980). "Environmental Policy and Competitive Structure: Implications for the Hazardous Waste Management Program," *Policy Studies Journal,* 8: 404–14.

GINSBERG, BENJAMIN and JOHN GREEN (1979). "The Best Congress Money Can Buy: Campaign Contributions and Congressional Behavior." Paper presented at the annual meeting of the American Political Science Association.

GLENDENING, PARRIS N. and MAVIS MANN REEVES (1984). *Pragmatic Federalism.* Pacific Palisades, Calif.: Palisades Publishers.

GOODMAN, ROBERT (1971). *After the Planners.* New York: Simon & Schuster.

GOODSELL, CHARLES T. (1983). *The Case for Bureaucracy.* Chatham, N.J.: Chatham House Publishers.

GORDON, GEORGE U. (1986). *Public Administration in America* (3rd ed.). New York: St. Martin's Press.

GRABER, DORIS A. (1980). *Mass Media and American Politics.* Washington: CQ, Inc.

GRACE, J. PETER (1984). *President's Private Sector Survey on Cost Control in the Federal Government.* Washington: U.S. Government Printing Office.

GRAVES, W. BROOKE (1964). *American Intergovernmental Relations.* New York: Scribner's.

GREENBERG, EDWARD (1979). *Understanding Modern Government: The Rise and Decline of the American Political Economy.* New York: John Wiley.

GREENBERG, EDWARD S. (1974). *Serving the Few: Corporate Capitalism and the Bias of Government Policy.* New York: Macmillan.

GREENBERG, GEORGE D., JEFFREY MILLER, LAURENCE B. MOHR and BRUCE VLADECK (1977). "Developing Public Policy Theory: Perspectives for Empirical Research," *American Political Science Review,* 71: 1532–43.

GREENSTEIN, ROBERT (1985). "Losing Faith in 'Losing Ground'." *New Republic*, March 15, 1985, pp. 12 - 17.

GRODZINS, MORTON (1960). "The Federal System," in the American Assembly, *Goals for Americans*. Englewood Cliffs, N.J.: Prentice-Hall.

GRODZINS, MORTON (1966). *The American System: A New View of Government in the United States*. Chicago: Rand McNally.

GROVER, STANFORD M. (1980). *Financial Trend Monitoring System: A Practioner's Workbook for Collecting Data, Charting Trends and Interpreting Results*. Washington: International City Management Association.

HACKER, LOUIS (1957). *Alexander Hamilton in the American Tradition*. New York: McGraw-Hill.

HAIDER, DONALD H. (1974). *When Governments Come to Washington*. New York: Free Press.

HAIDER, DONALD H. (1981). "The Intergovernmental System," *Proceedings of the American Academy of Political Science: The Power to Govern*, 34:2: 20–30.

HALL, JOHN STUART and ALVIN MUSHKATEL. "Local Influence over National Policy: The Case of Community development," in Dennis R. Judd (1985) *Public Policy across States and Communities*. Greenwich, CT: JAI Press.

HANUS, JEROME J. (ed.). (1981). *The Nationalization of State Government*. Lexington, Mass.: Heath.

HARRIGAN, JOHN (1981). *Politics and Policy in States and Communities*. Boston: Little, Brown.

HARRINGTON, MICHAEL (1987). *The Next Left: The History of the Future*. New York: Henry Holt.

HATRY, HARRY P. (1973). *Practical Program Evaluation for State and Local Officials*. Washington: Urban Institute Press.

HATRY, HARRY P. (1983). *A Review of Private Approaches for the Delivery of Public Services*. Washington: The Urban Institute Press.

HAWLEY, WILLIS D. and FREDERICK M. WIRT (1974). *The Search for Community Power*. Englewood Cliffs, N.J.: Prentice-Hall.

HENIG, JEFFREY (1985). *Public Policy and Federalism: Issues in State and Local Politics*. New York: St. Martin's Press.

HENRY, NICHOLAS (1987). *Governing at the Grass Roots*. Englewood Cliffs, N.J.: Prentice-Hall.

HERO, RODNEY (1986). "The Urban Service Delivery Literature: Some Questions and Considerations," *Polity*, 18:4: 659–77.

HOFSTADTER, RICHARD (1963). *The Progressive Movement*. Englewood Cliffs, N.J.: Prentice-Hall.

HOFSTADTER, RICHARD, WILLIAM MILLER, and DANIEL AARON (1959). *The American Republic*. Englewood Cliffs, N.J.: Prentice-Hall.

HOLCOMBE, RANDALL G. and ASGHAN ZARDKOOHI (1981). "The Determinants of Federal Grants," *Southern Economic Journal*, 48:2: 393–99.

HOLLI, MELVIN G. (1974). "Urban Reform in the Progressive Era," in Lewis L. Gould (ed.), *The Progressive Era*. Syracuse, N.Y.: Syracuse University Press.

JENKINS, J. CRAIG and TERI SHUMATE (1985). "Cowboy Capitalists and the Rise of the New Right: An Analysis of Contributors to Conservative Policy Organizations," *Social Problems*, 33:2 (December): 130 – 45.

JOHNSON, MICHAEL S. (1985). "Metropolitan Dependence on Intergovernmental Aid," *Social Science Quarterly*, 66:3: 713–23.

JONES, CHARLES O. (1970). *An Introduction to the Study of Public Policy.* Belmont, Calif.: Wadsworth.

JONES, CHARLES O. (1984). *An Introduction to the Study of Public Policy.* 4th ed. Belmont, Calif.: Brooks/Cole.

JUDD, DENNIS R. (1985). *Public Policy across States and Communities.* Greenwich, Conn.: JAI Press.

KEARNEY, RICHARD C. and ROBERT B. GAREY (1982). "American Federalism and Management of Radioactive Wastes," *Public Administration Review*, 42: 14–24.

KEARNEY, RICHARD C. and JOHN J. STUCKER (1985). "Interstate Compacts and the Management of Low Level Radioactive Wastes," *Public Administration Review*, 45: 210–20.

KLINE, JOHN M. (1984). "The International Economic Interests of the U.S. States," *Publius*, 14:4: 81–94.

KNEESE, ALLEN V. (1982). "Saliency in the Colorado River," *Resources*, no. 70, pp. 10–11.

KOLKO, GABRIEL (1963). *The Triumph of Conservatism: A Re-Interpretation of American History.* New York: Free Press of Glencoe.

KOTLER, MILTON (1969). *Neighborhood Government. The Local Foundation of Political Life.* Indianapolis: Bobbs-Merrill.

KOTLOWITZ, ALEX and DALE D. BUSS (1986). "Costly Bait: Localities Giveaways to Lure Corporations Cause Growing Outcry," *Wall Street Journal*, September 24, 1986, pp. 1, 27.

LADD, EVERETT CARL (1981). "The Brittle Mandate: The 1980 Presidential Election," *Political Science Quarterly*, Spring, pp. 1–25.

LASH, JONATHAN, KATHERINE GILLMAN, and DAVID SHERIDAN (1985). *A Season of Spoils: The Reagan Administration's Attack on the Environment.* New York: Pantheon.

LASSWELL, HAROLD (1960). "The Structure and Function of Communication in Society," in Wilbur Schramm (ed.), *Mass Communication.* Urbana: University of Illinois Press.

LEACH, RICHARD (1970). *American Federalism.* New York: W. W. Norton & Co., Inc.

LEARY, THOMAS J. (1985). "Deindustrialization, Plant Closing Laws, and the States," *State Government*, 58: 113–18.

LEISERSON, WILLIAM HENRY (1958). *Parties and Politics: An Institutional and Behavioral Approach.* New York: Knopf.

LESTER, JAMES P., JAMES L. FRANKE, ANN BOWMAN, and KENNETH KRAMER (1983). "Hazardous Wastes, Politics and Public Policy: A Comparative State Analysis," *Western Political Quarterly*, 36:1: 257–85.

LEVY, FRANK S., ARNOLD MELTSNER, and AARON WILDAVSKY (1974). *Urban Outcomes: Streets, Schools and Libraries (the Oakland Project).* Berkeley: The University of California Press.

LIGHT, ALFRED R. (1978). "State Agency Perspectives on Federalism," *Social Science Quarterly*, 59:2: 284–94.

LINDBLOM, CHARLES (1977). *Politics and Markets: The World's Political Economic Systems.* New York: Basic Books.

LINEBERRY, ROBERT (1977). *Equality and Urban Policy: The Distribution of Municipal Public Services.* Beverly Hills, Calif.: Sage Publications, Inc.

LINEBERRY, ROBERT (1982). *American Public Policy.* New York: Harper & Row, Inc.

LIPSKY, MICHAEL (1971). "Street-Level Bureaucracy and the Analysis of Urban Reform," *Urban Affairs Quarterly,* 6 (June): 391 – 409.

LOWI, THEODORE (1969). *The End of Liberalism.* New York: W. W. Norton & Co., Inc.

LUPSHA, PETER and WILL SIEMBIEDA (1977). "The Poverty of Public Services in the Land of Plenty," in David Perry and Alfred Watkins (eds.), *The Rise of the Sunbelt Cities.* Beverly Hills, Calif.: Sage Publications, Inc.

LYDEN, FREMONT J. and ERNEST G. MILLER (1972). *Planning, Programming, Budgeting* (2nd ed.). Chicago: Markham.

MCCONNEL, GRANT (1967). *Private Power and American Democracy.* New York: Knopf.

MCCOY, DREW (1980). *The Elusive Republic's Political Economy in Jeffersonian America.* Chapel Hill: University of North Carolina Press.

MCKAY, DAVID (1985). "Theory and Practice in Public Policy: The Case of the New Federalism," *Political Studies,* 33: 181–202.

MCKEAN, ROLAND N. (1968). *Public Spending.* New York: McGraw-Hill.

MCKENZIE, RICHARD B. (ed.) (1981). *Plant Closing: Public or Private Choices?* Washington: Cato Institute.

MACMAHON, ARTHUR W. (1955). *Federalism, Mature and Emergent.* Garden City, N.Y.: Doubleday.

MACMAHON, ARTHUR W. (1972). *Administering Federalism in a Democracy.* New York: Oxford University Press.

MADDOX, WILLIAM S. and STUART A. LITTLE (1984). *Beyond Liberal and Conservative: Reassessing the Political Spectrum.* Washington: Cato Institute.

MANLEY, JOHN F. and KENNETH DOLBEARE (1987). *The Case against the Constitution.* Armonk, N.Y.: M.E. Sharpe, Inc.

MANNING, BAYLESS (1977). "The Congress, the Executive and Intermestic Affairs," *Foreign Affairs,* 55: 306–24.

MARCH, JAMES G. and HERBERT A. SIMON (1958). *Organizations.* New York: John Wiley.

MARTIN, ROSCOE (1965). *The Cities and the Federal System.* New York: Atherton.

MASSEY, JANE and JEFFREY P. STRAUSSMAN (1985). "Another Look at the Mandate Issue: Are the Conditions of Aid Really So Burdensome? *Public Administration Review,* 45:2: 292–300.

MENDELSON, WALLACE (1965). *The Constitution and the Supreme Court.* New York: Dodd, Mead.

MOLOTCH, HARVEY (1976). "The City as a Growth Machine," *American Journal of Sociology,* 76 (September): 311 – 23.

MUELLER, KEITH J. (1984). "Local Government Implementation of National Inspired Programs: A Comparative Analysis," *Journal of Urban Affairs,* 6:2: 166–78.

NATHAN, RICHARD (1975). *The Plot That Failed.* New York: John Wiley.

NATHAN, RICHARD P. (1983). "State and Local Governments under Federal Grants: Toward a Predictive Theory," *Political Science Quarterly,* 98:1: 47–57.

NATIONAL RESOURCES COMMITTEE (1939). *Urban Government,* vol. I, part II. Washington: U.S. Government Printing Office.

NICE, DAVID C. (1987a). *Federalism: The Politics of Intergovernmental*

Relations. New York: St. Martin's Press.

NICE, DAVID C. (1987b). "State Participation in Interstate Compacts," *Publius*, 17: 69 – 83.

OAKERSON, RONALD J. (1987). "Local Public Economies: Provision, Production and Governance," in ACIR, *Intergovernmental Perspective*, Summer/Fall 1987, pp. 20–25.

O'CONNOR, JAMES (1973). *The Fiscal Crisis of the States.* New York: St. Martin's Press.

OFFICE OF MANAGEMENT AND BUDGET (1980). *Managing Federal Assistance in the 1980s*, vol. 1. Washington: U.S. Government Printing Office.

OSTROM, VINCENT (1971). *The Political Theory of the Compound Republic.* Blacksburg, Virginia: Public Choice.

O'TOOLE, LAURENCE, JR. (1985). *American Intergovernmental Relations.* Washington: CQ, Inc.

PALMER, JOHN L. and ISABEL V. SAWHILL (eds.) (1982). *The Reagan Experiment.* Washington: Urban Institute.

PALMER, JOHN L. and ISABEL V. SAWHILL (eds.) (1985). *The Reagan Record.* Washington: Urban Institute.

PARSONS, TALCOTT (1954). *Essays in Sociological Theory.* New York: Free Press.

PATTERSON, JAMES T. (1969). *The New Deal and the States: Federalism in Transition.* Princeton, N.J.: Princeton University Press.

PERROW, CHARLES (1983). *Complex Organizations* (3rd ed.). New York: Random House.

PETERSON, GEORGE E. (1986). *Reagan and the Cities.* Washington: Urban Institute.

PETERSON, MERRILL D. (1962). *The Jefferson Image in the American Mind.* New York: Oxford University Press.

PETERSON, PAUL (1981). *City Limits.* Chicago: University of Chicago Press.

PETERSON, PAUL E., BARRY RABE, and KENNETH WONG (1986). *When Federalism Works.* Washington: Brookings Institution.

PHILLIPS, KEVIN (1969). *The Emerging Republican Majority.* New York: Arlington House.

PILLAI, VEL and KEVIN BRONNER (1984). "State Monitoring of Local Finances: An Analysis of New York State's Financial Tracking System," *State Government*, 16:3: 108–14.

PRESSMAN, JEFFREY (1975). *Federal Programs and City Politics: The Dynamics of The Administrative Process in Oakland.* Berkeley: University of California Press.

PRESSMAN, JEFFREY and AARON WILDAVSKY (1973). *Implementation.* Berkeley: University of California Press.

QUINDRY, KENNETH (1971). *State and Local Revenue Potential.* Atlanta: Southern Regional Education Board.

REAGAN, MICHAEL D. (1972). *The New Federalism.* New York: Oxford University Press.

REAGAN, MICHAEL D. (1987). *Regulation: The Politics of Policy.* Boston: Little, Brown.

RIDGEWAY, MARIAN E. (1971). *Interstate Compacts: A Question of Federalism.* Carbondale: Southern Illinois University Press.

RIKER, WILLIAM (1964). *Federalism: Origin, Operation, Significance.* Boston: Little, Brown.

RIKER, WILLIAM (1975). "Federalism," in Fred I. Greenstein and Nelson Polsby (eds.), *Handbook of Political Science*, vol. 5. Reading, Mass.: Addison-Wesley.

ROSE, ARNOLD M. (1967). *The Power Structure.* New York: Oxford University Press.

ROSENBURG, PHILLIP and WAYNE M. STALLINGS (1978). *Is Your City Headed for Financial Difficulty? Guidebook for Small Cities and Other Governmental Units.* Chicago: Municipal Finance Officers Association.

ROSENER, JUDY B. (1980). "Intergovernmental Tension in Coastal Zone Management," *Coastal Zone Management Journal*, 7: 95–109.

ROURKE, FRANCES (1984). *Bureaucracy, Politics and Public Policy.* Boston: Little, Brown.

SALE, KIRKPATRICK (1976). *Power Shift.* New York: Random House, Vintage Books.

SALES, LEONARD and MARGARET CHANDLER (1971). *Managing Large Systems.* New York: Harper & Row, Pub.

SAVAGE, ROBERT L. (1982). "The Structure of Growth Management in the American States," *Publius*, 12: 99–110.

SAVAGE, ROBERT L. (1986). "When a Policy's Time Has Come: Cases of Rapid Policy Diffusion," *Publius*, 15:3: 111–25.

SAWHILL, ISABEL and CHARLES STOWE (1984). "The Economy: The Key to Success" in John Palmer and Isabel Sawhill, *The Reagan Record.* Washington: Urban Institute/Ballinger Press.

SCHATTSCHNEIDER, E. E. (1942). *Party Government.* New York: Henry Holt.

SCHATTSCHNEIDER, E. E. (1960). *The Semi-Sovereign People.* New York: Holt, Rinehart & Winston.

SCHEIBER, HARRY N. (1980). "Federalism and Legal Process: Historical and Contemporary Analysis of the American System," *Law and Society Review*, 14:3 (Spring): 663–722.

SCHWARZ, JOHN (1983). *America's Hidden Success.* New York: W. W. Norton & Co., Inc.

SHANNON, JOHN and SUSANNAH E. CALKINS (1983). "Federal and State Spenders Go Their Separate Ways," in ACIR, *Intergovernmental Perspective*, 8:4: 23–29.

SHANNON, JOHN and L. RICHARD GABLER (1977). "Tax Lids and Expenditure Mandates: The Case for Fiscal Fair Play," *Intergovernmental Perspective*, 3:3: 7–12.

SHARKANSKY, IRA (1970). *The Routines of Politics.* New York: Van Nostrand Reinhold.

SHARP, ELAINE and DENNIS PALUMBO (1980). "Process versus Impact Evaluation of Community Corrections," in David Nachmias (ed.), *The Practice of Policy Evaluation.* New York: St. Martin's Press.

SHERWOOD, ROBERT (1948). *Roosevelt and Hopkins*, vol. 1. New York: Bantam.

SMITH, MICHAEL PETER ET AL. (1985). "Capital Flight, Tax Incentives and the Marginalization of American States and Localities," in Dennis Judd (ed.), *Public Policy across States and Communities.* Greenwich, Conn.: JAI Press.

SMITH, ROBERT J. (1964). *Public Authorities, Special Districts and Local Government.* Washington: National Association of Counties Research Foundation.

STARLING, GROVER (1979). *The Politics and Economics of Public Policy.* Homewood, Ill.: Dorsey Press.

STARLING, GROVER (1986). *Managing the Public Sector* (3rd ed.). Chicago: Dorsey Press.

STENBERG, CARL (1981). "Federalism in Transition: 1959–79," in ACIR, *The Future of Federalism in the 1980s.* Washington: U.S. Government Printing Office.

STEWART, WILLIAM H. (1979). "The Function of Models and Metaphors in the Development of Federal Theory." Paper presented at the annual meeting of the American Political Science Association, Washington, D.C.

STEWART, WILLIAM H. (1984). *Concepts of Federalism.* Lanham, Md.: University Press of America.

SUNDQUIST, JAMES L. and DAVID W. DAVIS (1969). *Making Federalism Work: A Study of Program Coordination at the Community Level.* Washington: Brookings Institute.

SWEAT, JOSEPH and HERBERT J. BINGHAM (1987). "Municipal Politics and Power: A Casebook History of Intergovernmental Management," in ACIR, *Intergovernmental Perspective: Federalism in 1987.* Washington: U.S. Government Printing Office.

THOMPSON, FRANK J. and MICHAEL J. SCICCHITANO (1982). "OSHA, the States and Gresham's Law: From Carter to Reagan," in J. Edwin Benton and David R. Morgan (eds.), *Intergovernmental Relations and Public Policy.* New York: Greenwood Press.

THURSBY, VINCENT V. (1953). *Interstate Cooperation: A Study of the Interstate Compact.* Washington: Public Affairs Press.

TRUMAN, DAVID (1979). "Federalism and the Party System," in Aaron Wildavsky (ed.), *American Federalism in Perspective.* Boston: Little, Brown.

TUCKER, HARVEY (1984). "The Nationalization of State Policy Revisited," *Western Political Quarterly*, 37:3: 53 – 57.

USEEM, ELIZABETH (1987). "The Limits of Power and Commitment: Corporate Elites and Education in the 1980s," in G. William Domhoff and Thomas R. Dye (eds.), *Power Elites and Organizations.* Beverly Hills, Calif.: Sage Publications, Inc.

U. S. SENATE, COMMITTEE ON GOVERNMENT OPERATIONS, SUBCOMMITTEE ON INTERGOVERNMENTAL RELATIONS (1965). *The Condition of American Federalism.* Washington: U.S. Government Printing Office.

VALENTI, CARL F. and LYDIA D. MANCHESTER (1984). *Rethinking Local Services: Examining Alternative Delivery Approaches.* Washington: International City Management Association.

VAN Meter, DONALD and CARL VAN HORN (1976). "The Implementation of Intergovernmental Policy," in Charles Jones and Robert Thomas (eds.), *Public Policymaking in a Federal System.* Beverly Hills, Calif.: Sage Publications, Inc.

VEBLEN, THORSTEIN (1964). *The Theory of Business Enterprises.* New York: Scribner 's.

VITERITTI, JOSEPH P. (1982). "Bureaucratic Environment, Efficiency, and Equity in Urban Service Delivery Systems," in R. Rich (ed.), *The Politics of Urban Public Services.* New York: Lexington Books.

WALKER, DAVID (1981). "Dysfunctional Federalism: Congress and Intergovernmental Relations," *State Government*, 54:2: 53 – 57.

WALKER, JEANNE and DAVID WALKER (1975). "Rationalizing Local Government Powers, Functions and Structures," in *States Responsibilities for Local Governments: An Action Agenda.* Washington: Center for Policy Research of the National Governors' Association.

WARSHOW, ROBERT I. (1931). *Alexander Hamilton: The First American Business Man*. New York: Greenberg.

WEBER, MAX (1964). *The Theory of Social and Economic Organizations*, ed. Talcott Parsons. Glencoe, Ill.: Free Press.

WEINSTEIN, JAMES (1969). *The Corporate Ideal in the Liberal State*. Boston: Beacon Press.

WELLS, DONALD (1964). *The TVA Tributary Development Program*. University, Ala.: Bureau of Public Administration.

WELLS, DONALD (1982). "Site Control of Hazardous Waste Facilities," *Policy Studies Review*, 1:4: 728–35.

WELLS, DONALD T. (1986). "Statutory and Structural Determinants of State Response in Hazardous Waste Policy." Paper presented to the Western Social Science Association, Reno, Nevada.

WHITE, J. ALLEN (1982). *Urban Elites and Mass Transportation*. Princeton, N.J.: Princeton University Press.

WIEBE, ROBERT (1974). *The Search for Order, 1877–1920*. New York: Hill & Wang.

WILDAVSKY, AARON (1981). "Bare Bones: Putting Flesh Back on the Skeleton of American Federalism," in ACIR, *The Future of Federalism in the 1980s*. Washington: U.S. Government Printing Office.

WILDAVSKY, AARON (1985). *The Politics of the Budgetary Process*. Boston: Little, Brown.

WILLIAMS, WALTER (1982). *Studying Implementation: Methodological and Administrative Issues*. Chatham, N.J.: Chatham House Publishers.

WILLIAMSON, RICHARD S. (1983). "The 1982 New Federalism Negotiation," *Publius*, 13: 28–41.

WILSON, WOODROW (1908). *Constitutional Government in the United States*. New York: Columbia University Press.

WOODWARD, C. VAN (1966). *The Strange Career of Jim Crow*. New York: Oxford University Press.

WORTHELY, JOHN A. and Richard Torkelson (1981). "Managing the Toxic Waste Problem: Lessons from Love Canal," *Administration and Society*, 13: 145–60.

WRIGHT, DEIL S. (1982). *Understanding Intergovernmental Relations*. Monterey, Calif.: Brooks/Cole.

WRIGHTSON, MARGARET (1986). "Interlocal Cooperation and Urban Problems: Lessons for the New Federalism," *Urban Affairs Quarterly*, 22:2: 261–75.

WRONG, DENNIS (1978). *Power: Its Forms, Bases and Uses*. New York: Harper & Row, Pub.

YIENNAKIS, DIANA (1977). "Sunbelt vs. Frostbelt: The Evolution of Regulatory Conflict over Federal Aid to Cities," in David Perry and Alfred Watkins (eds.), *The Rise of the Sunbelt Cities*. Beverly Hills, Calif.: Sage Publications, Inc.

ZIMMERMAN, JOSEPH (1983). *State–Local Relations: A Partnership Approach*. New York: Praeger.

Index